Talent Management in India

Challenges and Opportunities

Talent Management in India

Challenges and Opportunities

Edited by

Masood Hasan
Anil Kumar Singh
Somesh Dhamija

ATLANTIC
PUBLISHERS & DISTRIBUTORS (P) LTD

Published by

ATLANTIC

PUBLISHERS & DISTRIBUTORS (P) LTD

7/22, Ansari Road, Darya Ganj, New Delhi-110002
Phones : +91-11-40775252, 40775214, 23273880, 23275880
Fax: +91-11-23285873
Web: www.atlanticbooks.com
E-mail: orders@atlanticbooks.com

Reprint 2016, 2018, 2019, 2023

Printed & bound in India by Atlantic Print Services

Dedicated to

Late Shri Ganeshi Lal Ji Agrawal,
a noted philanthropist and social
worker with vision and belief that true
knowledge should be promoted and
spread far and wide

Acknowledgements

The present work could not have been possible without constant encouragement and deep involvement in the promotion of academic pursuits of Mr. Narayan Das Agrawal, Chairman, GLA Group of Institutions, Mathura. We express our profound gratitude to him for his blessings and all possible support rendered for completing the book. We are especially grateful to Prof. Jai Prakash, Director General, GLA Group of Institutions, for his valuable suggestions and guidance provided during the course of writing this book. We also wish to record our debt of gratitude to Mr. Neeraj Agrawal, Secretary, Society, GLA Group of Institutions and Mr. Vivek Agrawal, Secretary, GLA Group of Institutions for their generosity and all possible support and assistance. Our thanks are also due to Prof. Anoop Kumar Gupta, Director, GLA Institute of Professional Studies and Mr. Ashok Kumar Singh, Registrar, GLA Group of Institutions for their keen interest and cooperation in the preparation of the book.

We are extremely thankful to all our colleagues in the Department of Management for their constant help, encouragement and advice offered during different stages of writing the book. Finally, we are also thankful to Mr. Rajendra Singh for neatly typing the manuscript.

Masood Hasan
Anil Kumar Singh
Somesh Dhamija

Preface

Talent management refers to the process of integrating new workers, developing and retaining current workers and attracting highly skilled personnel to work for the company. It is indispensable for survival and sustainable development of any business organization. Neglect of talent management is suicidal for the organization, particularly in the current business scenario of high competition. Opportunities to hire qualified and talented employees abound in India due to expansion of higher education and coming up of a large number of institutes promoting professional courses in various streams. But, it is important to train the employees and place them according to their suitability, aptitude and interest, so that the ill consequences of putting a square peg in a round hole—which leads to distortion in the organizational structure and low productivity—could be avoided.

The performance of talented employees is qualitatively superior to that of other employees. Giving encouragement, respect and recognition to the talented people and providing them congenial environment are in the interest of the organization because such employees are exceptional, having expertise in their respective fields, possessing entrepreneurial abilities and are highly mobile these days when opportunities both at the national and international levels are immense.

In view of the innovative aptitude and analytical mind of talented employees, an organization should develop ways and means for their retention because replacement of such employees involves enormous cost. The presence of talented people motivates other employees, carrying multiple effects on the growth of the organization due to their commitment, will power and aspirations. They are highly competent for the job and their effectiveness lies in their dedication which has far-reaching impact on the work culture of the organization resulting into good brand name for its products. Therefore, the organization should adopt a holistic approach for talent management right from the selection of talented people to their retention, development and promotional avenues.

This book comprises articles contributed by erudite scholars who are experts in their relevant fields. It is divided into seven parts covering various aspects of talent management in India such as talent management practices, developing talent for nation building, retaining talent through work culture, talent attraction and development, challenges and opportunities in talent management, and talent retention and development. The book provides a comprehensive study on talent management. It has been presented in simple language and lucid style and will be highly useful to the students and teachers of management, researchers in this field, business professionals, Human Resource managers and enterpreneurs.

Masood Hasan
Anil Kumar Singh
Somesh Dhamija

Contents

PART 4
RETAINING TALENT THROUGH ORGANIZATIONAL CULTURE

PART 5
TALENT ATTRACTION AND DEVELOPMENT

PART 6
TALENT MANAGEMENT—CHALLENGES AND OPPORTUNITIES

PART 7
TALENT RETENTION AND DEVELOPMENT

PART – 1
TALENT MANAGEMENT

1 Introduction

Masood Hasan

Talent Management implies the recognition of creativity, innovativeness, analytical ability and distinguishing qualities of a person, which are to be encouraged and respected for the sake of protecting human values and improving the living standards of the people. It happens because of multiple and widespread effects of such personnel in the organization increasing the productivity and motivating other employees. It is well known fact that everybody cannot do everything. Hence, it is extremely pertinent to place the employees according to their interest and suitability. Otherwise, the fate of putting a square peg in a round hole leads to distortions in the organizational structure and low productivity around. Employing people contrary to their liking and temperament results into negative attitude to work on the part of those employees. They hardly take interest in their job spilling over adverse effects on co-workers thereby spoiling the image of the organization. It lasts until such employees are shown the doors. It means neglecting talent management give rise to replacement of employees again and again, which causes further hiring, re-training and other wasteful activities.

Talented employees possess distinctive features. They are most superior in performance as compared to other employees of their age and experience. Their work exhibit creativity and they need congenial environment for carrying out their intellectual pursuits. It may be noted that outstanding talents is not the monopoly of particular casts, communities and regions. They exist among all social, economic and cultural groups. What is important is to locate them, encourage them and provide them excellent opportunities because of their diffusing and priceless contribution to the organization and the society around. They are knowledge owning entrepreneurial employees (KNOWEE). Their contribution to the organization is exceptional. Such employees are of T-shaped which means having command in their field represented by the vertical part of T and general knowledge of other areas displayed by the horizontal part of T signifying holistic view of the problems they come across in the organization. The important point is that talented employees can improve the overall performance of the organization through their entrepreneurship, willpower, determination, vision about the future and aspirations. Their presence brings prosperity and happiness to the organization and the employees. They are rare species and their mobility is immense at the global level discerned in the early years of 21st century. It becomes the sheer responsibility of the organization to manage them if they want to compete both at the national and international levels.

Those organizations realize the usefulness of talent management they do not only enjoy phenomenal growth but also harmonious relationship between the organization and employees. It is significant because howsoever effective the top management is the healthy growth of the organization depends on working together for success. It requires the management to be careful putting the right people in the right job. Talent management is also important because it is the quality of human capital, which plays a crucial role in the economic development of a country. There are physical, natural and human resources. The economic growth is more attributable to human resources rather than physical and natural capital. The World Bank study of 192 countries quoted by Human Development Report, 1996 concluded that 64 per cent of the growth occurs due to the human and social capital. The contribution of physical and natural capital is merely 16 and 20 per cent respectively.

Talent management benefits both the organization and the employees. The organization is benefited from the higher productivity, increase in absorptive capacity, dedication and commitment of talented employees, faster achievement of the goals of the organization due to innovative efforts of such employees, reduced cost of production and above all goodwill in the market due to superior quality of the products. At the same time, employees have job satisfaction, career development prospects, increased dexterity and knowledge and sustained efforts for increasing contribution to the organization. If it so then the organization should attach extreme importance to the talent related activities.

The effective management of talented employees requires the organization to adopt an integrated and strategic approach ranging from talent recognition to the change in the organization culture. In between, there are several other ingredients of talent management such as talent attraction, talent selection, talent retention and talent succession. Talent recognition is an uphill task, which needs full regards and affection to the talents, use of a variety of appraisals and unbiased approach of the management. Regarding the change in organization culture, the top management should adopt the magnanimity of tolerance towards talents and be visionary that the growth and goodwill of the organization depends on the talented employees. The organization should give thought as to why talented employees continue to work there especially these days when both the national and global business environment is highly competitive and rewarding.

Talented personnel are attracted towards those organizations, which builds up a good brand name for taking care of their valuable employees. It acts in the same manner raising the productivity and popularity of the organization as the good brand identity of the products between the customers and the reputed companies. Selection of talented employees should be transparent and take place according to the principle of meritocracy reflecting creativity for the sake of sustainable development of the organization. Selection should further be made on the basis of equal opportunity for all irrespective of cast, creed, colour and rural-urban bias because lotus grows in muddy water. All prophetic ideas took place far from the urban centers of their time. Retention of talent is comparable to the growth of infant, which needs all care of the parents. It becomes more significant especially these days when the mobility of such people is unimaginable. Replacement of talented employees involves enormous cost. Therefore, organization should evolve strategies and make efforts to retain people rewarding them for their high performance and providing them opportunities for their progress. Effective organization anticipates the emerging trends at the global level and undertakes measures to meet the challenges arising there. The organization plans the succession and trains the employees in a manner that the goodwill and brand name continues to dominate the market. It is an unending exercise to keep identifying potential talents and grooming the same for the future success of the organization.

To conclude, neglect to talent management is suicidal to the sustainable development of the organization especially during current business scenario when world market is highly competitive. No organization can survive even at the national level without talent management.

Talent Management in Self-Financing Institution

2

Jai Prakash

TALENT AND TALENT MANAGEMENT

"Talent" connotes different meaning to different people. It has different meaning in different contexts also. The meaning of talent is different for someone serving a corporate than someone serving defense services, serving civil services, etc. Therefore, it is germane to first decide in what context we are talking about then the meaning of talent would come. Here we are talking in the context of Academics and for Academic Institutions.

Talent Management in Academics

"What is talent?" has turned out to be a tough question, and we are not sure that we have an answer. It is defined by many in many ways.

Malcolm Cowley says "Talent is what you possess; genius is what possesses you".

Goethe says "Talent develops in quiet places, character in the full current of human life".

Talent to us is little like the person who climbed the Himalayas to the guru's cave to ask "what is the meaning of life?" and got the answer "Oh I was hoping you might be able to tell me dear son...." So, there is no one answer to this question. Just to cite the example from the *Gita*, which says that there is no plant that grows on the surface of the earth which does not have medicinal value; there is no sound in the universe that cannot form a *mantra* and I believe that there is no man born who does not have a talent, just we need to have an eye to recognize the hidden talent in him. So, with this paper of ours we seek you to let us try, and please permit us to ponder, ramble and philosophies a little along with you.

Talent Management in Self-financing Institutions

The use of the word "talent" has become almost jaded but not quite in the category of academics. We being in academics for more than four decades would like to make the judicious use of this word which is to us is extremely serious and sincere in its true sense. Because it is not only concerned with the society and country at large but with the entire human civilization. We feel talent management in academic institutions has never been more required before than today. Because, academics today is inextricably linked to the economic growth and development of the country. Talent management in academics is full of challenges and to come out victorious requires the talent to identify the talent and place them at the right position to reap the maximum benefits. In self-financing institutions it is much more important to do the justice with the job of managing talent. Because earlier there were less number of institutes and less number of people were required to manage the talent. But now we are more than 200 institutions in UPTU itself who are offering the B.Tech and other professional courses. The responsibility and expectations are too high but the people are less or difficult to manage.

Levels of Talent Management in Academics

One size fits all also does not apply to the talent management in the academic institutions. There are three levels in the academics for the management of talent. The first level is at the Management levels followed by the Head of Institution's level and the third level which is a combination of faculty, technical staff and students. Every level requires a different set of dexterity to manage the talent. The set of issues, problems, challenges all are different at different levels. Similarly the solutions of all those are also different at different levels.

We are going to take up these levels one by one followed with the deliberations on the talent management at every level. It is also pertinent to mention no level is more important than the other because level is important enough that it could make or mar any academic institute. Undoubtedly talent management is a double-edged sword. If used prudently at all the levels, could give very rich dividend otherwise could spoil a rising star.

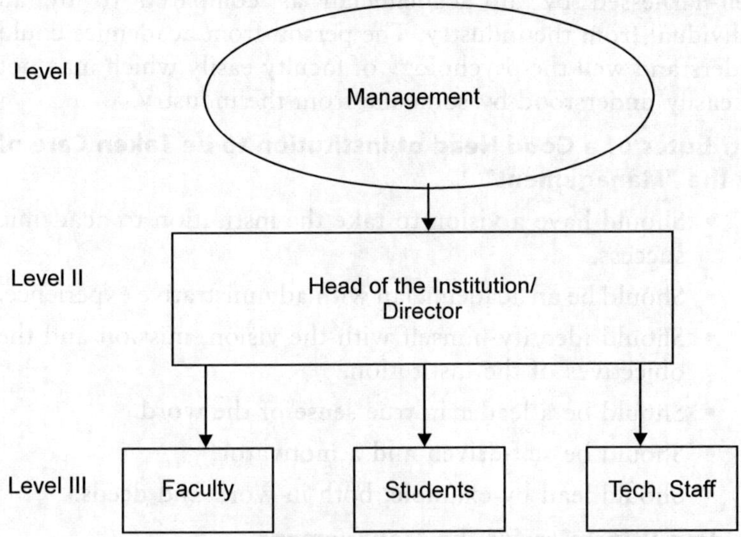

Fig. 2.1: Levels of Talent Management in the Self-Financing Institutions

Talent Management percolates from top to bottom. All the problems of level III is obviously included in the problem-set of level II and level I. But solving the issues at every level the solution also percolates from top to bottom. Solving issues at the level I would automatically take care the issues related to the issues of at level II and level III.

"MANAGEMENT" OF THE SELF-FINANCING INSTITUTION & TALENT MANAGEMENT

The main challenge before the management of the academic institution is the scarcity of talented people who could be made Head of the Institution or Director. As the number of Institutions is rising with a high speed with every passing day, this amounts to a monumental task in front of the management. But ultimately one has to be picked up from the available sample.

The main choice with the management is to take someone from either industry or academics. The latter happens to be better choice to us not because we are from the academics but because we have felt that the talent management of faculty and students—two pillars of any academic institution—could be well-harnessed by an academician as compared to by an individual from the industry. The person from academics could understand well the psychology of faculty easily which may not be easily understood by someone from the industry.

Attributes of a Good Head of Institution to be Taken Care of by the "Management"

- Should have a vision to take the institution to academic success.
- Should be an academician with administrative experience.
- Should identify himself with the vision, mission and the objectives of the institution.
- Should be a leader in true sense of the word.
- Should be self-driven and a motivator.
- Should lead by example, both in work and deeds.

Guiding Principles for the Management

- Management should have a clear vision.
- Management should act like a guiding star and not a dictator to the Head of the Institute or Director.
- If the Director is visionary, he is self-motivated and develops a kind of self-pressure to perform.
- If the Director is not a visionary but is ready to work hard then he needs to be continuously guided by the Governing Council to perform, so creating a kind of external pressure to deliver.
- If the Director is neither a visionary nor ready to work hard then no choice lies with management. (Hence, out of discussion.)

The Governing Council should meet regularly to review and analyze the performance of the institute at large.

HEAD OF THE INSTITUTION & TALENT MANAGEMENT

In any academic institution the Head of Institution or Director has to manage three different set of people. The first set of people is faculty, the second set of people is students and the third set of people is technical staff. The methodology to manage the talent with all the three set of people is different.

Head of the Institution and Faculty

The main challenges being faced by Head of Institution regarding faculty members are as follows:

- In the wake of growth of number of institutions it is difficult to find the adequate number of true talent, i.e. qualified and experienced faculty.
- Finding a good Head of Institutions is a difficulty, so imagine the situation of finding senior faculty in the ratio of growing number of institutions.
- Inability to attract a good response to job ads, both in terms of quantity and quality.
- Difficulty in motivating the young faculty and to balance the ego-state with senior faculty, i.e. with the professors and deans.
- Lack of aggression and proactiveness which is building among senior faculty members.
- Pyramid structure skewed to many junior faculty members, with too few teachers in the middle and higher level.
- Limited interaction with industry and external research teams, leading to inadequate exposure and visibility.
- To retain the faculty members.

The good qualities which should be looked for in a faculty by the Head of the Institution are as follows:

- Should be qualified and experienced.
- Should have a good academic background.
- Should have command, both in subject and communication.
- Should act as a role model to the students.
- Should be punctual and focused.

- Should understand the roles and responsibilities of a teacher.
- Should be updated and well informed.

In Govt. Institutions most of the liaison work is done by Head of the institute but in self-financing organizations he looks after the major academic work. The Head of Institution organize regular meetings with HODs and evaluate their performance. In turn HODs take meetings with faculty members for assessing students' attendance, course coverage and level of understanding to take remedial actions (if need be). The balancing of the policy of pressure and motivation should move from HODs to faculty and from faculty to the students. For better control the periodic feedback of the faculty should be done.

Good faculty members are invaluable asset to any good academic institution. The entire institute should try to stop them from leaving the institute. One methodology which could be followed in retaining of the good faculty members is as follows:

- To do an ABC analysis of the faculty.
- To identify the team of core teachers.
- To find those who are trainable and willing to see the institution as path to success.
- The A graders must be given full recognition in terms of their growth and promotions.
- The B graders can be invested in for the future. They will soon turn into A graders.
- To identify the C grade ones who neither have the necessary skills nor the motivation. There may be a need to hire in excess so that these C graders can be slowly phased out.

Head of the Institution and Students

Students could also be segregated into two groups. The first group is consisting of normal students and the second group is consisting of those students who are below average students. The important point for

- Students are to be motivated by telling them what their future prospects are and groom them accordingly.
- To devote more time with students (which would act as a pressure tactics).
- To give assignments and feedback at regular time intervals (even ask them to extend their stay in the institute and complete the assignments).
- Once the students get good marks they will be motivated.
- To conduct announced and unannounced subject based quizzes to make the students study continuously.
- To emphasize more on understanding than on mere course completion (on teachers' part).

Head of the Institution and Technical Staff

The motivational issues related to technical staff are much more difficult to resolve and manage. Before doing anything it would be prudent to understand that what motivates the technical staff employees. The counseling could be a very good start for motivating technical staff. The problems with them are more because of their availability. They do find industry as a better avenue than academics. Following are some of the solutions which can be utilized for the management of talent at the technical staff level.

- Provide clear job specifications.
- Give positive reinforcement for a job well done.
- To impart training to train them in relevant area of the subject.
- To motivate them by encouraging for higher education.
- To expose them to the new technologies for their career growth path.
- To provide them incentives and higher salary for better performance.

3

Designing a Framework for Mapping Talent Management Strategies

Solai Baskaran, Ashish Manohar Urkude and *Neha Agrawal*

The Origin

In the ancient times kings like Akbar used to keep Nine Genius with him. They were Super Stars of that time. The most famous among them were Birbal the Genius and Tansen the Music Maestro. Similar cases are there in all the pre-historic ages. In the Ramayan era King Dasharath had Top Talent with him in the form of Vasistha and Vishwamitra. In the Mahabharata era King Dhrutarashtra had Bhishmacharya, Dronacharya, Kripacharya, Karna, and other such stalwarts. So Talent Management is not new but it has taken a new dimension in the Global Village Era.

The Scenario

Earlier to Tech Revolutions and before the Liberalization, Globalization and Privatization (LPG) in India, people used to stick to one company and used to work for life. However, after this revolution most of the talent pool started changing jobs for growth, stability, security, challenge or for various reasons. Thus, see the Fig. 3.1, many organizations for example in our case we take an Software Development Company, faced a problem when, one of the Managers, one of the Team Leader (TL) of software (s/w), or Quality (Qlty), or System Administrator (s/a) or Hardware (h/w) professional left the job. The whole new team and their synchronization and the harmonization and orchestration used to be started from scratch. The situation before the Talent Management concept was taken seriously and was implemented full force in various companies is given in the Fig. 3.1.

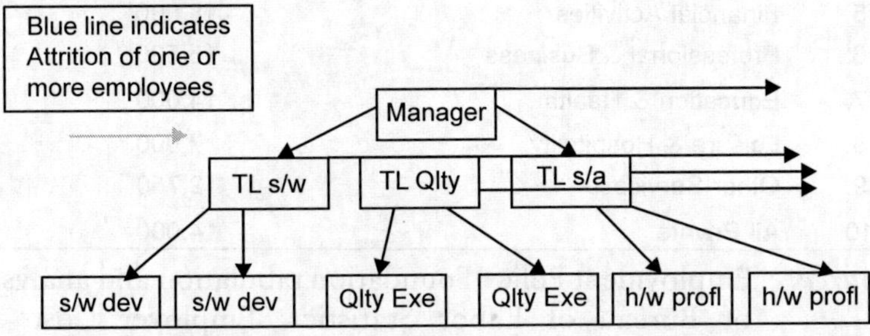

Fig. 3.1: Situation before Implementing Talent Management Programs

The Total Costing Disaster in Human Resource Management

The high attrition due to various reasons like increasing opportunities, poaching, family reasons, health reasons, vested interest, likings of individual or groups, has lead to this talent crunch as well as demand around the world. A continual effort to replace departing workers—to keep the revolving door full, instead of stopping it altogether—is bleeding organizations dry. It's expensive to constantly replace people that turnover. The cost of attracting, recruiting, hiring, training, and getting new people up to speed is tremendously more costly as well as tremendously more wasteful than most realize. Just consider these costs, SAP determined is cost $678,000 in recruiting, training, and missed sales opportunities every time an experienced sales person quit. Also, a typical medical center spends over $2 million each year replacing staff members. This cost include time spent by the HR department in hiring one person, training him/her, developing his skills, and up expertise him/her in their work.

Just consider the turnover replacement costs by industry.

Table 3.1: Cost Per Employee in Various USA Industries

Sl. No.	Industry	Cost Per Employee in U.S.D.
1.	Construction	14,500
2.	Manufacturing	14,500
3.	Trade & Transportation	12,500
4.	Information	19,500

(Contd...)

5.	Financial Activities	18,000
6.	Professional & Business	15,500
7.	Education & Health	14,000
8.	Leisure & Hospitality	7,000
9.	Other Services	12,750
10.	All Private	14,000

Source: Employment Policy Foundation tabulation and analysis of Bureau of Labor Statistics, Employer Cost of Employee Compensation Data.

Thus, from the Table 3.1, the conclusion drawn will be that the industries have realized the importance of only one Asset with them that is the Human Resources or the Talent.

Solution Found Out to be the Talent Management

Hence, the companies adopted various Talent Management efforts to really value their own people, by starting internal customers value adding programs. Indian Information and Computer Technology (ICT) giant Wipro implemented PCMM developed by SEI and attained 'Level-5' the highest maturity level in the human talent management, retentions and in HR practices. The strategy worked and the employees are not only satisfied but are keeping in the organization for longer time or even for the life. Other companies adopted new and innovative or standard practices around the world. However, it is predicted that if there will be any war in the world that will be on Talent Management only. The organization or the country which won this war will be the strongest in the world or at least the force to reckon with.

What is Talent Management?

According to Mr. Derek Stockley, Talent Management can be defined as, "A conscious, deliberate approach undertaken to attract, develop and retain people with the aptitude and abilities to meet current and future organizational needs". Talent management involves individual and organizational development in response to a changing and complex operating environment. It includes the creation and maintenance of a supportive, people oriented organization culture. Human Resources (HR) executives are starting to take a more strategic approach known as Human Resource Management (HRM). A key thrust is the quest to identify, recruit, develop, and retain highly talented individuals who can drive the company forward and provide competitive differentiation. 'People are our greatest asset' is a *mantra* that companies have been chanting for years. Yet it is only relatively recently that businesses have started putting HR systems in place that support this philosophy. A Enterprise Learning and Talent Management 2007 by Bersin and Associates, January 2007 study shows that 85 per cent of HR executives state that the "single greatest challenge in workforce management is creating or maintaining their companies' ability to compete for talent". Without question, effective talent management provides one of the most critical points of strategic leverage today. Offering enormous business value, talent management is complex and continually evolving. Research also, shows that organizations increasingly focus on talent management. Moving from reactive to proactive, companies is working hard to harness talent. According to SHRM's 2006 Talent Management Survey Report, fifty-three per cent of organizations have specific talent management initiatives in place. Of these companies, 76 per cent consider talent management a top priority. In addition, 85 per cent of HR professionals in these companies work directly with management to implement talent management strategies. Talent management is the integrated process of ensuring that an organization has a continuous supply of highly productive individuals in the right job, at the right time. Rather than a one-time event, talent management is a continuous process that plans talent needs, builds an image to attract the very best, ensures that new hires are immediately productive, helps to retain the very best, and facilitates the continuous movement of talent to where it can have the most impact within the organization. Organizational growth has transformed from quantity of talent to quality of talent. As organizations seek new ways of improving workforce productivity, "talent management" has become a vital element in establishing a Human Capital Management (HCM) environment talent management is more adequately defined as: "A continuous, integrated process that helps employers to effectively plan talent needs, attract the very best talent, speed time to productivity, motivate the right behavior, develop targeted capabilities and knowledge, retain the highest performers and enable talent mobility across the organization." The goal of the talent management process is to increase overall workforce productivity through the improved attraction, retention, and utilization of talent. The talent management strategy is superior not just because it focuses on productivity, but also because it is forward looking and proactive, which means that the organization is continuously seeking out talent and opportunities to better utilize that talent. It produces excellent results because it overcomes the major problem of traditional recruiting, which is isolation. It instead integrates the previously independent functions of recruiting, retention, workforce planning, employment branding, metrics, orientation and redeployment into a seamless process.

Four Steps of Talent Management Assessment Process

There are four steps that companies can take to quickly assess their talent management process and begin improving their talent management competency:

Step 1: Role Identification: Ensure and analyze the key competencies and responsibility required for each position at each stage. Ensure that there is no gap between responsibilities or overlapping of activities and responsibilities. The proper allocation of jobs to different line managers must be conducive to their skill set.

Step 2: Utilization of Talent Management Skills: Identification of the critical skills needed to play the key roles in the talent life cycle effectively is required to ensure that the company employs people who possess them; the methods need to be adopted to develop the employees and the clarification of the activities which need to be outsourced or made in house.

Step 3: Evaluation and Measuring Right Things: Assessment of the measures to evaluate the performance of the talent management process at each life cycle stage such as such as offer-to-hire ratios, average tenures of new hires, performance ranking, skill fit to job requirements, etc. such as offer-to-hire ratios, average tenures of new hires, performance ranking, skill fit to job requirements, etc. need to be evaluated in order to ensure that the measures are aligned with the overall talent management strategy.

Step 4: Aligning Work Forces with Business Objectives: Talent managers are required to apply different techniques and methods to connect their role and responsibilities to the overall objectives of the process to ensure that knowledge shared and experiences are properly utilized and communicated, to ensure that feedback mechanism is effective and to take corrective action for deviations.

Talent Management has Revolutionized HR Around the World

During the 1980s and 1990s, the focus shifted to a more "Strategic HR"—by turning outward, the HR organization established "business partner" relationships with business managers. In this era, the HR organization established new functions. We have put this Evolution in the form of Pyramid, Fig. 3.2.

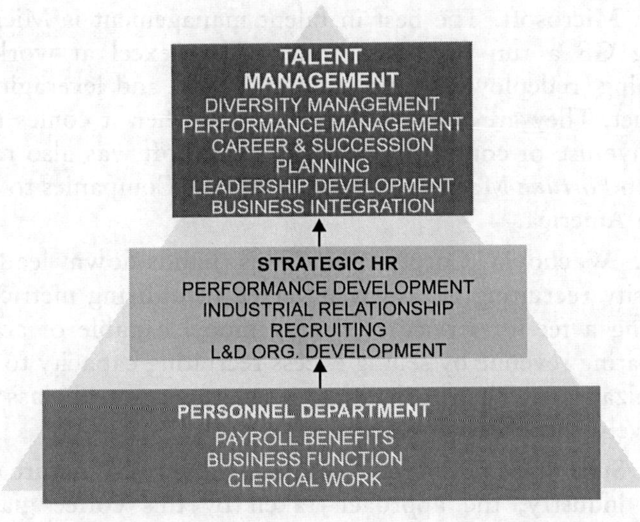

Fig. 3.2: The Pyramid of Evolution of HR

Talent Management Approaches in Various Organizations

The very best companies in recruiting are constantly striving to improve everything they do through continuous learning. One of the best learning tools at their disposal is benchmarking, which often provides learning that can be applied immediately. Dr. John Sullivan, has put it in the following way:

1. First Merit Bank. This bank headquartered in Ohio, is the most strategic and innovative approach to recruiting. They have a great referral program, the best in understanding how recruiting can adopt successful approaches such as data mining, customer relationship management, competitive intelligence, niche market targeting, and assessment metrics from other business functions.

2. General Electric. Long recognized as "the" benchmark firm when it comes to building a performance culture, GE wins hands down as having the best overall talent management strategy. They prioritize jobs and focus on "game changers". Their employer-of-choice brand is second to none and they are among the leaders (along with Home Depot) in recruiting from the military.

3. Microsoft. The best in talent management is Microsoft giving GE a run for their money. They excel at workforce planning, redeployment, utilizing analytics, and leveraging the internet. They are also truly world class when it comes to the effective use of contingent workers Microsoft was also ranked #57 on *Fortune* Magazine's 2005, 100 Best Companies to Work for in America.

4. Wachovia Corporation. This hands-down leader in diversity recruiting is also well versed in utilizing metrics and running a fee-for-service recruiting model capable of actually generating revenue by selling excess recruiting capacity to other organizations. Their recruiting strategy is world-class in a relatively conservative industry.

5. Starbucks. Given the "less than glamorous" nature of the retail industry, the approach taken by this coffee giant to employment branding and becoming an employer of choice is phenomenal. They also excel at high-volume hiring. Starbucks was ranked #11 on *Fortune* Magazine's 2005, 100 Best Companies to work for in America.

6. Marriott International. This hotel giant was one of the earliest adopters of employment branding, and one of the few companies to maintain a dedicated focus on the art. While they still excel in employment branding, their diversity recruiting and work with the disadvantaged are world class by any standard. Marriott was ranked #63 on *Fortune* Magazine's 2005, 100 Best Companies to work for in America.

7. South-West Airlines. The clear winner for innovation in recruiting, this company not only excels in selection but also scores huge in branding with the launch of its own TV show (*Airline*). Every employee periodically receives productivity and financial reports so they can act more like owners.

8. Wegmans Food Markets. Wegmans' ranking as the best company to work for in America by *Fortune* Magazine in 2005. Behind the long-standing reputation that has made these grocery stores tourist attractions are recruiting and talent management best practices in employment branding, workforce planning, redeployment, and alternative sourcing. Wegmans starts recruiting management in high school by bringing at-risk youth into its internship program and mentoring them towards college.

9. Corning. Corning's use of internal recruiters as placement experts during downsizing was both innovative and effective. They also effectively utilize service-level agreements and have a Six Sigma effort in their recruiting function (most HR functions teach Six Sigma, but they don't actually apply it to themselves).

10. Intel. Intel can be lauded for its scientific, "fact based" approach to recruiting and HR. Their workforce planning model has some excellent design features. Their culture of constructive confrontation also helps to drive an incredible rate of continual change.

11. Wal-Mart. When it comes to high-volume recruiting, nobody does it better. Wal-Mart's TV ads highlighting their great-place-to-work status are a bold approach to proactively defending their strong employment brand.

12. The Container Store. Its #1 ranking on Fortune's best-place-to-work list two years in a row is even more amazing given The Container Store's miniscule centralized HR and recruiting function. They have also done some work in candidate assessment and measuring the business impact of great recruiting.

13. Google. Google's ratio of recruiters to employees is mind-boggling. They also excel at candidate assessment and recruiting women engineers.

14. Baptist Health Care. Baptist excels at building a well-managed brand; the company ranks #6 among large companies on the Fortune best-place-to-work list. They are number one in recruiting and retention in an industry that has some of the most backward recruiters and recruiting practices on the planet.

15. PepsiCo. The leader in diversity recruiting, PepsiCo uses incentives to make diversity recruiting a standard business practice. It helps in building different perspectives and taking local decision at global level.

Talent Management Success Stories

1. Toyota Developing Exceptional People: The truth is that Toyota does like to start with good people who possess the *capability* to become exceptional employees. In Toyota people are carefully selected to join based on their potential and a judgment that there is a fit with the job and with Toyota's culture. They must have some general problem-solving capability and be willing to work as part of a team. People develop specific capabilities *after* they are hired at Toyota. It often creates situations in which there is an equal balance between reward and punishment in order to encourage the desired behavior. For example, given the critical nature of attendance on the performance of the system, a high emphasis is placed on having great attendance (perfect attendance is preferred). On the reward side, Toyota Motor Manufacturing Kentucky (TMMK) has an annual award ceremony for all employees who achieved perfect attendance in the previous year.

2. Intel is Melding Talent Management with Succession: Intel uses three systems that work together to allow leadership to emerge on the job and to be rewarded, for training and development. It starts with peers, real-life learning, and training culture.

The first system: It involves getting management experience at an early stage. Teams of 10 employees marked for promotions are called together to provide each other with peer-to-peer coaching on an ongoing basis.

The second system: It involves action-oriented learning. Groups of managers come together to solve real business problems by working in virtual teams. These teams can include members from locations around the globe. The teams operate proactively (senior leaders seek out projects that foster the members' management development) and reactively (the teams meet to address common business concerns).

The third system: In this senior managers teach or provide leadership training at least four times per year, and their participation is tied to their annual bonuses. Intel provides leadership assessment tools that are separate from the annual performance reviews. These tools pinpoint weaknesses in areas such as providing feedback or "living" the company's values. This culture has created leaders, who are highly promotable.

Talent Management Strategies in Indian Organizations

Hence, we have put some examples of the Indian companies who followed different talent management practices and was ranked as 'The Best Employers In India 2007':

1. Aditya Birla Group: It has created teams of Value Leaders and Value Facilitators—change agents who are in the forefront of role modeling and teaching values. The Corporate HR cell strategize and provide intellectual infrastructure, Engages with businesses at the operational and tactical level, Focus on drivers such as Leadership Development Reward Strategy Performance Management Competency Building. The Work Culture of company has a Concept of Life Long Employment, Meritocratic, achievement oriented organization, Create an ambience for talent to bloom. Senior managers arrange informal and formal meetings with the staff, Chairman shares the corporate policy with the middle and senior management—takes their views, Leadership Renewal. The reward program is designed to reinforce the HR vision. 'The Power of Five' honors what the company calls Value Champions, while 'Vision 2015' encourages dialogue about the group's future direction.

2. Infosys: It has a confidential instrument aimed at increasing self-awareness and hence the ability to manage one's stress more effectively. Organizations are offering yoga and meditation camps, employee counseling services, crèche and day care, extended maternity leave (even for adoption), paternity leave, concierge services, Employee Assistance Programs, relocation services, fully or partly paid sabbaticals, flexi time, telecommuting and involving families of employees as ways to convey caring. Infosys Women's Inclusivity Network (IWIN) is a team formed to address needs specific to women and promotes an "inclusive" workplace where the potential of women is leveraged for growth and every woman feels valued, heard and fully involved with the company.

3. TCS: It values every associate and employee care is a top priority. At TCS, they value every associate and invest in their personal and professional development and also have a number of associate engagement initiatives that bring associates and their families together in learning, fun and social activities. This enhances the bonding and commitment to the organization. They continuously revise HR policies, listen to the associates' opinions, make policies more people-friendly, and cater to varied needs of a diverse workforce. The company has associate-friendly policies, a dynamic focus on people as an asset, and a work environment, which is challenging and rewarding. Career growth and clear career tracks endear the organization to its people. The focus on Economic Value Added (EVA) to calculate variable performance pay makes TCSers among the most competitively paid in the market. TCS has a strong Academic Interface Program for creating synergy and forging strong relations with educational institutes, which brings TCS closer to the budding software engineering community.

4. Wipro: "Wipro's talent management and engagement has a two-fold approach. It contains the challenges by following best practices in two areas—compensation and non-compensation. Challenges arising due to compensation reasons are contained at Wipro by continuously benchmarking employees' salaries with their competitors and providing merit-based salary increases. In addition, for middle and senior management, they have equity-based compensation through Restricted Stock Units. They also have various employee benefit programs to ensure that they stay competitive on the compensation front." Wipro has following strategies such as 'Meet Your People Program', Wipro Listens & Responds, Best People Manager Awards, and Talent Review and Planning. Wipro has studied their best practices and created a framework called MYPP, which is an initiative launched to increase supervisory touch time and effectiveness with team members. It is a framework, which defines the various touch points that the manager needs to engage with the team. It enables every manager to connect the team to a bigger picture, create an understanding of the organization's objectives and the team members' role in the same, create fun at the workplace, work on the career aspirations of the team members, and conduct regular and periodic meetings that increase the productivity levels of the team. Talent engagement initiatives have always been a major thrust area, and will continue to be so. All its managers strive towards the same, with some of them going an extra mile to ensure superior levels of engagement, motivation and retention of their teams. The Best People Manager Award is an honor given directly by the Chairman and CEO to those managers who create a better workplace for their team members. These are managers who show high employee satisfaction, engagement, productivity and low attrition.

5. Godrej Consumer Products: It has different cross-functional teams that operate at different levels. Membership into these teams gives exposure to Senior Management and opportunities to work in strategic or cross-functional initiatives. The Young Executive Board—an initiative intended to energize and motivate young decision-makers respect for employees is visible in the Great Places to Work© in ways they try to make their employees succeed. Job rotations and international exposure is common, so is coaching, mentoring and structured leadership development. These Organizations do not hesitate to invest in training with almost half of the list spending more than six days a year on training. Practical help like concierge services and Employee Assistance Programs are offered, as is outplacement services for people who do not fit in spite of performance improvement plans.

6. SK Telecom: A supervisor can write comments into an online evaluation system as frequently as he or she wants, and HR collects the comments three times a year. This addresses leadership and employee issues raised by diversification beyond the core activity of this mobile carrier. The cultural focus has been shifted from employee seniority to performance and competence. The company has been a leader in reforming the traditionally hierarchical structure of Korean business. Satisfaction regarding compensation, benefits and employer reputation is extremely high and staff turnover extremely low. They activated open communication between top management and employees, and created a flatter organizational structure by abolishing traditional ranking of job titles. All of these were backed up with the promotion of a corporate culture based on challenge, creativity and teamwork. The four pillars of our employee orientation are "Earning, Learning, Pride and Fun". They believe in developing business through developing people. They have an in-house "Academy of Learning" and also have tie-ups with business schools, which help train our talent. To create a "Learning Organization" they created Knowledge Management function within the company just four years ago and feel amply rewarded by the journey because recently, at Seoul in Korea, they were given a MAKE (Most Admired Knowledge Enterprise) award for Asia".

7. FedEx India: It has a strong promotion from within philosophy, requiring that all permanent positions be posted internally to existing employees before external hiring may begin. Reserved parking slots, Executive canteens, Top Management Holiday Homes, separate washrooms for different levels in the hierarchy—are fast disappearing and performance and meritocracy is replacing these as the main differentiator. Equity also means that people are paid fairly for what they do. FedEx organizes road shows for the employees which are facilitated by the Compensation and Benefits representative and Managing Director to explain the pay review for the year. While sharing details of salary packages is fairly commonplace, in FedEx, employees can openly discuss any general issues with any level of management without the fear of discrimination, under the Open Door Policy. The Organization's grievance procedure called Guaranteed Fair Treatment Policy (GFTP). This includes a hearing at the management level closest to the employee and the opportunity for appeals up through the system.

8. Sapient: It has one of the most important recognition programs in the form of the core value award. These awards are run globally every quarter. People are recognized for living the core values of Client Focused Delivery, Relationships, Creativity, Openness, Leadership and People Growth. Winners of these awards get their place on the coveted "Core Value Wall of Fame" in the office. In order to support an individual's career aspirations, Sapient has introduced a Career Manager Program. Each individual in the company is assigned a career manager. This program focuses on an individual's long-term growth through frequent mentoring and developmental inputs provided by the Career Manager. Rather than taking pride in "weeding out" under performers Sapient takes pride in their successful performance improvement program that has been able to turn around 70 per cent of under performers Sapient has a Global Corporate Ethics Hotline where employees can seek restore of ethics violation in an anonymous manner.

Various Standard Practices and TM Methodologies

We have given few standard practices and methodologies which are practiced around the world as a bench mark.

1. Human Talent Management (HTM) using Competency Model: A "competency model" is a collection of competencies that also contains the related behavior which directly connects general strategic priorities with the work to be done to attain them, and the levels of competency to be reached for each item of behavior. An isolated profile of organizational strategy is not useful for achieving the results. Usually a competency is defined, for example, "Work with information", and a number of behavior indicators are associated with it, such as: (a) Appropriate identification and use of information sources, (b) Precise identification of the type and form of information required, (c) Obtain relevant information and maintain it in appropriate formats. The levels aim at describing the degree of development of the competency in terms of the extent of its performance and the possibility to undertake activities such as planning, decisions by resources, or the work of others. The application of competencies in HTM has become a good formula for taking better advantage of people's capacities. Incorporating competencies implies inquiring not only into the results which are expected but also into the way in which the different functions that work with the people in the company can help to achieve these results. To develop a style of HTM that identifies the competencies necessary for attaining the companies' objectives and facilitates the development of its people towards these competencies is to apply HTM by competencies. Successful experiences in human talent management by competencies are usually due to the skill with which the organization establishes a framework of competencies which reflects its philosophy, values and strategic objectives. This framework becomes the reference point for the various activities in the HTM work cycle.

2. High Impact Talent Management Framework: The latest research conducted by Bersin and Associates, is shown in the Fig. 3.3. It describes various factors and characteristics:

(i) Talent Strategy and Planning,

(ii) Sourcing and Recruiting,

(iii) Performance Management,

(iv) Succession Planning,

(v) Leadership Development,

(vi) Competency Management,

(vii) Compensation Management,

(viii) HR System Metrics, and

(ix) Learning and Development.

They provide HR Consultation. In that they find out the organization specific solutions on the following metrics:

(i) Business Problem Identification,

(ii) Business Related Talent Challenges,

(iii) HR Process Design, and

(iv) System Process and Implementations.

Fig. 3.3: Framework of Talent Management
(*Source*: Bersin & Associates)

3. PCMM (People Capability Maturity Model): PCMM, developed by SEI, is an acronym of People Capability Maturity Model, is a framework that guides organizations in improving the processes for managing and developing workforces. It's an integrated system for improving individual competency, developing effective teams, and motivating improved performance it "helps organizations characterize the maturity of their workforce practices, establish a program of continuous workforce development, set priorities for improvement actions, integrate workforce development with process improvement, and establish a culture of excellence". PCMM helps us "characterize the maturity of workforce practices, establish a program of continuous workforce development, set priorities for improvement actions, integrate workforce development with process improvement, and establish a culture of excellence". And these are key factors for human resource development, which is the most important competitive edge to a company's success, and to serve its client.

Framework of PCMM: The SEI who developed the PCM Model, see Fig. 3.4, believes that consistent improvement can be done only in steps. Hence, it developed five maturity level or five stages towards improvement. The five stages are as follows:

(i) Process Areas for Maturity Level 1: Initial: At the Initial level; an organization has no consistent way of performing its work. As a result, projects lose control of their schedule, costs, and product quality. Organizations must establish a foundation on which they can deploy common processes across the organization. To enable this repeatability, managers must get control of commitments and baselines which is developed in Managed level.

(ii) Process Areas for Maturity Level 2: Managed: At this level the Management has full control over the process by effect of controlled structured mechanism.

(iii) Process Areas for Maturity Level 3: Defined: At the Defined level, the organization identifies its best practices and integrates them into a common process.

(iv) Process Areas for Maturity Level 4: Predictable: At the Predictable level, the organization begins managing its processes through the data that describes its performance. When the organization can characterize the performance of its processes quantitatively, it has profound knowledge that can be used to improve them.

(v) Process Areas for Maturity Level 5: Optimizing: And finally at the Optimizing level, highest level of maturity, the organization uses its profound, quantitative knowledge to make continuous improvements in its processes. Based on its data, the organization can identify which processes can most benefit from improvement actions.

Thus, PCMM framework builds an environment in which:

(i) Practices can be repeated,

(ii) Best practices can be rapidly transferred across groups,

(iii) Variations in performing best practices are reduced,

(iv) Practices are continuously improved to enhance their capability.

Each maturity level provides a layer in the foundation for continuous improvement and equips the organization with increasingly powerful tools for developing the capability of its workforce. The nature of the transformation imposed on the organization's workforce practices to achieve each level of maturity is depicted in Fig. 3.4 given below:

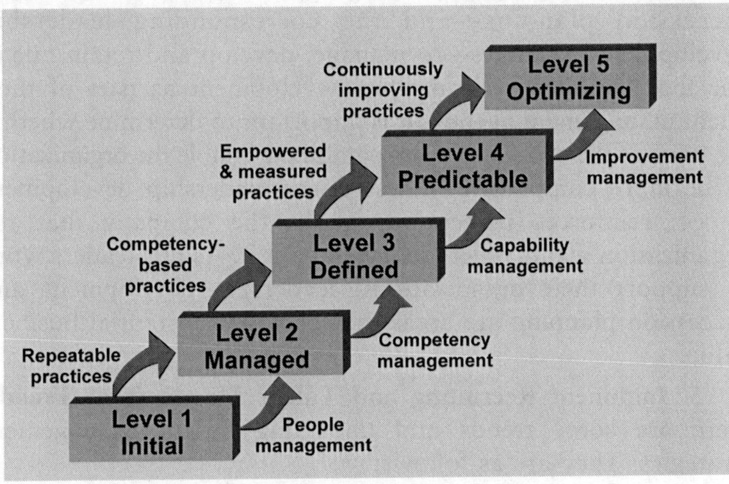

Fig. 3.4: PCMM Stages of Maturity

Few organizations that have achieved the PCMM level 5 are:

(i) Oracle, USA, and

(ii) Wipro Technologies, India.

4. Succession Planning Management and Leadership Development: Investment in human capital requires careful planning. Under the talent management umbrella, succession planning and leadership development are important organizational business strategies to develop and retain talent. As noted in the 2005 Human Capital Index Report, succession planning is also one of the key strategies to reduce turnover costs. While in the past succession plans were primarily focused on key leadership roles, organizations are now establishing leadership development and succession planning initiatives early in the process of employee career development. In addition, according to SHRM's 2006 Succession Planning Survey Report, 58 per cent of organizations have either a formal (29%) or informal (29%) succession plan and 26 per cent plan to develop one. The survey findings note that large organizations (500 or more employees) and publicly or privately owned for profit organizations are more likely to have formal succession plans. At the same time, organizations grapple with how to best utilize succession planning—and the corresponding leadership development initiatives—to manage, develop and retain talent. For that considering leadership development as part of their talent management agenda, it is important to determine whether the parts of the program, when combined, enable the organization to be more competitive; assess if the leadership development system reinforces perceptions about the company that the organization wants others to have about it. As HR leaders work to support their organizations, leadership development and succession planning are areas that provide substantial business value.

5. Imminent Recruiting and Talent Management Trends: Here are some trends and upcoming Talent Management strategies. They are as follows:

(i) An Increased Emphasis on Assessment: After sourcing, assessment is the highest impact area in traditional recruiting. Some of the areas in assessment include online technical skill assessments, the increased use of simulations (online and during interviews), improving the screening of diversity candidates, and better metrics to identify and validate the most effective screening tools and approaches.

(ii) Internet Networking Emerges: Firms and vendors to continue to explore Internet "social" networks, which can become an effective sourcing tool. Internet blogs are another area with unproven potential.

(iii) The Emergence of Workforce Planning: As the business environment and the world economy continue to change at a rapid rate (in particular, expect impacts from trade deficits, the strength of the dollar, government deficits, and increased free trade), recruiting and talent management managers will be forced to shift their focus to the future. That means an increased emphasis on forecasting, and workforce planning that is integrated into every aspect of recruiting and retention.

(iv) A Focus on Internal Redeployment: Recruiting can play a key role in moving key talent more rapidly within the organization. The proactive movement of employees to the "right job at the right time" increases retention, development, and employee productivity.

(v) Employment Branding: External employment branding is literally the only effective long-term recruiting strategy available to directors of recruiting. Top firms like Starbucks, Intel, Cisco, Marriott, Dell, Wal-Mart, and Microsoft have been focusing on employment branding for years. Closely working with product branding, PR, and marketing will help to develop an effective employment branding strategy.

(vi) An Increased Focus on "Selling": As the economy turns around, candidates will have many more job choices. Convincing them to take your job will become extremely difficult. New strategies and approaches will have to be developed to "sell" candidates on applying to your firm and get them to accept your offers.

(vii) A Laser Focuses on the Employed Top Performer: The time has finally come when the majority of recruiting and hiring managers will begin to focus the majority of their resources on finding currently employed top performers (some use the term "passive job seeker"). Because employed top performers are harder to convince, increased emphasis will be placed on market research tools to identify their job-switch criteria.

(viii) A Renewed Focus on the most Effective Sources: The new hiring boom will force corporate recruiting managers to

use metrics to identify the best recruiting sources for top performers. Most will find their very best sources for top performers to be targeted employee referrals, professional referrals, professional events, external employment branding, and Internet search engines that find information on candidates when they have not posted a resume. This also means a continued trend toward the decreased use of newspaper ads, brochures, ineffective job sites, and job fairs.

(ix) Tying Recruiting and Retention Together: As the economy improves and employee engagement continues to drop, there can be turnover among top performers to skyrocket (one recent study showed 75 per cent of employees are now willing to look for new job). Unless HR departments begin focusing on identifying individuals at risk of quitting and eliminating the causes of their frustration, recruiting will be stretched beyond its limits.

(x) A Continued Emphasis on Outsourcing: Although most outsourcing has failed to demonstrate its ROI, the continued emphasis on cost cutting and the need for a more strategic focus will keep this a hot area. Wise managers will examine outsourcing in the area of referral administration, "name identification", reference checking, and ATS outsourcing.

(xi) Referrals Remain King: Despite all the talk and the real advances in technology, nothing will come close to the effectiveness of a "no tech", proactive referral program, where employer directly ask its top employees to identify, screen, and pre-sell the best in their field.

(xii) Emerging New technology Arrives: Vendors have finally begun to realize that the current generation of technology has only made a minimal impact on recruiting. New technologies and approaches that will finally begin to meet their initial promise of revolutionizing recruiting. Recruiting managers must demand technology that's smart and that learns from its successes and mistakes. Their will be new breakthroughs in Internet search engines, candidate assessment, strategic metrics, and resume sorting technology.

(xiii) A Focus on Leadership Positions: As more senior leaders retire, there will be increased emphasis on recruiting

"potential leaders" from top firms both within and outside your industry.

(xiv) Strategic Metrics become King: This will be the breakthrough year when the focus will finally shift away from distracting and low impact "tactical" metrics (cost per hire, time to fill, number of hires, etc.) and toward more strategic metrics like quality of hire, hiring from competitors, ROI, and workforce productivity.

6. Talent Retention Exercises

(i) Employee Engagement: Employee engagement is best fostered through a meaningful and emotionally enriching work experience. Effective employee engagement—a mixture of tangible and intangible factors—fosters an environment of stimulation, development, learning, support, contribution and recognition. The impact of employee dissatisfaction varies, depending on work experience (e.g. overwhelming workloads, distant and non-communicative senior leadership, few developmental opportunities). The risk is that moderately engaged employees may move toward being disengaged. The opportunity and challenge for HR, working with senior management, is to increase the strength of employee engagement. Focus on engagement demands strong leadership, a sense of shared destiny, autonomy, accountability and opportunities for development and advancement. To better engage workers, companies must work harder to inspire people and provide a sense of passion, pride and mission. Ultimately, it is organizational culture that determines employee engagement and retention of talent.

(ii) Recruitment Strategies: In the war for talent, organizational success depends on effective recruitment and retention. To accomplish this goal, HR can provide value by focusing on five key areas: ensuring organizational stability, emphasizing employer brand and reputation, developing integrated talent strategies, supporting multilevel accountability, getting involved in talent management initiatives and offering opportunities for career and personal development.

To attract and retain talent, hiring for compatibility—the "fit" between employer and employee—is critical. In addition, companies with excellent reputations and strong brands are well positioned to attract top talent. Yahoo! Inc. exemplifies the organization that effectively links organizational culture and company values in its recruiting initiatives to determine the best candidates.

Another effective recruiting strategy is tapping into specific labor pools. By assessing the organization's areas of strength in its workplace programs and policies, HR may identify possible segments of the labor force to target. Some organizations focus on workers with disabilities, an excellent source of talent. For example, at IBM, 42 per cent of the organization's disabled workers possess key skills such as marketing, IT architecture and software engineering. By carefully assessing the organization's current and future talent needs, HR can develop recruiting and retention strategies that align with the company business goals, thus promoting organizational growth and sustainability.

(iii) Kaizen, Reengineering, Restructuring the Talent Management 24 × 7 × 365: Top Global Organizations like UNO, WB, ADB and the Fortune 500 organizations like GE, Ford, GM, Wipro, Infosys, Wal-Mart, United Airlines, which have become melting pots of diversity, multiple cultures, multiple civilizations, contrasts and who are working in several countries, but, still they are improving their talent management skills day in and out, 24 × 7 × 365. They are doing it:

- By adopting the best practices around the world,
- By generating new employee retention ideas,
- By updating employee retention plans, techniques and training programs,
- By keeping good employees,
- By keeping both ends open for discussion,
- By proper training and improving skills of employers and employees both,
- By keeping sense of understanding, direction, purpose and flexibility of demands, and

- By developing interpersonal excellence and organization belongingness.

Conclusion

Organizations continued to pursue high performance and improved results through HRM practices so, in talent management companies are taking a holistic approach—from attracting and selecting wisely, to retaining and developing leaders, to placing employees in positions of greatest impact. For organizations to succeed in today's rapidly changing and increasingly competitive marketplace, intense focus must be applied to aligning human capital with corporate strategy and objectives. It starts with recruiting and retaining talented people and continues by sustaining the knowledge and competencies across the entire workforce. With rapidly changing skill sets and job requirements, this becomes an increasingly difficult challenge for organizations. By implementing an effective talent management strategy, including integrated data, processes, and analytics, organizations can help ensure that the right people are in the right place at the right time, as well as organizational readiness for the future. To create a sophisticated talent management environment, organizations must:

(a) Explain a clear vision for talent management,

(b) Develop a roadmap for technology and process integration,

(c) Integrate and optimize processes,

(d) Implement robust technology to enable processes, and

(e) Prepare the workforce for changes associated with the new environment.

Wherever, you start with talent management, it should be clear that you ought to get moving! Talent management is here to stay and may well mark the future of HR itself. Technology is becoming rapidly enhanced or developed to support it. Senior management is aware of it and asking about it. The shifting employee base, with its special sense of employee value propositions, expects it. Also, we can't forget the personal impact it offers for HR professionals to enhance skills and visibility with senior management, as well to provide strategic impact on the organization. HR has long sought a way to do the latter; talent management is now offering it.

In crux, HRM has to develop a clear understanding among employer, employees and other stakeholders about short-term and long-term goals and have to mature their talented and skilled workforce with interpersonal excellence and organization belongingness through various innovative tools, techniques, models, means, competency frameworks, and measures.

REFERENCES

http://www.sei.cmu.edu/cmm-p/version2/faq.html

www.bersinassociates.com

Ashish Manohar Urkude, Ph.D. Thesis, submitted to Nagpur University in 2002, Management of indigenously built small car market in India with special reference to customer behavior, Chapter 1, Introduction, "Table: Jobs Associated with Automobile Industry", pp. 14-21.

Ashish Manohar Urkude, "Faster Development of India: Using Rapid Time Compression Technologies, Techniques, Tools and Talents", Annual Technical Paper Meeting, 2005, The Institute of Engineers (India), Nagpur, pp. 47-52.

www.chartcourse.com

www.highretention.com

A Study of Employees Attrition in Indian BPO Industry

4

Deepak Dixit and *Rachna Srivastava*

Introduction

Business Process Outsourcing (BPO) is the delegation of one or more IT-intensive business processes to an external provider that in turn owns administers and manages the selected process based on defined and measurable performance criteria. Business Process Outsourcing (BPO) is one of the fastest growing segments of the Information Technology Enabled Services (ITES) industry.

The Indian business process outsourcing industry, roughly around 5-6 years old, is growing at a phenomenal pace. The number of BPO companies in Indian cities has come from a handful a few years ago to about 500 in 2004.

The studies conducted by NASSCOM and the global consultants McKinsey & Co. brought to light certain amazing facts on the Indian BPO segment. According to a NASSCOM study, the country's flourishing ITES—BPO sector is estimated to have achieved a 54 per cent growth in revenue in 2003-04. A key employment—generating sector in the country; the BPO segment created job opportunities for around 74,400 additional personnel in India in the same year.

By the year 2008, the ITES-BPO sector is expected to employ over 1.1 million Indians, with its sales expected to touch an amazing 21 to 24 dollars. With 2,45,100 people employed at the end of March 31, 2004 against 1,71,100 last year, the industry witnessed a hiring growth rate of about 40-42 per cent. And the boom shows all signs of continuing considering that the cost per transaction in India is estimated to be the lowest at 29 cents compared to 52 cents in China.

Even after displaying impressive statistics about the growth and future, what is the biggest challenge for the BPO industry in India today? Well, it is a no-brainer Attrition!

The Business Process Outsourcing (BPO) industry in the country which is growing by leaps and bounds facing the challenge of finding quality human resources given the current attrition rate of around 50 per cent.

According to several recruitment firms in the country, attrition in the ITES (IT enabled services)-BPO industry is close to 35-40 per cent. The worse news is that, this is only the reported figure and the actual figures are much higher and can be as high as 80 per cent annually.

This impediment is likely to affect the industry severely in the long-run by creating a manpower shortage as well as bringing up the cost arbitrage on which the Indian industry is playing at the moment.

National Association of Software Services and Companies (NASSCOM) in a report said the outsourcing industry was expected to face a shortage of 2,62,000 professionals by 2012.

On the hiring front, the industry absorbed about 74,000 people in 2003 despite the attrition rate of 45-50 per cent being a matter of concern.

Attrition rates	%
US	42
Australia	29
Europe	24
India	18
Global Average	24

Source: Times News New York (2003)

India has one of the largest pool of English speaking graduate workforce. The challenge for the industry is not in employment but employability. The industry is also hiring professionals from outside the industry in order to meet its steady supply of manpower. NASSCOM ITES-BPO forum has identified HR as one of the key challenges of the ITES-BPO industry and has formed a special task force to address short-term challenges such as Attrition and also long-term challenges such as ensuring availability of a skilled talent pool.

Reasons for Attrition by Analyzing BPO Industry through Maslow's Hierarchical Model of Needs:

Maslow's Hierarchy Model of Needs basically concerned with revealing those needs; supposed to be main reasons of motivation for any person.

This theory can help us to know BPO industry's employee expectations and extent to which they are being fulfilled and where is still a gap. After identifying gaps, suggested actions can be taken to bring attrition rate down.

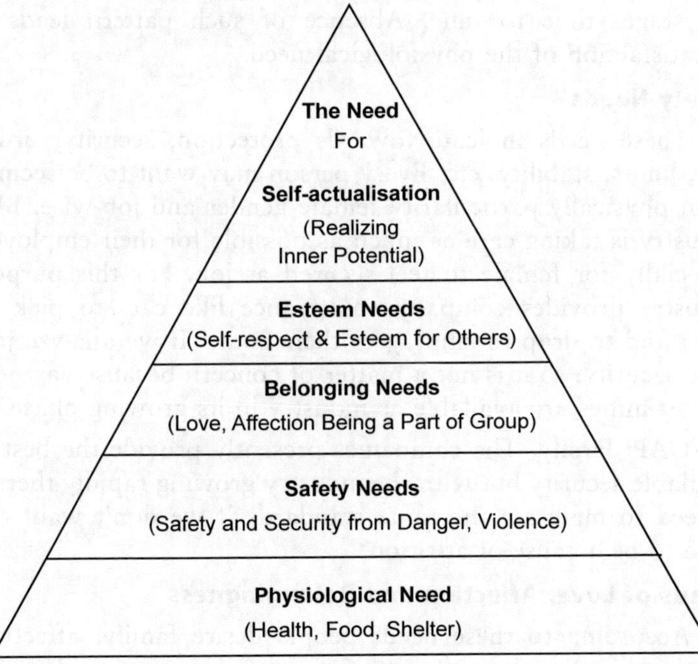

According to Maslow's theory following are the basic needs of human:

Physiological Needs

Human have some biological needs; those must be fulfilled otherwise other works cannot be completed effectively. BPO industry has been satisfying all these needs by way of providing compensation. Employees ask for sufficient compensation structure that can match with their physiological needs not only for a time being but also for a long period of time as various stages of his life comes.

Undoubtedly BPO industry provides better salary at entry level but proportionate increment in salary is not seen as experience gained by employees.

GAP: Hence, there is still a gap between employees' expectations and present condition. Even after getting high salary at entry level they want proportionate rise in salary according to their experience to cope with the needs of various life stages time to time. Absence of such pattern leads to dissatisfaction of the physiological need.

Safety Needs

These needs indicate towards protection, security, order, law, limits, stability, etc. Every person may want to be secured from physically particularity female gender and job-wise. BPO industry is taking care as much as possible for their employees especially for female to feel secured at job. For this purpose industry provides company conveyance like cars to pick up from and to drop to employees their home. If we analyze job-wise security; so it is not a matter of concern because vast jobs opportunities are available as industry in its growing phase.

GAP: Firstly, The companies presently provide the best of available security but with the industry growing rapidly there is a need to maintain the same standards if we don't want this need to be a cause of attrition.

Needs of Love, Affection and Belongingness

According to these needs people desire family, affection, relationships, work group, etc. Every person wants to share his feeling with others to avoid feeling of aloneness and also want to become acquainted by society members.

But this need in BPO industry is not being satisfied, reason being working in night shifts, isolates employees with their family, friends and society. After working in night shift employees feel fatigue and do not want anybody to disturb them in the morning.

Although industry try to provide casual and fun filled environment to their employees to enjoy the workplace, but there is a huge gap in expectation and fulfillment, which needs to be satisfied, because there cannot be any comparison between artificially created environment to make employees happy and getting satisfaction from that person they wish to have.

GAP: Definitely this is a matter of concerned for BPO industry and point to be remembered that what efforts industry has been making to create cool environment will not work for as long period of time because less interaction with family and society will definitely cause one day employees' frustration and feeling of being separated from affectionate persons.

Needs for Esteem

These needs are to feel satisfied because of some achievements, status, responsibility, reputation and recognition. After getting satisfied all these needs person feel him confident and valuable.

BPO industry unfortunately has been regarded by the Indian society as a low value industry with low-end work and which does not need high educational qualification.

Hence a person working in this industry is viewed as a person of less ability compared to others working in any other industry. This attitude has developed because of the mass recruitment undertaken by BPO firms during the initial days, where not much focus was laid on selecting highly capable person. This diminution in esteem sometimes leads to reasons for one to leave the industry. The industry presently requires an image makeover. Some of the present firms are focusing on creating a positive image of the industry by using the media in a positive manner, though much is yet to be done. Certain measure such as change in Job Title is a positive step in this direction. Providing great working environment in terms of infrastructure and facilities also acts as boost to ones esteem for the employees.

GAP: People working in this industry have an unsatisfied esteem need because of the general perception about the industry. As the industry matures, the industry's positioning needs to change from being a mere moneymaker option to an industry which provides immense learning, high growth prospects and opportunities for foreign experience.

Needs for Self-Actualization

Self-actualization need relates itself with personal growth and fulfillment. This is about being given the opportunity to develop to your full potential and will be different for every individual. Maslow describes self-actualization as a person's need to be and do what the person was "born to do".

The BPO firms nowadays are trying to provide Career growth path and higher educational opportunities for employees as a measure of retaining them. These steps are strides in fulfilling the discontented self-actualization needs of the employees. These are one of the few long-term motivations provided by companies.

GAP: Though recently companies have been trying to cater to the self actualization needs of their employees, this has been one of the major reasons for attrition. Industry workers are not able to envision the BPO industry as a long-term career option. They feel that a long-term career in the BPO industry is not feasible.

RECOMMENDATIONS

Definitely after finding all these gaps we can easily predict that the attrition problem will remain a hurdle for BPO industry in foreseeable future. The attrition in the BPO is consistent with what has been witnessed in any industry during its growth phase. The IT industry, manufacturing industry had seen similar high attrition during their growth stage which later reduces as the industry matures.

Therefore, this is the demand of time not to wait and watch but accept the challenge of attrition and keep on formulating best suitable strategies and plans to manage and minimize the impact of attrition as far as industry can do.

For this purpose BPO industry can have an advantage of suggested Win–Win model to satisfying the needs of both employer and employees.

Needs of the employer: To get maximum returns from each employee, recover training and development costs, minimize cost in terms of time in training new workforce, ensure that adequate number of people are there to carry on the process (proper manpower planning).

Needs of the employee: Enriched job profile, better career path, challenging work environment, future prospects of the job; in a nut shell a job that satisfies his overall needs as discussed earlier.

THE WIN-WIN MODEL OR (MUTUAL SATISFACTION MODEL)

In this model plans have been devised to minimize attrition in the BPO industry on the basis of dividing tenure in different possible stages of attrition and afterward taking suitable actions to retain employees.

Moderation Period or Short-term Mitigation Plan

According to this plan, for a specific period of time endeavors should be made to retain the employees to recover the total cost incurred. For this purpose small tenure bond can work to restrict employees for a time of bond duration and help the industry to recover at least its cost.

This may help to retain employee for specific time period. But it is very necessary to give them motivation and ease so that they should not feel trammeled or compulsive to do work forcefully. Otherwise, it will negatively affect the output and image of industry in the mind of current and prospective employees.

Short-term Contingency Plan

Work environment one of the most crucial factor may affect positively or negatively employees working. According to this plan assumption is that environment must provide motivation to the employees to work efficiently and some additional monetary and no monetary benefits on short-term basis.

BPO industry should try to incorporate informal, fulfilled and such environment which induces motivation to the employees particularly which suits to young employees along with some other following benefits for controlling attrition.

- Industry should devise Flexible Salary Structure to cope with changing needs of employees' time to time.
- Additional incentives and variable pay package based on performance also help to encourage employees and give a feeling of satisfaction to talented employees of being recognized.
- Sponsored vacations for employees can be planed to compensate work stress.
- If work does not get affected, than periodic job rotation amongst department such as quality, operation, etc. may provide zeal to employees and help to get rid of from same monotonous work.

Long-term Mitigation Plan

Long-term plan will affect long-term profit of industry, therefore long-term mitigation plan should be framed to minimize intensity of attrition's outcome. This plan may help industry by giving emphasis on job roles and their clear explanation.

Therefore this plan encompasses following aspects:

- Each and every employee should be made to understand about their job roles and responsibility very clearly.
- Industry try to do documentation and written elaboration of each process and job performed reduce severity of attrition as it will help new employees to understand job as soon as possible.
- Industry should be ready in advance for faster replacement of those positions which can have more adverse impact on operation.
- Continuous assessment and certification can also be helpful in creating an employable talent pool to cope with skill required for frontline management.

Long-term Contingency Plan

This plan attempts to provide some recommendation useful for long period of time. Some of these recommendations, which are worth implementing, immediately are:

- An ITES/IT awareness fund should be created with industry support to generate awareness about employment in these industries, especially in Tier II and III cities through advertisements, workshops, seminars and counseling sessions.
- Existing infrastructure in universities/colleges and existing vocation counseling centers should be furnished, especially in Tier II and smaller towns to provide career counseling in ITES/IT opportunities.

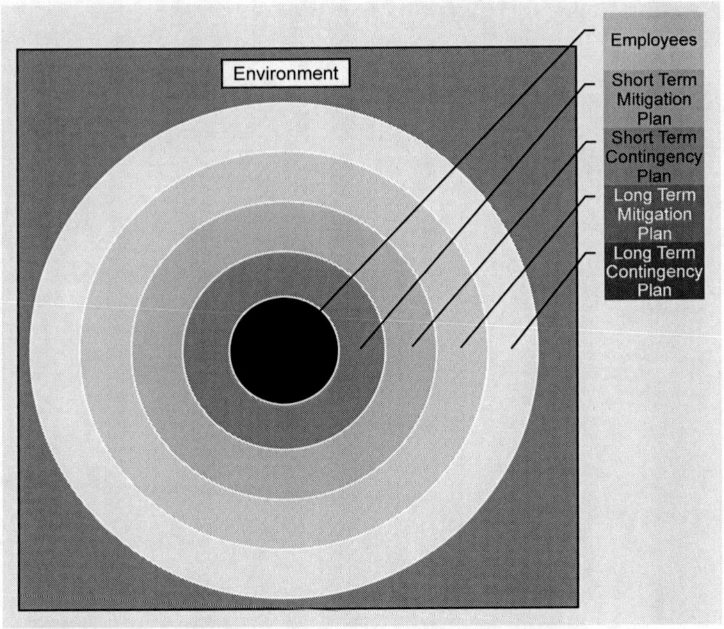

Source: http://www.coolavenues.com/know/hr/s_4.php

- In an intensely competitive environment BPO industry HR managers are poaching from each other, reduce poaching of employees within the industry bilateral agreements between companies should be signed. Basic norms are being put in place and code of ethics is being stressed upon by industry.

- Focus should be on having education and ongoing learning for the workforce, sponsoring employees on postgraduate programs and treating applicants and employees in the same way as one treats customers.

REFERENCES

http://www.coolavenues.com/know/hr/s_4.php
www.dqindia.com
www.bpoindia.org/

PART – 2
TALENT MANAGEMENT PRACTICES

5

Identifying and Nurturing Talent: Lessons from Talent Management Practices

C. Karthikeyan

Introduction

Across the globe, a new weapon is reemerging in the executive arsenal with powerful implications for driving and even predicting business success. Talent Management, variously called human capital management, employee relationship management and workforce management, among others, talent management is not a new concept, but one that in the past corporations haven't been prepared to embrace. In most functions such as recruitment and succession planning, learning and, performance management, workforce planning, compensation and other HR or training functions have often been sequestered in departmental silos. While important individually, these programs are usually a loose conglomeration of HR initiatives with little connection to each other, little alignment with the organization's vital few business goals and little real way of measuring their bottom-line impact. It isn't surprising, then, that senior management, whose daily challenge is to demonstrate progress toward bottom-line results, didn't consider these programs worth their attention.

Some Vital Statistics

The Global capability on Talent Management is Top Priority. Thirty five per cent of Asian Chief Human Resource Officers, 12 per cent of CHROs in North America, 10 per cent of counterparts from Europe.

Indian Specific Challenges

- IT/BPO Sector requires 2.3 million skilled by 2010 *vis-à-vis* 1.2 million at present.

- Estimated 1,30,000 graduates add to current base of 1.75 million engineers.
- Just 10-20% of workforce fulfills the qualification.
- English (Communicative and Spoken) skills inadequate.
- 195 million in India enroll at school and only 11 million to college levels.
- 2,00,000 enroll for university masters degree but only 16,500 opt for research, a sheer talent wastage.
- Every six out of 10 respondents (61.7%) issue comes under talent management.
- Other issues are; the cost of bad hire is 3 to 5 times.
- 40 per cent of employers struggle to find qualified candidates.
- Demographic Mix—To Maintain GDP growth of 7 to 8 per cent growth annually 16-20 million for next 10 years.
- Out of 8.5 million workforce—about 30 will refine in next five years.
- Working age group 25-60 years—swell to 600 million by 2020 nearly twice the current population of USA.
- These will include 200 million people.
- Presently 200 million people are presently in their childhood and Teens are the potential global knowledge workforce.
- Assuming just 50% of this workforce reaches a stage to be trained to generate revenues even a meager US $2 trillion per year.
- More than 50 times are current GDP.

Talent Retention Strategies; (graph shown follow).

Responses from 280 HR managers were asked about the factors relating talent management and responses were taken.

The strategies are:

- Retention of Talent,
- Staffing-identifying and Hiring of Right Talent,

- Leadership/Management Development,
- Compensation,
- Employee Motivation,
- Availability of Skilled Local Population,
- Culture Building,
- Succession Planning,
- HR Effectiveness Measurement,
- HR Technology Selection and Implementation,
- M&A Integration/Restructuring,
- Industrial Relations, and
- Others.

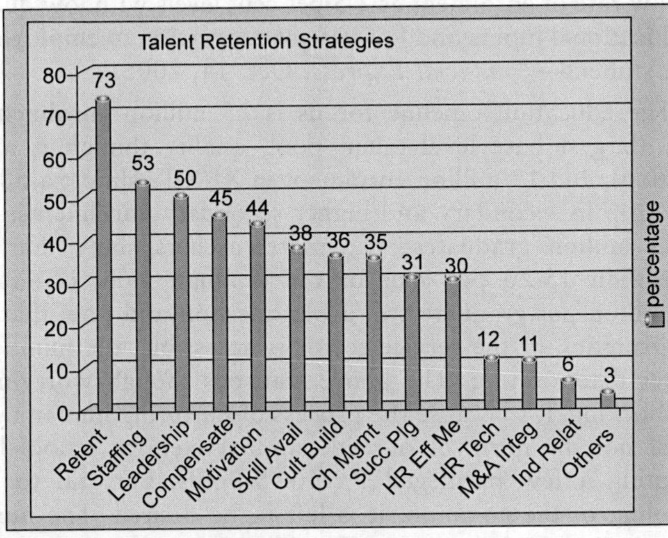

(*Source*: Article by J Karthikeyan in NHRD)

Ref: *NHRD Journal*, Issue 3, Vol. I, May 2007

According to Jack Welch; group the managerial talent into 20-70-10, and he calls it differentiation, approach to people management, the first group is 20 per cent they are "stars", the middle 70 per cent is critical.

Problem Areas: The problem areas can be seen in two ways, one is identifying and the next one is nurturing. The following generic problem areas would highlight where are the talent spots, where from sufficient resources can be tapped. The often unnoticed area where the talent growth needs to be mushroomed is not at all verified.

Fate of Base Level Talent Pool: "We are the youngest, but are we the smartest" was a statement that disturbes, say some of the reports recently, despite a surplus labour pool, 81 per cent of India Inc feels that the lack of skilled workers will be the single largest deterrent going forward (according to McKinsey Survey). Nearly 50 per cent of Indian Students drop out of School at high school stage and with a further drop out 75 per cent in class XII. Of the 3 million who the make it to the graduate pool only 15-20 per cent are hirable. India at present has low rate of enrolment at 2-5 per cent levels with low quality of educational inputs and low rate of conversion to employment for a student—(*Financial Express*, Oct. 14, 2006).

The education pipeline for us is 25 million enrolment in IX/X (largest base level talent pool, quality though is a big question), and 12 million enrolment in XI/XII. Almost a 50 per cent drop in secondary and higher secondary enrolments. Out of 03 million graduates—experts/researchers show that not more than 15-20 per cent of the graduate pool is hirable. 0.3 million postgraduate still a big question and now that job opportunities, at the service sector is accessible, the number is further deteriorating. The above statistics though worrying is not shocking, it's because the process of nurturing human talent is still not the norm of our education system at school level excepting a few privileged Private Schools, but still for the schooling of the common, it is left to be desired. The human factor in its initial shaping up is really now a cause of concern for the society, because there is a huge gap of "What is actually wanted and What is really made".

The "educational hinderosis" as put in by Dr. Irwin Flescher in the book *Children in the Learning Factories* is growing in leaps and bounds. The cause of concern is ingrained from the inception of learning inside the roof and something unusual practiced outside it. So the requirements of the hour are having some best lessons from the successful models and practices, and it's the only way to nurture. Benchmarking upon the best practice or shifting the entire paradigm is what is the crux of the problem. So the first and foremost is the Resource Analysis; Resource analysis takes place at two levels of aggregation. The basic units of analysis are the individual resources of the firm; financial, physical, human, technological resources and reputation. Organizational capabilities are bundles of resources such as capital assets, human resources, technological and routine, combined in path-dependent ways that make them difficult to unbundled or decipher. A key ingredient in those relationships is the management's ability to achieve cooperation and coordination between resources. Equally important are the implications for HRM.

A high quality workforce, available capital and access to markets and technology, are still likely to be significant source of competitive advantage. But none of these sources will be capable of providing a sustainable competitive advantage as even national boundaries are no obstacle to acquiring the human resources that are needed in order to be competitive....

Upgrading employees performances and improving their skills through training is necessity in today's competitive environment. Job demands are changing very rapidly as technology advances. A fundamental objective of training is the elimination or improvement of performance problems.

High-involvement organizations need a highly trained and skilled work force to be successful. Employees throughout these organizations must have extensive technical, business and organizational knowledge.

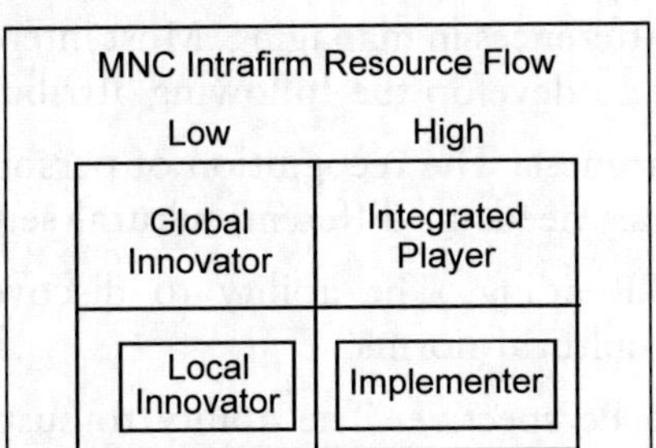

The success of MNCs global expansion therefore depends on its ability to adopt practical aspects of host countries' norms, while maintaining core aspects of the corporate culture that are the basis of its competitiveness.

Managerial Leadership in an International Context

The requirements for managerial leadership in an international context extend well beyond functional management practices to encompass a sensitivity to and empathy with cultural diversity. No global organization with continuous pressure for change can survive without clearly spelled-out standards of excellence. Excellence relates to substantive knowledge of the business, commitment to performance, accountability, concern for due process, interpersonal and intercultural sensitivity and the development of others. The initial ideas were highlighted at the Ohio University and the University of Michigan during the latter part of the 1940s. Since concern for people and concern for production are two separate dimensions, it appears that leaders can employ a combination of both. Such a combination is actually proposed under the title of "managerial grid".

To develop an indepth sensitivity to a culture's behavioral patterns, managers need specialized training that goes beyond a review of reports and instruction in foreign languages.

To overcome cultural biases and achieve a truly global perspective, international managers should receive international and intercultural management training. Through documentary programs, participation in business games and role-playing scenarios, managers can develop a better understanding of culture-based differences in managing. Most intercultural training programs hope to develop the following attributes and skills:

- Self-awareness: The recognition of personal assumptions and values needs in different cultural settings.
- Culture Reading: The ability to discover the inherent logic in cultural norms.
- Multiple Perspective: The ability to suspend judgement about other cultures and appreciate other's perspectives.

- Intercultural Communication: To send verbal and non-verbal messages in different cultures. Skills in building interpersonal relationships.
- Cultural Resilience: The ability to handle culture shock.

Now the Individualised Corporation

Percy Branwick, CEO of Asea Brown Boveri (ABB), who believes that managers spend too much time trying to squeeze the last percentage point of productivity out of their capital assets while ignoring the huge untapped potential of human resources.

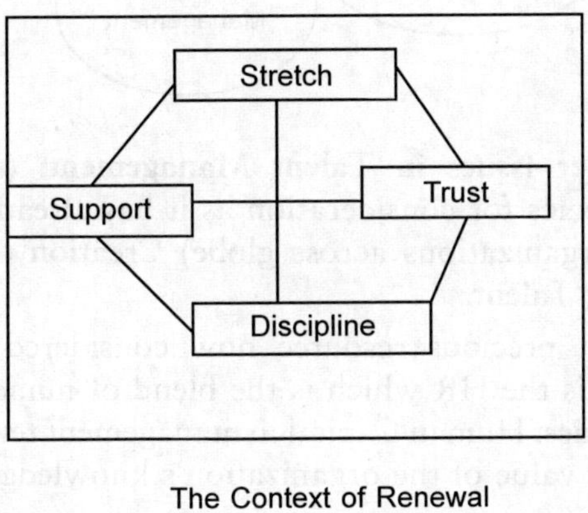

The Context of Renewal

There is tremendous unused potential in our people. Our organizations ensure that they only use 5 to 10 per cent of the abilities at work. Outside of their work they engage the other 90 to 95 per cent to run their households, lead a Boy Scout Troop, or build a summer house. We have to learn how to recognize and employ that untapped ability that each individual bring to work everyday.

"Successful Companies of the 21st century will be those who do the best job of capturing, storing and leveraging what their employees know."

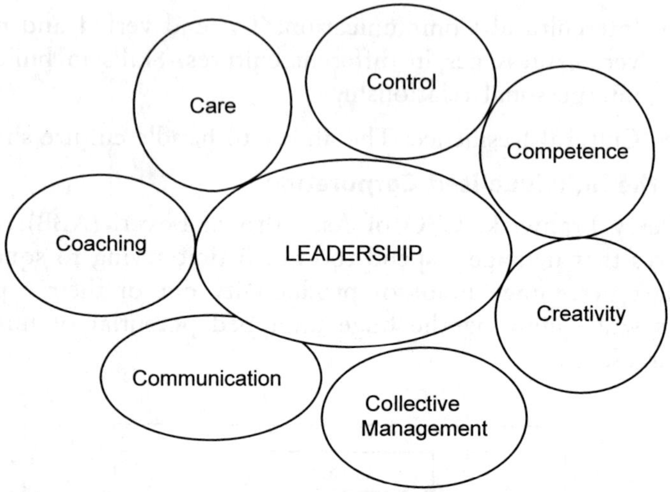

The Other Issues in Talent Management: (some of the success strategies for consideration as it has already been done by leading organizations across globe) Creation of Excellence by Nurturing Talent.

The most precious resource now considered almost any organization is the HR which is the blend of numerous factors known as values. Human Capital in management terms describes the economic value of the organization's knowledge, skills, and capabilities.

Trying Out Certain Practices

Reset Mind-set: Involves embedding the organization's value and behavior to all its employees. Potential about future performance and not past performance. Good technical knowledge is not the only criterion for a good managerial position but it has to be coupled with excellent people skills.

Set Focus: The HR managers need to discharge and need to identify jobs which make a difference and ensure that the right person performs the job at the right time.

Right Positioning: The HR managers need to position and talent management as a strategic issue with impetus coming from the topmost person in the organization.

Structure: A structure is to ensure the criterion of tools, processes and techniques with defined accountability to ensure that the work gets done through building contribution effectiveness at all levels and building a value proposition based on competitive compensation, flexible working, training, personal growth and multiple career opportunities in the same organization.

Systems: Facilitates a long-term and holistic approach to generate change, how efficiently organizations can manage their talent is dependent on the systems they implement.

Encourage employees to take up learning for anti-attrition or pro-retention. Invest scarce resources on the most promising talent.

Assessment of Talent: Employee performance assessment should be based on multiple assignments in different contexts. Employees should be sorted as high, medium or low talented so as to target rewards and plan future performance improvement programs.

Experiences

IBM: The top challenge for talent managers at IBM Business consulting services is focusing programes on what the business wants, according to Roger Metelerkamp, Leader of Human Capital Management.... Or else we are in danger of building the wrong kind of talent. He says striking the right balance between recruiting talent and growing talent also requires careful judgement. 'If you buy in too many people you run the danger of creating discontent among incumbents who feel they aren't getting enough opportunities', he says "the plus side of new recruits bring with them a fresh vitality and new ideas". Talent management at IBM Business Consulting is largely the responsibility of its line managers who are supported by HR Business partners.

Prudential: At insurance giant Prudential, Organization development leader Drew Watson says the company has been "serious about talent management for two years". The organization has a head of talent and succession, plus another full-time talent manager overseeing 7,500 employees based in

London, Reading, Sterling, Belfast in the UK and in Mumbai in India.

"In someway it's easier to identify senior talent" says Watson. The clues aren't as clear for the middle management roles. Here we look for people who are capable of promotion to the next level within two years.

"Having the most senior people in the organization looking at talent gives the whole process clout" says Watson. Prudential is now looking at bringing in a 'potential tool' a checklist of objective criteria against which potential top talent can be judged—to avoid objective criteria against which potential top talent can be judged—to avoid subjective nominations and cloning.

TNT: For Frank Keepers, Group Director of talent management at global delivery company TNT, talent management initiatives must be grounded in the day-to-day reality of what the business needs. We employ 1,65,000 practical people whose job its to move stuff around the world, he says. "I'm not paid to come up with conceptual ideas, but with practical programs related to the business". TNT says keepers, is the first company to be recognized as a worldwide investor in People Organization. It is structured into three divisions—logistics, express and mail—and each division has a head of talent management.

The key role is to articulate business needs so that the line managers understand the type of skills and people the company wants to develop, says Keepers, "You can have a great business plan, but you need the right people, in the right place, at the right time—and at the right cost—if you want it to succeed."

Intel Corp: Intel Corp uses three systems that work together to allow leadership to emerge on the job and to be rewarded, according to Kevin Gazzara, Program manager for training and development:

- It starts with peers: The First system involves getting management experience at an early stage. Teams of 10 employees marked for promotions are called together to provide each other with peer-to-peer coaching on an ongoing basis.

- Peers and Mentors: The second system involves support from peers and mentors. Each new manager is assigned a "buddy", who gives tactical advise on getting up to speed.
- Real-life Learning: The third system involves action-oriented learning. Groups of managers come together to solve real business problems by working in virtual teams. These teams can include members from locations around the globe.

The quest for talented workforce is never ending. Organizations need to formulate a model to value and benchmark a talented workforce and change the human capital existing with it rather than searching it.

- Create an employee value proposition that attracts new and talented people, striking a right balance between attracting talent and developing it in-house.
- Have a talent mind set pervading the organization rather than focusing on top talent.
- Build a long-term recruiting strategy. Ensure follow—through of the talent program to meet and heighten expectations, e.g. through training, promotion and peer coaching.

Other Strategies Could be

Competencies which are sets of behaviors (encompassing skills, knowledge, abilities, and personal attributes) that, taken together, are critical to accomplishing successful work and achieving an organization's strategy.

Competencies represent the most critical knowledge, skills, and commitments that underlie superior performance for your organization and or within a specific job.

Organizational—Core competencies identified strategic planning.

Leadership—Behaviors in the present organization expects all leaders to demonstrate or to develop.

Functional—Competencies that cascade from the core competencies are associated with specific work functions or business units.

Occupational—Competencies that cascade from the core and functional competencies and then are anchored directly to the needs of a specific occupation.

Individual—What each employee brings to his or her function, as this article suggests.

Team—What members of a team, in the aggregate, bring to their work in an organization will need to determine the competency definition levels essential to ensuring critical work gets performed. A competency model which is a map to display a set of competencies that are aligned with your organization's mission, vision and strategic goals.

Team Work—Another way to achieve human capital—TEAM—Together Everyone Accomplishes More. How to Perform better; Greater alignment with shareholder wealth; Designing better compensation plan; the EVA can be used as an incentive model for the organization. A typical EVA incentive plan can be represented as follows:

An EVA Incentive Model

Experience of Godrej with EVA—EVA has emerged as a clear winner when compared to compensation systems like ESOPs or the performance linked variable remuneration that was being followed at Godrej earlier. Also, EVA forced everyone to think long-term because it operated with a minimum three-year horizon; EVA seems to have importance for companies as a performance measurement and controlling tool. One of EVA's most powerful features is its suitability to management bonus systems.

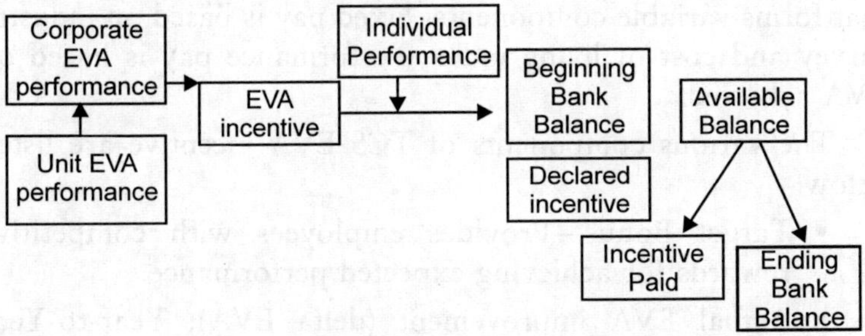

Typical EVA Incentive Pay-off Profile

To make managers behave like owners= Unlimited reward for success and Genuine Penalty for failure. Thrill of victory and Agony of defeat are Great Motivators. Thrill of victory and Agony of defeat are Great Motivators.

EVA and its Usage from Indian Companies

- Infosys—EVA is a tool to tell its clients that the value delivered by Infosys is greater than what the client pays for.
- MARICO—As a signaling device to tell its employees that capital is important.
- Dr. Reddy's—As a qualifying criterion to grant rewards such a variable pay.
- Laboratories—Stock options and performance bonuses.
- TCS and Godrej—Here EVA is linked to compensation and has been implemented in great detail.

The concept of EVA is catching on fast, and several Indian companies including TCS and Dr. Reddy's Labs have adopted it. The project of implementing EVA is of four phases; the first involve defining EVA for each of the company's businesses. The second phase, which is EVA management, focuses on training operating people on how to improve EVA. Then comes the motivational phase, which consists of evolving a variable remuneration plan to reward improvements in EVA.

Individual compensation consists of two parts: i.e. Fixed pay that reflects experience/competency and performance pay, that forms variable components. Fixed pay is based on industry survey and cost of living index, Performance pay is based on EVA achieved.

The various components of TCS EVA incentive are listed below:

- Target Bonus—Provides employees with competitive rewards for achieving expected performance.
- Actual EVA improvement (delta EVA); Year-to-Year change in EVA.
- Expected EVA improvement (EI)— Performance standard consistent with TCS owner's expected return.
- EVA interval.
- EVA improvement (delta EVA) above Expected Improvement (EI) that results in a 2 × Bonus declared and EVA below EI that results in a 0 × Bonus declared.
- Bonus Multiple.
- 1.0x + (delta EAV–EI)/EVA Interval.

Incentive Distribution in TCS

	Corporate	Unit Performance	Individual
Junior Level	Average %	Minimum %	Maximum %
Middle Level	Average %	Maximum %	Average %
Senior Management	Maximum	Minimum	Average

Synergies across cell — Avoid Free Riders — Be Good at Basics

Findings

On this analysis one aspect is very clear that talent management is not very new but the way it has to be approached is to be renewed. We have seen very existing models and examples of managing talent and the only concern can be knowing the pulse of the organization and acting accordingly.

REFERENCES

Al Ehrbar (1998). *EVA: The Real Key to Creating Wealth*, New York: John Wiley & Sons.

Arundhuti Dasgupta (2002). *Why Godrej is Captivated by EVA*, Indian Management.

BSE Training Institute (2001). *Fundamental Analysis*, BSE Stock Exchange Publication.

The Economist. 2nd August 1997, pp. 57-59. "Valuing Companies: A Star to Sailby".

Prasanna Chandra (2001). *Financial Management*, Tata McGraw-Hill Publishing Company Limited, New Delhi.

www.iimb.ernet.in

www.moserbaer.com

www.perterkeen.com/emgbp007.htm

www.garnet.acns.fsu.edu

www.investopedia.com

www.tcs.com

www.bsbmumbai.org

6

Spotting and Nurturing Talents through Practice School—An Excellent Example of Higher Education in India

P.N. Ramchandran

Introduction

There has been a great concern among industrialists, academicians and educational administrators in India, that there is big gap between what is being taught in the classrooms of higher educational institutes and what is actually required by industries and that graduates coming out of the universities are not adequately prepared to meet the challenges posed by real-world problems. In order to bridge this gap the Birla Institute of Technology and Science (BITS), an autonomous higher educational institute in India has been operating a Practice School (PS) scheme, wherein the first degree students have to spend a full semester in their final year in industries working on specific problems. This actually replaces the normal project work carried out in other institutions. The students are assisted by institute's faculty resident at the location as well as by experts from the industry in carrying out the PS assignment. In this process the students apply the theoretical knowledge gained in the classrooms and laboratories at the institute to solve multi-disciplinary problems and gain confidence in facing unknown situations. It is in this context that, the students get a chance to exhibit their talents, which is not normally possible in an institute-based routine project work. The resident faculty members get exposed to industrial environment, enriching their expertise. They also develop the capability of identifying and nurturing the hidden talents of their students. The industries stand to gain by finding workable solutions to some of their existing problems, as also by identifying suitably talented students to be absorbed in their set up for employment. The author was one of the resident faculty members for a period of 3 years in a large Viscose Rayon Manufacturing Unit, where such a PS scheme was operating. His experiences in identifying and developing talents in the young students are explained in the following pages.

The Setting

The sponsoring industry—the Gwalior Rayon Silk Manufacturing Company (GRASIM)—is the largest producer of Rayon Staple Fibre in India. Rayon grade pulp obtained from its sister concerns is converted into Viscose using Caustic Soda and Carbon-di-Sulphide as process chemicals. The Viscose is spun into Fibre in spinning machines using spin—both chemicals. The entire requirement of the main process chemicals is met by captive units set up at the plant site. A power plant using pulverized coal as fuel, a water treatment plant an effluent treatment plant are the other units of the complex. Modern chemical and research laboratories also form part of the set up. There is also an Engineering Development Division with a large workshop for designing and manufacturing Viscose Fibre-making machinery. A team of talented technocrats and managers run the plant very effectively. Thus this forms an ideal setting for the young final year students to explore and exhibit their talents, while trying to solve challenging practical problems.

The Scheme

Final year students of integrated degree programs of B.E. (Hons) in Chemical, Civil, Electrical and Mechanical Engineering; M.Sc. (Tech) in Computer Science and Instrumentation; M.Sc. (Hons) in Chemistry and Economics and MMS were attending PS programs for a full semester at Grasim. While the student batches changed every semester, the faculty team stayed for a longer period—two to three years at a stretch. A group of 3 students used to work on a project to be guided by a resident faculty and an expert from the organization. Projects were identified by the industries, care being taken to see that they were of immediate concern and relevance to the organization.

Also such problems need a team effort from students drawn from different disciplines, so as to ensure that all points of view are taken into account before arriving at the answer. Strategy for solution to real-life problems is often found in a peculiar mix of attitudes of scientific mind, respect for everyday routine and an element of adventure. Also they are open—ended in the sense that, one can rarely be sure that he knows the exact answer, thus introducing an element of decision-making in the face of insufficient data and uncertain parameters. With the help of host organizations and practice faculty information is collected in terms of the type of total integrated personality traits to be possessed by the student team, that could do the work at hand. Simultaneously the profiles of intending students are prepared at the institute incorporating their various capabilities and competencies. Information so collected are then matched to identify a suitable student team to tackle a problem. In short, the entire method is based on the theme emerging out of the experience that, it is not necessary to linearly order the students to say who is better than whom. Challenges in real life and hence choices are really complex and sufficiently varied to allow one merely to say who in his/her opinion is best suited for what, while providing a rational for it. This is how students are put on a platform, from where they can exhibit their talents while solving real-life problems of multi-disciplinary nature. To give an example one student each from Mechanical engineering. Chemical engineering and Chemistry were put on a project on The Analysis of Air Pollutants from various sections of the plant. Similarly a team of students from Chemical engineering, Economics and Management worked on a project on The Economic Utilization of Fly-ash from the Power House.

PS Evaluation

The evaluation process in PS seeks out and focuses attention on many latent attributes which do not surface in the normal classroom situation, such as intellectual ability, professional judgment and decision-making ability, interdisciplinary approach, skills for data handling, ability for written and oral presentation, initiative, ability for team-work, leadership quality, industry, sense of responsibility and ability to meet deadlines, etc. These attributes are judged by the faculty by various instruments of evaluation namely Quiz, Viva, Seminars, Group Discussions, Project Report, Observation of Student's Performance and Daily Diary. The weightages given for various instruments are as follows:

Quiz	15%
Viva	5%
Seminar	20%
Group Discussion	15%
Project Report	25%
Observation	15%
Diary	5%
Total	100%

The quiz is aimed at evaluating the students in terms of "knowing the organization" assignments, where they are expected to show acquaintance with the organizational structure, technical processes involved and historical development, etc. The viva voce tries to measure in-depth knowledge, self-expression, creativeness and originality. In the seminar on the projects that are carried out, one looks for technical credibility, expression and communication and organization of the material. Group Discussions are based on a topic of general interest. It will evaluate creativity, intellectual ability, approach to problem solving and group behavior. The project report prepared by a group is evaluated in terms of technical credibility, methodology, documentation and recommendations. In the observation component what one looks to evaluate are, initiative, self-reliance, co-operation, leadership, industry, sense of responsibility, social sense, etc. The idea of making a student write a diary is to judge him in terms of the ability to plan and meet deadlines and in organizing materials. Diary writing disciplines the mind in respect to the detailed routine and forces the habit documenting. It provides an opportunity to evaluate information gathering and documenting skills possessed by the students.

A matrix showing the evaluation instruments against the parameters is shown in Appendix I. This amply illustrates how opportunities are given to students to exhibit their hidden talents. The evaluation is done twice in a semester—one interim and then the final. After the interim evaluation a very constructive feedback is given to the students, explaining where they are lagging behind and how possible improvements can be made. Thus, they get a chance for talent development under the constant guidance of the faculty.

PS Rating Sheet

At he end of the PS module all successful students are give a rating sheet specifying the degree to which they are fulfilling the various traits. This is something very unique, which is not found on other degree transcripts. This in fact exhibits the talent mix of the students which can really be a boon to prospective employers to identify the right persons to fill their various openings. This can reduce the extra training that is to be given to the students before their actual employment. Thus this contributes greatly to the talent management, as in an organization the basic success lies in putting the right people in the right slot. Many organizations have accepted the validity of the rating sheet and BITS students are finding it very easy to get placements of their choice straightaway. The host organization is benefited is a big way by identifying the right talents for employment. Thus, talent transition is made very smooth. A typical rating sheet is shown in Appendix II. This is self-explanatory.

Talent Identification and Nurturing Through PS

It can be seen from the above sections that in PS method of education, if on the one hand one can assess highly subjective aspects of human personality, on the other hand one can also take care of issues such as objectivity, reliability and uniformity which have very high priorities in the minds of the students. They also will be glad to know about their strengths and weakness, so that they can develop into a much better personality. The continuous feedback gives them an opportunity firstly to experience the spirit of the endeavor and secondly to improve with time. The real gain is that, instead of restricting the scope to mere academic achievements, the PS evaluation methodology is integrated with priorities of overall conduct of the students in the professional world (which is based on talents), thus giving educational discipline a broader meaning. Talents have to be identified early and properly developed in students, so that they can be suitably utilized later on for personal and professional achievement. Talents are widely spread among students, but the problem is that mostly they are neither identified in time nor developed properly for gainful utilization. The PS scheme, while carrying out a very realistic evaluation of the student's performance from various angles, gives them a very good opportunity to experiment with their talents and exhibit them to a great extent. One of the most important themes emerging from the PS scheme is the positive role that students can play in the process of development during their educational years. Indeed their intense involvement in problem solving efforts at the practice stations has proved beyond doubt their ability for hardwork, sense of responsibility and their keen desire to achieve something concrete. In some sense such involvement seems to give them a sense of self-identity, thus enabling them to boldly face the unknown. Seen from a different angle, this means that PS method of education can provide a strategy for increasing the base of developmental type of activity by involving students and teachers and this in turn can resolve some of the major issues of higher education. Thus, it can be seen that practice schools are real fertile soils to sow the seeds of talents, nurture and grow young talents and subsequently have a rich harvest in the form of very competent manpower for deployment in the professional world.

Conclusion

The PS method of education virtually takes the university to industrial settings. This gives challenging responsibilities and opportunities to the students as well as the teachers and key benefits to the host organizations. This is an ideal technique for identifying the latent talents in young students undergoing higher education, for helping teachers to nurture talents in the students and for facilitating organizations to pick up talents suited to their requirements. It is heartening to see that this bold innovative experiment in higher education taken up in a big way by BITS, Pilani, has been proved to be very successful and other educational establishments have started using it and several organizations have welcomed the establishment of PS Stations at their premises. It is the higher educational institutes that should take the lead in spotting and nurturing talents in youngsters and the leading industrial houses should collaborate with institutes of higher learning to facilitate this process. In this context PS is the right vehicle to bring about the much needed transformation in our educational system.

7

Modern Practices in Talent Attraction, Selection, Recognition, Retention and Engagement in 21st Century Business World

Ashish V. Gadekar, Rimalini Ramesh Band and *Manika Sumani*

Extract. Talent is the exceptional combination of hard and soft skills. In reality there is no Talent Shortage, Just Talent Recognition Shortage. Attracting, recruiting and retaining talent to our region is a high priority for the organizations. Our economic development philosophy has been that if you can attract talent to a region, companies will follow. The organizations focus on attracting a diversity of talent from all ages with a particular focus on attracting the best and brightest recent college graduates and young professionals. While finding quality talent for your team is an arduous task, keeping them happy and developing their skills is a far more challenging endeavor. Organizations operate in a world of increasing complexity—intensified competition, globalization, and growing expectations. HR leaders must meet these business challenges as a partner in driving their organization towards its key goals.

Building and Retaining a World-Class Workforce—the Challenge for HR. Engaged, efficient, and flexible people are the core of any success story of a company. Following are the few guidelines:

- **Build Employee Skills.** You have talented people. Now you want them to learn, grow, and develop.
- **Build a Strong Leadership Pipeline.** You need strong leaders and a solid pipeline of high potential talent.

Developing a supply of superior leaders is critical, as population trends show talent pools shrinking.

- **Manage a High Performing Workforce.** HR must help people better understand performance expectations, career paths and talent development strategies. Organizational performance truly rests on workforce performance.
- **Enhance the Customer Experience.** You have a customer base to delight. The customer experience drives growth, retention, and financial performance. Maximizing the effectiveness of your customer contact center is a key imperative.

Talent Segmentation

The key idea that is very well explained here is how to think about "business critical" talent *versus* simple titles. This is leading savvy organizations to start thinking about talent in four general roles:

Those four roles are best explained by the authors. Here is a direct quote:

1. Creators devise and implement an organization's distinguishing value proposition or business model. They include senior executives and the chief designer in a fashion house. These are scarce resources with skills that take a long time to acquire and are costly to develop and maintain.
2. Ambassadors represent the organization's public face and are responsible for customer experience. Among other positions, they are bank tellers, supermarket cashiers, nurses, and field installation technicians. In most cases, these workers are easily replaceable and their skills do not have to be particularly sophisticated, but if they don't do their job well, the business can suffer significantly.
3. Craft Masters ensure the quality, timeliness, and cost-effectiveness of an organization—the essential ingredients for the faultless execution of a business strategy. These are the design engineers in a high-tech

business, the "nose" of a perfume brand, the whiskey blender in a distillery, and the auditor in an accounting firm.

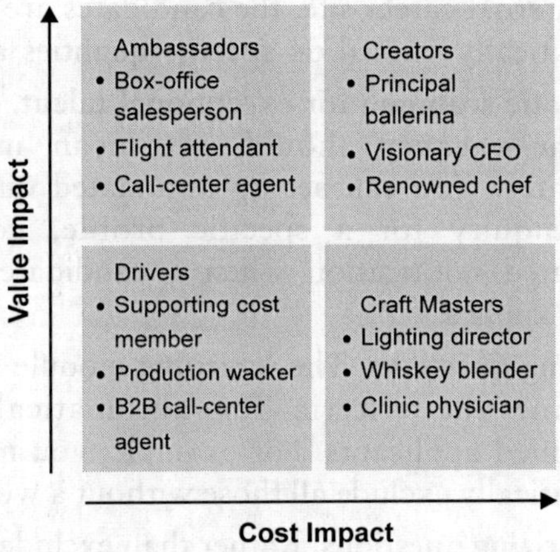

4. Drivers keep the business running. They are assembly-line operators, back-office agents, and administrative assistants. Although they are neither crucial to the success of a venture nor hard to hire, in most companies they represent the largest category of human capital, and bad management of this group can lead to operational disruption or quality problems.

Applying these four roles will lead to a refinement in all traditional talent management metrics that will give organizations more meaningful data and less meaningless averages.

Transition Coaching

Transition coaching provides an investment in key leadership talent by guiding newly appointed leaders through an established process that maximizes their likelihood of success in a new role of expanded scope and complexity. It minimizes the negative impact of failed transitions which can include turnover, poor financial results, negative employee morale or decreased customer satisfaction.

Talent Selection

What should you expect?

- **Ability to screen candidates using smart technology.** Whether candidates submit their applications using an online application form, through a job board or through your internal career site, the candidates are screened and automatically ranked on specific qualities and skills.
- **Automatic scanning for exceptional talent.** Not having a relevant vacancy should not mean missing good candidates. You can set up automated queries to scan each enquiry for a specific profile, generating an automated notification when a candidate fitting your profile applies.
- **Screening questions.** The screening module allows you to predefine the criteria for automatically rejecting unqualified applicants. For example, you might want to automatically exclude all those without a working permit.
- **Categorizing questions.** Rather than exclude applications, you can rank them by points based on answers given to specific questions. This allows you to priorities the most suitable applications.
- **Integration of third party assessment tools.** You may choose to increase the predictability of your screening and selection process by integrating market-leading tests and assessment tools from third party test vendors to help make more objective hiring decisions.
- **Automated profiling and talent pool creation.** Once you have built your talent pool searching within this invaluable resource will become your first step in uncovering talent for new opportunities. Our solution ensures that information from interviews and assessments are automatically added to the candidate's profile, providing you with an even wider criteria base for screening when searching in the talent pool.
- **Weighted scoring.** Step Stone's e-Recruitment solutions give you the ability to weigh questions with a score, based on responses, which allows the recruiter to assess applicants at a glance.

Talent Selection—A Critical Leadership Challenge

Getting the right person in the right job is what drives your business success, while having the wrong person in a key job has many costs to an organization. Every key role or job has a number of complex needs that might be difficult to pinpoint. Needs may include key accountabilities that require certain hard skills.

- Motivation that fits the culture and rewards the role.
- Behaviours that match the work environment.
- Personal skills that can make or break the job's success.

Effective talent management/talent selection must make the needs of the job the top priority. How do you find the best match for all these complex needs, especially the personal skill needs that are so critical to the role's success? How do you determine what all the needs are for a particular job?

Talent Recognition

July 13, 2007—CIO—The little-known truth in corporate America is that there is no talent shortage, just a severe shortage of people and systems that recognize, recruit and retain talent. Hiring managers have been told repeatedly that there is a talent shortage across all industries and that they should lower their expectations. Often, finding a qualified candidate turns out to be a long, drawn-out process at the end of which many hiring managers get less than what they deserve and pay more than what they would like. Sound familiar? If you are like most hiring managers, you have bought into the storyline of a severe talent shortage. It is time to challenge this widely accepted belief.

We live in times of sweeping and rapid global change. We work in a global marketplace that is driven by innovation; corporate wealth and growth is no longer driven by mega size, assets or past laurels. Instead, it is driven by the ability to innovate, innovate and innovate. Innovation rapidly shifts resource expectations and needs, often in unanticipated and unplanned ways, impacting the talent requirements of organizations all over the world. In such a climate, yesterday's talent requirements and hiring practices cannot meet today's needs. The ability to recognize and respond to global shifts is the key to locating the talent your organization needs.

Corporate America is missing out on some of the most creative and experienced talent because its hiring practices, policies, organizational thinking and, yes, HR systems are slow, parochial, outdated, and frankly sometimes obstacles to talent acquisition. Ask the innovative, dynamic and agile companies that easily attract the most creative talent about the secrets of their success.

There are four guiding principles to ensure that your organization has the ability to recognize talent when it sees it.

1. Talent is Your Most Valuable Asset? Prove it. While almost every company claims that human talent is its greatest asset, its actions don't always reflect this priority. Periodically it is important to reflect on what your company does to recognize talent. Companies must pay attention to the following four P's when it comes to talent acquisition:

Policies

Procedures

Practices

Performance

Companies must frequently review their hiring policies, procedures and practices to ensure they are not bureaucratic or detrimental to recruiting talent, particularly unconventional talent. Many hiring policies and procedures are archaic and limit hiring managers from being resourceful and agile. We have all come across policies and procedures that are devoid of any common sense, prompting the question, "Who wrote these policies?" Your hiring practices should be flexible and nimble. Setting and reviewing hiring policies, procedures and practices should not be just the prerogative of the HR department but must include organization-wide input and participation of all hiring managers. Finally, there must be an energetic reward system in place for talent acquisition. The talent recruitment incentives of the late 1990s need a boost if companies are to stay at the forefront of talent acquisition.

2. Web Cobwebs. A close analysis of the career websites of many large and small companies across a cross-section of industries reveals the painful truth that many sites are in need of a serious overhaul. There are many examples where a company's Web has become a cobweb! Here are a few examples: It is difficult to even locate the career link of a large global IT company because it is embedded many layers deep on its website. The career link of another Fortune company is found rock-bottom on its website! In the case of a major health insurance company, its career link is simply not there. If human capital is a company's greatest asset, why does talent acquisition receive a low priority on the company's website?

Best advice: Try applying for a job using your company's career link. Quite likely it will be a sobering experience! The labyrinth of links, tedious forms and tables, repetitious information requests and unfriendly Web practices reflect poorly on organizations. Of course, the standard response of many companies that "we don't expect to find good candidates through our career website" is both ironic and telling!

3. Seek Unconventional Talent. In today's economy, innovation is one of the highest priorities for business leaders all over the world. Senior executives are looking for ways to both strengthen and shorten the innovation cycle and to effortlessly repeat the cycle. Innovation of products, services, markets, operations and business models is high priority for senior executives. When creativity rocks industries, shatters establishments, and triggers unanticipated side effects on organizations and nations, the source of such far-reaching creative initiatives is often traced back to the company's talent pool. If a company's talent pool is cut from the same fabric, group think sets in. One way to get around this bottleneck is to hire unconventional talent. Unconventional talent refers to talent that is not a near-identical replacement of the person who just vacated the job! Look for individuals with leadership skills from other industries. Recruit those whose career paths are interesting and untraditional. Take the risk and hire someone who has never worked in your industry. Seek individuals who have a proven record as creative problem-solvers. Hire for creativity. The characteristics of what constitutes "unconventional talent" are likely to vary from company to company and industry to industry. Hence, a company should first carefully define what it considers unconventional talent and then make a concentrated effort to fill a certain percentage of its positions each year with unconventional talent from a cross-section of industries.

4. Train for Talent Recognition. The ability to recognize talent that may not be obvious from a cursory glance at a résumé can be acquired through training, brainstorming and careful mentoring. Studies show that many hiring managers are often not aware of biases and prejudices that may lead to the rejection of qualified candidates. More important, the over-emphasis on certain technical skills may lead to early elimination of highly qualified candidates. Hence, investments in talent recognition must be treated as an integral part of talent acquisition and retention. While it is understandable, given the intense pressures of today's markets, that most hiring managers look for potential employees who can "hit the ground running", it is important to actively recruit those who, even though they may have a slight handicap in the short-run, will in the long-term prove to be an invaluable asset to the organization. The initial investment in training and mentoring unconventional talent will yield rich dividends in the long-run, particularly on the innovation index.

It is easy to buy into the common belief that there is a severe global shortage of talent. While there is some truth to this, it is important to train people and invest in systems that recognize talent, including unconventional talent. Without such an approach, we all become part of the problem rather than part of the solution.

Young Professionals and Entrepreneurs

The countries young professionals and entrepreneurs who are in their 20s and 30s are an invaluable asset to our economic growth. These innovative young adults volunteer their time and energy to lead the group in endeavors of social activities, career development programs, and community service.

We know the lesson: if you ask your Talent to stay, they won't. So, the alternative is to create an invitation that "pulls" them towards your organization in a manner akin to the metaphor, care of Cognitive Edge, of a swarm of bees is a valuable metaphor: if the beekeeper can capture the swarm after it has left the hive, then it can be put in a new hive and will become productive. Swarming involves creating the equivalent of a bright light and seeing what comes to it.

Unfortunately, a "bright light" cannot be conscripted. One needs to tap into the informal talent network in one's organization to understand what that light may be...because that is where the answer lies, and it is there! Again, the argument is to really get into the mind of your talent before instituting cosmetic changes to your culture with regard to flexible working hours, relaxed dress code, etc.). Cosmetic changes are popular because they provide a false sense of security in believing "right, we have done something". While these changes have worked for other organizations, your organization is a different system.

Today's Talent Challenge—Engagement!

Is it possible to create a culture, in today's climate, that engages and retains talent? Can you foster loyalty and commitment in your workplace? Career Systems International addressed these critical questions with 25 global talent leaders, at their annual Retention Convention. After a day of discussion, debating, benchmarking and brainstorming, this group collectively recognized that the challenge today is not just about retaining talented people, but more importantly, about fully engaging them. It is about capturing their minds and hearts at each stage of their work lives. To be fully engaged requires emotional involvement in the work. This leads to increased productivity, higher customer satisfaction, and greater profits. Engaged employees bring value to organizations and improve the organization's competitive position. In turn they reap personal rewards from the work they do. Their engagement, commitment and loyalty are a result of being challenged, developed, appreciated, heard and respected.

All agreed that the term employee retention has acquired new meaning or, perhaps, new importance during recent economic turmoil. They saw the disengaged employee as a psychological casualty of talent mismanagement. Employees who leave are the physical casualties. Both drain the organization of the brainpower and commitment that is vital to ensuring productivity and profitability.

So, How to Keep Them?

The findings from Career Systems International's ongoing Retention Driver Survey supports what the talent leaders themselves have found: there is no real mystery about what keeps good people in their organizations. The key factors include: challenge, exciting work, career growth, development, a good boss, working with great people and, surprisingly at a lower priority, fair pay. The mystery lies in how to apply this knowledge in today's fast-paced, competitive work environments. It was interesting to note that these retention drivers had not substantially changed between 1998 and 2002, despite drastic U.S. economic and labor market shifts.

Key Findings and Best Practices

Once the current realities were discussed and both engagement and retention defined, these talent leaders shared key findings and best practices, some of which are listed below:

- Reciprocity is key. Employees are investors in the company and expect a return on investment.
- Retention must be part of the organization's DNA. Successful organizations have woven retention and engagement deeply into their structure.
- Loyalty is never a given. Loyalty must be earned; even satisfied employees sometimes leave.
- Organizations must be seen as employers of choice. You have to compete on compensation and benefits, but WIN on culture, learning and development.
- Mergers, downsizing and bankruptcies. Require leaders to re-motivate employees, both during and after the crisis.

- Stars include more than just the top 10%—or 1%! Stars are people at any level who bring value to the organization.
- High-potentials must be carefully managed. It's not uncommon to watch high flyers become willing victims of talent theft.
- A recovering economy spells choice. As the economy recovers, talented people will be even more in demand and will have greater choices. Talent will become harder to find, and even harder to engage.
- Each generation has different reasons for staying. For the first time in modern history, there are four generations working side-by-side in most companies. Generational differences continue to pose new challenges to today's employers.
- Make diversity an engagement and retention opportunity. One organization chose to weave key Love 'Em strategies into their diversity initiative.
- Mentor widely and in both directions. Build learning relationships in all directions and hold all partners responsible for the success.
- Train intelligently. Provide on going retention training in manageable bites—make it a continuous effort and find ways to size the retention plan to the specific demographics of the organization.
- Create a development culture. "Career development is the right thing for the organization (identifying and developing future leaders), the right thing for the employee (creating a development environment), and a key retention component."
- Recognize managers who keep employees. Meaningful recognition remains a potent energizer for employees and managers alike.
- Create the internal headhunter profile. When employers integrate retention efforts into the culture, headhunters have a difficult time prying talent out of the organization.

Conclusion

Today's leaders must manage the scarce commodity called talent to sustain their competitive edge. Brainpower remains a key differentiator in today's competitive markets. The organizations with the best talent win. In the midst of a slow economy and a take-no-prisoners stock market, attracting, recruiting, hiring, retaining and engaging top talent can make or break any organization. With a labor shortage expected to hit 10 million workers by 2010, and 43 per cent of our labor force eligible to retire in the next decade, the demand for talent is expected to outweigh supply by 20 per cent through 2005. Talent management remains one of management's highest priorities.

REFERENCES

Berger, Lance A. and Dorothy R. Berger. *The Talent Management Handbook: Creating Organizational Excellence by Identifying, Developing, and Promoting Your Best People* (Hardcover).

Byham, William C. *Grow Your Own Leaders: How to Identify, Develop, and Retain Leadership Talent.*

Charan, Ram. *The Leadership Pipeline: How to Build the Leadership Powered Company.*

Fulmer, Robert M. *Growing Your Company's Leaders: How Great Organizations Use Succession Management to Sustain Competitive Advantage.*

Rothwell, William J. *Effective Succession Planning: Ensuring Leadership Continuity and Building Talent From Within.*

—— *The Strategic Development of Talent.*

Schweyer, Allan. *Talent Management Systems: Best Practices in Technology Solutions for Recruitment, Retention and Workforce Planning.*

Chingosho, Elijah. *Enlightening books on Talent Management: A list by Elijah Chingosho.*

http://searchwinit.bitpipe.com/rlist/term/IT-Workforce.html

search.techrepublic.com.com/search/talent+management.html

whitepaper.techweb.com/.../Performance%20Management%20Tutorial%20On%20Talent%20Management

www.talentmgt.com/columnists/full-potential/2007/September

www.plateau.com/prod/talent-management.htm

blogs.zdnet.com/BTL/?p=4332

Sumser, John. Talent Management Interbiznet Special Edition March 2006.

http://www.interbiznet.com

whitepaper.optimizemag.com/cmpoptimizemag/search/tabsortbrowse/research/1767/26/2/index.jsp

Talent Management: A Tool for Differentiation

8

Seemant Kumar Yadav

Introduction

Talent management is all about the effective utilization human resource. But we can utilize only that resource which are actually we have, thus for this purpose we have to attract the right resource, cultivate them, and last but not the least retain them for a long time with the organization. This resource is nothing but "human resource", and this human resource is in common parlance is termed as "Talent". Thus talent management is nothing but the attracting the right talent, nurturing them and retaining them for the long term benefit to the organization. Human resource is the key for any organization and now HR Executives are using strategic approach to effectively utilize this resource, and they are using the concept of talent management for this purpose. Any organization can imitate other's technology, product specifications, policy but they cannot imitate the commitment and expertise of human resource of other's organization. Therefore, organizations can use the human resource as a tool for the differentiation. And this differentiation can be possible when there is a effective management of talent. That is why there is a war like situation among the organizations for Talent attraction. Once they attract the talent then by various means they try to retain them and nurture them to gain the competitive advantage.

Importance of the Study

There are basically four types of resources for the organization— Man, Machines, Material, and Money. All these resources plays a very significant role in the development of the organizations. Is it possible that we can utilize Machine, Material, and Money without the Man ? No it not possible, being a human we need some fuel in the form of our meal, which gives us energy and we execute our day to day activities, but in the absence of our hands we can't take our meal properly. Now in this situation either we will demolish or we have to be depend on others. In these circumstances we cannot competite with our rival. Similar situation will be infront of the organizations if they do not have the appropriate Man, i.e. Human Resource, human resource is just like the hand for the organization. In the absence of strong and capable human resource organizations cannot gain the competitive advantage over their rival firms. And Talent Management is a tool through which organizations can strengthen their hands, i.e. human resources. If we divert our concentration towards service sector—a sector having high potential and which have the capability to drive the economy, then the importance of HR (Talent) can be recognize easily. Unlike tangibles, the services are intangible in nature, they have the nature of heterogeneity also. Now due to these characteristics the quality of services depends not only the specifications of offering, but also up to a large extent on the persons who are delivering them. These persons are the talent for the service organizations. A service organization can achieve excellency and a distinct place by the performance of these talents. These talents plays a role of boundary spanners between organizational world and external world. If we will have a skilled, committed, and innovative talent then we can get a distinct place in the market and thus these talents can play a role of differentiator for the organizations.

Four Pillars to Manage the Talents

1. Recruitment: In this pillar we have to recruit those talents who have the capabilities to meet our requirements, who have the skills to performed the assigned task and who have the dynamic nature so the they can adjust themselves with changing environment.

2. Learning Management System (LMS): As I said earlier that the Talents should have the ability to change them with respect to the changing environment, now this ability can be strengthen. Our system should be designed in such a way that it can fulfill the requirement of the changing environment by the training and development programs.

3. Performance: Not only a LMS will serve the purpose, it also important to form some planning, so that the talents can perform well and contribute as maximum as possible. These planning may be career planning, succession planning and so on.

4. Compensation: Lastly on the basis of performance there should be a compensation scheme for the talents so that they can receive the monetory value for their performance. Monetory rewards also plays a role of motivational factor to the employees, and a appropriate compensation scheme can extract the valuable performance from the talents.

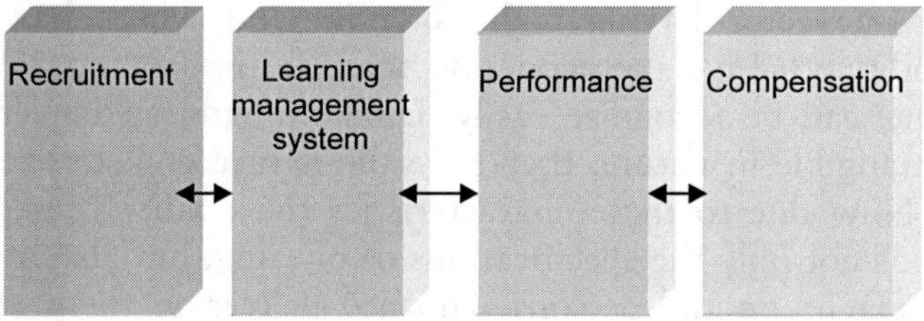

Source: March 30, 2007, Tech Choices "Learning and Talent Management Join Forces"

Now to achieve a distinct place, organizations have to adopt some very significant strategies, not only adopting these strategies will be beneficial for them but effective implementation is also has the same importance. There may be various strategies for this purpose but some basic strategies which are very significant for this purpose are discussed as follows:

1. Aligning the Individual and Organizational Goals: In common parlance the meaning of talent management is to attract, nurture and retain the talent-appropriate for the growth of organization. In addition to achievement of this goal, the individual goal of employees should also be incorporated with the organizational goal. That means if organization is achieving its goals through employees then employees can also achieve its goal through organization.

2. Effective Implementation of Feedback System: To make better understanding about employee's behavior organization can develop a feedback system. This system can take feedback from current employees, and former employees both. Although there are existence of some aluminy association in organizations, but there is a need to make them strengthen, because now they will learn from the past for the future.

3. Developing Proud of a Brand Image: Organization serving the society with accountability, playing their role of social responsibility, achieving corporate excellence, achieving operational efficiency, build a strong image in the society. It is not the only purpose of organization that they are merely producing the products, but if they are producing the product with high customer satisfaction, fulfilling their social accountability, etc., then it will creates a brand image of the organization in the society, and employees associated with this kind of firm feel proud to be a part of this kind of organization. This feeling bound the employee to the organization because they recognize themselves as a distinct person because of the image of their organization.

4. Intensify the Process of Talent Management: It is generally seen that the process of talent management is basically revolves around the some senior executives of the organization. To use the employee's talent for the sake of differentiation it is necessary that this approach should reach to the other members of the organization also, in addition to the senior executives. The result of this intensification will definitely gear-up the wheel of the organizational differentiation.

5. Implementation of Internal Induction Concept: The older and experienced employees of the organization have their own experiences and expertise; these people can motivate the younger talent, through proper guidance and counseling. This is very similar as to the employees from the employees concept.

Conclusion

Although we cannot confined the process of talent management in few points, but these points give a framework. Framework for utilizing the talent management to differentiate ourselves from others. A committed, skilled and satisfied human resource can provide the position of competitive advantage to the organization. Although it is true that there are many other factors also, when we talk about competitive advantage and differentiation, but the flagship factor is no doubt is human resource. An organization having excellent talent can easily make its different image with respect to its rival organizations. Human resources are just like the driver of a vehicle, more talented driver more safe journey without any hazard towards the excellence of the organizations.

Talent Recognition

9

Vijay Goyal

MNC's goals are the reduction of relative and absolute poverty, the increase of employment and the improvement of social welfare. Therefore, it leads to a higher standard of life to all. For that any company/organization has to work from head to toe in order to utilize the available constraint resources.

One of the important resources of any organization or the life of the organization to run or function the organization smoothly is talent/brain in the form of manpower.

So it is always very necessary for any organization to recognize the talent in this competent world to get ahead from others in order survives or to get the continuous growth.

The Main Features of Talent Recognition

- Need of Recognition/Why Recognition?
- How to Recognize?—Methods, Strategies.
- Prospects and Consequences.
- Benefits for Employee/Employer.
- Effects on Society, Nation, Economy.

Introduction

The changing demographics of the market, enduring skills shortages and employee demands for work-life balance have created a so-called 'war for talent'. In this 'war', successful MNCs look to improve their strategies, policies and practices for the attraction, development, deployment and retention of talent vital for their business needs. They, therefore have to aim to understand the capabilities needed in their organization and determine the actual or potential talents required of employees.

Talent Recognition is related to:

- Determining possible career paths,
- Planning of development and promotions,
- Encouraging employees to take responsibility for their development,
- Building self-confidence,
- Creating opportunities for developing skills,
- Goal setting,
- Appraisals.

1. Need of Recognition/Why Recognition?

In spite of recognizing the real/hidden talent of an employee hiring firing rule is in the practice in this competitive world for sustaining, surviving or in order to get ahead from others to get the ultimate objective of profit maximization/wealth creation or expansion of the organization.

Generally such MNC's Deviate from the long-term objectives for achieving the short run objectives which are not even short-term objectives, Employees are considered as the life blood of an organization, because they are the persons through which every work is executed or they put their brain to complete the work. An organizations success is always is in the hands of employees where some employees might be having some extra/hidden talent which may take the organization up to newer heights but which may not be utilized or unutilized or not recognized by the employer in a proper manner in the absence of talent recognition provisions or policies.

So the organizations should try to recognize the individuals who have specific talents rather than specific skills. One can teach the specific skills but one can't teach talents. Talents are something the individual is born with. Which is very much necessary for an organizations success in today's time?

It Helps In

To save the time energy and money of the organization, which were spend in making untimely recruitments due to the absence or escaping of employees to other organizations in the quest of job satisfaction (higher salary, perks, personal or family problems, etc.).

To fulfill the long-term or the ultimate objective of the organization of profit maximization and to be recognized in the leaders or to be considered itself as a brand company.

To build a strong reputation among the shareholders in order to raise the fund for further expansion of the organization.

2. How to Recognize?—Methods, Strategies

A. Competence model

Do the employees know what the organization expects with them?

The Competence Model is the example to be followed by all, and Competence is the quality of the best. Competence management and development of employees improve the quality of their performance.

Employees receive a clear picture as to the requirements of a given job and the awareness of possible career development.

B. *Coaching*

Achieving exceptional results requires the intensity, concentration, discipline and support offered by coaching.

Individual, concentrated coaching helps individuals to reach their professional goals.

It is an efficient method of building company success through developing current and future leaders.

Management system supported by coaching helps employees to recognize and use their strengths, to define obstacles on the way to success and to aim at maximizing their potential by four coaching methods:

- Induction Coaching,
- Executive Coaching,
- Team Coaching, and
- Coaching in the Organization.

Induction Coaching

The success of a newly appointed leader most often depends on the first few weeks in the new role or in a new organization. Induction coaching reduces the risk of new hires by offering them methodological support in the key first-three months in their new job.

The service is also addressed to leaders promoted within the organization.

Executive Coaching

Helps leaders to make use of their full potential. Top executives need neutral and objective discussion related to challenges and opportunities of the business. Executive coaching helps to realize objectives and to exceed expectations. Executive coaching is a successful tool to development of leadership skills and improvement of the relations with peers and bosses.

Team Coaching

Effective method of supporting team development. It uses team building tools while offering an individualized approach to press every team member to stretch far beyond their self-imposed limits. Examples of goals:

- Objectives reached in a more effective and timely manner.
- Improving motivation, creating team spirit.
- Clarification of mission, vision and objectives.
- Exchange of mutual expectations and feedback, clarification of teamwork standards.
- Support in managing change.

Coaching in the Organization

Organizations as they implement coaching is an effective method to manage staff and staff potential. Coaching helps to prepare management teams to take over the role of internal coaches of the organization.

Non-monetary Motives

How to get commitment and keep staff motivated?

Effective non-financial motivating system helps to attract and retain the best employees by stressing factors which are most influential in the choice of career. Implementation of a non-financial motivating system helps to obtain commitment and loyalty of staff. Non-monetary motives provide support to diagnose needs of staff in the organization. It assists in building motivating systems adjusted to their specific needs and situation.

EDP (Executive Development Programme)

Do we benefit from all the wealth of talent in our organization?

How do we unlock the potential and take our management to higher levels of capabilities?

For top management teams The EDP (Executive Development Programme). It usually covers areas such as Performance Management, Leadership Development, Team Building and Development, Creative Problem Solving and Thinking Skills. The sessions are facilitated by executives with minimum 20 years in line management and board experience in an international environment.

Opinion Surveys

Do we know what is the real level of commitment and motivation of our Employees?

Opinion surveys allow for an early diagnosis of potential threats such as growing conflicts, lowering level of identification with the company or occupational burn-out. It provides information that is otherwise difficult or impossible to gain, and therefore verifies previous assumptions towards the actual situation of the enterprise.

Actions that are taken as result of such surveys lead to expected positive change in attitudes and behaviors of Employees and in turn increase efficiency. And talent is recognized easily.

3. Prospects and Consequences

(a) Increased employee and employer satisfaction, mutual coordination between them which is beneficial for both of them.

(b) Decrement in the conflicts among employer and employees as now every employee who is working with full zeal and zest feel "Recognized and get noticed" by the employer or his/her immediate boss.

(c) Most of the employees now work with a positive spirit and treat the organization as a family, and in spite of seeking problems out of a given task as earlier now employees consider the problem as their own problem and try to find out the solution.

(d) When internally the organization get stronger as the spirit of family, harmony, amity prevails among the employees so they (employees) work harder and execute their respective tasks with their full potential. This helps the organization up to a great extent in the betterment of the organization in almost all areas related with the welfare of the organization and its employees mainly, this further helps organization in making high revenue and profits and the organization emerge as a "Brand" where again the share prices of the organization go high due to the popularity of the organization which again motivates other people to invest in the shares then the organization accumulate larger fund and may utilize it in the further expansion, investment or in JVs with big wigs or for some fruitful reasons for further profit making.

(e) Organizations Market share increases which in turn may allow the organization to raise the monetary benefits given to its employees in form of added perks, etc. So again the loyalty of the employee increases as in the form of increased monetary benefits given by the organization.

(f) The standard and ability to pay more allow the organization to hire the best talents available in the market for further expansion which almost ensure the success in the future and day by day reach to new heights of success which even it might not have thought of in the beginning to reach up to such heights.

4. Benefits for Employee/Employer

Benefits for Employee

An employee generally has two kinds of life and objectives:

1. Personal life and related objectives and goals.
2. Professional life and related objectives and goals.

Both lives and their respective objectives and goals are interrelated with each other.

If an employee is not satisfied or enjoying the one then definitely the other one will be effected by the first-one or very less chances would be there to achieve the goals of both lives due to the hindrance in the one, in today's cut throat competition and in the race of getting ahead from others every organization wants to utilize its available constraint resources optimally. One of the most important resources or the life blood of the organization is in the form of manpower/employees of the organization when this resource is recognized properly then the employee may enjoy or achieve the respective goals of life.

From employees point of view he/she would like to enjoy the both lives as both are very important for one to fulfill personal and professional goals. So in order to avail or reap the benefits of both he/she would try to make a balance between these two for making the balance. He will follow the rules and will work accordingly and will be rewarded accordingly

Reducement in the personal and family problems as earlier frequent job shifting in the absence of job satisfaction lead him/her to frequent shifting of places in order to join a new organization and live at that particular place with family

Long-term monetary benefits of sticking with an organization in the form of yearly company promotion, bonus, performance incentives, perks, pension.

Benefits for Employer

The organization save its precious three things—time, energy and money in making untimely recruitment to fill up the gaps/holes which were made by the employee's absence or escaping or switching over to other companies.

The cost which was saved from doing an untimely recruitment may be considered as "opportunity cost" for the organization which in turn may be utilized in the further expansion or in any other constructive activity of the organization.

A satisfied employee is always a "Win-Win" situation for any organization and the employee shows it by his performance and works with full potential where the 3D's (Determination, Devotion, Dedication) of the employee are applied towards the organization, and the employer reaps the benefits in the form of profits.

We have heard a lot cases about a satisfied customers "word of mouth" which provide, a great help in establishing and recognition of a product as a brand, and the respective organization reaps the benefits of the established brand equity in the form of profits with no extra efforts after that, likewise a happy or satisfied employee provides a great help for making or establishing an organization name and fame in the market in today's cut throat competition which helps in making the organization as a brand with its "word of mouth".

- Increased satisfaction and reduced attrition rate of employees.
- Short as well as long-term objectives of the Organization do not shatter.
- Good for the organization in terms of saving extra expenditure on untimely recruitment.
- More reliable talents at no extra costs and decrement in the expenditure.

5. Effects on Society, Nation, Economy

A healthy or satisfied individual creates a healthy environment in a society and such healthy groups forms a healthy society which in turn makes a healthy nation.

A satisfied employee gets the monetary and non-monetary benefits from the organization in the form rewards/recognition, etc. which increases the purchasing power of the individuals such flow if we consider in every part of the nation then the liquidity and flow of goods and services will take place which in turn will make the nations economy stronger and GDP would again increase, which again will promote the export and will get the foreign reserve, and the currency of the respective country will get stronger, which is the sign of the standardization or the level of standard of a nation.

- Increased per capita income.
- Higher level of standard of people, nation.
- Overall growth of the society.
- Increased GDP (gross domestic product).
- Reduction in the rate of brain drain.
- Overall development of the country.
- Economy Booms.

Conclusion

A company's success starts with its people, leaders must focus the majority of their time on their people because all else hinges on the ability of leaders to develop and retain their staff.

Talent is the power which can make or mar an organization, so the productive and timely use of talent by an organization by recognizing the talent and its hidden potential by nurturing the talent with different methods of recognition would be the success factor of any organization talent recognition is not only beneficial for a particular organization or its employees but it indirectly also affects a society, group, etc. and then a Nation and its Economy as a whole which is very crucial for a nation and its citizens to be categorized as developed, underdeveloped or undeveloped country.

REFERENCES

Srinivasan. *Managerial Economics*.

India Today Magazine.

Banking Services Chronicles.

PART – 3
DEVELOPING TALENT FOR NATION BUILDING

Business Process Outsourcing—Using Talent Management Technique—Impact on Indian SMEs Exports Growth in IT and ITES Segment

10

M.P. Dubey

Introduction

Small industry has been one of the catalysts in the growth of India's economic development strategy since Independence. India accorded high priority to Micro, Small and Medium Enterprises (MSMEs) from the very beginning and pursued support policies to make these enterprises viable and vibrant and overtime, these have become major contributors to the GDP. Despite numerous protection and policy measures for the past so many years, Small and Medium Enterprises (SMEs) have remained mostly small, technologically and lacking in competitiveness. The opening on the Indian economy in 1991 added problems to the SMEs. At the beginning, small scale enterprises found it difficult to survive. In the last decade, the economic environment has changed in favour of SMEs. Presently, the SMEs in India are at a cross-road and intense debate is centered on questions like what would be the future of the small enterprises? How these enterprises can survive in the international trade arena? What role can the government play in making these SMEs more competitive? In this context, it is important to relook into the basic issues of MSME, past, present and future prospects, especially in the policy framework.

The small and medium enterprises (SMEs) and entrepreneurs are today recognized as one of the key pillars of the world economy. SMEs provide vibrancy to the developed as well as developing economy by their dynamism, innovation and productivity. In most of the countries around the globe, SMEs provide the largest number of jobs, contributing over 95 per cent of the employment, over 50 per cent of production, and 40 per cent of exports.

Despite such a prominence of this sector, banks and financial institutions have not paid adequate attention to this segment. There is not even clear nationally or internationally understood definition of what constitutes a SMEs. SMEs are not a homogeneous lot, and hence, segmentation of the SMEs under various categories and then designing products and services to meet the requirement of each segment becomes an important factor. At a board level, SMEs may be segmented as traders, manufacturers, service providers and so on.

The SMEs Industry in India is currently at an inflexion point of growth and expansion. The most common definition of SMEs is the categorization based on revenues/turnover. There are times when businesses need capital, and SMEs are no exceptions. In fact, looking at the exceptional growth on India's SMEs segment, lending organizations are increasingly focusing their attention on SMEs sectors. SMEs have been called the Growth Engines of an economy. Of the many benefits associated with SMEs growth on the economy, a few visible ones are:

- More opportunities for low-skilled/high skilled (as to compete their product in the global business) workers since SMEs are labour-intensive.
- SMEs play an integral role especially in agriculture dependent nations making a shift gradually to an industrial and service-oriented economy.
- Small firms grow faster because of quicker adaptability and flexibility to the industry dynamics. With lower adaptation costs to the change environment, like demand and technology, SMEs respond/adjust more rapidly to the new circumstances.
- The major growth barriers that could obstruct the SMEs growth are primarily non-availability of adequate capital for investment including difficulties in accessing the capital market.

- Innovative both in technology as well as assimilation and Technology and business process.

Impact on SMEs—IT and ITES Industries

The recent World Bank's review on Small Business activity establishes the commitment of World Bank Group to the development of the Small and Medium Enterprises (SMEs) sector as a vital element in its strategy to foster economic growth, employment and poverty alleviation. The Indian MSME of the IT industry demonstrates the tremendous growth/value that the Indian IT industry provides to its customer/development effort which encourages existing MSME to do more business. The technology/business incubators have played vital role in success/growth of IT and ITES industry and has fuelled of SMEs segment in a significant manner. The sizeable gains made by Indian SMEs in information technology sector over last few years have caught international attention specially since they have managed ascend the so-called value chain of IT sophistication. Further they have laid the foundation of knowledge industry in India by responding to the technological needs of clients as they adapt themselves to a fast changing business environment.

The Indian IT and ITES industry market continue to enhance momentum, with offshore/outsourcing becoming a mainstream phenomenon. The IT sector was marked by sustained revenue growth, steady expansion of newer service lines and increased geographic penetration. A growth of about 30 per cent by the Software and Services industry places this sector among the highest performers within the Indian market. The Indian IT industry generally covers SMEs which accounts for 78 per cent of the total Industry. The MSME contribute around 26 per cent of the total national export in the IT and ITES industry.

This paper introduces a model on Indian SMEs exports growth using the Neural BACK Propagation Network and the need of the Technology Parks as the key success to the SMEs for the Indian IT and ITES industry and the need to focus on the facility provision in the technology incubator. It enables researchers to compare the extent of growth SMEs activity of a specific country with that of other countries in the same geographical region or the countries with similar level of expertise/facilitation in incubator and the impact in the income level. It also provides statistics on the contribution of the SMEs sector to the formal economy as well as the share of the economy.

Some of the very important and main reasons for India to focus on software industry can be summarized as below:

- The increasing request for software product locally and globally.
- The availability of qualified experts in the field of software.
- The low cost of the qualified Indian manpower in software makes the products of this industry very competitive.
- Establishment of unambiguous policy to stand up with Information Technology (IT).
- Knowing the degree of flexibility in applying the proposed mechanisms to achieve the required policies.
- The significant of STP Scheme and setting up of STPI across 49 locations, which is stated below.
- High level of IT Professional administrating the parks, who knows the complexity of IT and ITES and provide single window support during entire life cycle of this industry.
- The 100 per cent foreign investment is permitted.
- No corporate Income Tax until 2009.
- Provide and help companies with consultancy and services.

The main consequences of this development makes direct impact in the IT and ITES export market and following are few milestone achieved by the Indian SMEs in the domain area of IT and ITES industry, where the technology park also contribute a great help to grow:

- An interesting industry trend that has been noticed in recent years is the expansion of the Indian IT industry's presence from beyond traditional destinations, to newer geographies. The industry's focus is no longer on English-speaking countries alone, and a key strategy for Indian IT majors has been to harness local talent to tap domestic markets and de-risk the revenue model by reducing their dependence on one geographical region.

- The regions like Europe and US remain the key markets, accounting for over 90 per cent of IT-ITES exports. However, export earnings from markets other than the US and the UK are also witnessing significant double-digit year-on-year growth.
- While Indian service providers have built delivery centers in key source markets (e.g. US), they are expanding their footprints in specialist locations like China for engineering and design; South Africa for insurance, and near-shore locations like Eastern Europe and Mexico. Apart from companies in the US, organizations from Europe, South East Asia, Australia, Japan, Hong Kong, New Zealand, etc. are also reaching out for Indian software expertise, supported by the conducive policy environment and incentives for software exports offered by India.
- Demonstrated abilities of India-based firms to broaden their service portfolio, leverage productivity and utilization levels to sustain competitiveness and enhance their global service delivery capabilities—while maintaining high levels of growth.
- The total direct employment in the Indian IT-ITES sector is estimated to have grown by over a million, from 284,000 in FY 1999-2000 to a projected 1,600,000 in the current fiscal (2006-07) over next five years software industry sector double its revenue to US $86 billion and generate 18 million new jobs.
- Given the torrid pace of growth, it notes that at least the Indian companies could make it to world's top 10 in another two to three years.
- In addition to the nearly 1.3 million-strong workforce employed directly in the industry, Indian IT-ITES is

estimated to have helped create an additional 3 million job opportunities through indirect and induced employment. Indirect employment includes expenditure on vendors including telecom, power, construction, facility management, IT, transportation, catering and other services. Induced employment is driven by consumption expenditure of employees on food, clothing, utilities, and recreation, health and other services.

Category	No. of players	Share of India's total IT/BPO export revenues	Performance
Tier I Players	3-4	• 45% of IT Services • 4-5% of BPO	Revenues greater than USD 1 billion
Tier II IT Players	7-10	• 25% of IT Services • 4-5% of BPO	Revenues USD 100 million-USD 1 billion
Offshore operations of Global IT majors	20-30	• 10-15% of IT Services • 10-15% of BPO	Revenues USD 10 million-USD 500 million
Pure play BPO providers	40-50	• 20% of BPO	Revenues USD 10 million-USD 200 million (Excluding top provider with USD 500 million)
Captive BPO units	150	• 50% of BPO	Revenues USD 25 million-USD 150 million (top 10 units)
Emerging players	>4000	• 10-15% of IT Services • 5% of BPO	Revenues less than USD 100 million (IT) Revenues less than USD 10 million (BPO)

Source: NASSCOM McKinsey Report

The ability of most SMEs to survive, grow and generate new high quality jobs increasingly depends on their capacity to put innovation at the core of their business strategy in order to harness benefits from technological change and the globalization of markets for products and resources. In turn, small innovative firms, especially young ones (startups), play a vital role in ensuring the vitality of regional and national innovation systems, and thus enhancing significantly the growth potential in all economies. The Knowledge Based Economy is presenting new challenges as well as opportunities to SMEs.

However, many SMEs have not yet developed a culture of innovation and those that do invest in innovation may still face obstacles in pursuing this strategy. Here lies a huge potential source of technology growth, quality job creation and social well-being that can be met through technology incubators.

The Software Technology Parks (STP) Scheme has played a pivotal role in catalyzing the growth of the Indian IT and ITES industry and supporting its rapid proliferation across the country. The tax holiday has helped attract much needed investments (MNC and India) in the sector and the virtual model has allowed firms to avail benefits without constraints on their choice of location—encouraging Entrepreneurship and integrated growth. Although the existing term of the STP Scheme is nearing its end (in 2009) the government intends to continue the benefits offered, by introducing similar provisions in the Special Economic Zones (SEZs) policy and further relaxing the minimum area requirements (to qualify for an SEZ status) for the IT-ITES sector.

What Motivates Talent to Become More Engaged?

It has been widely demonstrated in employee surveys that country-specific cultural issues influence the key drivers of employee engagement. However, the research reveals that the key drivers of Talent engagement are similar across the Region. Career Development and Training is the number one driver of Talent engagement across the globe. This specifically refers to companies developing people to their full potential and assisting Talent to achieve their career objectives.

Leadership is also identified as a key driver of Talent engagement across the region. In particular, talented employees expect that management decisions will be consistent with the organization's values and that leaders will create a climate of continuous learning.

For many organizations the perennial problem is not just how to attract but also retain talented staff who are critical in making business success a reality specially in the IT and ITES segment. In responding to this long-term challenge, companies need to consider the cultural facilitators of Talent engagement.

Talented employees are more likely to want to stay and contribute in companies that foster an entrepreneurial, long-term oriented, proactive, participative, and flexible approach to management.

BPO Industry—Talent Management

At the core of the growth of strategic outsourcing is the realization that BPO could provide same service at lower cost and with better technology. According to a recent survey by IT toolbox, a major provider of information for IT industry, 36 per cent of the companies that outsource do so primarily to take advantage of cost saving. But reduced cost is not the only reason; the real benefit is about specialization. Across industries, successful companies are converging all their resources and energy on nurturing and strengthening their core business and outsourcing everything else. The core activity can be anything from brand management to product design.

The Indian BPOs (ITES) are moving up the value chain, handling high end data for airline information, insurance, banking sector and mortgage companies, enterprise resource planning, among others. Some of the companies have already moved into significantly higher value added segments such as mission-critical applications, development and support, product design, HR Management, knowledge process outsourcing for pharmaceutical companies and large complex projects.

The foundation of BPO-ITES success story in India was laid down by the subsidiaries of multi-national companies (MNCs) that were set up to cater to the offshoring requirements of their parent companies. Founders of Indian call centre industry were GE capital, American Express and British Airways, who created back-end operation infrastructure in India. Eversince Swissair, GE and American Express started their operation in 1992, captive BPO forms have dominated the structure combustion of low costs and quality manpower. Till the end of last decade most MNCs preferred to set up captive operation, as there was no other alternative. From risk perspective also setting up captive unit was safer.

By 1999 the industry structure had begun to change. With the entry of large number of third party BPO firms, some of which are backed by leading India IT software and service organization.

Projections about the ITES-BPO are sometime mind-bogging. According to a study by international DATA Corporation—ASSOCHAM estimates, the global BPO market is expected to touch $1.5 trillion by 2008. According to Nasscom-McKinsey report this segment will employ 1.1 million Indian and earn $24 billion by 2008. META Group, an IT research and advisory service in its report has predicted that offshore outsourcing market to grow at nearly 20 per cent annually through 2008. META Group believes that the average enterprise will ultimately outsource 60 per cent of applications work offshore. The report says that application development and maintenance constitutes approximately 30 per cent of spending of an average IT organization and off shoring it will typically reduce this expense by 30 per cent. Application development and maintenance are the most common service that majority of Indian Software service exporters provide. According to Gartner Dataquest study, India's revenues from BPO are expected to touch $13.5 billion mark in 2007, with global players contributing 65 per cent of the revenue and domestic companies 35 per cent.

While outsourcing has become imperative for industries to survive and remain competitive, there has simultaneously been an increased backlash against outsourcing in the US and UK markets. The New Jersey Bill in the US and UK's Financial Service Authority issuing new rules and regulations on outsourcing are indicators in this direction. Several associations and lobbies have sprung up to campaign against outsourcing.

The Mackinac report points out that far more Americans loose their jobs to technology, domestic competition and consumer tastes than to outsourcing or other forms of international competition. Think of all the former typists, telephone operators and bank tellers whose work has been replaced by computers and other machines. Job looses due to trade deficit with China has been far more significant.

Consolidation in ITES Industry

The real issue is value addition. To remain at the cutting, edge the captives would have to devote more time to compete with focused players like Accenture and Wipro Spectramind. British Airways recognized this early and have sold a major stake in its operation (now called WNS) to a private equity firm Warburg Pincus. The established players have to show that they can manage their Indian operations better than the independent players. For this they need to be at the cutting edge of technology to make their employees in India as productive and effective as possible.

The consolidation in ITES industry is witnessing a lot of action by way of Merger and Acquisitions (M&A). Things are beginning to hot up again. The trigger this time around of course is IBM's acquisition of Daksh eServices a Gurgaon based 600 employees BPO. Daksh with its huge workforce, international presence and big telecom, insurance and internet customers, makes it a prize catch.

Talent Management in BPOs

One major reason for high talent attrition rate is lack of career growth. Only 5 out of 150 employees progress from agents to team leaders. For those so don't make it, companies like Wipro Spectramind and Global Vantedge offer double pay against better performance. Exl's has the policy to fill at least 50 per cent of all senior positions from within the company. BPOs are adopting various methods to enable their employees to develop relevant expertise and competencies and enhance their knowledge base. Wipro Spectramind has tied up with Symbiosis and offer MBA course to their employees to upgrade their managerial skills and give them opportunity to grow within the organization. Chennai based office tiger has the lowest attrition rate of 8 per cent in the industry.

It uses career growth to retain employees. Here an employee can look forward to becoming a financial analyst or a research professional or anything he is interested in rather than just a call answering specialist. Some operators are offering huge cash incentives, while other use various fitters like psychometric tests to get people who can work at night and handle the monotony. Career counseling and planning career paths also helps. Employees are finally convinced that linking their medium to long-term career path is becoming possible in mature and long-gestation BPO ventures.

Conclusion

As the Indian BPO industry climbs the maturity curve it is realizing that some of the factors leading to its success in the past may not make them winner in the time to come.

India's relatively unsafe e-security environment is costing the BPO/ITES industry. The new IT Act (2000) needs to crucially define cyber harassment and cyber stalking to take care of cyber crimes in India. With the Indian IT/BPO exports to reach $60 billion by 2010, such companies need to invest in upgrading security measures for sustaining competitiveness.

Though India continues to be the top outsourcing destination of the world. It is bound to face growing challenge from new locations including Philippines, Mexico and Eastern Europe and China. The primary reason for this relocation is the growing demand for backup. The new clients handing over work to third party companies rather than their own subsidiaries and in counties where they have little experience feel more comfortable with suppliers who have good backup plans. They are insisting on 'Plan B' locations to hedge against risk of earthquake or civil disruptions disturbing back office work. September 9/11 has suddenly changed the risk perception of the clients. India BPO operators themselves have begun to set up centers outside Indian as backup. The dispersal of outsourcing business around the globe is expected to erode India's prominence as an outsourcing hub.

Apart from cost saving, quality, productivity and delivery have become equally important parameter for clients. Labour cost may not remain an advantage for long. With cost of BPO operates rising rapidly, the BPOs need to graduate to more value added business or contain costs.

India BPO industry is maturing very fast with each passing year. Outsourcing in India is not just a low and call centers chasing up credit card payments. India is rapidly moving up the value chain. The top 10 InfoTech Companies in the world have their second largest development centers in India. These centers have reached a critical mass in terms of the number of people and experience and are now delivering high-end innovative products or solutions in the industry jargon. The development centers of Microsoft, Oracle and SAP all are doing a large proportion of their cutting edge work in India. A much clearer shift is seen at Texas instruments, which was one of the pioneers in offshore hub for the development of its Digital Signal Processors (DSP) largest business for IT. The Indian centre of IT is also the second largest for the company and has filed more than 200 patents.

When it comes to providing specialized services and moving to verticals, which require delivery capabilities and domain knowledge, size becomes very important. The overcrowding of the BPO market has adversely affected the reliability and created unhealthy competition. The industry presently is experiencing a major consolidation, and only those with financial muscle and a record of service delivery will survive. The RBI annual report has suggested that, the BPO companies should go in for mergers and acquisition (M&A) both in India and other developed countries. M&A would help these companies to achieve cost efficiency and competitive price advantage. These companies also need to diversify their markets to other counties than depending only on US market. Manpower challenges are the most serious ones facing the ITES-BPO industry. While India has the advantage of a significant pool of educated English speaking talent for this industry, this base will be inadequate in the face to massive manpower requirement likely to emerge in the next few years. There needs to be a collective effort of the BPO players, the government and the support service industry. In order to transform trainable work force in to employable work force, initiatives like a university degree in BPO, voice assessment centers and workshops on customer care can be of great utility. It appears the NASSOM is already gearing up to address this issue. It proposes to build a robust work force development strategy for ITES-BPO sector. It has decided to fellow a multipronged approach to facilitate manpower development for the short-term and long-term.

Hiring and retaining talent by BPO is becoming another area of concern. The high end BPOs are employing postgraduates, MBAs, CAs, doctors and lawyers. As these jobs have intellectually oriented tasks along with good compensation, the attrition rate is low. Being a technology-dependent sector opportunities for highly qualified personal like computer engineers and network engineering are also increasing. BPO companies have made some headway in the areas of non-poaching agreements, sharing compensation data, notice period and relieving letters. NASSOM also proposes to run a media campaign to explode some of the prevailing myths about this sector. An attempt will be made through the above strategy to position BPO as a "career of first choice" for potential employees.

REFERENCES

Acemoglu, D., Johson, S., J.A. Robinson, (2001). "The Colonial Origins of Comparative Development: An Empirical Investigation". *American Economic Review* 91, 1369-1401.

——(2002). "Reversal of Fortunes: Geography and Institutions in the Making of the Modern World Income Distribution". *Quarterly Journal of Economics,* 117.

Beck, T., Demirguc-Kunt, A., Levine, R. (2002). *Small and Medium Enterprises, Economic Growth and Development.* World Bank Mimeo.

——(2002). "Law, Endowments and Finance". Working Paper.

Beck, T., Levine, R., Loayza, N. (2000). "Financial Intermediation and Growth: Casuality and Causes". *Journal of Monetary Economics* 46, 31-77.

Boyd, J., Levine, R., Smith, B. (2000). *The Impact of Inflation on Financial Sector Performance.* University of Minnesota, Mimeo.

Djankov, S. La Porta (2003). "MSME—the regulation entries".

Djankov, S., La Porta, R., Lopez-de-Silanes, Shleifer, A. (2002). "The Regulation of Entry", *Quarterly Journal of Economics,* 117, 1-37.

——(2003). "Courts", *Quarterly Journal of Economics,* 118, 453-517.

Dubey, M.P., Sunil K. Agrawal, Arun Mohan Sheery (2004). *Technology Incubator: The New Paradigm for MSME and Impact in Global Economy,* Intemac, 30-34, ISBN 81-89547-03-8.

—— (2005). "MSME Impact in Global Economy:Technology Incubator, WAMSME International Conference", Romania, 17th-19th May.

Dubey, M.P., et al. (2005). "Technology Incubator", ISBE 2005, Black Poll, UK.

—— (2006). "Benchmarking of Incubator", Inmantec, 99-107, ISBN 81-903615-0-3.

—— (2006). "Benchmarking of Technology Park/Incubator: the New Paradigm or MSME", IASP Asia Conference, Isfahan 2006, Iran. 1-8.

Dubey, M.P., Sunil K. Agrawal, Manu Pratap (2006). "Benchmarking of Incubator", ISPA Global Meet, Korea.

Dubey, M.P. et al. (2007). "Software Technology Parks/Incubators and Their Impact on Growth of MSME Using the Neural Back-Intelligent Propagation Network," Korea, 24-27 October, 2007.

Easterly, W., Loayza, N., Montiel, P. (1997). "Has Latin America's Post-Reform Growth Been Disappointing", *Journal of International Economics,* 43, 287-311.

Engerman, S., Sokoloff, K. (1998). "Factor Endowments, Institutions and Differential Paths of Growth Among New World Economies". In Haber, S.H. (Ed.). *How Latin America Fell Behind*, Stanford University Press, Stanford, CA, 260-304.

Friedman, E. et al. (2000). "Dodging the Grabbing Hand: The Determinants of Unofficial Activity in 69 Countries". *Journal of Public Economics,* 76, 459-93.

Hallberg, Kristin (2001). *A Market-Oriented Strategy for Small and Medium-Scale Enterprises*. IFC Discussion Paper # 48.

Hart (1999). *Different Approaches to Bankruptcy*. Harvard Institute of Economic Research Working Paper No. 1903.

Kaufman, D., Kraay, A., Lobaton, P.Z. (1999). *Governance Matters*. World Bank Policy Research Department Working Paper No. 2196.

Klapper, L. and V. Sulla (2002). *MSME Around the World: Where Do they Matter Most*? World Bank Mimeo.

La Porta, R. et al. (1999). "The Quality of Government". *Journal of Law, Economics and Organization,* 15, 222-79.

La Porta, R., Lopez-de-Silanes, F., Shleifer, A., Vishny, R. (1998). "Law and Finance". *Journal of Political Economy,* 106, 1113-155.

Nasscom (2005). "The IT Industry in India—Strategic Review".

—— (2006). "The IT Industry in India—Strategic Review".

—— (2007). "The IT Industry in India—Strategic Review".

Schneider, F. (2000). The Size and Development of the Shadow Economies and Shadow Economy Labor Force of 18 Asian and 21 OECD Countries: First Results for the 90s.

Schneider, F., D. Enste (1998). "Increasing Shadow Economies All Over the World—Fiction or Reality: A Survey of the Global Evidence of its Size and of its Impact from 1970 to 1995", IMF and University of Linz, August 21.

Sharma, N.K., Manish Mangal and M.P. Singh (2003). "Solution of Traveling Salesman Problem with Simulated Annealing of Meanfield Approximation Neural Network".

Snodgrass, D. and T. Biggs (1996). *Industrialization and the Small Firm*. International Center for Economic Growth.

Talent Hunt—How to Recognize Talent

11

Atul Narang and *Yogita Narang*

Vice Chancellor JNU in his one of the address at the International Human Resource Conference said that a 10 per cent investment in intangible resources (talent) leads to an 8.5 per cent increase in productivity, whereas 10 per cent investment in tangible resources leads to a 3.4 per cent increase in productivity. The fiscally prudent investment avenue is thus evident! It is indeed intangible talent pool. We have star companies that have consistently out-performed, and out-innovated their competitors. As to what drives their businesses, these companies have similar stories to tell. Today with large signing bonuses and very attractive salaries and benefits, the more perplexing question is how to best build the loyalty of our talented people. The more talent we retain, the more talent we'll attract. The question of attracting the brightest and best is a key issue for all these successful companies.

We have analyzed the performance of a few successful Indian companies from the talent management viewpoint and judged how well these companies have utilized the combination of their tangible and intangible assets. All the companies dwelt upon below are led by dynamic leaders and run by competent managers. As market leaders, these companies have access to low cost capital, yet they deliver above average returns on capital employed—and in the process, create extraordinary value for their shareholders.

The paper highlights a research study, through a questionnaire, conducted on few of these innovative, dynamic FMCG companies that how they attracted the most creative talent and about the secrets of their success in retaining, the response has been assimilated following in the form of guiding principles to ensure that the organization has the ability to recognize talent when it sees it. This research shows in today's corporate environment what are the most crucial talent challenges and what are the best practices which have been used by most successful companies to face the challenge. This benchmarking research helps organizations understand where they fit against the best practices of industry trends and better understand how these processes may be implemented in the organization. This research will help in understanding why talent recognition is not just a "new name" for HR, but has become imperative with very different challenges in each industry, with special reference to FMCG industry.

The representative companies are:

Dabur India Ltd.

Dabur India Ltd.—an Indian Multinational and leading consumer group with 2200 crore turnover is India's largest FMCG company. Dabur India Limited has marked its presence with some very significant achievements and today commands a market leadership status. Story of success is based on dedication to nature, corporate and process hygiene, dynamic leadership and commitment to partners and stakeholders. The results of policies and initiatives speak for themselves.

Hindustan Unilever Limited (HUL)

Hindustan Unilever's Ltd. with turnover 11566 crores-mission is to add Vitality to life. They meet everyday needs for nutrition, hygiene, and personal care with brands that help people feel good, look good and get more out of life. Hindustan Unilever Limited (HUL) is India's largest Fast Moving Consumer Goods company, touching the lives of two out of three Indians through its presence in over 20 distinct categories in Home and Personal Care Products and Foods and Beverages. Mr. Doug Baillie, CEO and Managing Director, Hindustan Unilever, said, "As India's largest FMCG company, we have been close to the heart of India for 75 years and we pledge to continue our commitment to 'Earn the love and respect of India, by making a real difference to every Indian'."

Tata Tea

Tata Tea with turnover 3107 crores, the world's second largest global branded tea operation, today announced its leadership position in terms of volume share in India in the packet tea segment. According to the AC Nielsen survey, for the first time ever, in the month of June 2007, the company outperformed its nearest competitor with a volume share of 19.2 per cent, as compared to the competitor's 18.6 per cent. For quite sometime, the competitor's leadership position in the branded packaged tea market was being challenged by Tata Tea. From a position 5 years ago of 16.3 per cent volume Tata Tea has grown to 19.2 per cent share in the month of June. In a recent survey by *The Economic Times*, Tata Tea has been ranked as the most trusted beverage brand in the country. Speaking on the occasion, Ms. Sangeeta Talwar, Executive Director—Marketing, Tata Tea Limited, said, "This is certainly a defining moment for us and one that will encourage us to work towards attaining greater heights. With this and more to come we have certainly created the momentum to continue on our aggressive growth path and deliver continuing value to our consumers." Tata Tea Limited is a group Company of TATA Group, one of the largest and most respected business houses of India. Tata Tea was formed in 1983 from the erstwhile Tata Finlay Company, a joint venture company formed in 1964. The current business interests include branded tea and tea extract business. Tata Tea Inc., a subsidiary company in US is involved in the marketing and value addition of tea extracts.

Nirma

Nirma turning over 2194 crores is a success saga of a first generation entrepreneur, on his way to create history in the Indian marketplace—that was Dr. Karsanbhai Patel. In a short span, he captured the domestic market, with a quality product. He swiftly crafted low-to-medium consumer pockets—a whole new consumer segment for detergent category. He took on mighty multinationals and rewrote the marketing rules. In true sense, he spearheaded the market revolution by offering innovative, 'value-for-money' products, and changed the cloth-washing habit of Indian housewives—the revolution called ..."Nirma".

Nestle India

With turnover 2477 crores Nestlé India is of Switzerland. With seven factories and a large number of co-packers, Nestlé India is a vibrant Company that provides consumers in India with products of global standards and is committed to long-term sustainable growth and shareholder satisfaction. The Company insists on honesty, integrity and fairness in all aspects of its business and expects the same in its relationships. This has earned it the trust and respect of every strata of society that it comes in contact with and is acknowledged amongst India's 'Most Respected Companies' and amongst the 'Top Wealth Creators of India'.

ITC Ltd.

ITC Ltd. with marked turnover 10318 crores and diversifying into all consumer goods market leader in each arena. The paper has specifically studied the 3 best practices of renowned FMCG companies with respect to two aspects:

1. Recognition of the External Talent:
   (a) Recognition of Prospective Talent.
   (b) Sourcing and Recruiting.
2. Recognition of Internal Talent Pool:
   (a) Performance Management.
   (b) Competency Management.
   (c) Leadership Development.
   (d) HR Systems.

The Analysis

Value creation is a dynamic process and requires not just a mathematical, but a holistic approach. Successful organizations are able to create value in the increasingly competitive and dynamic business environment because they realize the importance of intangible assets. Technology, leadership, relationship, talent recognition and management, brand value, knowledge—these factors, individually and jointly, have steered these companies to success. Business leaders and managers, who ignore this new and important dimension of business, might compromise the value creating potential of their respective companies.

1. To Prove that "Talent—a Most Valuable Treasure". While almost every company claims that human talent is its greatest asset, its actions don't always reflect this priority. It is important to reflect on what company does to recognize talent. Responses reflect that companies must pay attention to the following four P's when it comes to talent acquisition: Policies, Procedures, Practices and Performance. Companies must frequently review their hiring policies, procedures and practices to ensure they are not bureaucratic or detrimental to recruiting talent, particularly unconventional talent. Many hiring policies and procedures are archaic and limit hiring managers from being resourceful and agile. There are some policies and procedures that are devoid of any common sense. Hiring practices should be flexible and nimble and the responsibility of setting and reviewing hiring policies, procedures and practices is not just the prerogative of the HR department but must include input from entire organization and participation of all hiring managers.

Finally, there must be an energetic reward system in place for talent acquisition. The talent recruitment incentives must be brought in place to boost talent acquisition.

2. Defining the "Top Talent". Finding and keeping top talent is a strategic imperative. It's impossible to keep everybody at your company. But keeping the most talented employees is more important than ever. While key employees, by definition, are more productive than average employees but those who readily develop critical competencies and knowledge of unique business processes must also be considered. Some characteristics that can be used to identify talent within the workforce include the following:

- Comfort with Change,
- Clarity of Direction,
- Thoroughness,

- Participative Management Style,
- Persuasiveness, Persistence, and Discretion.

These indicate that talented people are not necessarily extraordinary individuals. People can be largely groomed to enhance these characteristics and become more talented themselves. As a way of involving employees in their own talent recognition and development, they can be asked to inventory and review their own achievements, assess their own interests and learning styles, and write personal goals (professional, career, and social). They are then asked to select resources-tangibles and intangibles, use experiences that are commensurate with their prior achievements, reflect the goals they have set for themselves, and are suitably challenging. Great talent managers do a highly controversial thing. They play favourites—they do not devote equal time to everybody. They devote most of their time to the best performers. Ironically, poor managers do the exact opposite. They devote the greatest amount of time to their worst performers, trying desperately to create some overall acceptable level of performance. Needless to say, in this process, they also lose their best performers. They believe that success is typically won by tapping into those in-built talents and turning them into real-world strengths. Attacking the myth that "each person's greatest room for growth is in his or her areas of greatest weaknesses", the authors maintain that the first priority for individuals as well as corporations must be to identify and then capitalise on the unique, enduring talents within each one of us.

3. Web Cobwebs. A close analysis of the career websites of many large and small companies across a cross-section of industries reveals the painful truth that many sites are in need of a serious overhaul. There are many examples where a company's Web has become a cobweb! It is difficult to even locate the career link of a large global IT company because it is embedded many layers deep on its website. The career link of another Fortune company is found rock-bottom on its website! In the case of a major health insurance company, its career link is simply not there. If human capital is a company's greatest asset, why does talent acquisition receive a low priority on the company's website?

4. Career Link Sites. The labyrinth of links, tedious forms and tables, repetitious information requests and unfriendly Web practices reflect poorly on organizations. Quite likely it will be a sobering experience!

5. Seek Unconventional Talent. Unconventional talent refers to talent that is not a near-identical replacement of the person who just vacated the job. Recruit those whose career paths are interesting and untraditional. Take the risk and hire someone who has never worked in your industry. Seek individuals who have a proven record as creative problem-solvers. Hire for creativity. The characteristics of what constitutes "unconventional talent" are likely to vary from company to company and industry to industry. Hence, a company should first carefully define what it considers unconventional talent and then make a concentrated effort to fill a certain percentage of its positions each year with unconventional talent from a cross-section of industries. While it is understandable, given the intense pressures of today's markets, most hiring managers look for potential employees who can "hit the ground running". It is important to actively recruit those who, even though they may have a slight handicap in the short run, will in the long-term prove to be an invaluable asset to the organization. The initial investment in training and mentoring unconventional talent will yield rich dividends in the long run, particularly on the innovation index.

To ensure this certain steps could be undertaken:

1. Bridge the Academia-Industry gap and create a constant interaction between the two. One should evolve as an extension of the other. Various corporates are into this in a big way.
2. Making significant and effective changes to the curriculum to make it more practical and industry-friendly. Today this measure is definitely being implemented in various streams and courses.
3. Coach students using e-learning as an effective mode for bridging the Academia-Industry gap.

4. Introduce more industry-oriented courses, so that the transition to the corporate world is easy.
5. Introduce soft-skills training at college levels like helping students to cope with job hunting, facing interviews, presentation, and honing good language skills etc.
6. Shift the focus from 'Tier A' cities to 'Tier B' cities, where there is definitely a huge and untapped talent pool whose skill sets have to be honed and developed.

6. Train for Talent Recognition. The ability to recognize talent needs talented eyes. It may not be obvious from a cursory glance at a résumé but it can be acquired through training, brainstorming and careful mentoring. Studies show that many hiring managers are often not aware of biases and prejudices that may lead to the rejection of qualified candidates. More important, the over-emphasis on certain technical skills may lead to early elimination of highly qualified candidates.

Once a person is gainfully employed, retention and job satisfaction is the next important factor. For this, constant mentoring, good and substantial salary hikes, talent recognition, constant training, upgrading job skills, mapping professional with personal terms, etc. should be undertaken to retain the talent pool.

1. Engage them within a very individualized way. One of the HR managers quoted "The first year I was a manager, I made the mistake of managing all of my staff the way I liked to be managed. It was quite a shock when I discovered that each of them had very diverse needs. It was a further surprise that they didn't want to do it 'my way'. I learned quickly that by taking the time to access individual styles, I was able to adjust my approach and retain and keep my talented staff motivated." It is essential for today's leaders to know how to manage situationally by understanding and respecting the diversity. Everyone has a distinct communication style which dictates how he or she likes to work, deal with conflicts, handle stress, is motivated, and likes recognition. Loyalty generally builds over time. And, we don't have the luxury of extended time or stability to build loyalty. We have to quickly catch the attention of our talent, give them an exciting vision of the company's future, and show them how they are an essential part of the success.

2. Identify the drivers of retention. Often these are subtle issues that don't require a lot of money. The immediate manager is still the strongest influence on whether an employee chooses to leave or stay with an organization. And today more than ever, they differ by individual. The adage that "employees leave managers, not companies" is borne out in exit surveys and other workforce polls and that the employees "liked the work and even the pay, they just could no longer stand the way their supervisor failed to involve them or recognize their contributions".

Another study of exit interviews found that good talent wanted to be part of a worthwhile enterprise, be influential in decision-making, and create and contribute to mutually agree upon objectives.

When people feel they are contributing to an exciting product or worthwhile service, their level of commitment increases. People want to be excited about their work. Loyalty also increases when people feel respected and acknowledged for what they do. People want to feel valued and that they are making a difference. Leaders need to recognize each person's need to feel like they count.

The most talented employees at large companies are increasingly demanding a better work/life balance, according to the response gathered. It has been found that "top talent places high value on flexible schedules", particularly when working for large corporations. These people also want a pat on the back; recognition and appreciation is far more important to them than money. The objective of employee recognition is to make employees (especially high performers) feel valued and appreciated. Recognition limited to a sincere "thanks" from a respected manager can be as effective as many tangible rewards. The challenge may be to find or develop skilled leaders who have the confidence, knowledge and experience necessary to know when to acknowledge excellence, and how to make it sincere and motivating.

The ability to motivate or engage others is fundamental to excellence in leadership. Motivational skills are, in part, knowing when and how to recognize and reinforce positive behavior. Assuming these skills can be learned, an organization may get the best results by teaching them to managers. If they cannot be learned, the investment might be better spent on figuring out how to recruit and retain managers who already have these skills.

3. Try uncovering information through one-on-one conversations. Which are critical to employee engagement and retention such as what makes or would make the employee look forward to coming to work, what skills they most like to use or would like to develop and what they would change if they could. One way to build an attractive company culture is through effective and open communication. Make your company a place that people want to join and stay. Continually identify ways to keep people in the loop. Even when there are setbacks, rumors of an acquisition, or anticipated changes in the environment, people want to know what's going on. As leaders, we may be tempted to keep information guarded until we have the full implementation plan. However, most staff want to be a part of the planning, want input into the decisions, and don't like surprises anymore than we do.

4. Credible development plan. It represents recognition of the individual's talents and interests, and the willingness to invest attention. The professional development conversation, coupled with individualized rewards and recognition, and a credible, individualized development plan will go far to secure top talent retention. A good development plan will connect to an individual's primary drivers. Primary drivers have to do with the deep motivations of the person. It focuses on more than competencies. Truly talented people often have "gifts" that they simply must express, and will express elsewhere if we can't tap into them. And why not customize jobs for your very best people? Investments in training, compensation and work-life programs, to name a few, can be of utmost importance.

5. Meaningful mentoring relationship. It's easy to undernurture top talent. Time and attention are scarce resources in the corporate world. But the mentoring role, the attention and the connection to your top talent, has never been more critical. Finally, there is no substitute for a meaningful mentoring relationship. Regularly discuss and review career goals with your organization's top talent, and have open conversations about the ups and downs of the individuals' career. Rather than judging a "down" in a talented person's career, or determining that perhaps a mistake was made in their designation as a high potential, recognize that the conversation never really ends. Check in again and again. Don't miss critical mentoring moments.

We have witnessed growing India, and it grooming-to-be. So in our quest for burgeoning heights and global recognition in all fronts, we have to ensure and take good measures so that our country's talent pool will live up to the name "Brand India".

Talent Management through Employee Engagement Means Higher Performance

12

Uma Sreedhar

In a speech at Harvard University in 1943 Winston Churchill observed that the empires of the future will be empires of the mind. He might have added that the battles of the future will be battles for talent.

Organizations that fail to engage their people fail to achieve their full potential.

Business today is dynamic, with a steadily increasing pace of change. Timely and actionable information is the best way to combat the elements. Peter Drucker said that just as marketing has 4 p's so does Human Resources have 4 e's. The 4 e's were empowering, engaging, enhancing and enabling. He said that having inducted an individual to the organization is not enough. Organizations need to help individuals to satisfy their personal vision by engaging them in activities which is close to their heart, not just that; they also need to help them enhance their skills by providing them opportunities and empowering and enabling them to utilize their skills to help reach the personal vision and also the organizational vision. This ensures greater commitment and enrollment rather than compliance to organizational vision. Individuals today are not loyal to their organization; they are only loyal to their profession. That being the case, what should the organization do to retain their employees?

It is important that the organization lives by the brand image that it wants to project—be it values, systems and practices, and treatment of all its employees, customers, vendors and investors. In case of any gap between the projected image and the actions, the brand building efforts will be futile.

A company which claims to place customers first, cannot treat its employees in a shabby manner. A company which touts quality in its products cannot ignore quality in its internal operations.

Retention, engagement and recruitment are all linked through the employer brand. Externally, candidates perceive the company brand as a promise for an expected employment experience. Internally, employees evaluate their company on the promise made by the brand *versus* how well the company delivers on that promise. Aligning what is promised and what is actually delivered is critical to strengthening the employer brand, and increasing employee engagement and retention levels.

According to the study of 2,000 employees by Hudson Institute and Walker Information in the early part of the new millennium had the following insight:

- 33 per cent are "high risk"—that is, they are not committed to their present employer and not planning to stick around for the next two years.
- 39 per cent are "trapped"—they aren't committed to the organization but are currently planning to stay for the next two years.
- Only 24 per cent are "truly loyal" both committed to the organization and planning to stay for the next two years.
- This is true of all out sourcing industry today. The high price of turnover is one of the major reason that retention matters. Employee turnover involves three types of costs, each of which saps bottom line results.

Research has proven that wholly engaged employees tend to be more self-motivated, reliable, and have higher levels of organizational loyalty. Additionally, studies have revealed that an engaged personnel tends to retain employment and has fewer absences. Plus, these engaged employees have higher levels of customer approval and service quality and they regularly achieve, and often surpass goals.

- Employee Engagement is the extent to which employees commit to something or someone in their organization and how hard they work and how long they stay as a result of that commitment.

- Employee Engagement is directly tied to key areas:
  - Intent to Stay - Retention
  - Discretionary Effort - Performance
- Engagement drives effort, performance, and retention. According to Corporate Leadership Council research:
  - Commitment can increase discretionary efforts by 57 per cent, which can improve performance by 20 per cent.
  - Every 10 per cent increase in commitment increase employee effort (performance) by 6 per cent.
  - Every 10 per cent increase in commitment decrease employee probability of departure by 9 per cent.
- Greatest opportunity for organizations to increase engagement is large group of 'moderates':
  - Degree of engagement impacted by many changes (e.g. restructuring, downsizing, leadership changes).

Engagement is a continuous process—management's credibility requires constant discipline and determination *over time.*

Engagement is defined as: 'A positive attitude held by the employee towards the organization and its values. An engaged employee is aware of business context, and works with colleagues to improve performance within the job for the benefit of the organization. The organization must work to develop and nurture engagement, which requires a two-way relationship between employer and employee. Engagement is two-way: organizations must work to engage the employee, who in turn has a choice about the level of engagement to offer the employer.

The Best Employers research effort has studied hundreds of organizations world-wide and millions of their employees. What is common to all Best Employers is great business results and a sense of passion, excitement and dedication that they are able to create in their employees—they don't just have "satisfied" employees, they have highly "engaged" employees. Engaged employees want to stay with the organization, say positive things about it, and strive beyond what is required to produce extraordinary results! And that makes all the difference.

Employee engagement is the state of emotional and intellectual involvement that employees have towards their organization or group. Engaged employees are those individuals who want, and who actually do take action to improve the business results of their organization. We observe three key behaviors in employees who have high levels of engagement. They:

STAY: They have an intense desire to be a part of the organization.

SAY: They are passionate advocates of their organization to all.

STRIVE: They go beyond what is minimally required to produce extraordinary service and results for customers and colleagues.

The organization must work to develop and nurture engagement, which requires a two-way relationship between employer and employee. Engagement is two-way.

Organizations must work to engage the employee, who in turn has a choice about the level of engagement to offer the employer.

Hewitt research has found that there are 16 "drivers" that influence employee engagement

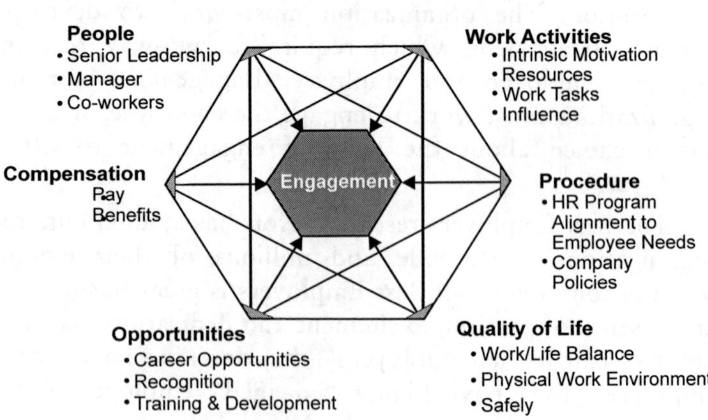

By drivers we mean those factors, which if were to increase, would have the most impact on raising the engagement score. These drivers are organized into six factors which have strong inter-linkages.

There are two commitment "Types": (1) Rational Commitment, (2) Emotional Commitment.

Rational Commitment: The extent to which employees believe that managers, teams, or organizations are in their self-interest (financial, developmental, or professional).

Emotional Commitment: The extent to which employees value, enjoy and believe in their jobs, managers, teams, or organizations.

In most organizations rational component is high, however, if the emotional component is high, the commitment is higher and the employees perception of the employer is better and his satisfaction is higher. Management should act as a facilitator to bring the best in the person rather than being an obstacle and start playing games which was referred too by Thomas Harris. This would only de-motivate people and bring down performance and reduce commitment, it would only lead to grudging compliance rather than willing compliance.

Engaged Employees Create Loyal Customers Who in Turn Create Bigger Profits

In short: Engaged Employees create Loyal Customers who in turn create Bigger Profits.

In the past, it has been labelled the biggest commercial untruth since "the cheque is in the post". Today, however, there is clear evidence that business leaders are not simply saying that "our people are our most important asset"—they are actually beginning to mean it too.

When asked which measurements "give the best sense of a company's health" in a recent Business Week advice column, former GE Chairman and CEO Jack Welch replied: *Employee engagement first.* It goes without saying that no company, small or large, can win over the long-run without energized employees who believe in the mission and understand how to achieve it.

Research also states that an energized employee is also the one who is also enthusiastic. That's why you need to take the measure of employee engagement at least once a year through anonymous surveys in which people feel completely safe to speak their minds.

If engagement can be defined and measured, what drives it? What persuades the employee to 'go that extra mile'—and what does the organization need to give in return?

The Loyalty Factor

The key to employee engagement is creating greater motivation for their work and commitment to their organization. Sudhalini Madhusudan, Assistant Vice-president, Talent Enhancement Group, Office Tiger concedes that it is not possible to retain professionals only by paying high salaries and offering attractive benefits. "We need to create enthusiasm for their roles, their work and the organization, and ensure they are well integrated. Employee engagement relates to the employee's commitment to the organization's success. Engaged employees who are inspired and guided by the leadership, equipped with the right tools and managed by the right systems and processes deliver superior performance." Employee engagement today encompasses training, development, work environment, leadership, performance management, work/life balance, communication, compensation, benefits, commitment, fun and social activities. This, asserts Madhusudan, enhances the bonding between employees and commitment to the company.

Research has clearly shown that the key reasons for attrition are lack of role and goal clarity, not having a challenging job, boss and his management style, lack of learning opportunities, lack of excitement and innovation in the job, lack of autonomy and freedom and no recognition. According to studies in the US, while firms go to great length to hire new employees, 80 per cent of pools of executives change their jobs within two years (HBR Article 2000, Issue 78). A successful organization is one in which both the individual and the organization are transformed for the better and are able to leverage from each others strength.

Employee engagement is a partnership between a company and its employees where everyone works together to achieve the business objectives of the company and the personal aspirations of the employees. It is therefore largely the organization's responsibility to create an environment and culture conducive to this partnership, and a win-win equation. Employee engagement is a barometer that determines the association of a person with the organization. An associated or engaged employee is, after all, a productive employee. However, in practice, engagement transcends this. It is about creating the passion among associates to do things beyond what is expected of them. A highly engaged employee will consistently deliver beyond expectations. A productive employee who has a sense of belonging and a strong bond with the company and its brand will create a ripple effect that results in a positively charged atmosphere in the organization.

Pioneering work from Gallup Research suggests that engaged employees are more likely to trust their companies and promote their business agenda. Beyond the common sense from Gallup is the bigger picture, that of developing the leadership mass and core of the organization through and beyond engagement.

Sudheesh Venkatesh, Head of Human Resources at Tesco HSC (Hindustan Service Center) views employee engagement as a psychological association. When the parent company did research on employee engagement in Britain it found that certain factors made a difference. "Our early experience in India has been similar", says Venkatesh. Employees want to work for an organization that:

- Is successful
- Is legal
- Provides opportunities to grow
- Has managers who help employees
- Is socially responsible.

Benefits to the Organization

- Employee engagement builds passion, commitment and alignment with the organization's strategies and goals.

- Attracts more people like existing employees. Increases employees' trust in the organization.
- Creates a sense of loyalty in a competitive environment.
- Lowers attrition rate.
- Increases productivity and improves morale.
- Provides a high-energy working environment.
- Improves overall organisational effectiveness.
- Boosts business growth.

Makes the employees effective brand ambassadors for the company.

Most organizations today realize that a 'satisfied' employee is not necessarily the 'best' employee in terms of loyalty and productivity. It is only an 'engaged employee' who is intellectually and emotionally bound with the organization, feels passionately about its goals and is committed towards its values who can be termed thus. He goes the extra mile beyond the basic job responsibility and is associated with the actions that drive the business. Moreover, in times of diminishing loyalty, employee engagement is a powerful retention strategy. The fact that it has a strong impact on the bottom line adds to its significance.

Engagement is about motivating employees to do their best. An engaged employee gives his company his 100 per cent. This is what makes the difference in an industry where the most valuable resource of a company walks out of the door every evening. "This is of particular importance in a knowledge industry. The quality of output and competitive advantage of a company depend on the quality of its people," says Anupama Babbar, Senior Manager, HR, at Flextronics Software Systems.

Investigating the engagement level at an organization can also lead to a more productive work force with fewer compensation and accident claims. HR Solutions has a survey tool that measures employee engagement. The survey items were developed in order to bring a method to examine the commitment, ownership, pride, loyalty, and satisfaction of employees.

Results

The information garnered from employee engagement surveys can give the management knowledge that directly impacts the bottom line and fosters positive employee relations in any or all of the following ways:

- Identifying cost-saving opportunities.
- Improving productivity.
- Reducing turnover.
- Curbing absenteeism.
- Strengthening supervision.
- Evaluating customer-service issues.
- Assessing training needs.
- Streamlining communication.
- Benchmarking the organization's progress in relation to the industry.
- Gauging employees' understanding of, and agreement with, the company mission.

Engagement survey will find out what engages the people within your organization, understand their perceptions, especially those that are driving the work behaviors that in turn drive business outcomes. This information will allow organizations to reinforce engaged employee behaviors and develop methods to repair areas with deficient engagement scores.

What is Engagement?

The first step in IES research was to investigate what HR professionals understood or meant when they used the term 'engagement'. A clear view of the behaviors demonstrated by the engaged employee emerged:

- Belief in the organisation.
- Desire to work to make things better.
- Understanding of business context and the 'bigger picture'.
- Respectful of, and helpful to, colleagues.
- Willingness to 'go the extra mile'.
- Keeping up to date with developments in the field.

Engagement has clear overlaps with the more exhaustively researched concepts of commitment and organizational citizenship behavior, but there are also differences. In particular, engagement is two-way: organizations must work to engage the employee, who in turn has a choice about the level of engagement to offer the employer.

IES' 2003 attitude survey of over 10,000 employees in 14 organizations, the full range of employee groups and job roles were represented—managerial, professional, technical and support (manual and administrative).

The study was funded and supported by IES' motivation, wellbeing and retention Research Network (Robinson D. Perryman S. Hayday S. IES Report 408).

The study revealed the following results:

Positive responses to the engagement statements indicate:

- A positive attitude towards, and pride in, the organization,
- Belief in the organization's products/services,
- A perception that the organization enables the employee to perform well,
- A willingness to behave altruistically and be a good team player, and
- An understanding of the bigger picture and a willingness to go beyond the requirements of the job.

Engagement Challenges

Further in-depth analysis of our NHS case study data revealed that engagement levels can vary, in association with a variety of personal and job characteristics and with experiences at work. Some key findings were:

- Engagement levels decline as employees get older—until they reach the oldest group (60 plus), where levels suddenly rise, and show this oldest group to be the most engaged of all.
- Minority ethnic respondents have higher engagement levels than their white colleagues.

- Managers and professionals tend to have higher engagement levels than their colleagues in supporting roles, although people in the latter group appear to owe greater loyalty to their profession than to the organization in which they practice their craft.
- Engagement levels decline as length of service increases.
- Having an accident or an injury at work, or experiencing harassment (particularly if the manager is the source of the harassment) both have a big negative impact on engagement.
- Employees who have a personal development plan, and who have received a formal performance appraisal within the past year, have significantly higher engagement levels than those who have not.

The above findings show that organizations need to work hard to prevent, and minimize the impact of, bad experiences. They also need to ensure that employees' development needs (including the special needs of professionals) are taken seriously; pay attention to, and value the roles of, support staff; and to maintain the interest of longer-serving employees. The relatively high levels of engagement of the oldest employees, and of minority ethnic staff, suggest sources of untapped potential within some organizations.

What Drives Engagement?

Research shows that committed employees perform better. If we accept that engagement, as many believe, is 'one step up' from commitment, it is clearly in the organization's interests to understand the drivers of engagement. Analysis of the NHS case study data indicates that opinions about, and experiences of, many aspects of working life are strongly correlated with engagement levels. However, the strongest driver of all is a sense of feeling valued and involved. This has several key components:

- Involvement in decision-making—the extent to which employees feel able to voice their ideas, and managers listen to these views, and value employees' contributions.

- The opportunities employees have to develop their jobs.
- The extent to which the organisation is concerned for employees' health and wellbeing.

The line manager clearly has a very important role in fostering employees' sense of involvement and value—an observation that is completely consistent with IES' research in many different areas of HR practice and employment, all of which point to the critical importance of the employee-manager relationship.

IES' Diagnostic Tool

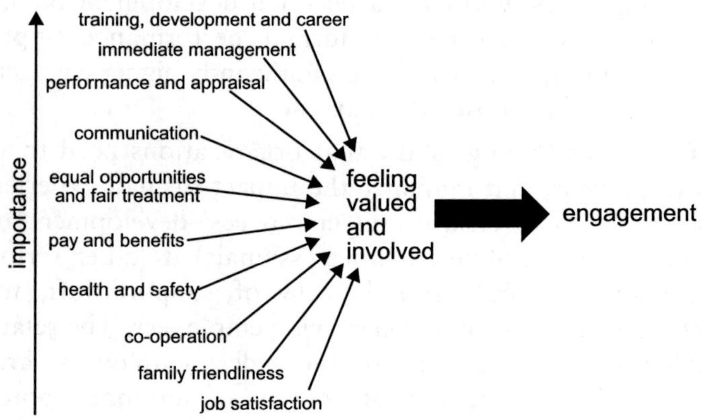

The diagnostic tool

Source: IES Survey, 2003

The IES engagement model illustrates the strong link between feeling valued and involved and engagement. In addition to the model, IES offers a diagnostic tool (above), which can be used to derive organization-specific drivers from attitude survey data. Our findings suggest that many of the drivers of engagement will be common to all organizations, regardless of sector; however, some variability is likely, and the relative strength of each driver is also likely to be contingent upon the organization being studied.

General Lessons

Attempts to raise engagement levels are likely to founder, unless the following 'building blocks' are in place:

- good quality line management,
- two-way communication,
- effective internal co-operation,
- a development focus,
- commitment to employee wellbeing, and
- clear, accessible HR policies and practices, to which managers at all levels are committed.

It looks easy, but of course it isn't; it requires a huge amount of effort and continuing investment to ensure that all of these basics are in place and working well. Embarking on a drive to increase engagement levels should not be undertaken lightly, bearing in mind the ease with which engagement (like the psychological contract) can be shattered.

Engaged employees create loyal customers who in turn create bigger profits.

For a few, including Richard Branson at Virgin, this simple premise was the basis upon which they had already begun to build their businesses. As Branson says:

"We embarked on consciously building Virgin into a brand which stood for quality, value, fun and a sense of challenge. We also developed these ideas in the belief that our first priority should be the people who work for the companies, then the customers, then the shareholders. Because if the staff is motivated then the customers will be happy, and the shareholders will then benefit through the company's success."

Others, however, would need a more rigorous analysis if they were going to commit their organizations to this somewhat radical vision of "the shareholders come last". Yet the Service-Profit Chain model's greatest problem was that it was only supported by data collected by different companies at different points on the chain.

For example, in the banking sector it was known that a 5 per cent increase in Customer Loyalty could produce

Profitability increases from 25 per cent to 85 per cent. Meanwhile, an insurance company had shown that when an experienced employee left the business Customer Satisfaction levels dropped from 75 per cent to 55 per cent.

In fact only quick-service restaurant chain Taco Bell had begun to do anything like an end-to-end analysis of the chain, observing that the 20 per cent of stores with the highest Employee Retention rates enjoyed double the sales and 55 per cent higher profits than the 20 per cent of stores with the lowest Employee Retention rates.

As a result, although the Service-Profit Chain model seemed logical and sensible, the potential return on investment was unknown. This made it difficult for business leaders to assess how much effort they should be making to embed it within their organizations.

Sirota Consulting studied 28 multinational companies through 2004 and found that the share prices of organizations with highly engaged employees rose by an average of 16 per cent compared with an industry average of 6 per cent.

Meanwhile, an ISR study published in August 2005 showed that companies with low levels of employee engagement saw net profit fall by 1.38 per cent and operating margin fall by 2.01 per cent over a 36-month period. In companies with above average levels of employee engagement profits rose by 2.06 per cent and operating margin rose by 3.74 per cent over 36 months.

And it gets even better, because the research has now been completed which identifies the key drivers of employee engagement. In other words, a "road map" for achieving outstanding organizational performance through the Service-Profit Chain has been developed and is ready for immediate implementation.

Summary/Conclusion

- Driving to Higher Levels of Engagement in a Journey.
- Engagement begins with the end in mind and requires a road map to get there.

- Alignment of practices, intent, process and discipline are must haves.
- Communication is a fundamental driver of understanding the work and its relationship to strategy.
- Leaders using high degrees of involvement, coaching, recognition drive higher levels of engagement.
- When understanding and involvement are high, discretionary effort increases and retention risk decreases.
- Only engaged employees can bring improvements in performance.

REFERENCES

Lowell L. Bryan, Claudia I. Joyce & Leigh M. Weiss, *Making a Market in Talent*, Indian Management, June 2006, p. 82.

John Hagel III, "From Push to Pull: The Next Frontier of Innovation", *The McKinsey Quarterly*, 2005. Number 3, pp. 82-91.

Pi Wen Looi, Ted Marusarz, and Raymond Baumruk, "What Makes a Best Employer?"

Insights and Findings from Hewitt's *Global Best Employers Study 2004,* Hewitt Associates LLC.

Optimizing Most Valuable Asset: An HR Perspective

13

Vibhuti N. Bajpai, Dhirendra Kr. Tripathi and *Anil Kumar Goyal*

Introduction

Human Resources (HR) as a function is fast changing since it works closely with senior management, business segments, line management and functional leaders in an IT organization. HR management is undoubtedly one of the major challenges ahead for Indian IT companies.

The IT industry is already under stress on account of persistent problems like attrition, confidentiality, loyalty, etc. Managing talent in the knowledge-based industry is not a cakewalk for HR managers as it is a multi-task responsibility. In the present scenario, HR managers are performing a variety of responsibilities. Earlier, their role was confined to administrative functions such as looking after manpower requirements and maintaining rolls for the organization. Now it is more strategic in keeping with the demands of the industry.

Talent has emerged as an extremely confident and sensitive entity. Its message to one and all is "better prefer, possess and pamper me or you will perish". In its new *avatar*, Talent is establishing itself as an extremely confident organism, no more willing to play a second fiddle and seeking a price without any compunction.

The momentous paradigm changes in the world have all been the outcome of human creativity, otherwise called talent. Consequently organizations need to put in place appropriate process, in other words strategies to enable and ensure talent to bloom and mature. The article under this section "Optimizing Most Valuable Asset: An HR Perspective "unequivocally puts that the winning organization is one, which has the clarity to define the role and then recruit. Employees are not to be treated as mere cogs in the wheel. The Organization needs to ensure that every person who gets selected is a champion of performance and result. Moreover this person needs to have in him team flair more than the individualistic streak.

From Personnel to Strategic HR to Talent Management

To understand why Talent Management has become so important, we must first look at the evolution of corporate HR:

Stage 1: Personnel Department

In the 1970s and 1980s the business function, which was responsible for people, was called "The Personnel Department". The role of this group was to hire people, pay them, and make sure they had the necessary benefits. The systems, which grew up to support this function, were batch payroll systems. In this role, the personnel department was a well-understood *business function.*

Stage 2: Strategic HR

In the 1980s and 1990s organizations realized that the HR function was in fact more important—and the concepts of "Strategic HR" emerged. During this period organizations realized that the VP of HR had a much larger role: recruiting the right people, training them, helping the business design job roles and organization structures (organization design), develop "total compensation" packages which include benefits, stock options and bonuses, and serving as a central point of communication for employee health and happiness.

The "Head of Personnel" became the "VP of HR" and had a much more important role in business strategy and execution. The systems, which were built up to support this new role, include recruiting and Applicant Trackings (ATs), portals, total compensation systems, and learning management systems. In this role, the HR department now became more than a business function: it is a *business partner*, reaching out to support lines of business.

Stage 3: Talent Management

We are now entering a new era: the emergence of "Talent Management". While strategic HR continues to be a major focus, organizations are now focused on a new set of strategic issues:

- "Competency-based" recruiting instead of sorting through resumes.
- Developing managers and leaders to reinforce culture, instill values, and create a sustainable environment.
- Identifying competency gaps.
- Identifying high performers and successors to key positions throughout the organization.
- Providing learning that is relevant, flexible, convenient, and timely.

These new, more challenging problems require new processes and systems. They require tighter integration between the different HR silos—and direct integration into line of business management processes. Today organizations are starting to buy, build, and stitch together performance management systems, succession-planning systems, and competency management systems. The HR function is becoming integrated with the business in a real-time fashion.

Evolution of the HR Function

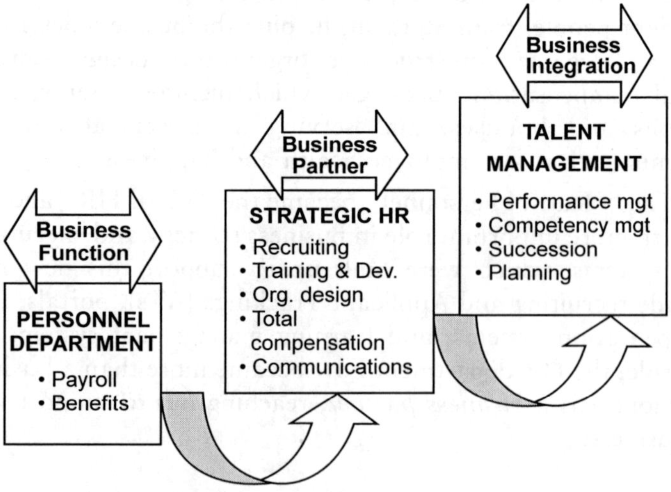

Talent Management Process: Adopted by IT Industry

Organizations are made up of people: people creating value through proven business processes, innovation, customer service, sales, and many other important activities. Some of the issues that the IT sector faces are managing people, motivation to adopt new technology changes, recruitment and training, performance management, development, and compensation management.

The following chart shows the complete process:

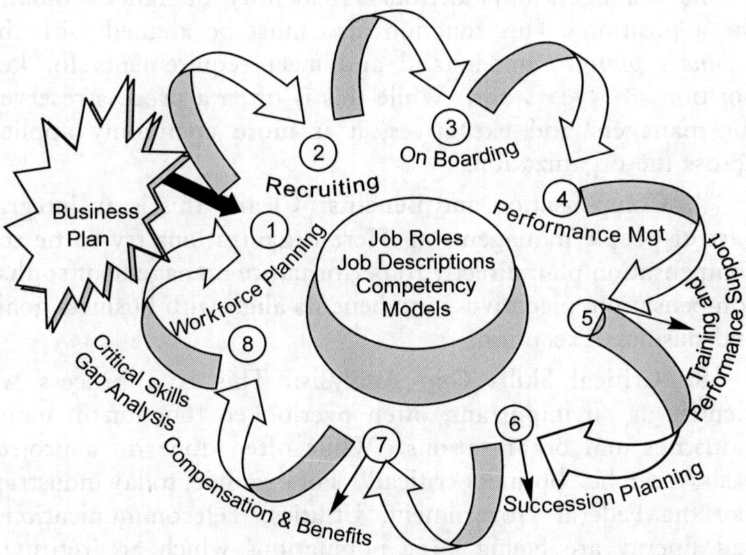

1. Workforce Planning: Integrated with the *business plan*, this process establishes workforce plans, hiring plans, compensation budgets, and hiring targets for the year.

2. Recruiting: Through an integrated process of recruiting, assessment, evaluation, and hiring the business brings people into the organization.

3. On Boarding: The organization must train and enable employees to become productive and integrated into the company more quickly.

4. Performance Management: By using the *business plan*, the organization establishes processes to measure and manage employees.

5. Training and Performance Support: Of course this is a critically important function. Here we provide learning and development programs to all levels of the organization.

6. Succession Planning: As the organization evolves and changes, there is a continuous need to move people into new positions. Succession planning, a very important function, enables managers and individuals to identify the right candidates for a position. This function also must be aligned with the *business plan* to understand and meet requirements for key positions 3-5 years out. While this is often a process reserved for managers and executives, it is more commonly applied across the organization.

7. Compensation and Benefits: Clearly this is an integral part of people management. Here organizations try to tie the compensation plan directly to performance management so that compensation, incentives, and benefits align with business goals and business execution.

8. Critical Skills Gap Analysis: This is a process we identify as an important, often overlooked function in many industries and organizations. While often done on a project basis, it can be "business-critical". For example, today industries like the Federal Government, Utilities, Telecommunications, and Energy are facing large populations which are retiring. How do you identify the roles, individuals, and competencies which are leaving? What should you do to fill these gaps? We call this "critical talent management" and many organizations are going through this now.

In the center of this process are important definitions and data: job roles, job descriptions, competency models, and learning content.

Developing a Competency based Recruitment System

What is a competency?

A competency is the capability to apply or use a set of related knowledge, skills, and abilities required to successfully perform "critical work functions" or tasks in a defined work setting. Competencies often serve as the basis for skill standards that specify the level of knowledge, skills, and abilities required for success in the workplace as well as potential measurement criteria for assessing competency attainment.

What is a competency model?

A competency model is a collection of competencies that together define successful performance in a particular work setting. Competency models are the foundation for important human resource functions such as recruitment and hiring, training and development, and performance management because they specify what is essential to select for or to train and develop. Competency models can be developed for specific jobs, job groups, organizations, occupations or industries.

Elements of a competency model

Competency models can take a variety of forms. Typically, they include the following elements:

- Competency names and detailed definitions. For example, a competency model could include a competency called "Teamwork" defined as follows:
  - Establishing constructive and solid interpersonal relationships;
  - Treating others with courtesy, tact and respect;
  - Working effectively with others, regardless of organizational level, background, gender, race or ethnicity;
  - Working to resolve disagreements, attempting to persuade others and reach agreements;
  - Biding by and supporting group decisions; and
  - Facilitating team interaction and maintaining focus on group goals.
- Descriptions of activities or behavior associated with each competency. For example, the following behaviors could be associated with the competency "Teamwork":

- Handling differences in work styles effectively when working with co-workers;
- Capitalizing on strengths of others on a team to get work done;
- Anticipating potential conflicts and addressing them directly and effectively;
- Motivating others to contribute opinions and suggestions;
- Demonstrating a personal commitment to group goals.

Methodology for designing

The following methodology for designing and developing competency frameworks is suggested by Martin. "In my experience, the most effective route is to employ recognized best-practice internal research methodology using behavioral event interview (BEI) techniques to selectively sample the target population (supplemented with expert panels and 'Competency Requirement Questionnaires' to engage wider population samples) and so build up the models from the data that emerges. This data should be triangulated against clear top-down input in terms of organizational strategy and business objectives, and also against external research relevant and analogous to the organization's situation—not as a driver, but as a reference point." He adds that once the behavioral data is collected, it should be sorted, categorized and leveled carefully to create models that are concise and comprehensive, simple and sophisticated. Developing BEI skills within the organisation has the added benefit that once the model is complete, it can be used more effectively by transferring these skills to selection interviewing, development assessments, and so on.

Martin cautions that international organizations must ensure that the methodology does not screen-out those competencies that do not match the culturally influenced pre-conceptions of the head office (wherever it is situated) of what high-performance competencies are. "This is a common error…the universalistic, all-powerful 'global leadership model'. There is so much evidence to support the idea that culture is a business issue, is a management issue, that it seems obvious that mono-cultural lists of 'exemplar behaviors' will work only to exclude those who do not conform to the originating culture. The point is not to get everybody to behave the same, but to get everybody to perform to the same high standards."

Identifying the Existing Talent

Tracking employee skills for business advantage

The activity of tracking down the competencies and skills (existing as well as unexplored), is becoming an integral program for many IT companies. Mapping the right skills to the right business requirement (which companies are fast realising is as critical to meeting business objectives as developing skills), leads to the creation and continuous tracking of the 'skills inventory'.

Maintaining a skill repository may not still be very common in many IT companies, but tapping into the power of skills (for business and competitive advantage) has put the exercise of skills tracking at the forefront of many an organizational agenda. Skills, which may otherwise go unnoticed, can be leveraged and canalized towards the company's benefits and improving employee productivity. And how can this be done? A little mix of intuition with science is the answer.

The significance of skills tracking

In the IT Industry you are in the business of your employees' skills and knowledge. This is the most important selling factor for grabbing a new business as well as for sustaining and growing the existing businesses. Competition is further forcing organizations to be 100 per cent aware of their employees' skills and abilities. With companies becoming aware of their employees' skills, more than ever before the skills tracking exercise has achieved serious proportions, almost at par with other regular internal employee programs.

While some progressive organizations had started the skills tracking exercise sometime back, others are now following suit. "These initiatives are becoming more integral to forward looking IT companies, who have the tremendous need to tap into the employee talent reservoir to provide value add to their business operations and customers. And, in turn, help employees to explore their potentialities," Most progressive organizations have skill evaluation as a formal program. An employee's customized development plans are made reflecting his/her skills and talents. These exercises are conducted in addition to the informal programs. Most large IT companies maintain a central skills inventory of their employees. Nirupama, V.G., Executive Vice-president of Team Lease elaborates, "Companies are currently conducting these programs from time to time as and when required, but the IT industry is looking at this with complete focus. Many companies are even introducing Web-based tracking system, which is more prevalent in the West." Employee-skill inventory is becoming a major source for designing training and development programs, as well as becoming an integral part of HRM systems—whether automated or otherwise—in IT companies. For organizations where formal programs are still a distant reality on account of resource constraints, conduction of informal exercises at least is becoming an acceptable norm.

Work Culture in IT Companies

Work culture highlights:

- **Results Oriented**
    - Deliver on commitments with speed and excellence.
    - Leverage our ability to respond to competitive challenges and grow our business globally.
- **Focused**
    - On maximizing client returns from outsourcing and offshoring
    - Provide best technology solutions to solve business issues.
    - Knowledge sharing through in-house-training and seminars to keep up-to-date with new technological developments.

- **People Centric**
  - Encourage and support people to achieve a qualitative work life balance.
  - Forming relationships based on openness and trust with the people.
- **Flexible**
  - Flexible working environment with flexi-hours boosts people's performance.
- **Fun @Work**
  - At India, Industry believes in having fun at the work place while focusing on complex business problems.

Following are some of the key initiatives at TCS, Wipro and Infosys in India:

- **New Employee Celebration:** The induction program for new employees at TCS is called the "New Employee Celebration". The name of the program is indicative of the approach of the company towards new joiners. It is a three-day program and includes meetings and presentations by the senior management, all departments and sharing of the organizational approach. Icebreakers, fun events, photo-session of the entire team are a part of the NEC.
- **Career Development Plan (CDP):** A career development plan jointly generated by an employee and his/her manager that documents the employee's short and long-term career goals and the training and developmental experiences necessary to mutually achieve these goals.
- **Mentoring:** Mentoring involves counseling others through formal or informal methods. A mentor willingly serves as a role model for his/her protégé, sharing company insights and lessons learnt. Mentors also provide advice on career development goals, strategies and options.
- **Competency Integration:** The purpose of competency integration is to improve the efficiency and agility of interdependent work by integrating the process of different work force.

- **Competency Analysis:** To identify the main tasks, skills, knowledge and attitude required for various roles in the organization that will be used in formulating job description, assessing employees' current level of competency, and in other activities like planning career development and coordinating competency development, etc.
- **Empowerment of Work Groups:** In TCS there are three types of workgroups in the organization: Departments, Projects and Taskforces. Department Heads (DHs)/Group Leaders (GLs)/Team Leaders (TLs) of departments and projects and sponsors of taskforces identify such responsibilities and authorities, which shall be delegated to a workgroup. The empowerment may be provided to an individual or a group and information about empowerment shall be given by concerned DH/GL/TL/ sponsor to their respective managers.
- **Continuous Capability Improvement (CCI) for Individuals:** CSC India has a defined and documented process for continuously improving individual capability of its employees.
- **Knowledge Management:** CSC India has defined a process for knowledge management and encourages capturing of knowledge assets and their use in organization (among individuals and teams/groups).
- **Sharing is Developing:** As another major employee initiative, with the objective to share the tools and best practices used in different projects, the Financial Services Group (FSG) division of CSC India has initiated a discussion forum called "Care to Share". Most of the tools shared in the forum are developed in-house to improve productivity, attain faster turnaround, and ensure efficient reporting. This is a new strategic initiative to share project experiences, ask questions, find solutions, plan together and coordinate activities. The discussion forum is attended by the Project Management Group (PMG) and the details of the discussion are mailed to all

the employees so that they can leverage this information to derive benefits in terms of saving cost and time in their projects.

Conclusion

Managing people in the knowledge-based industry is critical as the human resource is the soul of the organization. Since there is a high demand for knowledge workers, talented professionals often enjoy high bargaining power due to the knowledge and skills they have. The attitude is different for those who are taking up responsibilities at a lesser age and a lower level of experience. These factors have resulted in the clear shift to individualised career management from organization career commitment. Competency-based HR is considered the best HR. In India, however competency development and mapping still remains an unexplored process in most IT organizations despite the growing level of awareness. Is the underlying principle of competency mapping just about finding the right people for the right job? The issue is much more complex than it appears, and most HR departments have been struggling to formulate the right framework for their organization.

The management of the company encourages initiatives, recognizes individual contributions, treats each person with respect and fairness, and gives ample opportunity for individual growth.

REFERENCES

Agrawal, R.D. *Dynamics of Personnel Management in India.*

David. S. Cohen. *The Talent Edge: A Behavioral Approach to Hiring, Developing and Keeping Top Performers.*

Fiona Macleod Butts and Karen Gooch. *Building Tomorrow's Talent.*

Lance A. Berger, Dorothy R. *The Talent Management Handbook: Creating Organizational Excellence by Identifying, Developing and Promoting Your Best People.*

Mark Albrecht and Janet Clarey. *Talent Management: A Complete Guide to Strategies, Systems, and Issues.*

Nick van Dam. *25 Best Practices in Learning & Talent Development.*

Ramani, V.V. and K. Guruswam. *Talent Management—Concepts And Cases,* August 2003.

Paul Sparrow, Chris Brewster and Hilary Harris. *Globalizing Human Resource Management.*

'TCS continues to have the lowest attrition rate in the industry', *Hindustan Times*—February 27, 2007.

www.hrmguide.com

www.haygroup.cz

14

Next-Generation Talent Management

Satendra Kumar Yadav

Introduction

Now more than ever, it's imperative that organizations manage people well. In today's information economy, people's knowledge, skills, and relationships are an organization's biggest asset and main source of competitive advantage. Cost cutting and productivity boosting are corporate mainstays, while people related costs have risen to more than two-thirds of organizational spending. Increasingly, workforce optimization is viewed as a significant driver of shareholder value and bottom-line results. As the importance of people to the bottom line grows, the rules for managing people are dramatically changing. Demographic, economic, technological, and sociopolitical phenomena are driving the most drastic workforce changes in decades, creating a workforce that's more diverse, mobile, informed, and in demand than ever before. Alarmingly, most organizations aren't prepared to manage this new generation of talent. In fact, research suggests that most large organizations are currently underutilizing their managerial and professional talent, are failing to understand the kind of support knowledge workers need to perform at their best, and are continuing to use industrial-age talent management practices despite receiving less than optimal results. Numerous studies support these conclusions. A recent Conference Board survey reported that CEOs gave talent identification and growth, engaging employees in the company's vision/values/goals, and leveraging diversity surprisingly low rankings—sixth, eighth, and seventeenth, respectively—in their lists of top management concerns for the year 2008. A Society for Human Resources Management (SHRM) survey revealed that less than one-third of employers are adjusting their talent management policies and practices to the aging of their workforces and 60 per cent of organizations don't account for workforce aging in their long-term business plans. Recent surveys also indicate that most HR leaders are spending less than 25 per cent of their time preparing for the workforce of the future and that few organizations believe that HR has the skills required to manage a diverse and global workforce. Not surprisingly, many organizations are already struggling to effectively manage next-generation talent.

The United Kingdom's Chartered Institute of Personnel and Development (CIPD) reports that most employers are having difficulties recruiting skilled staff even in a down economy and half of employers are having difficulty retaining employees. Along a similar vein, Hewitt engagement studies indicate that one out of two workers worldwide is currently disengaged, 28 per cent of workers are actively in the job market, and 40 per cent of workers would like to be employed somewhere else within one year. Most of these trends will only be magnified as the global economy turns around. This report reveals five trends that are reshaping the workforce and outlines the unavoidable implications that these workforce changes will have for the practice of talent management. It also highlights examples of organizations already using innovative talent management practices to leverage the next-generation workforce.

Five Workforce Trends You Can Count On

Global organizations are awakening to the alarming realization that significant demographic, economic, socio-political, and technological changes are dramatically altering the workforce. Changes in birthrates, retirement trends, and job requirements are reducing the size of the workforce and creating significant skills shortages, while eased trade barriers, communications advances, and the knowledge economy are producing a highly global and virtual workforce. At the same time, loosened cultural norms, higher minority birthrates, and relaxed migration barriers are creating a workforce that's vastly diverse. And the knowledge economy, information technologies, and a changed employment contract are giving rise to the most autonomous and empowered group of workers ever. These changes are dramatic, and they're a reality that many employers have not yet grasped. The workforce is in the midst of an unstoppable and radical transformation. It is becoming:

1. Smaller and Less Sufficiently Skilled
2. Increasingly Global
3. Highly Virtual
4. Vastly Diverse
5. Autonomous and Empowered

Understanding the intricacies of these five workforce trends is critical, as these changes characterize the next generation of talent from which organizations will draw for years to come.

Workforce Trend #1—A Smaller and Less Sufficiently Skilled Workforce

For organizations across the globe, an immense and potentially long-term struggle to fill job openings is about to begin. A host of phenomena are coming together to dramatically alter both the sheer number of workers available, as well as the number of workers that possess the most in-demand skills.

There will not be Enough Workers to Fill Jobs

In industrialized nations, smaller, middle-aged population segments and early retirements are substantially reducing the size of working-age populations. When this decline hits bottom, member nations of the Organization for Economic Cooperation and Development (OECD) will have experienced a combined reduction in their working-age populations of 65 million people. In the United States alone, there will be 10 million more jobs than workers by the year 2010.

A 16 per cent drop in the number of middle-aged workers—a product of a developed world population bust between 1965 and 1976—is driving the decline in workforce size. In the United States, in just the next six years, the 30 to 44 year old workforce will decline by 3 million. A more pronounced drop is expected in most other developed nations, which have more restrictive immigration policies. As the middle-aged workforce in developed nations is shrinking, mature-aged workers in these countries are fleeing the work world. Encouraged by favorable pension plans and growing affluence, large numbers of workers are choosing to retire at younger and younger ages.

Today, the average OECD worker retires three to five years before the official retirement age. Half of European men aged 55 to 64 have stopped working. And, by 2050, one in three Europeans will be retired. To alleviate the worker shortage, growing participation from groups underrepresented in domestic labor markets—mature workers, women, and the disabled—will be critical. Also significant will be physical and virtual migration of workers and jobs across the globe. In fact, the developing world's 30 to 50 year old population is booming. Worker migration is expected to create a highly competitive global labor market at least until the year 2016, when the generation born in developed nations between 1977 and 1994 has fully entered the workforce. Often referred to as.

Generation Y, this group will bring roughly the same number of workers to the workforce as the baby-boom generation did years earlier and will offer significant domestic relief for worker shortages in the developed world.

There will not be Enough Workers with the Required Skills

Together, a rise in alternative labor pools and the entrance of Generation Y into the workforce may generate enough bodies for developed nations to make up for a dearth of middle-aged and mature workers. However, these phenomena will likely not generate enough workers with the skills and experience that employers need. As the workforce becomes more youthful and consequently less skilled, the demand for skilled labor will rise.

With knowledge and technology as the new economic currency, the majority of new jobs being created in the developed world require high skill levels and substantial knowledge expertise. And the fast pace of change requires that skill and knowledge levels be continually upgraded. Surprisingly, as demand for workers with higher skill levels rises, growth in worker educational attainment is falling short. In the United States, there will be demand for more than 30 million new college-educated workers in the next 10 years while only 23 million new U.S. college graduates are expected. In the European Union, younger workers are achieving high levels of education, yet demand for educated workers is still not being met. As workers pursue less formal education, many organizations are cutting back on corporate training programs, which is further contributing to the skilled-worker shortage.

In the United States and the United Kingdom, organizations have significantly scaled back training expenditures. And in the United Kingdom, inadequate corporate training has been cited as one source of current skill shortages. While some training program cuts have been the result of a weak economy and may eventually be restored, many are evidence of a growing trend for employers to source skills from the external labor market rather than develop them internally. Management expert Peter Cappelli notes that external sourcing of skills forces a constant churn in the skilled worker job market, and organizational hiring practices cannot keep pace. These skill shortages will create an intense global competition for the most valuable talent. In the end, each company, industry, and profession will experience the skilled-worker shortage differently. An organization's historical growth pattern, age, industry downsizing history, and skill requirements will ultimately dictate its experiences.

Workforce Trend #2—An Increasingly Global Workforce

Traditional geographic boundaries surrounding the workforce are crumbling fast. In their place, a truly global job market, the likes of which has never been seen before, is being built.

Worker Mobility and Migration are Gaining Momentum

Free-market economic reforms and technological advancements are creating a global labor market. No longer are workers limited to marketing their skills solely within one country or region. They can now market themselves to organizations based anywhere in the world. In this global labor market, workers are increasingly being reallocated to their most efficient uses. Worker mobility and migration are on the rise, with workers far less likely to remain in one physical location throughout their careers. During the past 40 years, global migration of less-skilled and highly-skilled workers has doubled. Among developed nations, the United States is by far the biggest recipient of labor inflows. However, other nations are likely to increase their share of migrant labor, as the impact of domestic labor and talent shortages heightens. Statistics show that electronic immigrants—"workers who take jobs in other countries without actually changing residence, much less citizenship"—are also becoming increasingly commonplace. Going forward, even workers from industries and professions that have historically been isolated will join the global labor market.

Job Migration has Become a Business Requirement

As with workers, jobs are also increasingly being relocated to the places that best match company needs in terms of labor, skills, costs, and capacity. Low-cost communications technologies and rising education levels in developing nations are making it possible and advantageous to move jobs across the globe in search of lower operating costs. A recent Hewitt survey found that 45 per cent of participant companies are currently offshoring or considering offshoring in the next three years. Companies are offshoring jobs in IT, call center support, HR, finance, and accounting to countries in the Asia-Pacific region, which have large populations of college-educated workers and low labor and operational costs.

In the future, the number of jobs offshored, the types of jobs offshored, and the nations to which they are offshored will broaden. Surveys show that more U.S. employers plan to offshore jobs. In the next three years, the number of jobs moved offshore will nearly double, increasing from an average of 13 per cent to an average of 25 per cent. By the end of the decade, this number will grow 30 per cent to 40 per cent. The jobs being sent offshore will become increasingly sophisticated and will more frequently shift to nations in Eastern Europe and South East Asia.

While offshoring is mostly an American practice—three-fourths of offshored jobs originate in the United States—other nations are expected to join the revolution. As this practice continues, so too will concerns about its negative impact on the workforce. Offshoring has reportedly boosted worker stress and competition and diminished worker engagement. These concerns, however, aren't likely to stop the trend, as a failure to offshore is increasingly equated with significantly diminished competitive advantage.

Workforce Trend #3—Highly Virtual Workforce

The definition of co-worker and the meaning of being "at work" are being completely redefined as workers across the globe connect via the latest communications technologies.

A Virtual Workspace is Taking Hold

Across the world and across industries, workers are being "freed" from their desks and "relieved" of their traditional nine-to-five schedules. Growing use of wireless phones, high-speed broadband connections, and personal digital assistants (PDAs), combined with the rising proportion of work products that can be transmitted electronically, is completely redefining the concepts of workplace and workday. No longer is a fixed physical location a requirement for work. Instead, workers are spending large portions of their time working in their cars, at client sites, in hotel rooms, at home, and even on vacation. A recent survey of senior executives found evidence of "a significant upsurge in remote working". In the next two years alone, the number of employers with no employees working from home on a regular basis is predicted to drop from 46 per cent to 20 per cent. Workers can now be accessible to work anytime. Growing numbers of workers are on call, all the time. Multitasking like never before, they seamlessly switch from work to non-work and back. They may respond to e-mails while waiting at the dentist's office and log back into work after the kids are in bed. For some workers, this capability is bringing a new level of work/life synchronization and satisfaction. For others, it's fostering unhealthy work-aholic tendencies.

Virtual Co-working is on the Rise

Growing numbers of online news groups, discussion forums, and social networks are making many geographic, social, and even corporate barriers of the past obsolete. Increasingly, workers are part of a global talent supply chain, participating in virtual teams composed of the best employees from around the world. In this supply chain, workers across disparate nations, social strata, corporations, professions, and job classes tap a common infrastructure and set of protocols to regularly connect based on mutual interests. No longer are workers reliant on having a common physical location or a similar place in the corporate hierarchy to interact in real time. With ease, they can now connect and collaborate with others doing the same job at other companies. Regardless of their position, workers can communicate directly with anyone in their organizations, even the CEO. Together, virtual co-working and the virtual workspace are creating an "always on" workforce that sees no limits to jobs. Many workers are simply afraid to slow down, afraid to disconnect from work at all for fear of losing job security in an increasingly competitive, global labor market. Unfortunately, the consequences of an "always on" workforce can be dire— "lousy employees: tired, depressed, mistake prone, resentful, and eventually burned out.

Workforce Trend #4—A Vastly Diverse Workforce

Prepare to experience the most diverse workforce in history in terms of age, gender, ethnicity, and life pursuits, as changes in birthrates, migration patterns, and cultural norms take hold.

There Are More Generations in the Workforce than Ever Before

Workers are entering the workforce earlier and staying longer. More generations are now in the workforce than have been in recent times. In the United States, growing consumerism, coupled with rising price tags for education, is motivating increasing numbers of teenagers to enter the workforce. Today, 70 per cent of 21 year old Generation Y Americans are in the workforce, and a similar trend has been observed in Europe. At the same time that younger workers are entering the workforce earlier, older workers—motivated by longer life expectancies, changing cultural expectations, and the availability of knowledge and service work—are staying longer. In the United States, workers are staying on the job for an average of 15 years beyond age 55, and growing numbers of workers aged 50 to 70 are returning to the workforce to fulfill needs for activity and income. Going forward, 80 per cent of U.S. boomer workers expect to keep working past age 65. Outside the United States, older workers aren't yet employed to such an extent, but this tradition is expected to change in the workforce at one time, workers are finding themselves the brunt of stereotypes and discrimination. In the United States, between 1999 and 2002, age discrimination claims rose from 14,000 to 20,000. In the United Kingdom, age discrimination claims have risen to the region's top workplace discrimination claim.

The Workforce is More Gender Balanced

Significantly large numbers of women, motivated by loosened cultural norms and economic necessities, have entered the workforce. According to the International Labor Organization (ILO), women now represent 40 per cent of the global workforce. Today, 70 per cent of women in the developed world and 60 per cent in the developing world are engaged in paid employment. Growing female workforce participation holds for married and single women, for women with and without children, and for women with both older and younger children. In OECD nations, female labor force participation rates are only expected to rise. By 2015, women will make up 48 per cent of the U.S. workforce. A similar trend is predicted for most EU-15 member nations. While more women enter the workforce, growing numbers of men and women are entering occupations previously reserved for the opposite gender. Today, women participate in all industries, professions, and job levels, while men are broadening the types of industries, professions, and job levels in which they participate. Increasingly, men are taking on traditionally female roles, becoming librarians, secretaries, nannies, preschool teachers, nurses, paralegals, and typists. Unfortunately, many men in historically female roles report high levels of stress and discrimination, while 56 per cent of women believe they don't have equal job opportunities compared to men.

The Number of Ethnic Minority Workers is on the Rise

Migration levels and birthrates are boosting the proportion of ethnic minorities in the developed world. Since 1975, global migration has doubled. Since 1970, US migration has tripled. Today, one in 10 people living in the developed world is a migrant, and 175 million people are living in a country different from the one in which they were born. At the same time, ethnic minority birthrates are increasing while majority birthrates are declining. In the United States, non-Hispanic whites are declining to just 50 per cent of the total population, while Hispanics, Asian, Americans, and African Americans are ascending to 25 per cent, 8 per cent, and 15 per cent of the population, respectively. As a result, minorities are the fastest-growing segment of the U.S. labor force. Half of new workers in the United States in the past 10 years were Hispanics and by 2010 the Hispanic labor force will be larger than the African American labor force. By 2025, close to 40 per cent of U.S. workers will be Hispanic, African American, or Asian American.

Workers are Leading More Complex, Less Uniform Lives

The workforce is not only diverse in terms of demographic characteristics such as age and ethnicity, it's also more diverse in terms of lifestyles or life patterns. Fewer workers are partaking in the traditional progression through life stages—education, work and family, followed by leisure. Instead, they're mixing up the pattern in unique ways. They're juggling, repeating, and changing stages more frequently in a lifetime. Older workers are staying on the job into their retirement years. Workers of all ages are departing their jobs for leisurely sabbaticals at different points in their careers. Parents are temporarily leaving the workforce while raising young children. And seasoned workers are going back to school while staying on the job. Altogether, increased diversity is creating a workforce that defines stereotypes and generalizations. As workers interact and pursue varied life paths, less can be surmised from outward identifiers such as age or race. Traditional notions regarding the attributes of older workers, male workers, and European workers, for example, must be abandoned or used with caution.

Workforce Trend #5—An Autonomous and Empowered Workforce

Workers are taking the driver's seat in controlling the direction and substance of their professional lives. Technological and economic forces are giving them the capacity for greater authority on the job and in the job market.

Workers have the Capacity and the Desire to be More Influential on the Job

Trends toward knowledge work and technology-based communications are giving workers the expertise and skills to make more decisions about how they do their work. Knowledge workers have job or profession specific expertise that's not possessed by management, making them the logical decision-makers in many areas. Via the Internet and intranets, workers have access to competitive intelligence, business trend information, and experts, increasing their decision-making capabilities. While the knowledge economy is producing workers with the expertise to make more decisions on the job, trends toward self-agency and free agency are giving workers the skills and desire to make these decisions.

As organizations encourage workers to take more responsibility for their career development and employee benefits, they're creating a class of self-agents—workers who have the skills and desire to be self-sufficient on the job. At the same time, corporate layoffs have pushed many workers into free agency. When the economy turns around, many free agents will again be employed by corporations and will have newfound skills and a desire for self-management.

Workers have More Authority in the Job Market

Information technology, the knowledge economy, and a changed employer-employee contract are giving workers more authority in the job market. Today, most workers have access to unprecedented amounts of high-quality employment information. On the Internet, workers find information on specific job openings, compensation and benefit options, and career paths. They can even obtain inside information on potential employers from current and former employees who share their employment experiences online. At the same time that access to employment information has proliferated, worker skills for accessing and applying this information have also grown. The increasingly knowledge-intensive nature of jobs has given most workers the skills they need to be proficient—and in many cases expert—at finding, evaluating, and responding to employment information on the Web. As the Internet and information literacy reduce job search costs, a changed employer-employee contract is minimizing the costs of job switching. Ushered in by the downsizing trend of the 1980s, this new employment contract is giving employees the ability to switch employers with relative ease and minimal sacrifice. No longer are employees limited to one corporation or career path as their sole route to promotion and increased rewards. Instead of being seen as an indicator of a problem employee, searching the external job market has become a sign of business acumen. Experience with other employers is now an asset as opposed to a limitation. And health and retirement benefits are more portable than ever. With job searching and switching costs dramatically reduced, it's becoming the norm for workers to continuously "comparison shop" the electronic job market for better opportunities. Rather than being "brand loyal", workers are increasingly using newfound employment intelligence to bargain with employers and switch jobs when they find a better deal. Many workers plan to use their employment intelligence to seek better offers as the job market improves. One survey found that 83 per cent of workers are extremely or somewhat likely to look for a new job when the economy strengthens.

Five Workforce Trends You can Count on—Summarized

Taken together, these five trends—smaller and less sufficiently skilled, increasingly global, highly virtual, vastly diverse, and autonomous and empowered—are creating a workforce that's so radically different from what employers have known in recent times that it will require them to entirely rethink their approach to managing talent. The next section of this paper will present the top implications this next-generation workforce poses for the future of talent management, as well as real-life examples of organizations that are pioneers in this arena.

Top Implications for Talent Management

The future of business is impossible to foresee; too many uncertainties remain. Far less mysterious, however, is the future of the workforce. As outlined in the previous section, a number of forces have set in motion a radical transformation of the workforce, the effects of which will be greatly magnified in the years to come. As this next-generation workforce takes hold, it will render traditional talent management practices grossly insufficient, and often detrimental to the bottom line. Past practices, designed for an abundant, isolated, homogeneous, and employer-dependent workforce, will no longer sustain organizations.

The new workforce will be smaller and less sufficiently skilled. It will be increasingly global, highly virtual, and vastly diverse. Autonomous and empowered, it will demand a new generation of talent management, one that embraces:

1. Predictive Workforce Monitoring and Strategic Talent Decision Making,
2. Flexible and Anticipatory Talent Sourcing,
3. Customized and Personalized Rewards and Communications,
4. Distributed and Influential Leadership,
5. Unified and Compassionate Cultures.

Adopting these practices now is critical for future-focused organizations. Only by perfecting them will organizations get the most from the force with the biggest impact on the bottom line—the workforce.

Talent Management Implication #1—Predictive Workforce Monitoring and Strategic Talent

Decision Making

Say good-bye to after-the-fact HR measurement and reactive workforce management. The scarce, global, and empowered workforce of the next generation will require that organizations embrace predictive workforce monitoring and strategic talent decision-making. Together, these practices will form the foundation of next generation talent management and ensure that organizations will have enough workers with the right skills, motivated to deliver desired results.

Embrace Predictive Workforce Monitoring

In the next generation of talent management, organizations will practice predictive workforce monitoring to anticipate future talent needs. Organizations will regularly gather information on workforce demographics, as well as worker attitudes, behaviors, and skills. They'll rely on both quantitative and qualitative information and will tap a range of information sources—including internal databases, email, the Internet, internal and external Web logs, newspapers, and internal business intelligence systems. Organizations will track broad workforce trends, as well as details on specific workforce segments. For example, energy provider PacifiCorp specifically tracks high-potential employees with leadership and technical talent. At its best, workforce monitoring will involve everyone in an organization and will be led by an individual or department whose sole charge is monitoring the workforce. Intel Corporation, the world's largest chipmaker, for example, uses a program called "Organization Capability Assessment", which allows the staffing department to work with the business twice a year to assess different workforce needs—immediate and up to two years out. Only by practicing workforce monitoring continuously and in real time will organizations have sufficient lead time for acting on the opportunities and challenges monitoring detects. For example, only with workforce monitoring was PacifiCorp able to see that 80 per cent of its workforce would be eligible to retire in the next 15 years and have time to implement a graduate recruitment and onboarding process to attract and retain young talent. At PacifiCorp, new graduate hires now spend their first nine months on the job learning the energy business and how to operate in a more seasoned work environment. During this time, PacifiCorp emphasizes to graduates that the company can be more than one stop in their careers; it can offer them multiple jobs throughout a career. To accomplish continuous, real-time monitoring, organizations will employ a variety of information technologies. They'll use tacit data collection software to gather workforce data behind the scenes as it's being input. They'll integrate workforce information platforms, combining external and internal workforce information in one, central repository. And, they'll take their human resource information systems beyond administration and self-service to become enterprise-wide workforce intelligence portals that have easy-to-navigate interfaces, advanced data analysis capabilities, and personalized reporting. Many organizations will turn to HR Outsourcing (HRO) to access real-time workforce information collection and reporting technologies. To reap the greatest benefit from HRO's data collection and reporting capabilities, organizations will outsource all workforce services to a single provider. For example, one of the top reasons Sony Electronics, Inc., a U.S.-based consumer electronics and entertainment company, choose total HR outsourcing—outsourcing of payroll, benefits, and workforce management services to one provider—was to improve the quality, timeliness, and access to its HR data. With total HR outsourcing, Sony has gained access to the hard data it needs to identify trends and make better workforce decisions. Organizations, like Sony, that choose HRO will not only gain real-time access to their own workforce data but will also obtain access to aggregate data on the workforces of their outsourcing provider's entire client pool. This aggregate data on benefits, HR costs and structure, employee engagement, employee demographics, and compensation practices will be an invaluable workforce monitoring tool.

Promote Strategic-Talent Decision Making

To take action on the issues and opportunities that real-time workforce monitoring provides, organizations will use a variety of strategic decision making techniques. They'll identify a relatively small number of critical talent measures and tie them directly to business performance outcomes. Moving beyond centrally appointed HR prevalence and cost metrics, organizations will measure key talent inputs and outcomes that have been identified by the talent decision-makers who rely on them. Talent decision-makers will establish measures of "at-risk talent"—employees who have a higher might consider how much the early retirement of a certain executive would cost department sales per year. Measures of "at-risk talent" enabled business consulting company Deloitte Consulting to determine that it needed to retain 40 per cent of its partners becoming eligible for retirement. Talent decision-makers will also use measures of "pivotal talent"—groups of employees with the greatest potential for improving business results. Decision-makers might look at how a change in a certain employee group's behavior would boost productivity per quarter. Pivotal talent measures allowed office furniture manufacturer Steel case Inc. to determine that it needed to retain or do succession planning for a top executive with significant expertise and a deep relationship base. To ensure that the information gleaned from business-outcome-linked talent measures and real-time workforce monitoring is turned into accurate talent forecasts and effective workforce plans, organizations will train talent decision-makers in hypothesizing, predictive modeling, and scenario planning. With seek the meaning behind and implications of workforce measures to ultimately identify workforce opportunities and challenges. Predictive modeling will help talent decisionmakers.

Scientifically identify which specific changes will generate desired business outcomes. Using computer models, talent decision-makers will simulate how even minute talent changes could significantly impact business outcomes. Finally, scenario planning will guide talent decision-makers in brainstorming a range of possible workforce and business futures, in assessing the likelihood of each happening, and in outlining how the organization can prepare for each.

At companies that master predictive workforce monitoring and strategic talent decision-making, workforce inputs will closely match talent requirements on a continuous basis. Those companies that become early masters of these techniques will be at a significant competitive advantage and reap benefits for years to come.

Talent Management Implication #2—Flexible and Anticipatory Talent Sourcing

The rigid and reactive staffing practices of the past will be grossly insufficient for tackling the staffing challenges posed by a smaller, more global, diverse, and empowered workforce. Going forward, organizations will need to abandon these practices for more flexible, anticipatory talent sourcing strategies.

Take a Flexible Approach to Talent Sourcing

To meet talent needs, organizations will leverage a broader spectrum of workers and employment relationships. From the external labor market, they'll recruit older workers, retired workers, and former employees. Home improvement giant The Home Depot, Inc., for example, is focusing its recruiting efforts on older workers, partnering with the older adult advocacy group the American Association of Retired Persons (AARP). The AARP makes referrals and trains members to work at The Home Depot. Today, 15 per cent of Home Depot's workforce is over-age 50-67. Retail Pharmacy CVS has a similar program. General Electric (GE) taps the long-standing experience and knowledge of veteran managers to help integrate newly acquired businesses. And global biotechnology firm Monsanto Company has a "Resource Re-entry Center" that allows full-time employees who have exited the organization in good standing to reapply after six months for part-time positions. Applicants are eligible for company savings and investment plans, as well as spot bonuses. Also from the external labor market, organizations will seek workers with disabilities, as well as the long-term unemployed. Computer hardware manufacturer International Business Machines (IBM) Corporation, for instance, is effectively leveraging the skills of disabled workers. IBM reports that "disabled workers contribute millions to the bottom line. Forty-two per cent of the company's disabled workers have key skill jobs such as software engineering, marketing, and IT architecture." Managers at IBM receive special training on recruiting disabled employees. In addition, organizations will court workers from many geographic locations and will tap the vast pool of women who either have yet to enter the global workforce or who want to re-enter the workforce after their childbearing years. Whirlpool Corporation, the top U.S. home appliance-maker, targets women in recruiting and promotion. It works to maintain a work environment that supports women's career development, conducting studies to reveal barriers female employees may face to career advancement. Computer hardware company Hewlett-Packard (HP) attracts an impressive number of female recruits by highlighting its impressive track record of women hires. Today, about 40 per cent of HP's top-level managers are women.

As they recruit from a broader spectrum of workers in the external labor market, companies will also recruit a wider talent pool from within the organization. They'll establish internal labor markets through which permanent employees continuously sell their services for short- and long-term engagements. With these internal, project-based employment systems, workers from anywhere in the organization will match their skills, interests, and capacity to open projects.

To support internal labor markets, organizations will establish talent match databases. They will regularly update these databases with worker skills and interests and continually cull them for talent matches. British Petroleum (BP) has a talent matching system where employees can post their résumés and receive weekly notification of jobs and projects that suit their abilities. Management consultants William Bridges and Susan Mitchell Bridges write that talent databases will be "a new organizational circulatory system that guarantees that when someone's work finishes here, it can resume somewhere else in (or around) the company without undue stress or delay". Some organizations will even employ inside move representatives to help employees market themselves in the internal employment landscape. As they leverage a broader spectrum of workers from the internal and external labor markets, organizations will also rely on different types of employment relationships. Nonstandard employment relationships, such as part-time work, flextime, temporary work, telecommuting, job sharing, nontraditional shifts, seasonal employment, on-call work, and ageless internships, will become the norm. JetBlue Airways Corporation, a leading low-fare airline, has had success with nonstandard employment relationships, offering remote work opportunities for call center representatives, many of whom are at-home moms working part-time.

With this strategy, JetBlue has eliminated call center expenses and boosted productivity and retention from a traditionally high-turnover position.

One non-standard employment model that organizations will rely upon heavily is free agency—a broad term describing a variety of contract and temporary employment arrangements. With free agency, organizations will tap the best talent on an as-needed basis. Organizations will connect open projects and available free-agent workers via temporary agencies, professional organizations, and even online networks such as Elance, Inc.,

Another non-standard employment model that organizations will rely on heavily is phased retirement—reduced-hour and flexible-schedule employment options for workers nearing or at retirement age. With phased retirement, organizations will retain mature workers and their irreplaceable knowledge. One organization that has used phased retirement to successfully preserve the skills and corporate memory of its retiring workforce is The Aerospace Corporation, which specializes in space-related research and development. Under its Retiree Casual program, Aerospace employees can retire at age 55 with full benefits and continue working on a project basis for up to 1,000 hours per year. Eighty per cent of retirees sign up for this program. Most work two days per week, but some work six months on, six months off. A majority work into their mid-60s, some into their 80s.

At radiotherapy system provider Varian, employees can initiate reduced schedules when they are three years away from retiring. Most working reduced-hour schedules work four days a week for a year and then drop to two days a week for the two years prior to retirement. Some work only half-time and some job share. Workers retain full medical and dental benefits throughout the reduced-hour years. Additionally, workers have the option to return to full-time status if reduced hours prove to be a financial strain.

Adopt Anticipatory Sourcing Strategies

In addition to using more flexible staffing models to secure next-generation talent, organizations will also adopt anticipatory sourcing strategies. They'll prepare workers in advance for potential roles and offer learning opportunities for people on a purposeful and continuous basis, thereby creating competency pools and talent reserves for later use. They'll help employees prepare long-term development plans and match these plans with existing work opportunities. They'll even create new job opportunities for employees whose development plans require them. In fact, Hewitt Associates has found that using such talent supply chains is a common practice at companies that consistently achieve double-digit growth in profits. These companies have highly integrated processes that yield a steady stream of talent. They stockpile talent and hire for current capability, as well as future potential. To reduce the time it takes to fill job openings with qualified candidates, organizations will pursue high-impact sourcing channels. Some organizations will use extensive and strategic candidate testing to identify the best talent. In preparation for its future needs, Hilton Hotels Corporation is working to "clone" its best employees. The company has used written tests to profile the behaviors and aptitudes of top performers. It has constructed a profile of the model employee that it evaluates new hire prospects against. Organizations will also develop stronger and more targeted relationships with recruiters and professional organizations. Telecommunications provider BellSouth Corporation relies heavily on relationships with community colleges, military installations, and community relations representatives to find the highest quality job candidates. In addition, organizations will partner with university professors to identify the best graduates and will keep in touch with organization alumni. Internet search firm Google Inc. maintains relationships with hundreds of university professors to stay abreast of future talent. Nationwide Insurance uses an exclusive in-house headhunter whose job is to apply in-depth knowledge of Nationwide's business to source external talent at the executive level. As a result of implementing this strategic model, costs have been significantly reduced and candidates are a better cultural fit. Some organizations will even hire workers they anticipate needing, even if there are no current openings. Some will use headhunters to keep tabs on external, as well as internal talent. Diversified Brazilian company Semco runs ads even when there are no job openings. The ads ask potential employees to present what they could do for the company. If Semco is impressed, they create a position for the worker.

Talent Management Implication #3—Customized and Personalized Rewards and Communications

Traditional, one-size-fits-all rewards and communications programs just won't cut it in the next generation of talent management. A workforce that's in short supply, empowered to switch jobs, and demographically and lifestyle diverse will require, and in many cases demand, that organizations take more than one approach to rewarding and communicating. It will require that rewards and communications not only be customized with high-tech tools, but also personalized in high-touch ways.

Use a High-Tech Approach to Customize Rewards and Communications

In the next generation of talent management, organizations will use consumer-marketing technologies to customize total rewards packages. Through personalized Web portals, organizations will offer rewards menus and associated dollar credits that are tailored to groups of workers and even individual workers.

Compass Group: Grooming Talent

Compass Group PLC, the world's largest food service company, has introduced a number of talent management initiatives to develop its talent pool in ways that ensure individual aspirations match organizational expectations. Compass identifies top performers who are both ready to assume more responsibility and aspire to advance. It assesses high performers for promotability, time frame, and leadership potential. It offers needed coaching and development opportunities and monitors progress. Career and performance information is presented at talent review meetings, where decisions are made on promotion readiness and leadership potential.

Compass also uses surveys to better understand and meet employee aspirations and capabilities. A career survey collects information related to education, experience, geographic preference, and career aspirations. Another survey measures job related qualities such as thinking and reasoning style, behavioral traits, and occupational interests.

The results are entered into a software program that generates individual qualification profiles for the employees, which are discussed at talent review meetings. Being in the service industry, Compass Group believes that people are at the heart of its business. The company's talent management initiatives are geared toward attracting the best people and realizing their full potential.

Dollar amounts will be tied to role and performance as opposed to age or seniority. Options offered will go beyond the traditional flexible benefits fare to include choice in work assignments and location, time and money for training, and working-time flexibility. With customized rewards menus, organizations will attract, motivate, and retain a broader spectrum of workers without increasing total rewards budgets. For example, pharmaceutical company AstraZeneca PLC offers workers customized rewards menus, giving employees their total cost of remuneration and allowing them to design the specifics of their rewards packages. Going even further, Semco offers a flexible rewards program through which employees determine their own compensation level. Semco keeps compensation amounts in check by providing detailed financial information upon which employees are encouraged to base their salaries. Semco also makes salaries public. As with rewards, employee communications will also be customized in the next generation of talent management. With the aid of technology, organizations will gather worker information and use it to create communications that resonate with specific group or individual needs. A wide range of worker communications will be customized, from messages about benefit offerings to messages about personal development and career progression. Rather than sending a generic mailing to all employees regarding the company's 401(k) plan, organizations will use employee segmentation technologies to target communications at groups of employees based on different factors, such as interest in saving or years until retirement. U.K. food retailer Tesco PLC, e.g. segments employees according to their personal and professional goals to better communicate and motivate its employees. In the end, customized rewards and communications will make individual employees feel valued by even large, distributed organizations and will elicit desired behaviors from a highly varied workforce. Increasingly, organizations will turn to sophisticated HR technologies to easily and cost-effectively manage customization. In addition, strategic and systematic outsourcing of noncore HR functions will give many organizations access to the latest customization technologies, while freeing HR's time to develop customized rewards menus and communications content.

Use a High-Touch Approach to Personalize Rewards and Communications

Organizations will use a number of high-touch approaches, including the manager-employee relationship and the organization culture, to personalize rewards and communications. Next-generation managers will develop personalized employment agreements with workers, outlining project details, deadlines, and personal development plans. Semco managers routinely ask employees to evaluate their job satisfaction and to consider changing positions to find the right fit. Another key role for next-generation managers will be developing more personalized incentives. For instance, Houston's Central Bank uses an assessment tool to determine what motivates individual employees.

In addition to leveraging the manager-employee relationship, organizations will also tap the power of organization culture to personalize rewards and communications. They'll create cultures that convey they care about employees' most basic and personal work needs. Humanity, respect, and dignity will be integral to these environments where basic worker rights will include opportunities to participate in productive, meaningful work, share ideas and receive acknowledgement, and be treated like an adult. Ultimately, employers will balance the benefits of customization and personalization with its costs. They'll invest only in the areas that make a difference to their employees and their business. Regularly, they'll assess the value of individual employees to the business, measure individual results, and make adjustments to customization and personalization strategies.

Talent Management Implication #4—Distributed and Influential Leadership

Out of the next-generation workforce, a radically transformed leadership model is emerging. To get the most from a workforce that's short on experienced talent, globally dispersed, virtually connected, and prepared to be authoritative on the job, organizations will distribute leadership responsibilities throughout the organization and transition traditional leaders from commanding to influencing.

Distribute Leadership Responsibilities throughout the Organization

The days of leadership's being defined as an individual quality or a job requirement are numbered. As we move into the next-generation of talent management, leadership will increasingly be viewed as an action that any worker or group of workers can take to meet the needs of specific business situations. Decision-making will grow highly decentralized. Deciding what to do and how to do it will be the responsibility of the every worker, as opposed to the sole privilege of executives and managers. Workers will make the decisions that are best made by them given their expertise and closeness to the issues at hand.

Decentralized decision-making is at the very core of how The AES Corporation, one of the world's largest electric companies, operates. In fact, one of the biggest decisions in AES history, to buy a power station, was not made by the CEO or the board, but by an employee who had been with AES for less than two years.

The person received advice, but the final decision was his. Whole Foods Market, Inc., the world's largest retailer of natural and organic pools has decentralized decision-making at its core, with a philosophy that "decisions should be made closest to the place they'll be carried out, should directly involve the people affected, and should leave out people who aren't involved."

At many organizations, decentralized decision-making will give way to much less hierarchical organizational structures such as those seen at W.L. Gore & Associates, Inc., and the Massachusetts Institute of Technology (MIT). At W.L. Gore, the manufacturer of Gore-Tex, there are no titles besides that of president and secretary of the company—two titles required by law. To manage at W.L. Gore, employees must find other employees willing to work with them. At MIT, senior faculty members are not bosses, but instead play a significant role in mentoring and promoting new faculty members. This loose management structure allows scholars to create and produce high-quality research and teaching. Some organizations will go beyond decentralization to incorporate elements of democracy into their decision-making practices. Democratic decision-making will aid organizations in unifying diverse workforces behind common goals. Organizations will employ a variety of democratic decision-making tactics, including informal worker polls and formal Web polling of stakeholders. They'll also have workers vote on job candidates, the hiring and firing of managers, and overall organizational strategy issues. Whole Foods and Semco have both incorporated elements of democracy into their decision-making processes. At Whole Foods, all new-hire candidates work a 30-day trial in one of the store's departments.

Then the entire department, whose bonuses depend on group performance, votes on whether to employ the candidate. At Semco, each department has a representative on the board of trustees. Two of the 117 trustees are on the board of directors and are given time at each board meeting to discuss issues of importance to their employee constituents. In addition, at each board meeting, two of Semco's nine board seats are available for any employee who signs up.

Together, decentralized and democratic decision-making will create more fluid and flat organizational structures, as well as more flexible and broad job descriptions. Ultimately, these forms of distributed leadership will allow organizations to subvert the most negative impacts of the experienced worker shortage, while more fully tapping their most valuable asset—the knowledge and experience of their people.

Transition Traditional Leaders from Commanding to Influencing

With the advent of distributed leadership, the roles of traditional leaders will dramatically shift. Executives and managers will stop commanding and start influencing. They'll promote a common organizational mission, using their passion for the business to excite employees. And they'll work to ensure that employees understand how they can contribute to the organizational mission.

Next-generation executives and managers will promote a few suggested protocols for how work gets done in the organization. They might put forth stringent hiring standards aimed at hiring only those capable of working in a decentralized organization. Or they might promote the regular practice of giving advice and seeking guidance. At AES, the main responsibility of leaders and managers is to champion the organization's core principles and processes, to maintain the organizational structure, and to serve as advisors. AES leaders, e.g. have established restrictive hiring standards, requiring job candidates to pass through a number of interviews and gain co-worker approval. At SAS, CEO John Goodnight is seen as a silent leader. Employees have much freedom to work without direct leadership oversight. Goodnight's philosophies strongly shape the practices within the company, and many consult him regarding decisions. SAS also has very selective hiring standards. Employees are noted for saying that the company hires hard and manages easy.

Another key role for next-generation executives and managers will be to ensure that information systems and knowledge-sharing incentives are in place. With these systems, they'll make available to the entire organization information that was once reserved for executives. They'll offer incentives for workers to act as knowledge stewards (subject experts) and brokers (knowledge stewards who connect with knowledge users). Information-sharing incentives will include public recognition and financial rewards. Ultimately, knowledge-sharing systems and incentives will ensure that all workers have the resources to make decisions and act as leaders. At AES, financial and strategic information is shared freely throughout the organization and employees are encouraged to share their perspectives. At Google, employees are asked to participate in weekly "Thank Goodness It's Friday" (TGIF) meetings where co-founders inform them about everything from finances to marketing to product development. Google employees also make use of Web logs to document work activities, discuss issues, and share information. Lockheed Martin Corporation, the world's leading defense contractor, has an information-sharing system that scans employee emails and matches employees who are doing similar work. Employees can search the system for co-workers with whom they can collaborate. Another crucial role for executives and managers will be to transform workers who are comfortable with traditional command-and-control leadership to be decision-makers and leaders themselves. Executives and managers will coach workers in information gathering, peer communication, and peer negotiation. They'll model how to cultivate stewardship, finding co-workers to partner with and setting an example of how to lobby for one's beliefs. Ricardo Semler, President of Brazil's Semco Corporation, e.g. does not typically make major decisions. Instead, he lobbies for what he believes in and contributes his viewpoints during discussions. Altogether, distributing leadership responsibilities throughout the organization will engage a workforce that's prepared for, and in many cases accustomed to, being authoritative on the job, while at the same time tackling the shortage of experienced talent. As more workers assume leadership roles, what has been described as a severe leadership crisis could be transformed into an unprecedented leadership boon.

Talent Management Implication #5—Unified and Compassionate Cultures

As the next-generation workforce emerges, threats to employee engagement are mounting. A workforce that's scarce in number and skills, globally and virtually dispersed, demographically and lifestyle diverse, and empowered in the job market is one for which the opportunity for organizational conflict and job-related stress is high. Organizations that want to motivate and retain next-generation workers will need to build unifying and compassionate cultures to combat the disengaging impacts that new sources of organizational conflict and job-related stress would otherwise have.

Build a Unifying Organizational Culture

Organizations will minimize self-interest, worker difference, and distance; build an organizational fabric; and work to make participation in these cultures more salient than membership in any demographic, geographic, or departmental subgroup. At telecommunications provider Cincinnati Bell Inc. diversity isn't emphasized because it calls attention to worker differences as opposed to worker similarities. Cincinnati Bell does not use employee affinity groups, because they highlight divisions between employees and take away from the company's culture of inclusion. Organizations will also promote collectivist values and reward collaborative contributions. They'll highlight the goals, standards, and destinies that all workers share and emphasize the commonalities among workers, such as the need to make a living and the desire to participate in fulfilling work. Many organizations will cultivate an "us" *versus* "them" mentality, rallying workers against the competition or behind a common cause. And most will rely heavily on rituals and celebrations to reinforce organizational belonging over individual difference. In addition, organizations will build cultures free of any kind of discrimination, including that based on gender, sexual orientation, age, employment type, and job location. They'll train workers on a broader definition of discrimination and will emphasize that discrimination doesn't just include big acts with obviously high costs, but also encompasses many small, everyday occurrences whose subtle costs add up.

Many organizations will set hard targets for hiring, rewarding, and advancing all kinds of employees. They'll tie manager and leader evaluations to the achievement of a broad range of diversity targets. They'll frequently review policies and workforce composition for signs of covert discrimination and regularly survey workers regarding their perspectives on discrimination at the organization. At carmaker Volkswagen AG, workers are encouraged to submit ideas for eliminating age barriers. Seasoned managers are asked to train newer managers on ways to meet older workers' needs. Energy Company Shell Oil Company holds managers accountable for developing diverse pipelines of future talent, tying compensation to hiring, development, and promotion of minorities.

Going even further, health care provider Baptist Health Systems, Inc., requires actions that could negatively impact employees with 15 or more years of tenure be approved by the president, the head of HR, and the vice-president of the employee's department. In addition, Baptist Health employs two inside move representatives to assist older employees in making internal job moves. Today, 24 per cent of Baptist Health workers are over-age 50. Many organizations will move beyond formal discrimination programs toward more grassroots efforts to eliminate discrimination. Some will utilize self-appointed discrimination stewards to educate and correct peers. Others will have peers review one another on how well each supports efforts to eliminate discrimination, tying worker compensation to the results.

Create Cultures that Minimize Stress from Work/Life Conflict and Job Insecurities

Global competition for jobs, workers' growing responsibility for their own careers, and expanding life choices are creating a workforce that is highly stressed. Organizations will take steps to minimize this stress by putting workers incharge of arranging workdays and workweeks according to both work and personal demands. Ricardo Semler, CEO of Semco, calls this practice "reinventing the workweek". He notes that workers will still meet their job commitments in the reinvented workweek. People want to work when work is not the enemy of personal freedom and legitimate self-interest. In the reinvented workweek, organizations will offer more workers a choice of where to work—from home, at the office, or even at a coffee shop. Health insurer Cigna Insurance has an e-work program set up to allow employees to "work wherever work occurs".

The program has cut employee turnover in half and boosted productivity.

Organizations will also reward based on results achieved, not hours worked, and will ensure that career progression isn't contingent upon putting work before one's personal life. At Ernst & Young LLP, an accounting, consulting, tax, and legal services firm, employees create flexible schedules to accommodate personal and professional needs. Some work full-time for part of the year and part-time for another part of the year. Numbers show that employees using flexible scheduling are not hurt in terms of promotions and rewards. Ernst & Young has a philosophy that workers will be more productive and will produce higher quality work if they're not distracted by work/life balance concerns.

In addition to reinventing the workweek, organizations will also become experts at minimizing job insecurities within their workforces. They'll present an accurate picture of employees' job security at all times. Managers will be responsible for having ongoing dialogues with workers regarding individual employment situations. Workers whose jobs are not secure will be informed. Workers whose jobs are secure will know it and be spared needless preparation for job change. In making decisions regarding job elimination, outsourcing, and offshoring, organizations will make it policy to obtain perspectives of potentially affected workers and managers. Organizations will also make it policy to announce job changes well in advance of the actual events taking place. Workers will know they'll be given adequate preparation time should they ever lose their job. For workers whose jobs aren't secure, organizations will offer opportunities to build job market security. They'll help workers maintain up-to-date skills and external marketability with continuous, personalized development support and projects divided into distinct parts that individuals can manage and add to their résumés. The most progressive organizations will make these employability-enhancement opportunities a regular part of their employee-value propositions, giving all workers, not just those whose employment is insecure, the peace of mind that comes from maintaining job market value.

IBM, for instance, has adopted new Global Redeployment Principles to help those whose jobs are being outsourced find jobs within the company. The emphasis of this program is on re-development and reskilling. IBM is creating software to help match the skills of these employees with job openings and is requiring managers to hire internally if a qualified candidate is available. IBM has also created the $25 million Human Capital Alliance Fund to counsel and train employees whose jobs may be outsourced. In the end, efforts to counter next-generation threats to employee engagement by building a unifying and compassionate culture will stave off what could be a huge drain on corporate bottom lines—disengaged workers, often star performers, withholding talent due to mounting dissatisfaction.

Tips and Take-Aways: Closing Thoughts on Ushering in Next-Generation Talent Management

Our research clearly indicates that over the next decade a significant corporate change will be in progress. Organizations will confront challenges relating to demographic trends, global mobility, diversity, a virtual workforce, work/life issues, and technology changes. In this new era, competition will be global, ideas will be developed swiftly, and talented people will be keen to change jobs frequently. In this environment, a prime resource that will become increasingly scarce is people. Questions organizations must ask themselves include these: Are we prepared for the new global workforce revolution? What can we do to be winners in this race toward managing next-generation talent? Truth be told, our research on leading organizations revealed no single company that has planned a holistic approach to address all of the coming workforce changes. It showed that while many organizations are aware of the unstoppable workforce trends identified in this report, they fall short in terms of preparing for the talent management implications these trends present. In fact, many organizations fail to comprehend the intensity of these workforce changes. Some are complacent, assuming the workforce changes will have little or no impact on them. Some have dismissed these workforce trends as "hype" or exaggeration. Only a select few have begun planning "combat" strategies. But even they are still predominantly focused on addressing one or two workforce trends. A pioneer of next-generation talent management, Semco is embracing innovative talent practices more than most organizations. Semco does not define its business or industry. It does not have a stable organizational structure, nor does it have business plans. Semco purposely does not define these operational aspects, leaving them open for employees to shape as they pursue their own ideas, interests, and instincts. At Semco, major decisions are made democratically and information is shared freely. Managers focus on employee outcomes, learning what motivates individual employees, and making sure specific employee needs are met. Workers determine their own schedules, working when it fits and working, wherever they choose. The ultimate goal at Semco is to give workers a satisfying and challenging work experience. Semco's philosophy is that profits will come if workers' needs are put first. A model of next generation talent management, Semco's productivity, growth, and profits have all benefited significantly from its approach. Yet even with models such as Semco, for many organizations there exists a wide gap between ambitions and accomplishments. This gap can be fatal for organizations looking to attract, retain, and motivate the best-in-class talent in this dynamic and competitive environment.

Organizations that are ignoring or procrastinating on these issues will almost certainly—at first slowly and then with exponential speed—face a severe talent crisis. Today's organizations need to heed the warnings. They need to build upon the few bright sparks of action relayed throughout this report and begin to proactively usher in the next generation of talent management.

REFERENCES

"A Different Track," *Chief Executive,* May 2004.

Armour, Stephanie. "Higher Pay May Be Layoff Target," *USA Today*, June 22, 2003.

Armour, Stephanie. "More Men Train to Be Nurses, Midwives, Secretaries," *USA Today*, July 10, 2003.

August 2004 interview with David Binkley, SVP Global HR, Whirlpool Corporation.

Balu, Rekha. "The New Face of Leadership," *Fast Company*, May 2001.

Bankert, Ellen, Mary Dean Lee, and Candice Lange. SAS Institute, The Wharton Work/Life Roundtable, Wharton Work/Life Integration Project, University of Pennsylvania, 2000.

Bonabeau, Eric, and Valdis Krebs. "Model Behavior," *Optimize*, October 2002.

Bonabeau, Eric, and Valdis Krebs. "Model Behavior," *Optimize*, October 2002.

Bridges, William, and Susan Mitchell Bridges. "Transforming Your HR Department into a Start-Up Professional Services Firm," in *Human Resources in the 21st Century*, eds. Marc Effron, Robert Gandossy, and Marshall Goldsmith, John Wiley & Sons, Inc., 2003.

"Britain: Skills Filled", *The Economist*, February 7, 2004.

Brown, Jeff, and Lindy Williams. "People: HR's Bottom-Line Asset," in *Human Resources in the 21st Century*, eds. Marc Effron, Robert Gandossy, and Marshall Goldsmith, John Wiley & Sons, Inc., 2003.

Budman, Matthew. "Will We All Be Unemployed?" *Across the Board*, January 1, 2004.

Bulkeley, William M. "IBM Now Plans Fewer Layoffs From Outsourcing," *The Wall Street Journal*, July 29, 2004.

Cappelli, Peter. "What Labor Shortage?" Knowledge@Wharton, August 27, 2003.

Census Releases Immigrant Numbers for Year 2000, Center for Immigration Studies, June 4, 2002.

Chatman, Jennifer A. Jeffrey T. Polzer, Sigal G. Barsade, and Margaret A. Neale. "Being Different Yet Feeling Similar," *Administrative Science Quarterly*, December 1998.

Davidson, Paul. "Tacit Finds Matches in Company Email," *USA Today*, June 14, 2004.

"Different Views Drive Results," *Hewitt Magazine*, Vol. 7, Issue 2, 2004.

Dolliver, Mark. "Just Think How Cheery They'd Be If They Weren't Discriminated Against," *Adweek*, December 1, 2003.

Dychtwald, Ken, Tamara Erickson, and Bob Morison. "It's Time to Retire Retirement," *Harvard Business Review*, March 1, 2004.

Dychtwald, Maddy. *Cycles*, The Free Press, 2003.

"Employer Perspectives on Global Sourcing", Hewitt Associates, 2004, and also see Gandossy, Robert and Tina Kao, "Overseas Connections", *Across the Board*, November/December 2004.

Fishman, Charles. "The Anarchist's Cookbook," *Fast Company*, July 2004.

Fullerton. Howard N., and Mitra Toossi. "Labor Force Projections to 2010," *Monthly Labor Review*, November 2001.

Gandossy, Robert, and Tina Kao. *Channels to Anywhere*, Hewitt Associates, 2004.

"Global Survey Predicts Upsurge in Telework", ITAC (International Telework Association & Council) *Telework News*, Issue 3.3, Summer 2003.

Gratton, Lynda. "Free to Choose," in *Human Resources in the 21st Century*, eds. Marc Effron, Robert Gandossy, and Marshall Goldsmith, John Wiley & Sons, Inc., 2003.

"Grow Faster Together, or Grow Slowly Apart", The Aspen Institute, 1998; and Training & Development 2003, Chartered Institute of Personnel and Development, April 2003.

Grow, Brian. "Hispanic Nation," *BusinessWeek* Online, March 15, 2004.

Heet, Justin A. *Beyond Workforce 2020: The Coming (and Present) International Market for Labor*, Hudson Institute, 2004.

Hewitt's Human Capital Foresight TM service uses predictive analytics to turn a company's massive amount of HR data into actionable insights on "How Key Characteristics of Human Capital Impact the Bottom Line".

Hymowitz, Carol. "In the Lead: Baby Boomers Seek New Ways to Escape Career Claustrophobia," *The Wall Street Journal*, June 24, 2004.

"Innovation: Remote Working in the Net-Centric Company", The Economist Intelligence Unit Executive Briefing, July 15, 2003.

Johnson, Lauren Keller. "Four Practices for Great Performance," Harvard Working Knowledge, August 23, 2004.

July 2004 interview with Dorenda Kettman, Human Resources Director, Global Staffing, Intel Corporation.

June 2004 interview with Elaine Dixon, Director, Organizational Development and Training, and Erich Wilson, Director, Compensation, Pacific Corp.

June 2004 interview with Robert Puccio, Vice President, Associate Services and Patti Cotter, Vice President, Human Resources, Nationwide Insurance.

Kaihla, Paul. "The Coming Job Boom," *Business 2.0*, September 2003.

Karoly, Lynn A., and Constantijn W.A. Panis. *The 21st Century at Work*, Rand Corporation, 2004, and Thomas J. Donohue, "Falling Behind", Training, October 2003.

Karoly, Lynn A., and Constantijn W.A. Panis. *The 21st Century at Work*, Rand Corporation, 2004.

Leibfritz, Willi. "Retiring Later Makes Sense," *OECD Observer*, January 13, 2003.

Lockwood, Nancy R. "The Aging Workforce," *HR Magazine*, December 2003.

Loughlin, Catherine, and Julian Barling. "Young Workers' Work Values, Attitudes, and Behaviours", *Journal of Occupational and Organizational Psychology*, November 2001.

Malone, Thomas W. *The Future of Work*, Harvard Business School Press, 2004.

Map of the Decade 2003, Institute for the Future, 2003.

Martin, Susan F. "Heavy Traffic", *The Brookings Review*, Fall 2001.

"Meeting the Challenges of Tomorrow's Workforce," Supplement to *Chief Executive*, August/September 2002.

Mullich, Joe. "Hiring Without Limits," *Workforce Management*, August 2002.

Mullich, Joe. "They Don't Retire Them, They Hire Them," *Workforce Management*, December 2003.

Nielsen, Jeffrey. "Ten Key Questions Regarding Leaderless Organizations," *CEO Refresher*, 2004.

Niesse, Mark. "Home Depot Seeks Older Workers for Jobs," Associated Press Online, February 6, 2004.

Prencipe, Loretta W. "Disengaged," CNN.com April 17, 2001.

"Preparing for the Workforce of Tomorrow", Hewitt Associates *Timely Topic Survey Report*, February 2004.

Raphael, Todd. "At Google, the Proof is in the People," *Workforce Management*, March 2003.

Recruitment, Retention and Turnover 2004: A Survey of the UK and Ireland, Chartered Institute of Personnel and Development, June 2004.

"Rise in Hispanics and Asian-Americans is Predicted," *The New York Times*, March 18, 2004.

Salter, Chuck. "Calling JetBlue," *Fast Company*, May 2004.

Salter, Chuck. "Solving the Real Productivity Crisis," *Fast Company*, January 2004.

Schwartz, Karen. "Some Finding Retirement is Only Temporary", *Chicago Tribune*, March 17, 2004.

Schwartz, Peter. *Inevitable Surprises*, Gotham Books, 2003.

Semler, Ricardo, *The Seven-Day Weekend*, Penguin Group, 2004.

Society for Human Resource Management and *The Wall Street Journal* Job Recovery Survey, 2003.

Speizer, Irwin. "By Adding More Women to its Workforce, HP Sees Customer Needs More Clearly," *Workforce Management* Online, September 2004.

Speizer, Irwin. "Hilton Tries to Clone the Model Employee," *Workforce Management* Online, August 2004.

Taylor, Craig R. "Retention Leadership", Training & Development, March 2004.

Temple, Paul. "No Retirement for Boomers," *Workforce*, July 2000.

The American Workplace 2003, Employment Policy Foundation.

The Challenge of Age: The Change Agenda, Chartered Institute for Personnel and Development, November 2003.

The Social Situation in the European Union 2003, European Commission, 2003.

Wallace, Patricia. *The Internet in the Workplace*, Cambridge University Press, 2004.

Ware, James, and Charles Grantham. "The Future of Work," *Journal of Facilities Management*, September 2003.

Weber, Gretchen. "Adelphia's 'Rent to Own' Recruiting Solution," *Workforce Management*, August 2004.

Weiss, Michael J. "To Be About to Be", *American Demographics*, September 1, 2003.

"What's Behind the 4-Minute Mile, Starbucks and the Moon Landing?" Knowledge@Wharton, July 14, 2004.

"Youthful Demographics of Developing Countries May Be Their Economic Salvation," *Institute of Public Affairs Review*, March 2003.

Changing Complexion of India Inc. and Talent Management: Discovery and Development

15

Bhavesh P. Joshi, *G.S. Rawat* and *Vikas Kumar*

With the increasing acceptance of 'India Shining' empowered by the accelerating growth rate at 9.2 per cent for the period 2006-07, prevailing in both the services and manufacturing sectors, India is becoming a destination 'not be ignored'. Souring heights of US $199.2 billion as foreign exchange reserves were touched by the end-March, 2007 making ample space for the international financial resources to be absorbed, utilizes and earn. Offshoring of financial services to India are saving a good amount to the foreign financial institutions in India, as per a survey conducted by NASSCOM American BFS companies have saved about US $6 billion in the past four years of offshoring to India. With the high-end offerings in the form of infrastructure, IT, financial reforms and availability of critical support system the financial services India is being considered to be the hub for the offshoring of financial services. Ongoing research both on International and Indian has gone into determining the factors that affect the performance of India INC.

The other facet of India Inc., a buoyant nation in a booming economy, is the Employability crisis. As per the Teamlease Labour Report 2007, the Indicus Analytics based on government and other data and employer surveys, the 53 per cent or 71.4 million, of India's young workers (15-29 years) face some degree of Employability Crisis. Of these, 55.4 million need 1-2 years of structural repair, 21.9 million need 6-12 months of interventional repair, and 5.3 million needless than six months of last mile repair.

Brighter prospects in all sectors are encouraging sense of optimism within the economy. With the Indian customer increasing demands, complexities in relations and need of product differentiations to meet the specific needs, companies are competing for their share and success. Competition had even forced the Indian companies to look the talent with a different angle, because even they are not left untouched because of improvement in technological developments, liberalized markets, competition, shrinking boundaries, improving infrastructures, and financial stability of Indian economy. Even the managers are in dilemma with the number of options like quality, price or convenience, services, customized products, long-term relationships, variety and problem-solving. In other words the Indian customer's facets are changing from product centric to customer centric, so is the role of talent managers.

So at this juncture differentiating between the leaders and the followers is the need of the day to be handled in the most effective and efficient way with the use of Human Resources, Information Technology, Capital Base Products while overcoming the cut throat competition. In the fiercely competitive business environment the need of the day is for sustainable competitive advantage through the matchless customized services to the customer.

This study is minuscule effort to analyze and understand the chemistry and the success of Talent *mantara* so that the predominant role of Talent Management can be understood carefully, cherished and the charisma of it will empower the India's growth story.

Introduction

Febrile competition for the talent is on high rise, development of a corporate culture of employee's commitment had made the organizations to think out of box with a creative approach. Focus is on increasing employee's satisfaction, turnover reduction, improved production, sustainable growth with transparency in organizational working. Organizations are at stake with the changes taking internally and externally. Economic pressures are compelling across the sections of almost all the organizations.

Problems and Prospects

India is a dynamic economy, but without a linear growth, where the economy is supposed to grow at 9 per cent the importance of substantial growth requires substantial resources exploration, retention and development. Today at the crossroads, from rural to urban, non-farm to farm, across India Inc., the need of the day is employable, efficient and effective utilization of available resources. It not only requires infrastructure on financial and operational turnarounds but also the same is needed for the human capital also.

Today India Inc. requires talented people though the workforce is expected to grow up to 300 million new workers by 2025, with barely 9-10 per cent of employable graduates. Many of the corporate entities feel that the multilingual transitions are happening without any improvement in the quality of workforce. On the same side, the lack of employability of the resources across the sectors had led to the manpower crunch. Lacuna to the growth is being considered is the employability of manpower, near about 56 per cent, in agriculture who is contributing only 18 per cent of the GDP.

Information Technology industry had felt the need in the recent past now the sectors like construction, real estate, education, etc., are also facing the same situations. They are asking for focused restructuring, technological upgradation, improved production lines, liberal and favorable governmental policies and in house development of talent. The looming shortage of talent with the organization emphasizes on its being savvy to attract and develop the best talents within the organization.

For a better understanding of the problems of talent in India we must see the other side of the coin, i.e. from the talents side in India. In a recent study by Hewitt Associates on attrition and retention in the Asia-Pacific region it was found that compensation inequality (external) is contributing the most, i.e. 22 per cent of the total factors affecting. The others are Limited growth opportunities (21%), Role stagnation (15%), Underutilization of skills (9%), Lack of recognition (8%), Work life balance (6%), Performance assessment (6%), People managers (5%), Compensation inequality (internal 5%) and Business instability (3%). With the open/slightly opening boundaries for the external world to trade with, the global cosmopolitan presence is the need of the day. But this leads to complexities arising out of multilingual cultures, identity clashes and other HR issues with certain financial issues like salary in perquisites, differential packages, organizational costs, etc. this intangible asset, talent, requires tangible approaches to manage and maximize towards higher productivity and profits.

For this study we had considered talent as the Intangible Capital of the organization. This capital had various dynamic issues concerning which should be managed in the most efficient manner. The portfolio of organization had to be balanced with the increasing opportunities and threats. An aggressive and active approach towards this capital can synergize the existing ones and attract the others from the open markets. This minuscule effort of ours is towards a better understanding of the problems and utilization of this capital within the available resources and timeframe.

As far as the concepts and approaches towards talent management are often loosely defined and difficult to pin down analytically, so there is a tendency to make ad hoc decisions grounded more on experiences and gut feelings of the decision makers than the available actual data. Looking forward for a cohesive approach based on the facts and figures. For this, the study is based on the Delphi method, talent managers of different organizations from different streams were consulted and the outcomes emphasizes on the three approaches to talent discovery and development.

Decision Initiative Model

The four principles of enduring success followed by the Great Companies had emphasized on exploitation before you explore. Their growth is through the discovery of efficiency to the fullest potential with in the organization and then looking beyond that. So understanding the talent and then expecting performance can make the difference.

Our research was to understand why some of the talents are considered as good and paid and served better than the others? How different they are from the others and to whom and at what stage the development is needed? To answer these questions, we made a survey and asked the real talent managers to give answers how does a talent perform exceptionally and on which dimensions they are different from others. The result is in the form of Decision Initiative Model (Figure 15.1).

The model distinguishes between the talent and the workforce. The two dimensions of the model include Decision and Initiative. The first dimension is Decision: What does organization mean to the worker? (Clarity of importance and responsibility associated with Job, here considered as an External Force). The second is Initiative: Can their be a different approach? Will the new approach help the organization? (Initiative towards growth of individuals as well as organization, considered as the Internal Force).

These two dimensions generate a matrix with the differentiation of workforce into four categories: The Laggard (Ambiguous Decision and Uncommitted Initiative); The Facilitator (Ambiguous Decision and Committed Initiative); The Developer (Focused Decision and Uncommitted Initiative) and The Generator (Focused Decision and Dedicated Initiative)

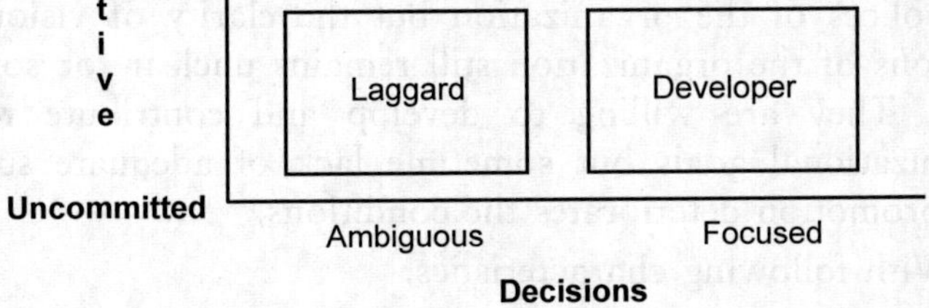

Fig. 15.1: Decision Initiative Model

Based on this there are two dimensions which generate this matrix with four categories/stages:

1. The Laggard

With the dynamically changing environment, cross culture shifting, salary structures and such other reasons, the talent feels tough to work as a dedicated employee. That too at that stage when the worker feels for the organizations that voluntary severance and retirement package or reduction in workforce are considered as the time tested method of cost reduction, it becomes tougher.

This Stage has the following characteristics:

1. Searching for answers within but not able to discover them.
2. Lack of clarity about their life purpose, values and aspiration.
3. Tug of war is between their views and the perspectives created by the environment.
4. Expansion or challenges of their visions are at nascent stage, but with a huge expansion scope.

Due to the organizational structure and policies at the workplace they found it a bit tough to cope up their perspectives with organizations expectations of result.

Talent at this stage requires awareness, open experimentation, promotion to creativity and networking between the official hierarchy and departments. In absence of these the talent tries to quit or perform inefficiently.

2. The Facilitator

With the passage of time the workforce get acquainted with the polices of the organization but the clarity of vision and missions of the organization still remains unclear for some of them. They are willing to develop and contribute to the organizational goals but sometime lack of adequate support and promotion deteriorates the conditions.

With following characteristics:

1. Dedicated workers, with the passage of time and little adjustments with the organizational structure.

2. Mismatch of expectations of theirs and perspectives of organization.

Mostly they feel underutilization of skills, lack of recognition, compensation inequality (internal) comes into the mind of the workers.

At this stage recruitment and retention of like minded people and support from the senior management can help in the organizations strategic frame. Promotion to new ideas, new trainings, team building, concept exploration and experimentation are the high needs of this category. For a mature business this is most valuable group of people, a higher rate of retention rate is necessary to gain economically in the form of market share or expansion.

3. The Developer

For the Developer, the focused decision-making is possible as he had an experience of working under favorable and adverse circumstances.

Characteristics of Developers:

1. Neglected but not negligible.
2. Require sharpening of management skills, but lack opportunities.

So assigning of organizational ownerships, responsibilities, benefits (tangible, intangible or combination of both) and team work to the Developer envisages growth of the unit with the organization. Co-creation of plan for action, expansion to their vision and identification future directions helps and motivates these Developers to move to the next stage of individual and organizational development.

4. The Generator

At this stage, the development of talent is in the way of strategic innovation while keeping in mind the competitor's strategy. The Generator may lead as a facilitator of understanding of needs to identify resources required or obstacles to be managed with in the organization or arising out of the external complications.

Characteristics:

1. Well accepted within the organization.
2. Creative, Encouraging and Decisive.

Unutilised/Unnoticed potentials and creativity of Generator may make them feel; Role stagnation, underutilization of skills and lack of work-life balance. At this juncture the cosmopolitans presence, who had failed to integrate with the local community, and lack of their acceptance by the expatriates make the situation more critical.

Taking Advantage

With the discovery of talent within their development makes the possibilities of looking forward for attraction of new talent. With this understanding of the talent, positioning of them in the Decision Initiative Model and provision of needy inputs based on their functions is the next step. So that accordingly their training needs must be identified, up graded and enhanced. But the inputs for all the stages are different. Varying from Orientation amd Induction for Laggard to Involvement of, due recognition and reintegration with the rest of the teams are needed for the Generator (Table 15.1 Approach to talent discovery and development).

The other side of the coin is the involvement of different sets of inputs the Risk and loss of the Talent. If at any of the stages the talent leaves the organization there is a loss but the intensity is different for different stages. As at Stage IV this is the highest due to the integration of individual's goals with the organizational goals and their involvement as a strategic partner.

The success of these approaches will depend on the External factors, provided by the culture with in the organization and Internal factors developing with the past experiences and knowledge (explicit and tacit). Organizations focusing on the promotion of these External factors can promote a culture of in-house development of talent which in a long-run will attract the others from the external environment.

It is very clear that talent had really unique to deliver for the organization; diversity, richness of concepts and views, tacit

Table 15.1: Approach to Talent Discovery and Development

	Stage I	Stage II	Stage III	Stage IV
Parameters[1] Stages	Laggard	Facilitator	Developer	Generator
Organizational Goals	Lack of clarity	A bit clear, but lack of vision	Clear	Clear
Function	Encouraging, But lack full utilization	Encouraging & utilized	Encouraging, but less Decisive	Encouraging & Decisive
Inputs needed	Orientation, Induction & Mentoring	Promotion to creativity	Reintegration, Responsibility and Cross cultural handling	Strategic Partnership, Recognition & Reintegration
Risk and Loss Involved	Moderate & Less	Moderate but more	High with hidden cost Which appears in long run	High & Very high
Success Factor (External)	**External:** Innovation, Structural flexibility, Communication, Team facilitation, & Corporate Entrepreneurship			
Success factor (Internal)	**Internal:** Leadership & Skill sets			

wealth that enhances the performance of the organization inspite of location, size and structure. Difference comes out with the discovery of the talent and a push to deliver that extra mile. In an organization talent is who can cognitively mobilize the resources within the context of business entity, enhance them and perform.

REFERENCES

"Attrition rate increases 14 p.c. in Asia", http://www.ciol.com/content/developer/2006/106101204.asp

Dwivedi, R.S. (1983). "A Comparative Study of Managerial Styles, Leadership and Trust among Indian Managers", *Lok Udyog* 27(1), 7-17.

Financial Express. "Rural India will be Growth Engine: Purwar" 22nd March, 2005, Net Edition.

Kanungo, R.N. and M. Mendonce (1996). *Ethical Dimensions of Leadership*, Sage, Thousand Oaks.

Nilkantha, V. and S. Ramanarayan (1990). "Managers in the Middle: A Case of Underdevelopment and Underutilization", *Vikalpa*, 15(2), 3-12.

Ramalingaswami, Vulimiri and Jonsson, Urban., and Rohde, Jon (1996). "The Asian Enigma." *The Progress of Nations*. 1996, New York: UNICEF.

Stadler, Christian (2007). "The Principles of Enduring Success," *Harvard Business Review* July-August, pp. 62-72.

Sahay, Arvind (2007). "How to Reap Higher Profits with Dynamic Pricing," *MIT Sloan Management Review*, Summer.

Developing Talent Factory

16

Gitanjali Singh

Introduction

Growth in the global marketplace depends on putting the right people in the right places fast. Large number of companies still struggle to fill key positions. The challenge of filling these positions has become much more strategic concern for the organizations. Due to demographic changes—impending retirement of baby boomers—along with changing business conditions, such as significant growth in largely unfamiliar markets, like China, have combined to produce something of a perfect storm. Faulty processes and executive inattention now carry a tangible cost for the organizations. Therefore, the talent development is the critical success factor for the growth of the companies.

For example, One London-based real state firm, for instance, was gearing up for a major reconstruction job in Berlin—an effort that would represent not only a € 500 million boost in revenues over two years, but also an opportunity to get the base of many other projects in that part of the world. When executive committee reviewed the list of people who might be ready to take such an assignment, the CEO noticed that the same names appeared as the only candidates for other critical efforts under consideration. And when he asked his business unit heads for additional prospects, he was told that there were not any. The firm's growth strategy hinged on these projects, but the company had failed to groom people to lead them.

Some companies, by contrast, face the future with confidence because they don't just manage talent; they build what we call "Talent Factories".

Consider, for example, consumer products icon Procter & Gamble, found a leader for a burgeoning joint venture with an entrepreneur in Saudi Arabia. The role required someone with emerging markets experience, who had worked in other countries and in the laundry detergent business and was ready to relocate on short notice to Saudi Arabia. For most companies' HR departments, finding and hiring such a senior manager would entail protracted dialogue with internal and external candidates and might well end in failure. P&G, however, searched its global database of talent profiles and came up with five very strong potential candidates in just a few minutes. In the end, they found just the right fit, and the new manager was fully on board three months after the start of the search.

In this paper, we look at the people processes in two talent factories: Procter & Gamble and financial services giant HSBC Group. We selected these companies because even though they approach talent management from slightly different directions, both illustrate the power of a twin focus on functionality and vitality.

Functionality: Business processes for recruiting, training, and succession management that are designed to align with real strategic objectives.

Vitality: A commitment, addressing how leadership's daily actions foster passion and engagement.

The functionality and vitality of a company's talent management processes determine how well company can groom its high-potential employees to fill strategic management roles. Through a structured questionnaire company can assess these processes and map the strengths and weaknesses. For example, a company strategy is to achieve better global integration. In other words, it wants to be able to serve its customers anywhere they do business. Clearly, this requires a talent pool that can easily move across regional, functional, and unit boundaries, as well as the capacity to find and develop local talent "on the ground".

The functionality wheel shows that this firm is weak on sourcing, deployment, development and rewards; better at retention, assimilation, performance management and engagement. The firm may be able to keep its local talent happy and productive, but it struggles to place people in key positions or move then across unit or geographic borders.

Corporate vitality is manifested by the passion for talent management among four constituencies: the top team, line management, human resources and talent itself. As the vitality Wheel shows, this company neither champions the process nor holds other key stakeholders accountable for developing talent. Despite high commitment, all the segments in this firm are weak on accountability and the top team is weak on engagement as well. Since a company's talent management process is only as strong as its weakest link, and vitality falls apart without mutual accountability, this company plainly has a lot of work to do. Identifying weaknesses in functionality and vitality can help a company clarify its talent management agenda.

P & G has established a plethora of elaborate systems and processes to deploy talent; HSBC has worked mightily to incorporate talent processes into the firm's DNA.

Both companies can claim a free-flowing pipeline of current and future leaders.

Functionality: Effective Execution

It refers to the processes themselves, the tools and systems that allow a company to put the right people with the right skills in the right place at the right time, as P & G did in Saudi Arabia. Good design isn't just a matter of technical excellence; clearly linking processes to the company's objectives is equally important. In particular, processes should support most CEOs' top concerns: driving performance and creating an effective climate.

So, for example, after years of growth through acquisition, HSBC in 2002 shifted its strategy to focus on organic growth. The goal was to strengthen local resources in multiple geographies for the firm's increasingly global customers. Achieving this objective required an accompanying cultural shift, since HSBC had always operated as a confederation of fiercely independent, stand-alone businesses. As part of the move, the bank committed to a new brand promise: to be "The World's Local Bank", guaranteeing the availability of local resources for the customers, wherever they do business. Stephen K. Green, HSBC's chairperson, views performance and climate as inextricably linked: "if we don't create the proper climate internally and live up to our brand promise, we won't be able to achieve our strategic objective-managing for growth".

To develop local talent while maintaining global standards, HSBC centrally designed its human resources practices and policies but built in some flexibility to accommodate local variations. The firm now has company wide processes for assessment, recruiting, performance and career management, and leadership development, but local offices can adapt them (within limits) to their own resource capabilities and cultural requirements. When making assessments, e.g. each office must choose at least two from a menu of tools, such as psychometric tests, individual interviews that probe people's aspirations, and 360 degree feedback. They must also use a standard rating scale and include performance data from the most recent three years. This way the company can ensure a degree of objectivity and establish a common measurement language across all the businesses and locations.

To help instill a global mind-set, HSBC created a system of talent pool that track and manage the careers of high-potentials within the firm. After those employees have been identified, they are assigned to regional or business unit talent pools, which are managed by local human resources and business unit leaders. Employees in these pools are then selected initially for a new assignments within their region or line of business and, over-time, are given positions that cross boundaries. They are viewed as having the potential to reach a senior management role in a region or a business. Managers of the pools then single out people to recommend for the group talent pool, which represents the most senior cadre of general managers and is administered centrally. These managers are considered to have the potential to reach the senior executive level in three to five years and top management in the longer term.

Leaders maintain talent relationship dialogues with members of each pool, in face-to-face conversations where possible, to address their development needs and concerns. In new relationships, the dialogues are time intensive and available to the employee on demand; in established relationships, the conversation tend to occur two to four times a year, as needed. The aim is to structure a set of experiences that leads to a deep knowledge of all aspects of the business as well as an understanding of the many different cultural environments in which HSBC operates.

In fact, people are told that if they want to reach the highest levels of management they must expect to work in at least two very different cultural environments. The number of people making such moves has increased exponentially over the past few years. "We have a Brazilian working with one of our affiliates in China, our insurance affiliate", Green told us. "We have an Armenian working in India in the IT function, a Turk working in New York. There are...hundreds and hundreds of examples of this." Green acknowledges that this approach is expensive—it's nearly always cheaper to fill a role with someone local— but considers it a vital investment in achieving the firm's global goals.

HSBC is still tweaking the process. The bank learned, for instance, that assessing each employee on a scale of one to five was demoralizing for some people, so it modified the process to rate only people in the top two levels of some areas. Feedback for the rest is framed in terms of development needs and support, rather than "you haven't made it in to a talent pool". This change takes into account early-stage career development, which entails gaining a certain amount of expertise before a person is ready to advance.

HSBC also learned that, talent pools notwithstanding, leaders of the local units still behaved as princes of their domains—they weren't connecting across units in ways that would benefit the firm overall. In short, the model of international teamwork was still more an aspiration than an operating principle. To close this gape between aspiration and reality,

HSBC resolved conflicts in its reward system and took steps to build relationship on a more personal basis.

So, for example, the top executive team launched what it called collective-management conferences, where employees could learn about the company's strategic objectives and operations around the world—another way to help people feel like part of an organization that extends beyond their own unit or locale. Each conference is attended by about 40 senior managers, who have been nominated by their country, functional, or customer group leaders because they've demonstrated a potential for growth and because their roles have policy implications across the enterprise.

These meetings, which are held twice per year, have become a vehicle for senior people in the company to share knowledge and ideas across corporate borders and customer groups. During one conference, the General Manager for Mexico told his colleagues how he managed to rebrand a recent acquisition, Group Financiero Bital, literally overnight. His story shed light on the value of collaborating across company boundaries. At another gathering, one of HSBC's senior executives explained how acquiring the U.S. firm Household International gave the organization much deeper capabilities in customer analytics and buying behavior. During yet another meeting, a couple of general managers explained how they built on their preexisting relationship to ease the transfer of a client from commercial banking to private banking. (In the past, the client would have been jealously guarded because this profitability would have been attributed to whichever group "owned" that customer.) After each conference, participants are asked to commit to doing one or two things differently to strengthen the firm's collaboration capabilities.

The company also established network across countries, so that, for instance, the head of personal financial services in Hong Kong knows her counterpart in Mumbai, in Mexico City, in Sao Paulo, in Vancouver. These networks allow executives to participate in important virtual meetings on a regular basis for each line of business and provide them with opportunities to gather face-to-face in occasional offsite meetings.

Like HSBC, Procter & Gamble has tied its talent management processes to its strategy for growth, which means a focus on winning in the emerging markets of China, India, Latin America, and the Middle East, and Eastern Europe. The company is building what amounts to a global talent supply-chain management process, coordinated worldwide but executed locally. Hiring and promotions are the responsibility of local managers, but high-potential prospects and key stretch assignments are identified globally. New hires tend to be local talent. Line managers in China, for instance, hire Chinese recruits. That's been the case for sometime, but it is used to be that key corporate roles in emerging markets went to expatriates. Now, local hires are considered growth prospects for the firm; those Chinese recruits are expected to become managers in that market. Key stretch assignments and senior positions, however, are managed globally, at the executive level. The emphasis on hiring nationals translates into a diverse pool of leadership talent for the entire corporation, especially at more senior levels. At the geography and country leader level, there are almost 300 executives who come from 36 countries, and 50 per cent are from outside the United States. The top 40 executives come from different nations, and 45 per cent are from outside the United States. As high-potential employees advance, they move through a portfolio of senior-level jobs that are categorized according to strategic challenges, size of the business, and complexity of the market. Leadership position for businesses or countries is earmarked for either novice or experienced general managers. A relatively small country manager position—in Taiwan, for instance,—is considered appropriate for first-time general managers. Such assignments then set up the incumbents for placement in larger countries, like Italy or Brazil, which in turn can lead to roles in clusters of countries, such as Eastern Europe or the United Kingdom. Those last roles then become springboards or crucibles for leaders who demonstrate the potential to become senior executives.

P & G offers formal training and development programs and sometimes sends managers to external executive education programs. The lion's share of development, however, takes place on the job, with the immediate manager's support and help from mentor's teammates. A typical marketing manager, e.g. will have worked with a number of different brands over a period of time. A finance manager will have gone through various assignments, ranging from financial analysis to treasury to auditing to accounting. Most managers are also placed on important multifunctional task forces or project teams from time to time. New postings and task force participation are expected to challenge employees, and they signal to managers that P&G will always offer new opportunities.

Consider the career progression of Daniela Riccardi, who has been with the company for 22 years. She started as an assistant brand manager in Italy, where she stayed for six years, advancing to branding manager, a three-year stint in Belgium as a marketing manager for cleansers and bleach followed. She then spent seven years in three Latin American countries, holding the positions of marketing director, general manager, and vice-president of ever-larger divisions. From there, she became a vice-president of Eastern Europe, and in 2005, she was promoted to her current position—resident, Greater China. When the development of a career like Riccardi's has to be managed across business units and countries, the planning process is led collaboratively from the center by the company's CEO, A.G. Lafley; the vice chairs; the global HR officer; and the global leaders of the various functions for their people. All this is done in partnership with the president and human resources manager at both ends of the reassignment.

People and positions are tracked in a technology based talent management system that is sufficiently robust to accommodate all the company's more than 1,35,000 employees but is primarily used to track 13,000 middle and upper management employees. The system captures information about succession planning at the country, business category, and regional levels; includes career histories and capabilities, as well as education and community affiliations; identifies top talent and their development needs; and tracks diversity. It also makes in-house talent visible to business leaders, who no longer have to scour the company to find candidates by themselves. To keep the systems relevant, P & G has instituted a global talent review—a process by which every country, ever function, and every business is assessed for its capacity to find, develop, deploy, engage, and retain skilled people, in light of specific performance objectives. For example, if the company has stated diversity hiring objectives, the review is used to audit diversity in hiring and promotions. Determinations made in these reviews are captured in a global automated talent development system and can be accessed by decision-makers through their HR managers.

The company also pays close attention to the effectiveness of its recruiting processes. P & G interviewers record detailed assessments of each candidate and assign them a quantitative score, using uniform criteria. The company then regularly assesses performance against the baseline set during the interviews. P & G also evaluates the success rate of its key promotions, using quantitative and qualitative measures that cover a three-year period. Managers who improve the business and its capabilities are deemed "successful"; the company has a success rate that exceeds 90 per cent. When derailments occur, P & G conducts a thorough "lessons learned" review.

Vitality: The Secret Weapon

If functionality is about focusing your company's talent management processes to produce certain outcomes, vitality is about the attitudes and mind-sets of the people responsible for those processes—not just in human resources but throughout the line, all the way to the top of the organization. Unlike processes, which can with some effort be copied by competitors, passion is very difficult to duplicate. Nevertheless, there are measures that companies can take to build it into their cultures.

Our research shows that the vitality of a company's talent management processes is a product of three defining characteristics:

- Commitment
- Engagement
- Accountability

Fostering Commitment

P & G hires and develops people through a set of principle—such as the rules to hire at entry level and build from within—that are specifically designed to foster commitment. While people typically have long careers with the company, the average age for all employees is only 39; 38 for all managers. More than half the organization has been with P & G for less than five years. That's because the company constantly pumps in new talent and has integrated huge numbers of people through its acquisitions of Clairol, Gillette and Wella. So, even with the relatively low attrition rate of 7.5 per cent (including retirements), more junior managers are always coming in. P & G hires 90 per cent of its entry-level managers straight from universities and grows their careers over time. (The relative youth of the workforce may also reflect that this approach often allows for retirement earlier than usual.) All the vice chair and corporate officers either joined the company from universities or arrived via acquisitions. Lafley himself joined P & G right out of Harvard Business School an over the subsequent 25-plus years, went through numerous assignments before becoming CEO.

To gain commitment early, the company also established a college intern program that offers the chance to assume real responsibility by working on important projects with the full resources of the company. Extensive intern programs can be drain on an organization because of the time that managers must spend sponsoring, coaching, and advising the interns. P & G, however, converts former interns to full-time employees at a percentage well above that of most competitors, so the company is compensated for its investment with high-quality hires that can hit the ground running. It also assigns interns to multifunctional teams that work on business and organizational issues and present solutions to the CEO and senior management sponsors. The company often ends up implementing the suggestions those teams come up with. One of the four ideas presented in 2006, for instance, may result in accelerating the launch of a new brand; two other projects have been partially implemented.

At HSBC, commitment to talent is personified by Green, who explains, "There is noting more important than getting the right…all the way from intake through the most influential senior positions." Line executives participate directly in the process, partnering with the central and regional HR functions to fill important positions.

Building Engagement

Engagement reflects the degree to which company leaders show their commitment to the details of talent management. P & G engages in their own career development the day they start with the company. They work with their hiring managers to plots moves that will build what the company call "career development currency". For high-potentials, P & G identifies "destination jobs", which are attainable only if the employee continues to perform, impress and demonstrate growth potential. The purpose is to view job assignments through a career development lens. For instance, a manager whose destination job is to become a president of one of P & G's seven regions will go through assignments in different locations to acquire international experience and work in a global business unit with responsibility for a major product category.

University recruiting is a line-led activity at P & G, and many senior managers personally lead campus teams at top universities around the world. These executives are held accountable for hiring only graduates with outstanding track records in both academic and non-academic performance (such as summer jobs, clubs, and entrepreneurial activities). To bolster ties with these institutions, the campus team leaders also fund research, make technology gifts, participate in the classroom, and judge case study competitions.

As for HSBC, a conversation with Green makes his engagement immediately clear. Green has a remarkable knowledge of the company's day-to-day people processes and can speak at length about how the company approaches recruitment, where managers are deployed, how their careers are progressing, and what they need to do to continue advancing. Down through the ranks, line engagement in talent management is ensured by specific policies and practices, such as the requirement that each unit have a talent implementation strategy. These plans explicitly link a unit's growth objectives to its people development, so the company won't be surprised by any deficits. Barbara Simpson, HSBC's group head of talent, works closely with each unit to develop its proposal and presents the aggregated plans to the group head office, highlighting any gaps in talent to meet the firm's growth objectives. This process keeps talent management high on the agendas of line and corporate leaders and prevents them from getting distracted by seemingly more pressing problems. What's more, talent management, succession planning international moves, and senior-executive development are standing agenda items at meetings of business executive committees and the group's board.

The bank fosters engagement in new hires by sending them to the United Kingdom for a seven-week training program, typically in groups of 30 to 40, whose members represent about 20 nations. At these sessions, held several times a year, new employees have a chance not jut to meet one another and members of the leadership team—Green or his most senior colleagues spend sometime with them—but also to share their own ideas about the bank.

Ensuring Accountability

Talent factories hold all stakeholders (including talented employees themselves) accountable for doing their part to make systems and processes robust. At P & G, Lafley claims ownership for career planning of all the general managers and vice-presidents and for the talent pools that comprise what he refers to as the company's "top 16s": P & G's preeminent 16 markets, 16 customers, and 16 brands. He reviews the top talent assignment and succession plans for each business and region annually. Along with the company's vice-chairs and presidents, he personally sponsors and teaches all the leadership development courses for the company's most senior 300 leaders, signaling that talent management is both a leadership responsibility and a core business process. All of P & G's managers and executives understand that they will be held accountable for identifying and developing the firm's current and future leaders. They are evaluated and compensated on their contributions to building organizational competence, not just on their performance.

HSBC's Green holds his group management board, which comprises about a dozen executives, accountable for the company's talent pools. Each member is responsible for a region, a customer group, or a product. Members oversee the list of people in their own business in the regional talent pool as well and select mangers for the group pool.

Executives are also held accountable for maintaining honesty in the talent management process, which is easier said than done, says Green. "We've had people who got into talent pools who shouldn't have. You can either let it ride, or you have that hard conversation saying, 'Sorry, this wasn't right', or 'you were a legitimate member of the talent pool but you started to coast and lost it a bit'. You don't do people a favor by being nice all the time."

Leaders have long said that people are their companies' most important assets, but making the most of them has acquired a new urgency. Any company aiming to grow—and, in particular, to grow on the global stage—has little hope of achieving its goals without the ability to put the right people on the ground, and fast. Companies apply focus and drive toward capital, information technology, equipment, and world-class processes, but in the end, it's the people who matter most.

REFERENCES

Case Study—*Harvard Business Review South Asia*, 2007.

Gregerson, Hal B., Morrison, A.J. and Black, J.S. "Developing Leaders for the Global Frontier", *Sloan Management Review*, 1998.

Tapomoy Deb. *A Conceptual Framework to Strategic Talent Management*", *Indus Publishing Company*, New Delhi, 2005.

http://www.deloitte.com

http://www.marceffron.com

http://www.newtmn.com

http://www.ddiworld.com

PART – 4
RETAINING TALENT THROUGH ORGANIZATIONAL CULTURE

Retention of Talent through Organizational Culture

17

S.S. Narula and *Bhawna Jaiswal*

Introduction

Our economy is growing at a scorching pace. Indian companies are competing aggressively in global markets, snapping up large multinationals, hiring thousands of young people every month at hitherto unheard of salaries and turning investors into multimillionaires overnight. Indian entrepreneurs are gaining respect across the world for their abilities to combine vision and ambition with execution. In today's scenario, shareholder value of an organization is driven by knowledge and innovation and it is no more measured by the value of its physical assets. Encouraging key talent to continue to generate fresh perspectives and innovative ideas to maintain competitive edge has become critical to business success. The dynamic nature of global business is putting an ever-increasing pressure on companies to be constantly on the lookout for exceptional talent in a market where demand far exceeds supply. The jobs are plenty and so are the job seekers. However, it is the talented manpower which is not easily available. Retaining talent has never been so important in the Indian scenario. When people do jobs which don't suit their inclination or temperament, the results are disastrous. Low productivity, dissatisfaction, low morale, absenteeism and other negative behavior will become typical till the employee is shown the door. A wrong fit will result in further hiring, re-training and other wasteful activities. Perhaps, there is another option—Talent Management. Talent management implies recognizing a person's inherent skills, traits, personality and offering him a matching job. Pressing business imperatives, such as increasing turnover as the economy improves, globalisation of markets/labour forces and aggressive competition have intensified the need to acquire, develop, deploy, motivate and retain key talent. It is therefore vital to innovate and formulate strategies to create positive organizational culture for retaining talent.

Talent Management Process

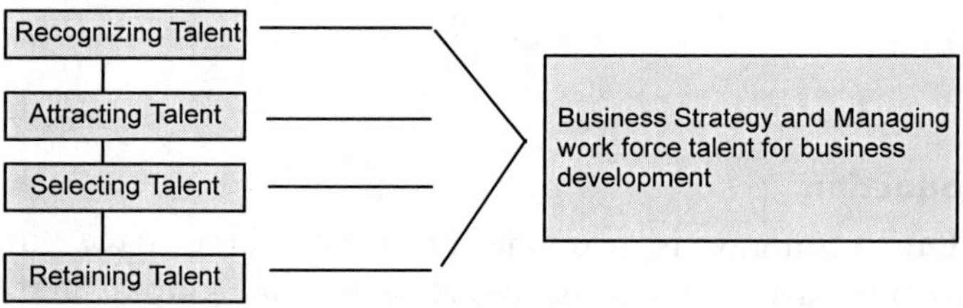

Fig. 17.1: Systems Approach to Talent Management

Recognize Talent. Try to discover strengths and interests of employees. Also, encourage them to discover their own latent talents. For instance, if an employee in the operations department convincingly explains why he thinks he's right even when he's wrong, consider moving him to sales!

Attracting Talent. The Organizations must create a strong brand identity. The right people will automatically choose to join the organization.

Selecting Talent. Management should implement proven talent selection systems and tools to create profiles of the right people based on the competency of high performers. It's not simply a matter of finding the "best and the brightest", it's about creating the right fit—both for today and tomorrow.

Retaining Talent. It's critical to hold on to the key people. These are the people who will lead the organization to future success, and you can't afford to lose them. We shall dwell on this aspect in the paper.

Why Employees Leave

Most employees leave their work for reasons other than money and an organization can correct these reasons. Most leaving employees seek opportunities that allow them to use and develop their skills. Leaving employees want more meaning in their work. They often indicate that they want to use their qualities and skills in challenging work led by capable leaders. Some of the common reasons given by different levels of employees for leaving an organization are:

- **Managerial staff** cite "career growth" and "leadership" as the major factors that influence attrition and retention, together with "opportunities for management" "ability of top management", "use of skills and abilities" and work/family balance.
- **Professional employees** cite concerns about "supervisory coaching and counseling", "company direction" and interesting work.
- **Clerical employees** voice concerns such as "type of work", "use of skills and abilities" and opportunities to learn.
- **Hourly employees** notice whether they are treated with respect, have capable management and interesting work.

Causes of Employee Turnover

Exit interviews provide an excellent source of information of internal problems, employees' perceptions of the organization, underlying workplace issues, and managers' leadership abilities. This avenue must be fully utilized and not allowed to degenerate into a mere formality. Some of the major causes of employee turn over are:

- **Lack of Proper Employee Orientation.** Lack of proper employee orientation on induction is one of the major causes of employee dissatisfaction. New employees who attend a positive orientation program are more likely to remain longer with the company.
- **Ineffective Managers.** High employee turnover can be recognized and properly attributed to poor managerial performance, emotional intelligence and ineffective leadership. Poorly selected or improperly trained managers can be expensive.
- **Growth Opportunity.** Every employee looks forward to grow in the organization and career progression. Lack of these opportunities lead to dissatisfaction and turn over.

- **Competitive Compensation Package.** An attractive compensation package commensurate to an employee's capabilities and matching industry trends is essential. HR Managers have to use their ingenuity to design compensation package to retain talented employees.
- **Higher Education.** Some employees leave an organization to enhance their qualifications for improving their career prospects. The organizations not only have to encourage such endeavors but also provide some incentives for such employees to rejoin the organization on completion of their study program.
- **High Stress.** Soaring expectations keep people on edge and create unhealthy stress. They rob the employee of internal security and make the employee feel unsuccessful. It is not intended to advocate unchallenging jobs, but there is a need for a specific framework within which people clearly know what is expected from them. Physical strain and excessive job related stress could also contribute to employee turn over.
- **Work Environment.** Conducive work environment is vital for talent retention. Company policies, procedures, relationship with peers or managers and work place facilities play a major role in employee retention.
- **Work Life Balance.** A human being cannot be treated like a machine lest it breaks down. Organizations have to ensure proper work life balance leaving adequate time for the employees to attend to their personal and family requirements.
- **The Trust Factor.** Too many broken promises and commitments lead employees to feel distrustful of the company. Trust and loyalty have to be a two-way street.
- **Poor Fit between the Employee and the Job.** Employees who dedicate themselves in their organizations need to feel that their values and principles match those of the organization and that their skills and talent match those required for the job. A poor fit in this regard causes dissatisfaction leading to turnover.

- **The Emotional Factor.** Employees need to be recognized, rewarded and encouraged to grow. When employees leave an organization, they often cite lack of recognition, inadequate compensation and rewards, no opportunity for advancement and too little focus on their personal development as reasons to move on.
- **Mergers/Acquisitions.** Far more employees leave following a restructuring than are laid-off or terminated as a result of downsizing. This lost talent and cost can be minimized through good communication.
- **Poor Internal Communication.** Lack of transparency in personnel policies relating to future career path of employees invariably leads to sense of insecurity and gives rise to unnecessary rumours. Feeling of job insecurity among the employees' results in increased turnover.

Cost of Employee Turnover

Direct Costs. Cost of turnover that can be measured directly falls in two areas: separation costs and replacement costs. Separation costs may include severance pay, costs associated with an exit interview, outplacement fees and possible litigation costs, particularly for involuntary separation. Replacement costs are the well-known costs of a hire, including sourcing expenses, HR processing costs for screening and assessing candidates, the time spent by hiring managers for interviewing candidates, travel and relocation expenses, signing bonuses, orientation and training costs.

Indirect Costs. There are a number of other areas too in which turnover indirectly impact a corporation, although the effect is difficult to quantify. Indirect costs actually represent the greatest losses for the organization. Turnover results in a loss of productivity, since it results in lower productivity of the departing employee, unproductive time for both colleagues and managers, and a general disruption of the team dynamics. Potentially even more damaging to a corporation are lost sales and even lost customers resulting from the departure of an employee. Employee retention is not only critical for cost-efficiency but an important factor in revenue growth as well, because of its direct link to customer acquisition, satisfaction and retention.

Talent Retention Strategy

One of the things we learn in business is that customer is the king. If customer does not feel like a king, won't he run to our competitors? Absolutely! That's why we have to treat our employees also royally. This spirit of bonhomie will naturally get passed on to the customers. How we treat our people will determine whether or not they treat the customer like a king. A simple example given below illustrates this Imagine that you are a manager of restaurant, and you have the world's best customer. This customer eats in your restaurant three times a day, 365 days a year; you cannot have a better customer than that. On the other hand, you also have the world's best hostess. This hostess gets to work on time everyday, she's never sick. She can keep track of a restaurant full of people without missing a beat. What's more, she always has a smile on her face and can remember every regular customer by name. You are managing a restaurant that has world's best customer and world's best hostess. Tonight, one of them has to go. You pick!

Most of you would vote to save the hostess. The bottom line is that good hostesses are a lot harder to find than good customer. As a restaurant manager, if you want your hostess to treat the customer like a king, then you need to make sure that your world-class hostess knows that you think she's more important to you than any customer. That's how you can ensure great customer experience and also keep your world class hostess.

To achieve a true competitive advantage through the employees, talent strategy must align with the organizational strategy and objectives. With a clear understanding of the organizational environment and challenges, design a strategy that will effectively guide individual talent programs and decisions. This strategy will reduce the risk to the organization's 'people portfolio', and minimize the threat presented by transition and enable employees to be ready for change, career progression and long innings with the organization.

Key Factors Influencing Employee Retention

It is the employees who make an organization successful and competitive. Therefore, organizations have to consider various factors which influence employee retention and provide positive organizational culture to nurture and hold talent. The measures to address these factors form integral part of talent retention strategy. A brief survey was conducted on impact of some of the key factors on Employee Retention. It was found that attractive compensation package and growth opportunities were two most important factors leading to 91 per cent and 81 per cent employees respectively to remain committed to the organization. Details are shown in the graphical form below:

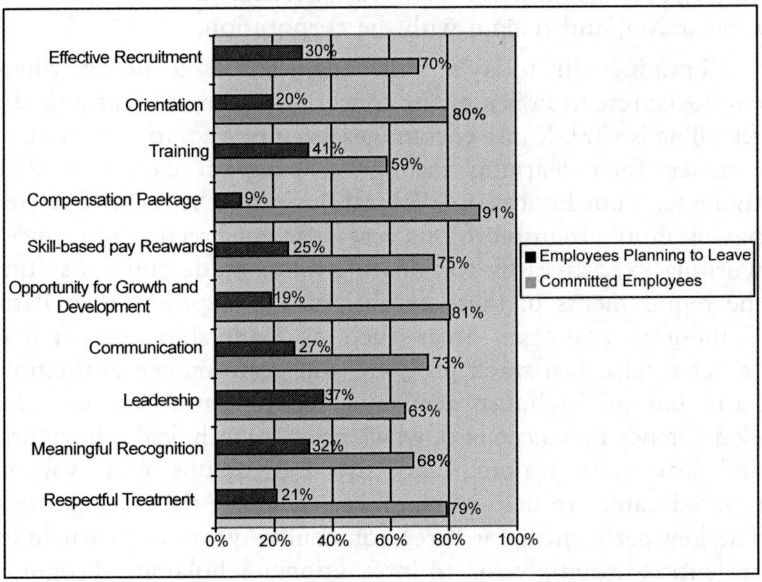

Fig. 17.2: Key Factors in Employee Retention

Effective Recruitment. Effective recruitment is the beginning of effective retention. Therefore, retaining an employee starts with a recruitment strategy. This includes identification of key positions, turnover risks associated with these positions, and competency/behavioural-based selection criteria that support the retention strategy. Hiring the right person saves everyone a lot of headaches. It is important to go beyond the basic interview and try to find out more about the candidate before you know if there is going to be a good match between them and the company. Person to person job interviews fail to give you enough information to make a good selection. Anybody can put on a "show" during an interview.

Orientation. Induction of new recruits with the potential for leadership positions in the future will bring their own expectations of the business. New talent must be inducted with care, sometimes through a carefully designed program undertaken months prior to the actual joining date. It is important to avoid bringing new people into old ways of working and thinking unless it adds value to business. By making this initial investment, employees are more likely to succeed, achieve personal satisfaction, and remain with the corporation.

Training. In today's knowledge based economy where employee retention is a major concern, continuous learning and reskilling is vital. Xansa encourages its employees to continuously enhance their learning through a program called as EYE (Enhance Your Education). Several Business schools have started paying more attention to this very different breed of students—working executives by formulating tailor made courses suiting the requirements of these executives. LEAP program of Patni Computers addresses areas such as leadership competency, career tracks, fast track program and performance evaluation. Patni has an in house academy, PACE (Patni Academy for Competency Enhancement), which provides technical behavioural and leadership training and also has tie-ups with various reputed names to help its employees enhance their capabilities. The key performers for three consecutive years at Cairn India are entitled to apply for an International Scholarship Program. Through this scholarship program, an employee can pursue a year of higher studies at a leading global institution and the successful employee is eligible for a full sponsorship for the course in addition to his/her salary.

Compensation Package. Every one wants to feel that he or she is being paid appropriately and fairly for the work he or she does. Be sure to research what other companies and organizations are offering in terms of salary and benefits. It is also important to research what the regional and national compensation averages are for that particular position. Flexible Salary Benefits may be offered to the employees to plan a tax-effective compensation structure by balancing the monthly net income, yearly benefits and income tax payable. Creative benefits include anything that doesn't fall into the traditional benefits category. This is an area where companies may provide significant retention incentives, often at a lower cost than more traditional benefits. Six-digit salaries and lucrative stock options are not the only things that the key employees want. Employees in the age group of 25 to 30 years inveriably get married. They are always on the look out to enhance their monetary status by a job with higher pay package. People are also looking at skipping posts as they want to rise to the top fast. So most of the time, the decision to switch job is taken as a higher post is offered in the new organization. You can be sure that if your compensation package is not competitive, team members will find this out. With the availability of information today through professional organizations, Internet and salary surveys, employees have little trouble finding out their true market worth. If the incentive is large enough, they will seek to be compensated at these values either within the corporation they are currently employed or elsewhere.

Skill-based Pay Rewards. Companies should focus on improving the quality of thinking within their organizations and reward those who make an extra effort to broaden their knowledge base. By rewarding people for making this extra effort, employees will feel appreciated and continue to strive to expand their capabilities. Skills-based pay encourages employees to learn and enhances employee satisfaction, thus decreasing turnover. Companies like Apollo Tyres, Ranbaxy and Dabur have successfully and tactfully implemented this approach.

Opportunities for Growth and Development. Offer opportunities for team members to acquire new skills and knowledge useful to the organization. If an employee appears to be bored or burned out in a current position, offer to train this individual in another facet of the organization where he or she would be a good fit. Nobody wants to feel stuck in his/her position with no possibility for advancement or new opportunities. Corporations can offer many means for advancement of employees such as internal job postings, identification of competency gap, nomination for required training to fill the competency gap and internal promotions. Employees must feel as if they can advance within a corporation or they will move to another corporation where they can advance. Leading companies like GE, Motorola, etc. have been trying to improve retention by providing their staff with extensive learning and development opportunities. This benefit could as well be extended to the employees family by providing them with similar growth opportunities like providing free subscription to 24×7 guru.com for his/her child.

Communication. An essential element in a retention strategy is communication, specifically a communications process that's structured to inform, emphasize and reaffirm to employees that their workplace contributions are having an impact. Since we're dealing directly with how employees feel about their performance, the company and their work environment, the question becomes, "How do the employees feel about these matters?" It is important that employees feel free to criticize and comment for betterment of the organization. They should not bite their tongues or find themselves constantly "in trouble"—until they leave.... An effective and sensitive communication plan can provide you with insight on exactly what's driving employee morale and how your staff members feel about your company.

Leadership. The supply of leadership talent is critical to any organisation's prosperity and is, therefore, a central element of talent management. Leaders/Managers have to be people oriented and provide value based leadership. They should be capable of motivating their employees through personal example to give their best to the organization. The manager has to build a sense of belonging towards the organization and make every employee feel valuable. The quality of the leadership an employee receives is critical to employee retention.

Meaningful Recognition. Employees want to be recognized for the work they do and the goals they accomplish. Short-term rewards for employees include such things as retention bonuses, annual or quarterly bonuses, and financial target bonuses. Retention bonuses are paid to employees once they have completed some length of employment with the company. Motorola, e.g. has a benefits package that includes a bonus for employees who have remained with the company for ten years. Retention bonuses are also designed to encourage employees to stay throughout some project or throughout such things as a corporate merger or takeover. Annual and quarterly bonuses focus on the short-term goals and can be linked to financial targets such as sales or economic profit. Meaningful recognition should occur in a timely and equitable manner. Such things as spot cash awards, certificates presented at department meetings, recognition meals, or even a simple verbal "Thank You" can go a long way to increase employee satisfaction and improve employee morale. Meaningful recognition can also come in the form of what people are recognized with. By understanding the hobbies and interests of employees, meaningful recognition can include tickets to sport events or theatre events or gift certificates to fancy restaurants. Without meaningful recognition, employees may begin to feel their accomplishments and contributions are going unnoticed and are unimportant. With increased dissatisfaction comes an increased chance of turnover.

Respectful Treatment. Employees want to be treated in the same manner as customers would be treated. Employees demand open and honest communication along with unrestricted information required for superior job performance. If employees feel that they are not being treated respectfully, they may seek another position.

Retention Through Positive Organization Culture

Happy employees make productive employees. One of the most important factors is the work environment itself, i.e. how employees "feel" about the company. The impact of work environment on employee attitudes can be seen in improved customer satisfaction consequently increasing revenue. Seeking ways to motivate and build worker morale pays dividends to any business or organization. The motivated worker is more committed to the job and to the customer. Providing a positive work environment pays off financially. Most employers do not know how much turnover is costing them. A company experiencing high turnover faces a financial crisis. Taking care of your employees' saves money.

Ask yourself, "Why would a talented person choose to work here?" If the organization wishes to substantially strengthen its talent pool, it should be prepared to change things as fundamental as the business strategy, the organization structure, the culture and even the caliber of leaders in the organization. Some of the aspects which assist in talent retention through improved organizational culture are discussed in succeeding paragraphs.

Competitive Advantage. The most important element in your strategy to retain employees is your competitive advantage. The image of the company plays an important role as people want themselves to be associated with established names. While this may seem odd at first, think about it: People want to work for a winner. What sets your company apart from your competitor? How are you—and as a result, your employees—making a difference in your industry, in your community, and for your customers? Take time to identify and inform your clients and your employees about your unique competitive advantage. If your product is similar to others in the marketplace, your service can be what distinguishes you from others.

Empowerment. Too many rules and regulations may overwhelm employees and inhibit their judgment and individuality. Provide them with the necessary tools and authority to serve the customer. Employees must have all information readily available at their fingertips to make the decisions necessary to complete their jobs effectively and efficiently. Oren Harari says in an April 1998 *Management Review* article, "You can't have people taking on the responsibilities of business people if they don't have free, unfettered, unfiltered access to the information and conversations that business people require. Trust is lost when people are kept in the dark and not provided the information they need to perform. When trust is lost and individuals are not able to adequately perform their jobs due to the corporate infrastructure, norms and procedures, the frustration rises leading to increased turnover.

Mentoring. The Mentoring programs foster a learning environment within an organization and provide employees with a confidant and an advisor. Mentoring allows new employees to learn how to be productive at the start of employment, thus providing employees greater satisfaction and a greater sense of connection to the organization. Employees with mentors may be able to obtain career guidance, project assistance, and corporate culture advice that cannot be obtained easily from a manager. Figure 17.3 shows some of the direct benefits of having a mentor as given from a mentoring survey. This increased satisfaction and increased productivity at the beginning of a new position helps address some of the key retention issues with employees.

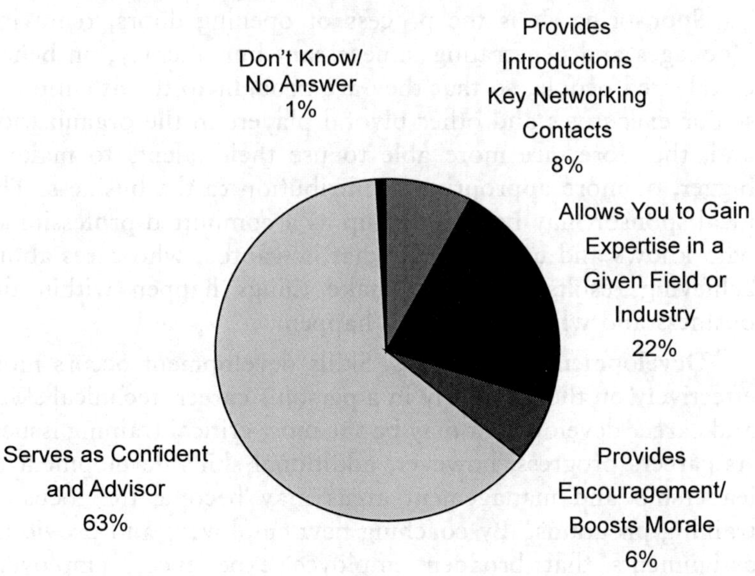

Fig. 17.3: Benefits of Having a Mentor

Source: Mentoring: Building Your Company's Intellectual Capital. HR Focus, Sep. 1998.

Skill Assessments. Employees should have the opportunity to assess the current skills they possess so that the skills can be compared to those required in desired positions within an organization. Skill assessments provide means for employees to learn where they stand and provide a basis for goals that employees may develop for advancement and additional career opportunities. Companies such as Union Carbide and The DOW Chemical Company offer employees the opportunity to take skills assessment tests to determine areas of strengths and weaknesses. By understanding their strengths and weaknesses, employees can determine what they need to do and what they need to concentrate for their development in order to broaden their career advancement opportunity. Organizations have to encourage employees to take up distance learning program to pursue PG in technical or management courses to enhance their skills and abilities by providing extraordinary leave, free subsidy and pay increment/promotion on completion of these courses.

Sponsoring. It is the process of opening doors, removing blockages and penetrating unnecessary bureaucracy, on behalf of talented people, so that they are brought to the attention of senior executives and other pivotal players in the organization and, therefore, are more able to use their talents to make a bigger, or more appropriate, contribution to the business. The ideal sponsor may be summed up as a committed professional, who knows and understands what is wanted, who cares about achieving results, who can make things happen within the business and who will make it happen.

Developmental Resources. Skills development occurs most effectively on the job. Early in a person's career, technical skills and career development may be the most critical training issues. As careers progress, however, additional skills development in leadership and management areas may become the focus of training programs. By coaching new employees and providing assignments that broaden employee experiences, employees continue to learn and contribute to the corporation. Classroom training on specific items may also be required and memberships to professional associations, subscriptions to journals, access to industry experts, and online resources can help extend the development capabilities of an organization. Nothing can be more frustrating to an employee than a lack of training or the proper tools to successfully complete his or her duties. You wouldn't try to build a house without a hammer, so why should an office job be any different? Providing a team member with the tools and training he/she needs to be successful shows a commitment and investment in that employee and will encourage the team member to stay with the organization.

Shorten the Feedback Loop. Do not wait for an annual performance evaluation to give feedback on an employee. Most team members enjoy frequent feedback about how they are performing. Shortening the feedback loop will help to keep performance levels high and will reinforce positive behavior. Feedback does not necessarily need to be scheduled or highly structured; simply stopping by a team member's desk and letting them know they are doing a good job on a current project can do wonders for morale and help to increase retention.

Employee Inputs and Involvement. Everybody has opinions and ideas, some are better than others. However, every team member wants to feel that their input is welcome and will be taken seriously without ridicule or condescension. Some of the greatest ideas can come from the most unlikely of places and people. Creating a culture where input is welcome from all levels of the organizational chart will help your organization grow and encourage employee retention. Studies show that having workers involved at all levels has a major impact on improving profit and productivity. A good example is Guardian Industries, an 800 person glass plant in Indiana. They decided to start listening to their employees to find their opinion on how to staff the plant's 24 hours work shifts. The employees decided that instead of working rotating day and evening shifts, they would rather work permanent 12 hours shifts. The result—turnover fell by 50 per cent.

Beware of Burnout. Staff adequately to reduce the amount of unwanted over-time a team member must work. Some employees enjoy the extra money that accompanies over-time hours, while others would rather spend their time with their families or doing other activities they enjoy. Burnout can be a leading cause of turnover. Recognize the warning signs and give employees a break when they need it.

Management to Get to Know Team Members. It's not a big surprise that one of the greatest complaints that employees express in exit interviews is a feeling that management didn't know they existed. Nobody wants to feel like just another spoke in a big wheel. Managers are very busy—everybody is busy, but it is crucial that managers and supervisors take time to get to know the team members who work under them. Learn and remember a team member's name, what skills and talents they bring to the table, and what their business interests are. The time spent by management in getting to know team members is well invested and can eliminate the headaches caused by having to continually hire and re-train new employees.

Internal Promotions. Companies such as MOBIL have searched through their corporate layers to identify the leaders of the future for the company. By providing these internal leaders with increased opportunities within the company, retention of the best and the brightest employees increases. With MOBIL, each identified future leader rotates through various functional areas across the business and is assigned to a manager who is not his or her supervisor. Without an internal promotion strategy, employees will begin to see leaders come from external organizations and understand that their advancement opportunities are limited since outsiders move into the key leadership positions. By promoting from within, corporations provide opportunities internally that employees may have otherwise sought externally.

Succession Management. Planning future leadership needs is a huge concern for today's senior leaders. To identify and close executive talent gaps, it is essential to accurately predict leadership potential, improve the quality of executive promotion decisions, and accelerate the performance of senior leaders. By ensuring strong supply of leaders today to meet tomorrow's challenges, you reduce the risk of executive failure. Effective organizations need to identify potential talent and groom it.

Make Use of a Team Member's Talents, Skills, and Abilities. All team members have knowledge, skills, and abilities that aren't directly related to their job description, but are still useful to an organization. Utilizing a team member's talents in areas other than their current position will indicate to an employee that management appreciates and recognizes all that an employee has to offer to the organization. This can also provide work variety and helps to break up the everyday grind of work.

Job Redundancy. The job scenario today is a paradox. On one hand you have a surplus of jobs but on the other hand, executives are biting their nails due to the fear of job redundancy. Job redundancy is typical situation which arises in corporations, where a particular job is no longer relevant to the enterprise. Sometimes jobs are made redundant when there is no need for a specialized skill/delineation of role or when the organization's needs—because of growth or downsizing—requires a less/more qualified person. A lot of activities, today, are occurring around mergers and acquisitions (M&As) resulting in job redundancy. The organization cannot dump such employees and leave them to fend for themselves. Typically people below 40 are more open to change and hence redundancies do not hit them hard. Employers are also willing to retain younger employees who are eager to learn and have the right attitude in the person. However, employees in the later age bracket are the worst affected. A person's job gets redundant, not because she/he is incompetent; it is just because the organization could not offer a role befitting his specific skill sets or it failed to foresee such contingencies. This creates job insecurity leading to avoidable turnovers. The organizations have to plan ahead and equip persons likely to be affected with required skills or arrange their lateral absorption.

Sense of Belonging. Leaders/Managers must develop a sense of belonging to the organization among their employees. A corporation's vision must be inspirational and shared with all employees. When employees help to define the corporate vision and the corporate goals, employees feel more connected to the corporation and more committed to their work. Harley-Davidson inc. has employees so connected to its purpose that many employees have the company name tattooed on their bodies. Employees are energized by the sense that they are somehow making a contribution. Empathising/Joining the employees in their moments of joy and sorrow create a deep sense of belonging to the organization.

Perception of Fair and Equitable Treatment. If you have a staff person who views his/her role as important and he/she brings ten years of experience, an M.B.A. and a great contribution record to the table, but he/she finds he/she is making less money than another employee, just a year or two out of the college, his/her morale and motivation will take a big hit. He/She is likely to look for a new job. Did the staff person deserve the raises? Yes. But, recognize that there will be impact on others. There should be no double standards with regards to application of rules/regulations, rewards and disciplinary norms.

Analyse an Employee's Failure. Most frequently, if the employee's failure is analysed, the answer lies in time, tools, training, temperament or talent. The easiest to solve, and the ones most affecting employee retention, are tools, time and training. The employee must have the tools, time and training necessary to do their job well—or they will move to an employer who provides them.

Never Threaten a Team Member's Job or Income. While threatening an employee with termination or demotion might seem like a surefire way to get the results needed from him or her, doing so is likely to make the employee to leave the organization. Put yourself in the employee's shoes, what is the first thing you would do if your job was threatened? Odds are that you would probably update your resume and start checking for open job postings expecting the worst. If a team member's performance is not what you had hoped it would be, it is better to work with that team member on ways to improve his performance, saving termination only as a last resort.

Intervention. Effective management within a corporation must be able to identify potential retention issues before they arise and address issues with employees before they give their resignation notices. Signs will be evident when employees are beginning to evaluate other opportunities and look outside their current opportunity. Employees may begin to withdraw from others and reduce participation with team members and fellow employees both inside and outside the work activities. Productivity may begin to decrease and work hours may begin to fluctuate or suffer due to increased discontentment. By paying close attention and approaching dissatisfied employees prior to announcements of departure, managers may be able to retain more employees. Sometimes a simple effort by the manager and some quality listening time may be all that is required to relieve the frustration of the employee and to convince him/her to remain with the organization.

Flexitime. The main objective of the flextime policy is to provide opportunity to employees to work with flexible work schedules and set out conditions for availing this provision. Flexible work schedules are initiated by employees and approved by management to meet business commitments while supporting employee personal life needs. The factors on which Flexitime is allowed to an employee include: Child or Parent care, Health situation, Maternity, Formal education program and so on.

Telecommuting. Companies like Gandalf Technolgies inc., a computer networking company in California, are allowing employees to spend several days each week telecommuting. Employees are finding that they are spending more quality time with their families and working longer hours than they were previously. Thus, employers are left with happier, more productive employees. By allowing employees to be flexible and acknowledging the technological advances available, employers can retain employees who may have otherwise looked for positions closer to their homes or families.

Welfare Measures. Apart from the legal and mandatory benefits such as provident-fund and gratuity, the organizations may offer other welfare measures for employee benefit such as personal accident insurance, medi-claim, subsidized food and transportation, company leased accommodation, recreation, cafeteria, corporate credit card, cellular phone, soft loans and scholarships for meritorious children of employees. Organizations which offer such employee benefits are unlikely to have problem of retention of their employees.

Balance Work and Personal Life. Family is incredibly important to team members. When work begins to put a significant strain on one's family, no amount of money will keep an employee around. Stress the importance of balancing work and one's personal life. Small gestures such as allowing a team member to take an extended lunch break once a week to watch his son's baseball game is likely to be repaid with loyalty and extended employment with an organization.

Entrepreneurial Attitude. Minimal layers of bureaucracy and a free flow of information between employees who need to communicate in order to effectively complete their jobs are required in today's new business model. Employees need to be free to make quick decisions and to be accountable for them. Top performers typically want to get out there and try things as quickly as possible when they see the potential for great gains. The mindset must be there for employees to gather information, generate a hypothesis, test it quickly, gather feedback, and start all over again. The let us try it entrepreneurial attitude must prevail and companies must encourage employees to act on their own when they feel that they can make a difference and contribute to the company's bottom line. If employees are not able to get out there and try things and act as entrepreneurs within the corporation, they may end up on their own as entrepreneurs competing for the same customers and same markets.

Regular Get Together and Other Cultural Programs. The companies organize cultural programs as and when possible in which all the employees are given an opportunity to display their talents in dramatics, singing, acting, dancing, etc. Apart from that, the organizations also conduct various sports programs such as cricket, football, etc. and regularly play matches with the teams of other organizations. This helps in strengthening bonds of employees with the organization.

Birthdays/Anniversaries. It is a nice feeling to be greeted on birthdays/anniversaries. Employee may be presented bouquet or given a gift voucher based on their level in the organization. Such small gestures go a long way in building bonds among employees.

Sabbatical Programs. Some companies are introducing sabbatical programs in order to recruit and retain top employees. The program improves employee morale, increases their loyalty to the company and, in turn, probably makes better workers. Xerox's sabbatical program allows several employees each year to take paid leave of absence to work for charitable organizations. The belief by Xerox is that, while the bottom line impact to the company is not measurable, the benefit to the company comes in the ability to attract and retain top people and the new skills that the employees bring back to the organization after a sabbatical.

Wellness and Fitness Centers. By keeping their employees fit and providing means of achieving personal wellness goals, companies are finding that employees are more satisfied and more productive and perhaps less likely to defect. American Bankers has a fully equipped gym which the employees are encouraged to use before/after work and during lunch. Northern Telecom also found the benefits of a fitness center when a survey of employees indicated that 91 per cent felt the facility would reduce stress and increase the quality of work time (Dutton, The Re-Enchantment of Work). DOW Chemical offers a fitness center at its corporate headquarters and offers subsidized membership to a local fitness club at its Freeport facility. All these wellness and fitness facilities cost the corporations money, but the benefits of employee satisfaction, commitment, and retention outweigh the expenses.

Household Chore Assistance. Many corporations are beginning to offer household chore assistance such as laundry services and handyman services. Solutions to employee household problems and challenges that could decrease employee productivity are typically minimal in cost to the employer, yet provide incredible benefits through increased productivity and increased employee satisfaction. Productivity stays high when people do not have to worry about the little things in life. Wilton Connor Packaging Inc. and Andersen Consulting are companies offering such household chore assistance.

Child Assistance. Understand employee child-care needs and provide such things as sponsored public schools, on-site day care, or child care subsidies. Companies such as American Bankers Insurance Group and Hewlett Packard have schools on site that meet the educational requirements of the local school district. At American Bankers, parents are encouraged to visit children at lunchtime and after school and the company has seen employee turnover drop from 13 per cent, on average to 5 per cent for employees with children in the school (Dolan). When employees are satisfied with the care and education of their children, they are less likely to move elsewhere where child assistance may not be equivalent.

Corporate Culture. Corporations such as Ernst & Young have come to the realization that keeping good employees is key to business success and are making retention a part of their corporate culture. Ernst & Young has created an office for retention to evaluate retention strategies and to assist in the customization and individualization of policies and strategies in order to retain the best employees. Companies should believe in reciprocal investment where employers invest in the professional and personal development of employees with the intent that employees will invest their energy and abilities within the company. The companies have to adopt the attitude of "We Care" for the employees and their family. NIIT is a good example of this which has schemes like contributing a sum as investments for the new born. Corporate culture is so important to employee retention, that companies are even joining together to share notes on effective programs. For example, in 1995 twenty-six firms including Marriott and Conagra formed a consortium in New York called the Employer Group to provide a forum for personnel managers to compare notes on affordable programs for worker recruitment, retention, and reliability. These companies are committed to learning from each other and modifying their culture in order to retain top employees and provide employees with greater opportunities.

Conclusion

Take a look at your organization. Are you doing your best to retain your top talent? Employ the factors discussed in the paper in your organization to retain your desired employees and attract the best talent. Off course, there is no end to ingenuity and innovation on the part of HR Managers to create conducive organizational culture in tune with specific needs of the industry and the workforce. The final tip on retention list is that your staff members must feel rewarded, recognized and appreciated. Frequently saying Thank You goes a long way. Monetary rewards, bonuses and gifts make the Thank You even more appreciated. Understandable raises, tied to accomplishments and achievement, help retain staff. Commissions and bonuses that are easily calculated on a daily basis, and easily understood, raise motivation and help retain staff. You can bet that work is about the money and almost every individual wants more. Besides the money, it is the positive organizational culture which attracts and binds the employees to an organization and propels them to give their best for making it "A Successful Organization with the Competitive Edge".

Talent Acquisition from Indian B-Schools: Role of Employer Brand Image and Word-of-Mouth Endorsements*

18

Rakesh Kr. Agrawal and *Pragati Swaroop*

INTRODUCTION

India Inc., riding on a booming economy with high annual growth rate of nearly ten per cent, is suddenly grappling with the problem of finding the right talent to sustain the momentum in a competitive environment. This talent crunch is not confined to the top only, but spills over to the bottom of the pyramid (*The Economic Times*, 2006). The National Association of Software and Service Companies has estimated that by 2010, India could face a shortfall of 500,000 IT professionals alone which could seriously threaten India's position as a leading provider of IT and ITES services. And the crisis is not limited to the IT sector alone; the talent crunch haunts even the financial, manufacturing and marketing areas (*Business Week*, 2005; *The Telegraph*, 2007). Many Indian companies have in fact, started recruiting personnel from other countries to meet their needs of skilled manpower.

As the demand for skills continues to rise, the competition for available workers will intensify. Given the war for talent (Michael *et al.,* 2001; Woodruffe, 1999), organizations that are able to attract larger pools of quality applicants from a limited talent pool can be more selective in their hiring decisions and increase the effectiveness of their staffing systems (Boudreau & Rynes, 1985; Murphy, 1986). Since talented people can be an

*The authors would like to acknowledge the assistance provided by Mr. Michael Joseph, a former part-time student at Institute of Management Technology, for his help in collecting the data.

important source of competitive advantage over rivals, studies of issues that can influence applicant attraction to a firm become very important both for the practicing manager and the academic researcher.

University students are a major source of hiring for skilled jobs such as managers, professionals and technical workers (Rynes *et al.,* 1997). Although a costly process (Stevens, 1997; Rynes and Boudreau, 1986), campus hiring is strategically important for organizations as university students have been found to be more eager to learn and are more easily socialized into an organization's norms and culture as compared to traditional hires (Loughlin and Barling, 2001; Van Vianen, 2000), in addition to being technologically savvy (Burke and Ng, 2006). In a stiff and fiercely competitive recruiting environment, recruiters need to understand how different organizational actions and social networks affect career choices of students and hence the outcomes of the recruitment process during its various phases. The first phase of the recruitment process is the period when the firm uses an array of different practices to attract individuals to the organization (Barber, 1998). An organization's success is important in this first stage of recruitment because the effectiveness of later stages will rest upon the outcomes of this first stage. A decision not to apply for an opening is tantamount to a rejection decision.

While some studies have investigated early recruitment practices and their outcomes (Collins and Stevens, 2002; Collins & Han, 2004; Taylor and Bergmann, 1987), their models have not investigated the role of employer brand image and word-of-mouth endorsements (and hence, role of social networks) in the job-seeking behavior of prospective managers, especially in the Indian context. Specifically, the purpose of this paper in three fold: (i) to investigating factors during the first phase of recruitment that affect the application intentions of students in business schools; (ii) to investigate the role of employer brand image in the application intentions; and (iii) to investigate the role of word-of-mouth endorsements in the relationships between early recruitment practices, employer brand image and students' application intentions in Indian business schools.

The paper is organized as follows. First, we draw on theory and findings from previous literature to identify early recruitment strategies and to develop hypothesis regarding how these strategies may affect individual intentions to apply. We then identify the dimensions of employer brand equity and frame hypothesis how these dimensions may affect application intentions. We also develop a hypothesis on the role of word-of-mouth endorsements. Then we test our hypothesis with data collected from five premier business schools spread across India. These graduates are in very high demand and many students get multiple offers during the placement process. Finally we discuss the findings and the various implications and limitations of the study.

THEORETICAL BACKGROUND AND HYPOTHESES

Literature suggests that job seekers develop and rely on a number of different beliefs when making application decisions (Barber, 1998; Rynes, 1991). According to Cable and Turban (2001), applicants broadly evaluate a firm based on the physical attributes of the employer, job attributes and people information. Because applicants often do not have complete information about a firm, these categories of organizational information provide insights about the firm (Ng and Burke, 2006). It is critical for recruiters to understand how to systematically influence these beliefs through different recruitment activities meant to enhance the knowledge about the employer and the employer image (Collins, 2007). Different recruitment strategies may be more or less successful depending on the extent to which job seekers have already developed employer knowledge through exposure to the company's products, services, and advertising (Rynes and Cable, 2003).

Early Recruitment Practices

During the first phase of the recruitment process, a firm uses an array of different practices to attract talented individuals to apply to the organization (Barber, 1998). Some of these recruitment practices are designed to require few searches and processing on the part of job seekers, but others require a greater degree of search and processing (Cable and Turban,

2001). Low-involvement recruitment practices provide general positive cues and signals regarding the company as an employer and communicate positive images that can be processed incidentally or subconsciously (Collins and Han, 2004). Such practices include general recruitment advertisements such as banner ads on websites and recruitment posters, and sponsorship. On the other hand, high-involvement recruitment practices contain detailed specifications and arguments regarding the job and company and require a greater degree of search and processing (Collins and Han, 2004) and affect individuals by creating positive affect toward the company and by signaling the presence of important attributes (Collins, 2007). For example, companies communicate positive details about salary, growth opportunities, company culture, etc. through detailed recruitment ads (e.g., recruitment brochures) and employee endorsements (e.g. company executives, university alumni).

Marketing literature suggest that mere exposure to a company can increase consumers' attraction to its products (Mitchell & Olson, 1981). Collins and Stevens (2002) found that publicity—defined as information about a product or service communicated through editorial media that are not paid for by the organization (Cameron, 1994)—affected job seekers application intentions through their general attitudes toward the company. Barber (1998) suggested that media publicity about firm may have spillover effects on their recruitment efforts.

Organizations can also use sponsorships to influence job seekers which fosters positive affect among individuals who attend sponsored events or become aware of the sponsorship (Johar & Pham, 1999). Many organizations in India give scholarships to needy and/or meritorious students, sponsor events during college festivals and intercollegiate sports meets and encourage students of professional courses to take up short-term live projects. Such sponsorship on the part of industry helps to create positive signals without requiring active search on the part of job seekers (Poe, 2000).

In addition, organizations can also undertake activities like research grants for faculty, building relationships with the faculty and staff, sending alumni for recruitment and other industry-institute activities like seminars by industry experts, jointly organizing conferences, etc. to create positive beliefs in the minds of students and attract them to apply for possible job offers (May, 1998). Collins and Stevens (2002) have found a positive relationship between such relationship building activities (which they have termed word-of-mouth endorsements) and intentions to apply. Our discussions with the campus recruiters also indicated that it was an important strategy for organizations and the recruiters intended to created positive attractions in the minds of students through such activities.

Based on the above discussions, we hypothesize that early recruitment practices would be positively related to students' intentions to apply.

Hypothesis 1: Early recruitment practices will be positively related to students' intentions to apply.

Employer Brand Image

Brand equity has been defined as the marketing effects uniquely attributable to the brand—e.g. when certain outcomes result from the marketing of a product or service because of its brand name that would not occur if the same product or service did not have that name (Keller, 1993, p. 1). Brand-equity literature suggest that brands are important to consumers because (a) brand names offer signals that consumers use to make inferences about the attributes of the product, and (b) consumers endeavour to associate themselves with certain brands to improve their self-esteem (Cable and Turban, 2003). Strong brands can generate a competitive advantage for organizations because they initiate consumer purchase decision, they improve the efficiency of marketing programs, and they allow firms to charge more for their products (Aaker, 1996; Keller, 1993; Cable and Turban, 2003).

Brand equity concept can be generalized to recruitment contexts in which job seekers confront issues similar to those faced by consumers (Backhaus and Tikoo, 2004; Cable and Turban, 2003). As consumers do with products and services, job seekers form beliefs about potential employers; these beliefs provide the basis for decisions about whether to pursue or accept employment offers (Barber, 1998; Rynes, 1991). If such beliefs, called employer brand image, are similar in structure and impact to produce brand images, then recruitment researchers can gain insights by examining analogous dimensions of these beliefs and the marketing activities known to affect those dimensions (Collins and Stevens, 2002).

Drawing upon the accepted models of associative memory in marketing research (Anderson, 1983; Wyer and Srull, 1989) to understand the key dimensions of brand image, Collins and Stevens (2002) have conceptualized that information and memory of a product brand (and presumably an employer brand) has two key dimensions: the awareness of the brand/employer, and the associated feelings and knowledge of the brand/employer (Keller, 1993). In our study, the respondents evaluated only the firms they were aware of employers or potential employers, and focused our investigation in the associated feelings and knowledge about the brand.

Two aspects of brand image are important: (a) attitudes, or general affective responses associated with the brand (Wilke, 1986), and (b) perceived attributes, or beliefs about the brand's specific features that are relevant to the purchase decision (Keller, 1993). As in Collins and Stevens (2002), we define employer brand image as potential applicant's attitudes and perceived attributes about the job or organization.

Inexperienced consumers find it difficult to cognitively compare available products or services on key attributes (Aaker, 1996; Cobb-Walgren *et al.*, 1995). The impact of branding is likely to be greatest among such consumers who then use their perceptions of brand image to evaluate brands against their needs (Aaker, 1991; Keller, 1993). Drawing parallels with the recruitment literature, the student job seekers in campus face similar situations. Many of the students do not have any prior work experiences, while others have a few years of exposure to work. For inexperienced job seekers, it is difficult to compare the available options on the basis of true attributes of the job and company, and many attributes may not be known to them. They may rely on employer brand image for guidance in decision-making. Cable and Turban (2003) found that job seekers' reputation perceptions affected job pursuits because reputation was used as a signal about job attributes and affected what they expected from organizational membership. Based on the above arguments, we hypothesize that brand equity would be positively related to application intentions, and would mediate the relationship between early recruitment practices and application intentions of student job seekers:

Hypothesis 2: Dimensions of employer brand image (i.e. attitudes and perceived job attributes) would be positively related to the student job-seekers application intentions.

Hypothesis 3: The relationship between early recruitment practices and application intentions would be mediated by employer brand image (i.e. attitudes and perceived job attributes).

Word-of-Mouth Endorsements

According to Defillippi and Arthur (1994), 'know-whom' competencies aid careers and capitalize on 'social capital' (Burt, 1992) that include contacts drawn from personal experiences with family, friends, colleagues, fellow alumni and teachers and mentors. Studies have examined these types of relationships within the context of boundaryless career concept. Social networks have been found to support high rates of job mobility, career advancement and learning [Burt, 1997; Saxenian, 1996; Jones, 1996 (quoted in Sullivan, 1999)]. Extending the results to students-managers' job seeking behaviors, one can hypothesize that their application intentions through the campus placement process will also be influenced by social networks. The organization one intends to join can have significant implications for later career moves. The beginning stage (getting access to industry or profession) can affect the later stages of career development. Being unsure, the student-managers may like to rely on information and endorsements about a company's employment brand from others in their network. Kilduff (1990) has found that graduating MBA students showed strong preferences for organizations that were most preferred by their peers. Thus many job applicants gather information and form their opinion about organizational values and job attributes through informal social networks of individuals who are not affiliated with the company, such as friends, family and professors (Cable *et al.*, 2000). Information collected from word-of-mouth sources is likely to be salient and credible to applicants because it is communicated by a friend or an expert (Fisher *et al.*, 1979; Popovich and Wanous, 1982).

Helm and Schlei (1998) have referred to 'word-of-mouth' to describe verbal communications (either positive or negative) between groups such as the product provider, independent experts, family and friends and the actual or potential consumer. Arndt (1967) has described word-of-mouth advertising as "oral, person-to-person communication between a perceived non-commercial communicator and a receiver concerning a brand, a product or a service offered for sale" and describes informal conversation as probably the oldest mechanism by which opinions on products and brands are developed, expressed and spread. Given that word-of-mouth is a highly informal style of communication, managing the process is quite difficult simply because the communicator is not within an organization's direct sphere of influence (Ennew *et al.*, 2000). Yet, within the recruitment context, the early recruitment activities can be used to positively impact word-of-mouth endorsements, both within and outside the campuses. Advertisements in newspapers and magazines can be viewed not only by the student job seekers but also their family and friends. Sponsorship and relationship building activities within campuses can create positive affect not only amongst the possible applicants but also faculty and peers. Thus social networks and word-of-mouth advertisements can affect the student job-seekers' perceptions of employer brand and thus their application intentions.

Thus, we hypothesize that word-of-mouth endorsements will mediate the relationship between early recruitment practices and employer brand image.

Hypothesis 4: The relationships between early recruitment activities and employer brand image will be mediated by word-of-mouth endorsements.

The proposed model is shown in Figure 18.1

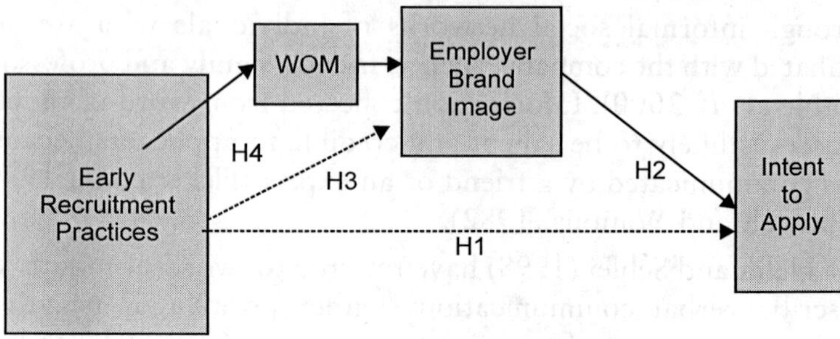

Fig. 18.1: Proposed Theoretical Model

Methods

The data was collected in the first half of 2007 from 130 students of five premier schools in India, randomly chosen (one each) from the northern, southern, eastern, western and central parts of India. These schools have consistently ranked amongst the top business schools in India in different surveys. Our study was confined to respondents from business schools due to our own interest in management education and human resource issues.

The students were contacted through emails and requested to mark their responses in the questionnaire attached as an MS word file. The marked questionnaires were returned through emails. Only 73 students responded to our initial request. A second reminder was sent after a week. The final sample consisted of 130 students. Five of the returned responses were incomplete and were not considered in the final analysis. We also checked for outliers in the remaining 125 response sets. One of the respondents (case no. 30) had standardized score beyond ±4 on age, experience and a number of other items. This case was also not considered in the final analysis. Thus the final sample consisted of 124 respondents.

Only the students in the first year of their business education were selected as the target respondents, as they would be applying for placements in the coming year. Males comprised of about 85 per cent (n = 106) in the final sample, while females formed the remaining 145 (females = 18). 26.7 per cent of the respondents (24 males and 9 females) had no prior work experience. Table 18.1 shows the mean age and work experience of the sample. Overall, the mean age of the respondents was approximately 24 years and the average work experience about 1.5 years. While the study is not necessarily 100 per cent representative of student population of the business schools in India, it nevertheless furnishes a data set on which reasonable conclusions about the influences of early recruitment practices on students' intentions to apply can be made.

Table 18.1: Mean Age and Work Experience and Genderwise Distribution of Respondents

Gender	Age (yrs)	Work Experience (yrs)
Male (106)	24.02 (1.51)	1.51 (1.16)
Female (18)	23.06 (1.16)	0.96 (1.13)
Total (124)	23.88 (1.50)	1.43 (1.17)

Note: Figures in brackets are the standard deviations

Measures

The most widely accepted conceptualizations of memory structure involve some type of associative model formulation (Anderson, 1983; Wyer and Srull, 1989; Keller, 1993). The associative network memory model views semantic memory or knowledge as consisting of a set of nodes and links. A spreading activation process from node to node determines the extent of retrieval in memory (Keller, 1993). Consistent with the models of associative memory, the respondents were asked to think about a real world (not hypothetical) organization X, Y or Z as follows: they were supposed to think about an organization which was likely to visit their campuses for placement purposes during the next placement season (organization 'X'); if they could not recall such an organization, they could had to think about an organization which had visited their campus during the last placement season (organization 'Y'); else, if they could not recall such an organization, they were simply asked to think about an organization which they would like to come to their campuses for placements in the coming year (organization 'Z'). It was not necessary for the respondents to name the organization. All the subsequent questions in the questionnaire had to be answered with respect to this organization. This approach helped us to control for awareness of the brand/employer

(Collins and Stevens, 2002). In our study, 53.2% (66) had opted for 'X', 32.3% (40) for 'Y' and 14.5% (18) for 'Z'.

Independent Variables

Early Recruitment Practices: Prior research in the field of recruitment (e.g. Taylor and Bergmann, 1987) has identified a number of early recruitment practices that could be used to attract talent to organizations. We identified the measures for early recruitment practices through a survey of existing literature and through personal interviews with recruiters and students. We adapted a number of items from Collins and Stevens (2002) and Collins and Hans (2004) (e.g. items on sponsorship). We also generated some items, based on the feedback received in our interviews with the recruiters and student job seekers, to include those practices that had not been identified but were relevant in the current context (e.g. visits of company executives to campuses as guest speakers). Finally, a total of 15 items were written to tap the relevant activities. The student respondents were asked to rate each item on a scale ranging from 1 (strongly disagree) to 5 (strongly agree).

A principal components analysis with varimax rotation was performed on the students' responses in order to reduce the data to a distinct set of predictors and distinctly identify the early recruitment practices. This yielded five components when the eigenvalue criteria (eigenvalue >1) was adopted to retain the factors. An item was included in a component if (a) its highest loading was 0.40 or greater on a component and (b) its second highest loading was at least 0.20 less than the highest. The five components together accounted for 70.68% of variance in the data. Bartlett's test of sphericity (approx. Chi-square = 687.867, df = 105, $p<0.01$) rejects the null hypothesis that the population correlation matrix is an identity matrix. The value of KMO statistic is also large (>0.5), and equal to 0.713, indicating that the principal component analysis is appropriate.

The results of the principal component analysis are shown in Table 18.2. The components are assigned names considering the list of items under each factor and the respective loadings of the items. Thus the various dimensions of job attributes

Table 18.2: Results of Principal Components Analysis for Early Recruitment Practices

Factors & Items	Loading	Rotated Eigenvalue	% of Variance	Alpha Coeff.
Factor 1—Sponsorships		2.525	16.832	0.789
This organization has sponsored events (sports, cultural, etc.) on my campus.	0.868			
This organization has sponsored scholarships at my university.	0.837			
This organization has organized tours (e.g. adventure tours) for students of our campus.	0.759			
I have worked on projects (excluding summer projects) sponsored by this organization.	0.613			
Factor 2—Media Presence/Publicity		2.133	14.219	0.782
Top officials from this organization (e.g., its CEO) are often quoted in newspaper and business magazines.	0.910			
I have read or listened to news stories about this organization.	0.879			
I have noted in the media that this organization sponsors important business events and seminars.	0.590			
Factor 3—Corporate-Institute Relation Building		2.133	14.217	0.728
Alumni of this university work in this organization and come to the campus for relation building and placement purposes.	0.807			
This organization has a good relationship with the placement office.	0.805			
I have listened to executives from this organization who have visited our B-school as guest speakers.	0.769			
Factor 4—Detailed Recruitment Ads		2.013	13.419	0.876
I have seen recruitment advertisements of this organization in business magazines.	0.867			
I have seen eye-catching recruitment advertisements of this organization in newspapers.	0.860			
Factor 5—General Recruitment Ads		1.799	11.991	0.652
I have seen display advertisements on websites for job opportunities about this company.	0.847			
This organization's recruitment brochures caught my attention.	0.697			
I have seen recruitment posters on our placement office/hostel notice boards.	0.560			

emerging from the analysis can be labeled as Sponsorships, Media Presence/Publicity, Corporate-Institute Relation Building, Detailed Recruitment Ads and General Recruitment Ads. Reliability analysis indicated reasonable item convergence for all the components: Sponsorships (α = 0.789), Media Presence/ Publicity (a = 0.782), Corporate-Institute Relation Building (α = 0.728), Detailed Recruitment Ads (α = 0.876) and General Recruitment Ads (α = 0.652).

Dependent Variable

Application Intentions: Student application intentions was the dependent variable in our study. To reasonable capture this variable, we adapted one item—"I intend to apply for a position with this organization"—from Taylor and Bergman (1987) [quoted in Collins and Stevens, 2002] and generated two more items through interviews and discussions with recruiters. All the items were measured on a five point scale (1 = strongly disagree, 5 = strongly agree). The a reliability of the scale was found to be 0.766.

Mediating Variables

Employer Brand Image: As mentioned earlier, employer brand awareness was controlled for, while associated feelings and knowledge about the employer was measured along two dimensions:

(a) *Attitudes:* The attitude dimension of employer brand image was measured through three items on a scale of 1 (strongly disagree) to 5 (strongly agree). One item was adapted from the scale used by Harris and Fink (1987) [quoted in Collins and Stevens, 2002]. The other two items were generated through the process mentioned. Reliability estimates yielded a Cronbach a score of 0.848.

(b) *Perceived job attributes:* Prior research (e.g. Ng and Burke, 2006; Harris and Fink, 1987; Powell, 1991) have identified a large number of job attributes that influence the applicant's decision-making process. As job seekers are unlikely to have knowledge of many attributes prior to their applications, after an initial survey of available literature, we conversed with student job seekers, recruiters and placement service officers to identify 13 items about which potential applicants might have some rudimentary knowledge. These 13 items related to salary and compensation, nature of work and organization, growth prospects, etc. Some of these items (e.g. job security) are similar to those identified by Harris and Fink (1987); others have been modified (e.g. good salary and compensation, comparable with the best internationally) or added (e.g. strategic responsibilities early in one's career). The respondents were asked to rate on a scale of 1 to 5 as to how likely it was (1 = very unlikely; 5 = very likely) that the organization they had identified possessed the attribute in question.

The 13 items were subjected to principal components analysis with varimax rotation. This yielded four components having eigenvalues greater than 1, which together account for 65.97 per cent of variance in the data. Bartlett's test of sphericity (approx. Chi-square = 543.463, df = 78, $p<0.01$) rejects the null hypothesis that the population correlation matrix is an identity matrix. The value of KMO statistic is also large (>0.5), and equal to 0.754, indicating that the principal component analysis is appropriate.

The results of the principal component analysis, the respective items under each component, and the item loadings are shown in Table 18.3. The components were named considering the list of items under each factor and the respective loadings of the items. Thus the various dimensions of job attributes emerging from the analysis can be labeled as Nature of Assignments ($\alpha = 0.797$), Growth Prospects ($\alpha = 0.733$), Compensation ($\alpha = 0.678$), and Social and Cultural Factors ($\alpha = 0.648$).

Word-of-mouth endorsements: We generated four items for word-of-mouth endorsements which captured the endorsements of relatives and family friends, peers, faculty and friends in other B-schools. For example, one of the items was 'Many of my peers in my B-school think that this would be a great organization to work for'. The responses were taken on a five

Table 18.3: Results of Principal Components Analysis for Perceived Job Attributes

Factors & Items 0	Loading	Eigenvalue	% of Variance	Alpha Coeff.
Factor 1—Nature of Assignments		2.399	18.455	0.797
50. Challenging assignments	0.887			
49. Interesting work	0.840			
51. Strategic responsibilities early in one's career	0.642			
Factor 2—Growth Prospects		2.125	16.346	0.733
42. Career growth prospects	0.855			
41. Rapid advancement opportunities	0.768			
43. Opportunity to learn new skills	0.648			
Factor 3—Compensation		2.101	16.162	0.678
37. Good salary and compensation, comparable with the best internationally	0.871			
38. Good salary and compensation, comparable with the best nationally	0.802			
40. Location in advanced countries	0.636			
Factor 4—Social and Cultural Factors		1.950	15.000	0.648
53. Job security	0.724			
55. Appropriate sized company	0.706			
54. Sociable co-workers	0.638			
45. Good corporate culture	0.505			

point scale (1 = strongly disagree, 5 = strongly agree). The scale had an a reliability of 0.807.

Control Variables

Five control variables were included during the analysis to control for differences in gender, age, work experience of respondents and the organization choice (X, Y, Z). Thus the control variables are gender (male = 0, female = 1), age (in years) and work experience (in years). Organization choice was accounted for through two dummy variables (X = 0, Y = 1, Z =0 and X = 0, Y = 0 and Z = 1).

RESULTS

Table 18.4 shows the means, standard deviations, and correlations among the variables of interest. Some of the early

Table 18.4: Means, SDs, Alphas & Intercorrelations of Study Variables (N = 124)

	Mean	S.D.	1	2	3	4	5	6	7	8	9	10	11	12	13	14	15
Control Variables																	
1. Gender#	0.15	0.354															
2. Age (yrs)	23.88	1.501	-.227(**)														
3. Work Experience##	0.73	0.444	-.218(**)	.562(**)													
Independent Variables																	
4. Sponsorships	1.46	0.736	0.116	0.134	0.054	(0.789)											
5. Media Presence/ Publicity	3.60	0.952	0.140	0.048	-0.039	0.089	(0.782)										
6. Relations with Institute	3.46	0.978	.165(*)	0.005	-0.076	0.111	.330(**)	(0.728)									
7. Detailed Recruitment Ads	2.44	1.134	0.022	0.113	-0.032	.334(**)	.350(**)	.233(**)	(0.876)								
8. General Recruitment Ads	2.98	0.897	0.030	0.001	-0.090	.179(*)	.316(**)	.253(**)	.441(**)	(0.652)							
Mediating Variables																	
9. Nature of Assignments	4.23	0.663	0.112	0.042	0.015	-.256(**)	0.064	-0.029	-.253(**)	0.002	(0.797)						
10. Growth Prospects	4.23	0.593	.178(*)	-0.103	-0.120	-0.054	.348(**)	.247(**)	0.141	0.084	.392(**)	(0.733)					
11. Compensation	4.18	0.727	0.119	-0.054	-0.027	-0.137	0.114	-0.127	0.056	0.006	.259(**)	.274(**)	(0.678)				
12. Social & Cultural Factors	4.03	0.609	.236(**)	0.066	-0.040	-0.005	.461(**)	.253(**)	0.069	0.148	.402(**)	.423(**)	0.157	(0.648)			
13. Attitude	4.47	0.609	0.121	-0.142	-0.145	-0.110	.249(**)	0.085	-0.051	.166(*)	.506(**)	.464(**)	.240(**)	.472(**)	(0.848)		
14. Word-of-Mouth Endorsements	4.18	0.666	0.136	-0.096	-0.033	-0.138	.335(**)	.183(*)	-0.035	.220(**)	.363(**)	.292(**)	.290(**)	.422(**)	.564(**)	(0.772)	
Dependent Variable																	
15. Intent to Apply	4.65	0.616	-0.050	-0.146	-0.078	-.321(**)	.160(*)	0.033	-.161(*)	-0.022	.475(**)	.432(**)	.302(**)	.288(**)	.498(**)	.354(**)	(0.700)

** p < 0.01; * p< 0.05 # 0 = Male; 1 = Female; ## 0 = No; 1 = Yes

Alpha reliabilities are shown in parenthesis along the diagonal recruitment practices showed significant intercorrelations amongst themselves, with the absolute values ranging from 0.002 to 0.461. All the dimensions of employer brand image had positive significant correlations with application intentions as well as with word-of-mouth endorsements, the coefficient of correlation varying between 0.288 and 0.564. Three of the recruitment practices (media presence/publicity, relation building and general recruitment ads) were significantly correlated with word-of-mouth endorsements. However, there was no significant correlation of word-of-mouth endorsements with detailed recruitment ads or sponsorships. Intent to apply had negative and significant correlations with sponsorships ($r = 0.321$, $p < 0.01$) and detailed recruitment ads ($r = -0.161$, $p < 0.05$), while it had positive and significant correlation with media presence/publicity ($r = 0.160$, $p < 0.05$) and word-of-mouth endorsements ($r = 0.354$, $p < 0.01$).

Before testing the hypothesis, we checked for normality assumptions for the variables to be included in further analysis using both the graphical methods (histogram and normality plots) and rule of thumb (variable is reasonably close to normal if skewness and kurtosis lie between -1 and +1). Three of the variables were subjected to transformations to ensure that they satisfy tests of normality. Thus sponsorship was inverse transformed ($x \rightarrow 1/x$), perceived job attributes was subjected to reflection & logarithmic transformation ($x \rightarrow \log(6-x)$, while intent to apply was subjected to 'reflection + inverse' transformation [$y \rightarrow 1/(6-y)$].

We tested hypotheses 1 and 2 through hierarchical regression analyses. To test for hypotheses 3 and 4, we adopted a three step process as outlined by Baron and Kenny (1986) by estimating a series of regression models. First, we regressed the mediator (employer brand image/word-of-mouth endorsements) on the predictor variables (the different early recruitment practices); second, we regressed the dependent variable (intent to apply/employer brand image) on the predictors; and third, we regressed the dependent variable on both the predictors and the mediator. In each regression, we also included a dummy code for differences in the gender, measures for age and dummies for work experiences and organization choice to control for any differences on these variables amongst the student job seekers.

Table 18.5—18.8 show the results of the hierarchical regression analyses. Gender, age, work experience and dummy variables for organization thought about were entered as control variables in Model 1 (Tables 18.5 to 18.8). In Table 18.5, the results of regressing intent-to-apply on the early recruitment practices are shown, while Table 18.6 summarizes the results of regressing intent to apply on dimensions of employer brand image. In Table 18.7, regression results with perceived job attributes and attitude as dependent variables are shown, while in Table 18.8, word-of-mouth endorsements is treated as the dependent variable.

Table 18.5: Results of Hierarchical Regression Predicting Intent to Apply (Inv_reflect) [independent variables: early rectt. Practices] (N = 124)

Variable	Model 1 Beta	Model 2 Beta	Model 3 Beta
Gender	–.112	–.128	–.186
Age	–.208	–.181	–.175
Work Experience	.026	.023	.052
Org Dummy 1	.013	.025	–.021
Org Dummy 2	.040	.031	–.044
inv_Sponsorships		.131	.097
Media Presence/Publicity		.286**	.129
Corporate-Institute Relation Building		-.006	–.025
Detailed Recruitment Ads		-.163	–.095
General Recruitment Ads		.018	–.041
log_refl_Perceived Job Attributes			–.228**
Attitude			.295**
R^2	0.044	0.141	0.314
Adj. R^2	0.004	0.065	0.239
ΔR^2	0.044	0.097	0.172
ΔF	1.088	2.559*	13.924**
Durbin-Watson		1.840	

*p<0.05; **p<0.01

Table 18.6: Results of Hierarchical Regression Predicting Intent to Apply (Inv_reflect) [independent variables: Employer Brand Image] (N = 124)

Variable	Model 1 Beta	Model 2 Beta
Gender	–.112	–.199
Age	–.208	–.204
Work Experience	.026	.066
Org Dummy 1	.013	–.035
Org Dummy 2	.040	–.022
log_refl_Perceived Job Attributes		–.269**
Attitude		.302**
R^2	0.044	0.283
Adj. R^2	0.004	0.239
ΔR^2	0.044	0.238
ΔF	1.088	19.276**
Durbin-Watson	1.875	

*p<0.05; **p<0.01

Table 18.7: Results of Hierarchical Regression Predicting Dimensions of Employer Brand Image (N = 124)

Dependent Variable	Perceived Job Attributes (log_refl)			Attitude		
Control & Predictor Variables	Model 1 Beta	Model 2 Beta	Model 3 Beta	Model 1 Beta	Model 2 Beta	Model 3 Beta
Gender	–.226	–.191	–.153	.085	.048	–.001
Age	–.052	–.048	–.075	–.059	–.058	–.023
Work Experience	.038	.021	.045	–.097	–.082	–.114
Org Dummy 1	–.138	–.147	–.175	.034	.043	.079
Org Dummy 2	–.110	–.140	–.093	.106	.145	.084
inv_Sponsorships		–.114	–.078		.026	–.020
Media Presence/Publicity		–.356**	–.231*		.254*	.092
Corporate-Institute Relation Building		–.022	.031		.048	–.020
Detailed Recruitment Ads		.050	–.032		–.193	–.087
General Recruitment Ads		–.028	.061		.178	.062
Word-of-Mouth Endorsements			–.399**			.517**
R^2	0.081	0.212	0.336	0.043	0.148	0.356
Adjusted R^2	0.042	0.142	0.270	0.003	0.073	0.292
ΔR^2	0.081	0.130	0.124	0.043	0.105	0.208
ΔF	2.091	3.739**	20.888**	1.070	2.777*	36.102**
Durbin-Watson		1.611			2.121	

*p<0.05; **p<0.01

Table 18.8: Results of Hierarchical Regression Predicting Word-of-Mouth Endorsements (N = 124)

Variable	Model 1 Beta	Model 2 Beta
Gender	.143	.094
Age	–.076	–.068
Work Experience	.038	.061
Org Dummy 1	–.087	–.070
Org Dummy 2	.039	.119
inv_Sponsorships		.088
Media Presence/Publicity		.313**
Corporate-Institute Relation Building		.131
Detailed Recruitment Ads		–.205*
General Recruitment Ads		.224*
R^2	0.035	0.223
Adjusted R^2	0.006	0.154
ΔR^2	0.035	0.188
ΔF	0.856	5.465**
Durbin-Watson	1.760	

*p<0.05; **p<0.01

Hypothesis 1: Early Recruitment Practices and Intentions to Apply

As shown in the results of the second regression equation (Table 18.5, Model 2), the combined direct effect of the early recruitment practices explained a significant amount of variance for application intentions ($\Delta R^2 = 0.097$, $p<0.05$).

In hypothesis 1, we predicted a positive relationship between various early recruitment practices and students' intentions to apply. As shown in Table 18.5 (Model 2), media presence/publicity was significantly related to intent to apply ($\beta = 0.286$, $p<0.01$). However, other early recruitment practices (sponsorships, relation building, detailed recruitment ads and general recruitment ads) are significantly related to intentions to apply. Thus we found partial support for hypothesis 1.

Hypothesis 2: Employer Brand Image and Intentions to Apply

In hypothesis 2, we predicted that the dimensions of brand equity, i.e. attitudes and perceived job attributes would each significantly affect the student job seekers intentions to apply. As shown in the results of the second regression equation (Model 2, Table 18.6), the combined direct effect of these predictors explained a significant amount of variance for application intentions ($\Delta R^2 = 0.238$, $p<0.01$).

Specifically, we found the 'attitude' dimension of employer brand equity to be significantly related to application intentions ($\beta = 0.302$, $p<0.01$). We also found perceived job attributes to be significantly related to intent to apply ($\beta = 0.269$, $p<0.01$). Thus hypothesis 2 is supported, and employer brand image (attitude and perceived job attributes) significantly predicts student-managers' intentions to apply during campus placements.

Hypothesis 3: Mediating Role of Employer Brand Image

In hypothesis 3, we predicted that dimensions of employer brand image, viz. attitudes and perceived job attributes would mediate the relationship between early recruitment practices and students' intentions to apply. As already explained we tested this hypothesis through a series of regression models. The results are shown in Table 18.7 (Model 2) and Table 18.5 (Models 2 & 3).

Table 18.7 (Model 2) shows that shows that 13 per cent of the variance in perceived job attributes is explained by the early recruitment activities combined ($\Delta R^2 = 0.130$, $p<0.01$) while 10.5 per cent of the variance in attitude about the organization is explained by the early recruitment activities combined ($\Delta R^2 = 0.105$, $p<0.01$). We also found significant positive relationships between media presence/publicity and perceived job attributes ($\beta = 0.356$, $p<0.01$), and between media presence/publicity and attitude ($\beta = 0.254$, $p<0.05$). However, the relationships of sponsorships, relation building, detailed recruitment ads and general recruitment ads with perceived job attributes and attitudes were not found significant ($p>0.05$).

In the second step, we established the relationship between intentions to apply and the early recruitment activities. As discussed in the findings for hypothesis 1, we found significant relationships between media presence/publicity and intent-to-apply.

In the third step, we found that perceived job attributes and attitudes were significantly related to students' intentions to apply. Model 3 (Table 5) shows the regression results of the analysis when the mediator variable is included along with the predictors ($\Delta R^2 = 0.172$, $p<0.01$). Both the dimensions of employer brand image were significantly related to intentions (b = 0.228, $p<0.01$ for perceived job attributes; $\beta = 0.295$, $p<0.01$ for attitude). We also found that the inclusion of the mediators reduced the significant effect of media presence/publicity ($\beta = 0.129$, $p>0.05$) in Model 3; $\beta = 0.286$, $p<0.01$ in Model 2). These results imply that the relationship between publicity and intentions to apply are mediated by employer brand image, thus supporting our mediation hypothesis for one of the early recruitment practices.

Hypothesis 4: Mediating Role of Word-of-Mouth Endorsements

As earlier, we first established the significant relationships between the independent variables and the mediator. Table 8 (Model 2) shows that 18.8 per cent of the variance in word-of-mouth endorsements in explained by the early recruitment activities combined ($\Delta R^2 = 0.188$, $p<0.01$). We also found significant relationships between three of the early recruitment practices, viz. media presence/publicity ($\beta = 0.313$, $p<0.01$), detailed recruitment ads ($\beta = -0.205$, $p<0.05$) and general recruitment advertisements ($\beta = 0.224$, $p<0.05$), and word-of-mouth endorsements.

In the second step, we established the relationship between the dimensions of employer brand image and the early recruitment activities. As discussed in the findings for Hypothesis 3, we found significant relationships between media presence/publicity and perceived job attributes and between media presence/publicity and attitude.

In the third step, we found that word-of-mouth endorsements were significantly related perceived job attributes and attitude. Model 3 (Table 18.7) shows the regression results of the analysis when the mediator variable is included along with the predictors ($\Delta R^2 = 0.124$, $p<0.01$ for perceived job attributes;

$\Delta R^2 = 0.208$, $p<0.01$ for attitude). We also found that the inclusion of the mediator reduced the significant effect of media presence/publicity (for perceived job attributes: $\beta = 0.231$, $p<0.05$ in Model 3; $\beta = 0.356$, $p<0.01$ in Model 2; for attitude: $\beta = 0.092$, $p>0.05$ in Model 3; $\beta = 0.254$, $p<0.05$ in Model 2). These results partially support our hypothesis and imply that the relationship between publicity and dimensions of employer brand image are mediated by word-of-mouth endorsements.

DISCUSSIONS

The purpose of this research was to study the effect of early recruitment-related activities on students' application intentions, and the mediating role of employer brand image and word-of-mouth endorsements in the relationship. We verified this empirically through data collected from students of five premier business schools in India. Our results indicate that the hypotheses we had framed are partially acceptable—only one of early recruitment practices (media presence/publicity) significantly and positively predicts the application intentions of business school students. The mediating roles of the dimensions of employer brand image—perceived job attributes and attitude—and word-of-mouth endorsements is also significant for 'publicity' dimension of the early recruitment practices, revealing the importance of social networks in the choice of organizations by the students. The resulting model is shown in Figure 18.2 below:

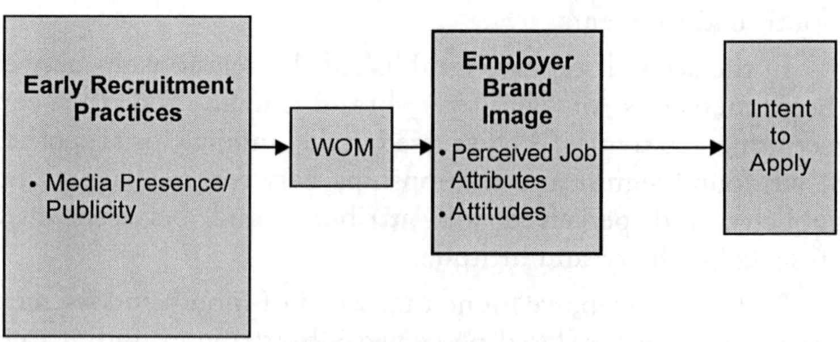

Fig. 18.2: Resulting Model

Our study contributes to the literature in several important ways. An intention to apply is the first part of any employment decision process and indicative of the occupational choices the student is likely to make during the initial part of his career goals. Any negative intention of the prospective candidate forecloses his employment prospects with the organization, thus also reducing the application pool for the recruiting organization. Our study examines this important first phase in the applicant's decision-making process in the Indian business school students, an area hardly researched in literature.

In addition, our study examines the role of different early recruitment practices in the students' intentions to apply for possible job offers. Earlier studies (Collins and Han, 2004; Collins and Stevens, 2002; Collins, 2007) have suggested that early recruitment practices affect students' intentions to apply and in increasing the applicant pool quantity and quality. Five factors emerged in our analysis, out of which only one was found to be significant in the Indian context.

Specifically, Collins and Stevens (2002) predicts that publicity, word-of-mouth endorsements (not used in the same sense as ours—we have termed this corporate institute relation building) and advertising affect intentions to apply, through the attitudes and attributes dimensions of employer brand equity. However, our study reveals that advertising (both general and detailed recruitment ads) does not affect students' intentions to apply, although it does predict word-of-mouth endorsements.

Secondly, corporate's relation building activities with the institute do not affect the students' intentions to apply. This result contradicts the results of Collins and Stevens (2002) wherein he surveyed 133 engineering students in the United States (*Note*: They used 'word-of-mouth endorsements' instead of 'relation building' to label an almost similar set of items). A perusal of the items of relation building (Table 18.2) will indicate that this includes such activities like maintaining good relationships with the placement office, sending alumni to their alma-maters, and giving invited lectures. This aspect of our result needs to be researched further for understanding the factors which could influence such contradictory results.

Another important finding of our research is the role of 'sponsorships' in affecting students' intentions to apply. Our study suggests that sponsoring student activities does not influence their application intentions either, nor does it appear to generate positive word-of-mouth endorsements. The results support the findings of Collins and Stevens (2002) who, in their study of engineering students, did not find any significant relationships between sponsorships and both application intentions and decisions. The items in the 'sponsorship' factor (Table 18.2) refer to sponsoring campus events, scholarships, projects and tours. It is doubtful whether organizations should spend money in college campuses to attract talented applicants. In this study, sponsorship is treated as a separate and distinct factor from relation building. Maybe sponsorship can be used for relation building and increasing awareness, but it does not seem to have an impact on attracting any talent. Collins and Stevens (2002) study suggests that it does not even have an impact on building the employer brand. Students working on sponsored projects may not be interested in working for or build up a part of their career through the sponsoring organization.

In addition, our study examines the role of employer brand equity in the applicants' intentions to apply for possible job offers. Earlier studies (Cable and Turban, 2001; Cable and Turban, 2003) have suggested that employer image and firms' reputation matter to job seekers because individuals use reputation as a signal about job attributes and reputation affects the pride that individuals expect from organizational membership. They are willing to pay a premium in the form of lower wages to join firms with positive reputations (Cable and Turban, 2003). In our study, it was found that attitudes towards employer significantly affected the application intentions of the students. This implied that a favorable impression of the company and high regards for the company (constituent items of 'attitudes' dimension of brand equity) are important predictors of students' intentions and thus job seeking behavior.

The positive and significant effect that publicity has on the job-seekers' application intentions confirms the results flowing from earlier studies (Barber, 1998; Collins and Stevens, 2002). However, our study additionally finds that publicity/media presence strongly predicts employer brand image and that word-of-mouth endorsements mediate the relationship between publicity/media presence and job attributes and attitude. We can conclude that the students intend to apply for employment in those organizations who have strong brand equity. The perception of the students about the employment brand is built upon strong media presence are influenced by recommendations from peers, friends, family and other well wishers. Indians are still influenced a lot by the opinions of family and friends, and our results are a pointer to this social phenomenon.

The findings are also a pointer to the fact that student job seekers relay heavily on personal networks for career choice decisions. They use their know—whom competencies to maximize their subjective return on investment in job search. The recruiters would also need to influence the social networks of the prospective applicants, perhaps using the organizational social capital apart from media publicity. Cameron (1994) suggests that although publicity is not under the direct control of the organizations, they can nevertheless influence the publicity they receive through press releases and public relations campaigns. Gaining insights from our results, corporate houses should strategize to make their presence felt in the media. The human resource departments of organizations should coordinate with the public relations offices (or public relations) and undertake strategic public relations exercises from time-to-time. Through such processes, they can create a favourable impression about the company in the minds of the friends, family and well wishers of the job-seekers and gain a competitive advantage over their rivals by attracting the best graduates of premier business schools.

Limitations

This study is not without its limitations. The sample has been taken from only five business schools in India, and we cannot claim the results to be completely generalizable. While the results can be said to be somewhat applicable to premier business schools in the country, they cannot be directly applied to a large number of other business schools. In addition, we have used the responses of only 124 students. Further studies with a larger sample size and in a larger number of schools would be required to come to any conclusive evidence. Thirdly, we have relied on the respondents' recall of a single employer instead of a number of possible employers through a within-subjects design. By asking job seekers to consider one form, the between-subjects approach may fail to capture the larger context in which multiple options are considered. In addition, the restrictions that may be placed by the campus placement cells (for example, a student who has already been offered a job through the placement process may not be allowed to participate further in the selection process of other companies) have not been considered. However, in spite of its limitations, the study gives valuable insights into the effects of early recruitment practices and employer brand image on the application intentions for campus placements in business schools. It also highlights the role of social networks on students who are at the starting points of their professional careers. The results can be used by prospective employers to improve their recruitment success rates.

CONCLUSION

Student at the beginning of their careers may not be sure of what companies they should join after their degree. They may rely on their well-wishers for guidance. This can influence the application decisions during placements, and organizations may find that the quality and quantity of applicant pool is below their expectations. In an environment where students are opting for alternate career paths and talent crunch haunts the different sectors of the Indian economy, it would be prudent for organizations to adopt strategies that can attract and retain the best talent from the campuses and derive the necessary competitive advantage. In this study, we have offered interesting and vital insights to employers to enable them to strategically focus on those recruitment activities that are effective. Our study suggests that employer brand equity can influence the application intentions of the student job seekers. It also concludes that media plays an important role in building up the employment brand equity thorough word-of-mouth endorsements by well-wishers. Organizations should work closely with public relations agencies, and human resources departments should interact closely with the public relations cells, to increase visibility and presence in the media and create a unique brand image in the hearts and minds of potential applicants.

REFERENCES

Aaker, D.A. (1991). *Managing Brand Equity: Capitalizing on the Value of a Brand Name,* Free Press, New York.

——(1996). *Building Strong Brands,* Free Press, New York, NY.

Anderson, J.R. (1983). *The Architecture of Cognition,* Harvard University Press, Cambridge, MA.

Arndt, J. (1967). "Word of mouth advertising and informal communication", in Cox, D. (Ed.), *Risk Taking and Information Handling in Consumer Behaviour,* Boston, MA. [quoted in Ennew *et al.*, 2000].

Backhaus, K. and Tikoo, S. (2004). "Conceptualizing and researching employer branding", *Career Development International,* Vol. 9, No. 5, pp. 501-17.

Barber, A.E. (1998). *Recruiting Employees: Individual and Organizational Perspectives,* Sage Publications, Thousand Oaks, CA.

Baron, R.M. and Kenny, D.A. (1986). "The moderator-mediator variable distinction in social psychological research: Conceptual, strategic, and statistical considerations", *Journal of Personality and Social Psychology,* Vol. 51, No. 6, pp. 1173-82.

Baruch, Y. (2004). "Transforming careers: from linear to multidirectional career paths", *Career Development International,* Vol. 9, No. 1, pp. 58-73.

Boudreau, J.W. and Rynes, S.L. (1985). "Role of recruitment in staffing utility analysis", *Journal of Applied Psychology,* Vol. 70, pp. 354-66.

Burt, R.S. (1992). "The social structure of competition", in Nohria, N. and Eccles, R.G. (Eds.) *Networks and Organizations,* Harvard Business School Press, Boston, MA.

Business Week (2005). 'India: Desperately Seeking Talent', Nov. 7.

Cable, D.M. and Turban, D.B. (2001). "Establishing the dimensions, sources and value of job seekers' employer knowledge during recruitment", in Ferris, G.E. (Ed.), *Research in Personnel and Human Resource Management,* Elsevier Science, New York.

Cable, D.M. and Turban, D.B. (2003). "The value of organizational reputation in the recruitment context: A brand-equity perspective", *Journal of Applied Social Psychology,* Vol. 33, No. 11, pp. 2244-66.

Cable, D.M., Aiman-Smith, L., Mulvey, P.W. and Edwards, J.R. (2000). "The sources and accuracy of job applicants' beliefs about organizational culture", *Academy of Management Journal,* Vol. 43, No. 6, pp. 1076-85.

Cameron, G. (1994). "Does publicity outperform advertising: An experimental test of the third-party endorsement", *Journal of Public Relations Research,* Vol 6, pp. 185-207.

Cobb-Walgren, C.J., Ruble, C.A. and Donthu, N. (1995). "Brand equity, brand preference, and purchase intent", *Journal of Advertising,* Vol. 3, pp. 25-40.

Collins, C.J. (2007). "The interactive effects of recruitment practices and product awareness on job seekers' employer knowledge and application behaviors", *Journal of Applied Psychology,* Vol. 92, No. 1, pp. 180-90.

Collins, C.J. and Han, J. (2004). "Exploring applicant pool quantity and quality: the effects of early recruitment practice strategies, corporate advertising, and firm reputation", *Personnel Psychology,* Vol. 57, pp. 685-717.

Collins, C.J. and Stevens, C.K. (2002). "The relationship between early recruitment-related activities and the application decisions of new labor-market entrants: a brand equity approach to recruitment", *Journal of Applied Psychology,* Vol. 87, No. 6, pp. 1121-33.

Defillippi, R.J. and Arthur, M.B. (1994). "The boundaryless career: a competency-based perspective", *Journal of Organizational Behaviour,* Vol. 15, No. 4, pp. 307-24.

Ennew, C.T., Banerjee, A.K. and Li, D. (2000). "Managing word of mouth communication: empirical evidence from India", *International Journal of Bank Marketing,* Vol. 18, No. 2, pp. 75-83.

Fisher, C.D., Ilgen, D.R., and Hoyer, W.D. (1979). "Source credibility, information favorability, and job offer acceptance", *Academy of Management Journal,* Vol. 22, pp. 94-103.

Harris, M.M. and Fink, L.S. (1987). "A field study of applicant reactions to employment opportunities: Does the recruiter make a difference", *Personnel Psychology,* Vol. 40, pp. 765-86.

Helm, S. and Schlei, J. (1998). "Referral potential—potential referrals. An investigation into customers' communication in service markets", *Track 1 Market Relationships, Proceedings 27th EMAC Conference, Marketing Research and Practice,* pp. 41-56. [quoted in Ennew *et al.*, 2000].

Johar, G.V., and Pham, M.T. (1999). "Relatedness, Prominence, and Constructive Sponsor Identification", *Journal of Marketing Research,* Vol. 36, pp. 299-312.

Jones, C. (1996). "Careers in project networks: The case of the film industry," in M.B. Arthur and D.M. Rousseau (Eds.), *The Boundaryless Career,* pp. 58-75, OUP, New York, MA.

Keller, K.L. (1993). "Conceptualizing, measuring, and managing customer-based brand equity", *Journal of Marketing,* Vol. 57, pp. 1- 22.

Kilduff, M. (1990). "The interpersonal structure of decision-making: A social comparison approach to organizational choice", *Organizational Behavior and Human Decision Processes,* Vol. 47, pp. 270-88.

Loughlin, C. and Barling, J. (2001). "Young workers' work values, attitudes, and behaviours", *Journal of Occupational and Organizational Psychology,* Vol. 74, pp. 543-58.

May, K. (1998). "Work in the 21st century: Recruiting in a tight labor market", *The Industrial-Organizational Psychologist (TIP),* pp. 39-41. [quoted in Collins and Stevens (2002)].

Michaels, E., Handfield-Jones, H. and Axelrod, B. (2001). *The War for Talent,* Harvard Business School Press, Harvard.

Mitchell, A.A. and Olson, J.C. (1981). "Are product attribute beliefs the only mediator of advertising effects on brand attitudes?" *Journal of Marketing Research,* Vol. 18, pp. 318-32.

Murphy, K.A. (1986). " When your top choice turns you down: Effect of rejected offers on the utility of selection tests", *Psychological Bulletin,* Vol. 99, pp. 133-38.

Ng, E.S.W. and Burke, R.J. (2006). "The next generation at work—business students' views, values and job search strategy", *Education + Training,* Vol. 48, No. 7, pp. 478-92.

Poe, A.C. (2000), "Face value: Snag students early by establishing a long-term personal presence on the campus", *HR Magazine,* pp. 60-68.

Popovich, P. and Wanous, J.P. (1982). "The realistic job preview as persuasive communication", *Academy of Management Review,* Vol. 7, pp. 570-78.

Powell, G.N. (1991). "Applicant reactions to the initial employment interview: Exploring theoretical and methodological issues", *Personnel Psychology,* Vol. 44, pp. 67-83.

Rynes, S.L. (1991). "Recruitment, job choice, and post hire consequences", in Dunnette, M.D. and Hough, L.M. (Eds.) *Handbook of Industrial and Organizational Psychology,* 2nd ed., Consulting Psychologists Press, Palo Alto, CA, pp. 399-444.

Rynes, S.L. and Boudreau, J.W. (1986). "College recruiting in large organizations: Practice, evaluation, and research implications", *Personnel Psychology,* Vol. 39, pp. 729-57.

Rynes, S.L. and Cable, D.M. (2003). "Recruitment research in the twenty-first century", in Borman, W., Ilgen, D. and Klimoski, R. (Eds.) *Handbook of Psychology, Volume 12: Industrial and Organizational Psychology*, Wiley, New York, NY.

Rynes, S.L., Orlitzky, M.O. and Bretz, R.D. Jr. (1997). "Experienced hiring versus college recruiting: practices and emerging trends", *Personnel Psychology,* Vol. 50, No. 2, pp. 309-39.

Saxenian, A.L. (1996). "Beyond boundaries: Open labor markets and learning in Silicon Valley", in M.B. Arthur and D.M. Rousseau (Eds.), *The Boundaryless Career,* pp. 23-39, OUP, New York, MA.

Stevens, C.K. (1997). "Effects of preinterview beliefs on applicants' reactions to campus interviews", *Academy of Management Journal,* Vol. 40, No. 4, pp. 947-66.

Sullivan, S.E. (1999). "The changing nature of careers; a review and research agenda", *Journal of Management,* Vol. 25, No. 3, pp. 457-84.

Taylor, M.S. and Bergmann, T.J. (1987). "Organizational recruitment activities and applicants' reactions at different stages of the recruitment process", *Personnel Psychology,* Vol. 40, pp. 261-85.

The Economic Times (2006). *Talent shortage haunts India Inc: CII,* Nov. 9, New Delhi.

The Telegraph (2007). "Talent shortage perks up India Inc pay", May 28, Kolkata.

Van Vianen, A.E.M. (2000). "Person-organization it: the match between newcomers' and recruiters' preferences for organizational cultures", *Personnel Psychology,* Vol. 53, No. 1, pp. 113-49.

Wilke, W. (1986). *Consumer Behavior,* John Wiley & Sons, New York.

Woodruffe, C. (1999). *Winning the Talent War,* Wiley, New York, NY.

Wyer, R.S. and Srull, T.K. (1989). "Person memory and judgment", *Psychological Review,* Vol. 96, pp. 58-83.

Talent Management: A Road Map to Success

19

Shubhada Mohan Kulkarni

Introduction

It is always said that change is the only permanent thing. This fact is brought out very emphatically in the field of management. If we look at the changing paradigms, we observe a sea change in the manner business is done. There are many paradoxes that we come across. Especially in India, our population is very large and yet when organizations want to recruit, getting right kind of person is not an easy task. Lot of efforts and systematic approach is essential to find persons fitting the bill. The problem doesn't end here. The person who joins, may or may not stay. If the new recruit leaves, the search begins again and again. Recruiting to retain requires to be handled seriously. As the attrition rates in some industries have sky-rocketed, they realized that something must be done to control the problem before it becomes a crisis. We will learn from experiences of others, how to manage talent; how to attract and how to retain.

Employee Engagement

Microsoft India Global Support Center has developed a cohesive employee engagement program termed 'You and Microsoft' designed to connect employees psychologically and intellectually to the organization. 'You and Microsoft' program is based on the premise that employee motivation is a function of multiple factors that go far beyond just tangible benefits. Microsoft India GTSC has identified eight critical needs that employees value and has integrated these in its program to ensure that employees are satisfied with their work and with the organization. They are:

1. **Making a difference through work:** Personal Contribution, Accountability, Performance.
2. **Recognition:** Monetary and Non-Monetary Rewards, PR-External Visibility.
3. **Career Growth:** Opportunities, Training, Coaching and Mentoring, Career Counseling, Job Enrichment, Knowledge Resources.
4. **Fun:** Events, Youth and camaraderie, Creativity boosters.
5. **Environment:** Facilities and Infrastructure, Dress Code, Interest groups and CSR, Communication channels, Transparency.
6. **Care:** EAP, Medical Benefits, New Employee Orientation, Help line, Tuition assistance program.
7. **Technology:** Innovation, Cutting-edge platforms and systems.
8. **Money**: Competitive Compensation, Flexible pay package, Transparency—No valuation of benefits.

By devoting equal attention to all elements holding significance for employees, Microsoft India GTSC has succeeded in demonstrating that sometimes money alone is not enough.

Too much Competition

In April 2005, Jet Sahara, Indian Airlines, Air-India, Kingfisher, Spice Jet and Deccan Air came together to sign a non-poaching pact to protect their business interests. Under the code of the pact, the member airlines have agreed to refuse jobs to pilots and engineers who have not given a minimum four month notice to their previous employer.

Wipro Spectramind, the business process outsourcing and call centre arm of Wipro Ltd. recently signed no hiring pacts with nine BPO and call centre firms in an attempt to control its attrition levels.

Major players in the print media, *The Times of India*, *Hindustan Times* and *The Telegraph* entered a pact, which prevents dipping into each other's manpower resource pool, with the objective to avoid turnover troubles in Mumbai, where all three were planning entries.

Dr. Sullivan defines poaching as the practice of proactively targeting and hiring top talent away from a competitor or top firm, with the specific intention of:

- Securing skills or capabilities faster than would be achieved by developing talent internally.
- Securing expanded capacity that will require less time.
- Mitigating high level talent losses due to attrition.
- Damaging competitors' ability to achieve strategic objectives.

According to Dr. Sullivan, there are three categories of poaching activities, differing in terms of their ethical exposure, timeline and cost. These include:

- Direct sourcing: where organizations handle the entire process internally, including data-mining.
- Third-party poaching: where vendors are used to identify targets.
- Attracting them with honey: where honey refers to various aspects of employer branding.

Source: www.drjohnsullivan.com

Legal bindings can only go so far, when it comes to retention and protection against poaching. There is something uniquely cultural about retention and protection against poaching. Retaining employers is not as simplistic as replicating tested formulae as best practices across companies. It can be pretty hardwork!

Many educational institutions have also observed the problem in recent times. Right from KG to PG there is dearth of good teachers. Lot of outsourcing is taking place. Virtual classrooms are becoming more common. E-learning and distance learning are alternatives preferred to overcome some problems. The problem is more acute in higher and professional education as the experts get offers from corporate world as well. The competition for talent is all pervasive.

The Right Choice

Talent management begins only after getting the right choice. But how do we ensure that our choice is right? The more candidates you compare probably you have better chance. How to ensure that more than enough prospective employees approach you? You need appropriate marketing in the job market. One should rely on conventional as well as unconventional sources of manpower supply. One may try these sourcing tips:

1. Try market networking.
2. Ask ex-batch mates in the same profession to suggest a perfect candidate.
3. Browse industry, trade and alumni directories.
4. Search internal directories of companies with likely candidates.
5. Read newsletters of other companies.
6. Keep track of patent ownerships to find out intelligent candidates.
7. Scan through visiting cards from your companies trade show.
8. Participate at job fairs.
9. Use personal visibility at industry events for candidate referrals.
10. Re-hire retirees to lead critical projects and act as technical lead on projects.
11. Consider the 50+group for their maturity, experience and loyalty as part of think tanks.
12. Try fresh graduates with high energy levels and enthusiasm for project-based work.
13. Build a strong internship program to create a pipeline of talent for future.
14. Track award winners in professional competitions.
15. Take references from new hires about outstanding performers at their ex-employers.
16. Use online search engines for news and names of top talent.
17. Liaise with outplacement agencies to pick suitable candidates from those who have been displaced.

18. Hunt for potential candidates from various alumni directories and forums.
19. Tap the power of internal career movements.
20. Get aggressive with innovative job ads to reach out to passive candidates.
21. Keep a list of candidates who were selected but did not join earlier due to some reason.

Catch them Young

Avaya Global Connect won the 2005 Recruitment and Staffing Best in Class award for the most Innovative Recruitment and Staffing programme.

Avaya selects students in their third year of engineering instead of their final year and invite them to do summer internship for a period of 6 to 8 weeks. During the summer projects students are required to undertake specific projects relevant to their specific curriculum and Avaya's business. On completion of their internship, the interns are evaluated and pre-placement offer is made accordingly. The inters have choice to accept or reject the offer. Candidates who have accepted the offer are not allowed to participate in the placement program in the final year.

This process gives Avaya an advantage in getting the cream of the crop for almost two years in advance, another advantage of this model is that fresh engineers who agree to join have better cultural fit, tend to stay longer and become productive faster since they have hands-on experience of working with the company. The system also provides a unique opportunity for the organization to evaluate the student over a longer period of time in terms of aptitude and cultural fitment. It is a win-win situation.

The driving force behind this initiative was to address the issue of how to attract best talent. They conduct pre-recruitment engagement program. This acts as bridge building and creates awareness about organization.

The Indian Experiment

Bharati Enterprises is set to train and employ engineers from the SC/ST bracket on the preferential basis. The social justice ministry and Bharti Enterprises are joining hands in an endeavour that was set rolling by Infosys last year. The IT giant trained 88 engineers in its Bangalore premises of which 79 have found work in top industrial houses.

Bharti has taken a cue from Infosys. In the wake of the success of its six-month training program and the goodwill generated for the firm, the IT giant has expressed a desire to devise ways to institutionalize it. The firm has decided to spread the training for 2007-08 to five new places, including Bhuwaneshwar and Pune.

The Retail Sector

According to a recent CII employment report, organised retail is estimated to grow from a Rs. 36,000 crore industry in 2005-06 to Rs. 110,000 crore by the year 2010. Business giants like Tatas, Birlas, Reliance, RPG, ITC, and HLL are entering the Indian retail arena in a big way as are global players in the league of Wal-Mart and Carrfour. Investments into the sector are estimated at Rs. 2000-2500 crore in the next 2 to 3 years and over 20,000 crore by the end of 2010. There are huge untapped retail opportunities in grocery, apperal, electronics, entertainment and even niche segments like education. CII's employment report predicts that in India up to 70 million square feet of the retail space will be created by 2007. Assuming one front-end customer associate for every 300 square feet of retail space created, India would need about an additional 210,000 customer associates in the next three years. How is India Inc. bracing up to the talent challenge?

Rituparna Chakravarty, Vice President, Teamlease Services Private Limited, believes that there is dearth of qualified profiles at all levels when it comes to large retailing formats and primarily at middle and senior level. "Lack of education and training in retail is creating a huge gap between supply and demand. "Most organizations are filling up the gap by hiring talent from US and Europe where retail industry is far more mature. This not only helps bring in the desired experience but also helps in forming a platform to groom future prospects from within the country over a period of time. Companies are also hiring from industries with higher focus on customer service and or operations like BPO, ITES, hospitality, FMCG, aviation and the service sector.

There is an increasing trend for back-end and non-core jobs like infrastructure maintenance to be temped as they don't require specific skills related to retail. More and more retailers are hiring temps specifically in malls to replace regular workers during lean hours as well as during peak hours to provide extra hands. TeamLease predicts that by 2007, roughly 15 per cent of direct jobs and most indirect jobs would be temped.

Internal Grooming

Leading retail organizations have been quick to realize that they need to build talent internally given the growth that is expected within the industry in the long run. Pantaloon, Shopper's Stop, Aditya Birla Group are focusing on customizing in-house and on-the-job training programs and initiatives. Most of these organizations have charted out a defined growth path for employees to control attrition. Pantaloon has initiated full-time course and training programs along with a few colleges in Mumbai to groom and nurture talent. Similar initiatives are being taken by most of the leading retailers in the country. Preempting the industry need, TeamLease is providing retail clients with candidate pre-trained in basic soft-skills in customer service and communication to provide greater value to clients and to enable the temps hired by them to hit the ground running.

Retail corporations like Spencer's and Shopper's Stop that have been smart enough to invest in talent building will probably give new entrants a run for their money. Research shows that about 50-60% of the difference in the performance is the result of effectiveness of front-line staff. Retailers who do not systematically build relevant sales skills and increase selling capacity across the frontline may be missing a hugh opportunity.

Talent Management

An organizations most valuable assets are its talented human resources. Knowing how to attract, retain and assist talent to expand their skills is essential to the successful operation and growth of the company. Development Dimensions International (DDI), Asia Pacific International Ltd. (APIL) Australia, General Manager, Mark Busine says, "An organization needs to develop a pool of people who are ready to take on new opportunities and roles as they emerge in the organization. We refer to this as an 'acceleration pool'. You are accelerating the development of talented individuals towards senior roles."

The factors driving the popularity of talent management today are:

1. Scarcity of talents.
2. Increasing complexity of the role of leadership.
3. Increased demands in technology.
4. Employee and shareholders expectations.
5. Growth of knowledge.

The costs of replacing executives far outweigh the investment in talent retention. Hong Kong conglomerate of companies, Jardine Matheson Limited, Group Head of Human Resources, Dr. Richi Bent, says the cost of replacing decent managers is roughly 2-3 times the annual outlay of retaining staff. Expenses include talent search, recruitment and the learning curve.

Succession of internal talent is encouraged. Employees are assessed for their potential to take on a larger role. Those who are ready for promotion are evaluated by top management.

Talent Management at AIM

Director of Business Development, Australian Institute of Management (AIM)—Victoria and Tasmania, Serge Sardo says that AIM delivers a variety of company specific talent development programs for its clients, These include:

- Establishing the talent pool-identifying who the talent is through assessment and profiling.
- Analyzing strengths and developmental areas.

- Establishing professional development plans, pathways, etc.
- Creating succession management processes and career paths.
- Establishing competency frameworks and success profile.
- Training and coaching programs.

They have an internal process called the Management, Motivational and Mentoring plan where twice yearly, they review employees performance and provide opportunities for their development.

Developing Key Players

National Australia Bank is an International financial services organization and is organized around three regional businesses; Australia (including Asia) the UK and New Zealand. The NAB employees around 22,000 employees in Australia and around 39,000 globally. Executive General Manager, People and Culture, Elizabeth Hunter says, "Talent Management is about everything that we do recognizing that people are our business. It is our people who deliver our brand and purpose."

The need to develop talent is more intensively felt by service industry. They make conscious efforts to manage their pool of talent. NAB needs talent at all levels and all functions to achieve their goal. Graduates to seasoned performers, form their leadership pipeline, providing richness of experience and education for the future success of the operations. It is the attraction and retention of talented people that contributes to success.

Executive talent management is conducted at a global level in order to build a pool of highly talented, capable organizational leaders, who can move into critical roles across the group. Regional talent management builds a strong pipeline of local talent. There is a focus on talent management across NAB on assessment, career management, succession planning and talent development. These processes ensure that NAB has the capability ready and able to deliver on its broader business unit strategies.

Group and Regional Talent Management teams exist to support talent practices and talent outcomes. Asia is part of NAB's working environment and it has a presence in Asia Pacific region. The approach to talent management is consistent.

The way Japan does it

Talent management is viewed as being extremely important in Japan, but is conducted in a patriarchal, autocratic environment. It means that staff are managed top down and are often not party to their own development directions.

Terrie Lloyd, President of LINC Media Inc. says that talent management helps promising staff to move up and assists companies to recover after setbacks, by focusing on key staff members. In times of stress and performance demands, companies need to focus on key individuals more than the group as a whole. Regular promotions and ongoing expansion ensures new talent can move upwards.

IBM Story

In IBM the focus is on expanding and nurturing the teams. They have access to growth opportunities. IBM provides effective mentoring, coaching and training programs to enhance skills so the team reaches its full potential. The Singapore based HR Director says, "Talent management really begins at the marketplace." We start by attracting the best talent into IBM. We are acutely aware of the value of talented people in our organization. It is an investment in our future and we work to get the best of the best talent to grow in an environment with unlimited opportunities.

The challenge for HR professionals is to stop being reactive and be proactive and strategic. It is vital to have a good mix of talent groups that complement the strength of each group. In south-east Asian countries plus India and China, major strength is a team of young, enthusiastic, and committed IBMers. In Australia, the workforce is more mature that provides invaluable experience to the existing talent base. All learn from each other.

Conclusion

Success is not by chance but by choice. There are various success mantras tried and tested by organizations over a period of time. What was a sure fire way may not work in a changed circumstances. Medicines have expiry date. The effectiveness is reduced over a period of time: same way concepts and ideas also have limited life. What worked in the past may not work now. What gave spectacular results in one organization may not have same impact in another, as they are not identical. To remain as front runner you have to think out-of-box. Trail and error method may prove too costly. So one tries to learn from others and adapts these learning to suit their specific requirements.

I have tried to find out from practitioners their views and tried to share experiences of many. Talent hunt is becoming more and more important. Organizations want to be first time right. When they have the right person, they want to hold on to him as long as it benefits them. The journey begins with recruitment and how long they will travel together is dependent on retention policies. Only fairy tails end up saying 'and they lived happily ever after'. Organizations who dream of such fairy tail endings, will have to be proactive and pragmatic.

REFERENCES

Balasaheb Sonawane. *Attracting and Retaining Talents—HR Challenge*, NIPM 25th WRC Souvenir.

Gary Dressler. *Human Resource Management*, Prentice Hall India Ltd.

Ram Marlapalle. "ABCDnRoadmap to Attract and Retain the Talent", NIPM 25th WRC Souvenir.

Steven L. Mcshane, Mary Ann Von Glinow and Radha R. Sharma. *Organizational Behaviour*, Tata McGraw Hill.

PART – 5
TALENT ATTRACTION AND DEVELOPMENT

Validating E-Learning as a Tool for Talent Development*

20

Sanchita Ghatak and *Satyendra Kr. Singh*

Overview of Talent Development

Every role performed at excellence, requires talent, this is so because role performed at excellence requires certain recursive pattern of thought, feeling and behavior.

Thus talent development can be defined as a regular pattern of thought, feeling or behavior which can be applied productively.

Since it is not possible to excel or perform at excellence without talent, organizations are finding new and innovative means for talent development so that new capabilities can be developed and the genuine intent of fostering long-term learning and development can be easily attained.

Talent development has nowadays become a major issue to be addressed in any organization. This is very important because it is needed for managing careers of the personnel, and ensures that they develop the skills and judgment they move into leadership role, and this is the major challenge of an HR system to design and deliver such program and making the above mentioned things happen.

Talent development can be taken as a meta system containing 7 smaller systems which are actually aligned, as depicted in the figure.

---

*This study would have remained incomplete without the help of my friends and students from IISE and Jaipuria Institute of Management, who have helped us to collect the data.

Special thanks to our friend Ms Shruti and Dr. Rastogi who have been a great help in doing with the empirical part.

We really count on the support of our friends and colleagues of IISE and JIM as well.

Fig. 20.1: Talent Development System

Failure of any unit in this system blocks or breaks the talent pipeline and discourages the organization to achieve the goal of talent efficacy.

Studies say that giftedness and intelligence are the major factors on which a talent development program succeeds. But further study suggests that the above parameters are not the only deciding factors (Baird 1985) for success in talent development program.

It has been further studied that talent development process can be used for increasing Creativity (Pirto, 1992; Tannenbaum 1998), Passion for work in a domain (Benbow, 1992); Perfections (Silverman, 1993), Persistence (Renzulli,1978), Risk Taking (Torrance, 1987), Self Discipline (Renzulli, 1978), Self Efficacy (Zinnerman *et al.* 1992), and Will Power, (Corno and Kanfer 1993).

These studies suggest that effective adults can be achieved by force and also those talented adults possess many of the qualities mentioned above.

Presence of talent is very common. Every individual may possess some talent or the other. Thus, it is truly said that talent is not sufficient for excellence. In a study by James Hillman (1996), it was found that the talent of a person can be developed by means of training, when he learns to work according to a given situation.

Every field or domain develops talent in a different way. Sometimes direct teaching is useful, sometimes learning by doing method works best.

In an organization the basic reasons for having talent development programs are broadly categorized as:

- When performance improvement is needed as indicated in performance appraisal.
- As a part of overall professional development.
- As a part of succession planning to help an employee to be eligible for a planned change in role in the organization.
- Specific training needs in:
  - Communication,
  - Computer skills,
  - Customer service,
  - Human relations,
  - Quality initiatives, and
  - Product/Service updates.

It has been found that the benefits that organizations reap out of TD process are myriad. Some of which can be broadly viewed as—

- Job satisfaction increases and there is an increase in the morale of the employees, further resulting in increased motivation level towards work.
- Talent development process leads to increased efficiency leading to financial gains to the organization. Yet another aspect of this is that the process increases the capacity to adopt new techniques and methods.

Researchers say that talent development actually increases innovation in strategies, production and services. Not only this proper development program also leads to enhancement in computer skills.

Need for Talent Development in Insurance Sector

Insurance sector has witnessed significant development and now it is in a state of growth. The companies of both life and general insurance are facing tough competition from their competitors because there has been a remarkable change in the sector.

The market has become more buyer driven and customer focused which requires a tremendous improvement in the services and solutions provided by the company (Balasubramanium, 2007). Further concepts like customer delight, customer centricity, CRM, customer experience management are causing substantial pressure on the sector.

The knowledge about the insurance products and services, ability to customize according to the need of customer involvement, and participation in devising the cover and working of premium differentiates one insurance company from the other.

Viewing all these, it becomes necessary that there should be massive talent development programs in this sector which will cater to the training needs on the insurance products, concepts, information, development of skills to be more customer focused, to have confidence and ability to convince and inform the customer about the choices they have, the risks they have and how to avoid them by taking or planning proper insurance for themselves and their family.

Insurance business remains to be complex in nature because of complexity of the market and heterogeneity of the service providers along with the variety of products and their complexity.

On the other hand surveys reveal that:

- Customers lack general awareness of various risks and which to prioritize and when.
- Customers do not possess sufficient understanding about the providers.
- Customers are not willing to take policies or subscribe coverage.
- Customers have lack of insurance culture.

Because of the above mentioned reasons substantially the major problems an insurer faces are:

1. Less developed market.
2. Tough competition.
3. Costs of claims, litigation and complaints arising from badly understood products.

The ultimate solution to this problem is that the training program in the insurance sector should be strengthened so that quality information and objective advices can be provided to the customers where various risks, products, services, and coverage, etc. can be introduced.

Training as a Mode of Talent Development in Insurance Sector

There are around 50 major established companies in insurance sector in India, specializing either in product related life insurance or general insurance.

Though most of the products offered by the insurance companies are similar in some respect but there are wide variations in their product pricing, schemes, policies, etc. Thus the training needs for various companies become different.

Howsoever, the training needs differ as the companies need training for:

1. The entry level professionals which are provided by various institutes approved by IRDA which is a 100 hours mandatory training program for those who are aspiring to become an agent.
2. The existing employees and agents on various aspects of products and specializing related to the following issues:
   (a) Medical billing expertise.
   (b) Language of medical billing.
   (c) Privacy policy.
   (d) New product training.
   (e) Policy and schemes.
   (f) Modification and moderation of existing products.
   (g) Communication and convincing skills.
   (h) Modules of travel insurance issues.
   (i) Modules of medi-claim issues, etc.

All these kinds of trainings are provided by organizations as a step towards developing talent. Currently these trainings are provided using online mode, instructor led classes, self-directed classes and even through CBT (computer based training) which comprises learning using CD and e-Books.

Personal interviews with employees of various insurance companies located in Lucknow—the capital city of Uttar Pradesh, revealed that mostly CBT, online training using V-SAT or video conferencing is mainly provided to the employees with profile of mid to top level managers.

Agents or advisors are trained on various new products and policy schemes using traditional or classroom based training. Some companies do provide E-Learning to its agents but undergoing training is not compulsory. They get updates on the existing and new products from the business development manager who is a regular employee of the company.

Recently some companies have started to do product training or sometimes as they term it as "progress tracking" by means of video conferencing.

E-Learning as a Mode of Conducting Training

E-Learning is a mode of learning which utilizes the capability of ICT, i.e. Information and Communication Technology.

It has been found that ICT enables us to do things easily, flexibly and faster. Moreover ICT helps us do things differently. So is E-Learning. With the help of ICT, learning can take place in an entirely different way which can give different learning experiences than what is usually obtained in a traditional classroom curriculum and text based method.

In E-Learning, the teaching-learning method is assumed to be self directed. It is believed to be an active process because in this process, the knowledge generation is accomplished through individual experience, maturity and interaction.

In the early phase of evolution of E-Learning, the process was conducted by posting e-copy, i.e. digital manuscript of learning material to the WWW. The learner would open, read and learn according to his interest and self regulatory method (it's a learning pattern where there is a learner's intended effort for learning subjects).

Today all organizations are making big efforts to adjust and excel in the changing business scenario and enhance their competitiveness. With the advent of WWW and ICT, the traditional mode of training and development is getting modified and find e-mode, i.e. E-Learning a better way of conduction of training. In this mode, the training and development process is being conducted using various ICT tools like internet, V-SAT, Multimedia based websites, blogging sites and sometimes even through interactive CDs and DVDs.

Several factors are involved in the process of e-learning. Researches broadly identified the following factors (Lim *et al.*, 2006) which should be kept in mind while designing a training module to be carried out using E-Learning like the trainee, training content, level of communication between trainee and trainer, ease of use of ICT resources and organizational environment. Some of the dimensions of these factors have also been studied under TAM, i.e. Technology Acceptance Model (Davis, 1989).

Success of such kind of training can only be found if there is perceived usefulness from the user's side (Theory of Reasoned Behavior—TRA-Fishbein and Ajzen, 1980).

Quality of system and information quality also determines the success of e-learning as a mode of training. Components like content, accuracy, format, timeliness and ease of use are some other factors determining E-Learning success (Doll and Torkzadeh, 1988).

Some other researches identify 5 dimensions which affect the efficacy of online training and these dimensions are based on motivation theory (Compeau & Higgins, 1995).

In a situation where training is being conducted using E-Learning mode, the ability to handle computers is one big challenge (Chau, 2001). Further it was found that a training program to be successful should be administered in a similar environment like the actual work and surrounding condition (Bramley, 1991).

Conventional medium of training as face to face interaction, telephone contact increase reliability in a training program, but the success of training lies in the mental set up and education background of the trainee (Leduchwicz, 1982).

Thus in a training program using e-mode, the ease of interaction becomes the most important factor for the success of such program. Online training must facilitate communications between physically and geographically separated trainers and trainees. Technologies like simulation and 3D virtual reality act as a part of ease of interaction design process (Leidner & Jarvenpaa, 1995).

Results of a study by Hayashi *et al.*, 2004 suggested that perceived usefulness of E-Learning is directly related to the satisfaction of the trainee which further determines the success of the training program.

Scope of Study

The literature review shows various aspects related to E-Learning, thus the study is focused on finding the following:

- What is the awareness level of e-learning as a mode of training in insurance sector?
- How is this mode of training perceived by the employees of insurance sector?
- Find out the perceived usefulness of this training mode.
- For effectiveness of such a training mode what factors are involved?
- Does this kind of training increase the productivity and efficiency towards job?
- Does this have any effect on the motivation level towards work in this sector?
- Satisfaction level of the trainee by this mode of training.
- What is the acceptance level of E-Learning as a conduit for providing training?

Based on the above mentioned dimensions, the study mainly aims to find out the future scope of E-Learning as a mode of talent development and suggest how companies involved in providing E-Learning can tap this sector which requires frequent training on various aspects of insurance.

Empirical Methodology

The research is descriptive in nature where various aspects of E-Learning as a mode of training for talent development in Insurance Sector have been investigated.

Data Collection

Data obtained for this research has been obtained from all the major insurance companies located in Lucknow using a structured questionnaire. The questionnaire designing was done by interviewing employees of various insurance companies and previous research work on E-Learning and talent development.

Sampling method used was judgmental on the basis of whether the respondent has got any kind of exposure to any training program. Sample size is 140 respondents from 11 companies present in Lucknow. Since training using computer based online mode, V-SAT or video conferencing (various companies use various modes of E-Learning amongst the mentioned methods) is being provided mostly to employees of higher managerial level and sometimes to entry level managers who are on rolls, therefore the sample constituted 60 per cent employees and 40 per cent advisors.

Before finally getting the data filled up in the questionnaire, a pre-testing was done on few advisors and employees to check the probable or most potential errors. Unwanted and ambiguous questions were removed and some new alternative questions were introduced in the questionnaire after conducting the reliability analysis.

The study has been performed only on the basis of primary data collected through survey. Different scales like nominal scale, ranking scale, rating scale, 5 point likert scale was used for measuring various attributes.

Analysis

1. Awareness of E-Learning in Insurance Sector

Regarding the awareness level of E-Learning as a mode of training it was found that about 86 per cent of the respondents are aware of this mode and only a small percentage of people are not aware, i.e. 13.7 per cent which has been depicted in the pie chart.

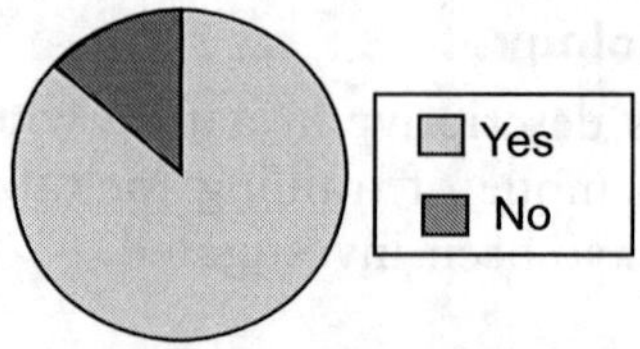

Chart 1: Awareness of E-Learning

This finding led to the conclusion that the maximum number of people working in this sector are aware of this kind of training mode.

Though most of the organizations provide such training and that too is not limited only to the employees of higher level, still the percentage of respondents saying that they did not have such kind of training is very high (70.5%), and believe that it is for employees of higher level.

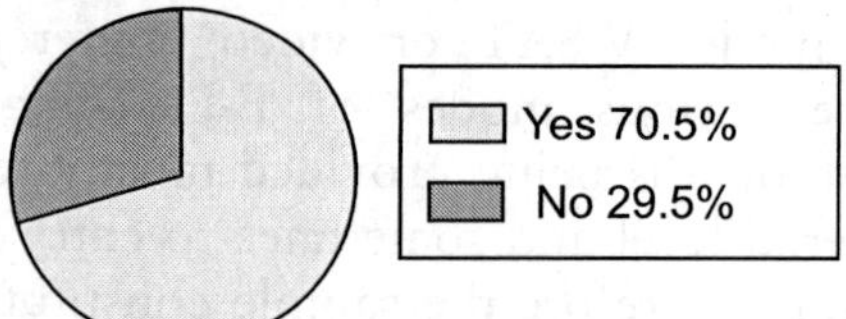

Chart 2: Current Organization Providing E-Training

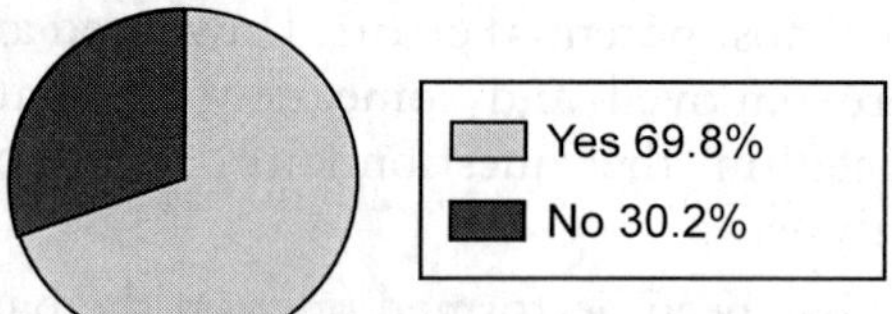

Chart 3: Training Provided to Employees of Higher Level

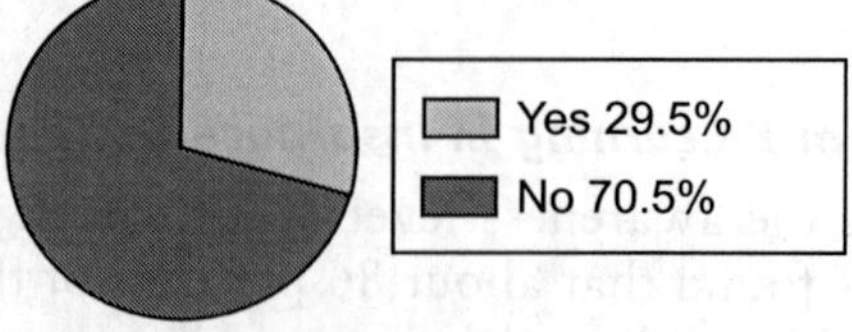

Chart 4: Respondents Undergone E-Training

2. Perception of Employees Regarding this Kind of Training

Since maximum respondents said that they are aware of E-Learning, it was necessary to find out that what according to them is E-Learning. The basic intention of finding out this is to change the perception of the people regarding E-Learning, so that this training mode can be promoted in insurance sector.

Responses for all the factors stated in the questionnaire were tested to find out what according to maximum people, is this mode of training all about.

Table 20.1: Employee Perception about E-Learning

Learning by own pace but appear in exam through online mode	***0%***
Learn using tools like Chatting, Video Conferencing, email and various IT Tools	***4%***
Learn in the absence of a trainer there is learning by browsing the internet	***9%***
Learn using a computer where study material is provided in a CD or DVD	***6%***

Though from the interviews it was revealed that insurance companies who are currently providing E-Learning, do it by using V-SAT where the trainer and trainee are distance apart, yet from the data collected this fact shows least knowledge regarding mode of such training program.

3. Usefulness of this Training Mode

The literature review reveals that training (by any mode) will be useful only:

- if the trainee feels that the training will be good for his development,
- if the training is good for the job type,
- if the trainee is able to judge his performance,
- if the trainee experiences a good learning environment,
- if the trainee can find current training mode better than what was provided earlier, and
- if the trainee is able to exchange ideas without the fear of getting criticized openly.

Therefore, some variables were identified and factor analysis was performed on them. The variables were reduced to 3 factors—

F1: factor which signifies learning environment,

F2: factor which signifies job and performance,

F3: factor which signifies self-development.

Further calculating the mean rank on the 3 identified factors using Kendall W test, it was found that relationship between the cases is very high (.903).

Table 20.2: Kendall W: Usefulness of this mode of training

F1	*2.95*
F2	*2.00*
F3	*1.05*

Note: F3 has been positioned as the most determining factor for usefulness of training program).

4. Factors for Effectiveness of Training

A training program is considered to be effective on the basis of how good is the lecture content, personal touch from the trainer and final outcome of the training.

If the variable lecture content was considered, Friedman test was run to rank for each case in the variable. It was found that content variety scores the least (2.76) and recent and upgraded scores the most (5.05) which can be interpreted as Case 1 has been considered as the most significant for training.

Table 20.3: Friedman Test

	Mean Rank
content variety	2.76
new problems solve	3.45
as for job type	3.45
abundant content	4.66
various learn method	4.13
well communicated	4.50
recent and upgraded	5.05

5. Effect of Training on Productivity

Productivity variable has been defined according to ten factors, i.e. effort free work, improved communication, improved customer conversion, improved attitude towards work, good relationship with peers, motivated towards work, fast and quality work, more work in less time.

Plotting a productivity matrix based on all the variables, we get an output within the range of 1-10. It was found that majority of the respondents feel that their productivity has increased.

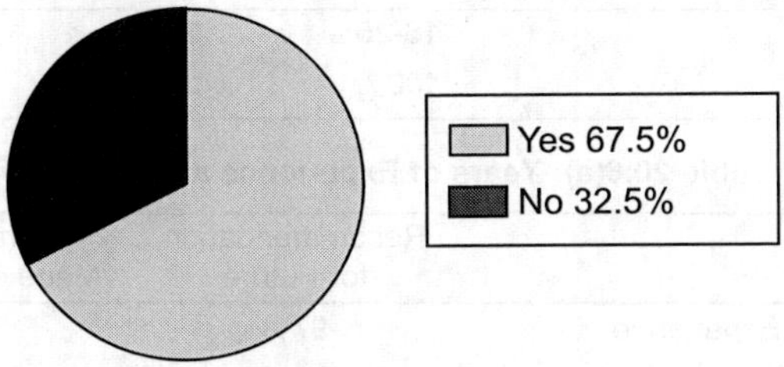

Chart 5: Respondents whose Productivity has Increased

6. Motivation towards Work

The data showed that the respondents who have undergone training by this mode feel motivated towards work. The percentage of motivated respondents is more compared to the other group.

Table 20.4: Motivation for Work

	Per cent
Not Motivated	35.0
Motivated	65.0
Total	100.0

7. Satisfaction Level of the Trainee by this Mode of Training

Satisfaction has been measured indirectly using two variables, i.e. future recommendation of the program and willingness towards such a mode of training. This is true for only those who have attained a training by this mode.

Running cross tabulation against the mentioned variable and demographic variables namely age, years of experience and position in the company. The Tables 20.5 and 20.6 show the description of the data.

Table 20.5(a): Age Wise

	Recommendation For Future	Willing for this Mode of Training
Age Wise	97%	3%

Majority of the respondents according to age seemed to be satisfied by this training. Further the description shows that the age group of 18-25 and 34-41 comprise the largest group.

Table 20.5(b)

	18-25	26-33	34-41
Age Wise	100%	95%	100%

Table 20.6(a): Years of Experience and Position

	Recommendation for Future	Willing for this Mode of Training
Years of Experience	97%	3%
Position	97%	3%

Data shows that majority of the respondents are satisfied according to their years of experience and position. Further classifying the data, we have:

Table 20.6(b)

	0-5	6-15	16-20
Years of Experience	97%	100%	100%

The data depicts that the respondents with experience 6-15 and 16-20 years have greater satisfaction level.

Table 20.6(c)

	Advisor	Employee
Position	100%	95%

The data depicts that the respondents who are advisors have greater satisfaction.

8. Acceptance Level of E-Learning as a Conduit for Providing Training

The literature review shows that the acceptance level of training is directly related to the satisfaction level of the respondents. More satisfaction will result in more recommendation. Thus, it can be concluded that there can be a good future scope of training using this mode in this sector.

For finding this, the mean response of respondents who have undergone training by this mode was calculated and was found to be:

Table 20.7: Mean Satisfaction

Variable	Mean
satisfied	1.5750

Based on the mean, one sample T test was run to check whether the mean of the single variable differs from a specified constant. The observation is as follows:

Table 20.8: Significance Test

	T	df	Sig. (2-tailed)
Satisfied	–6.481	39	.000

The low value of Sig.-2-tailed (.000) shows that the value is highly significant, i.e. respondents undergone such type of training are highly satisfied.

Further studying the recommendation percentage and percentage of willing respondents for such a training program, the following observation is obtained:

Table 20.9: Recommendation for E-Training

	Per cent
Yes	97.6
No	2.4
Total	100.0

Table 20.10: Willingness to Do E-Training Again

	Per cent
Yes	92.7
No	7.3
Total	100.0

Tables 20.9 and 20.10 show high level of willingness to do such a program and recommend it for future.

Summary of Findings

With this empirical study, it was found that majority of the people are aware about the E-Learning process. Though most insurance companies provide training by VSAT and Videoconferencing to employees at higher level, study reveals that majority of the respondents feel the same way proving that the response from a pilot group regarding availability of training by E-Learning mode is true. Interestingly, there is such a high awareness level but merely 30 per cent have attended such a training program.

The general perception about this mode of training is that, it is a way to get training where the trainee learns by his own determined pace and appears in exam through online mode. This is what happens for the entry level candidates for this sector who have to pass a certification course from IRDA. Respondents seemed not to have any other perception regarding the modes available for E-Learning.

Literature review reveals that usefulness of a training program depends upon the learning environment, relevance of the training in the existing job and level of self-development.

It was found that majority of the respondents feel that usefulness of training program through E-Mode is when it shows significant self-development and further if there is any relevance of the training in the existing job.

Effectiveness of training program is decided by a lot of factors but according to this study majority of respondents feel that variety in training content decides its effectiveness.

It is thought that productivity of an employee is incremented by training program. This thought has been endorsed by this study as 68 per cent respondents feel that their performance have increased by undergoing training by this mode.

Satisfaction level of trainees was found more in the age groups of 18-25 and 34-41. Trainees who have more job experience and do not hold a higher position have greater satisfaction. Motivation level of the respondents also seemed to be increased by such a training program.

Past researches show, more the satisfaction, the more is the acceptance level of a training program. Thus, this study suggests that majority of the people who have undergone such a training program are satisfied and are willing to undertake such training program again and will be recommending this for their organizations.

Conclusion

Almost all the factors studied in this research showed a bent towards a positive side proving that this mode of training can be very effective for this industry and training by E-Learning has immense scope in insurance sector in the future.

To study the acceptance level of training program by E-Mode, efficiency, productivity in work and usefulness were considered as some of the major determining factors. However, some other factors like previous knowledge and efficiency level of handling computer are also said to be very important. This, however could not be covered in this study and remains as a scope for future research.

An effective training depends upon the content of the training and how it is communicated to the trainee. Further the training becomes effective if the knowledge and experience gained in the process can be transferred in their performance, which is a direct dependent of learning performance. The study focused on the content of the training but transfer performance and learning performance needs to be studied.

Motivation level after attaining training was also given due importance, which was found to be very high.

This kind of study finds scope of research in all the service sectors where development of talent becomes very necessary for managing the human resource, which is a very important factor for survival and growth of an organization.

REFERENCES

Baird, L. (1985). "Do Grades and Tests Predict Adult Accomplishment?" *Research in Higher Education*, 23(I)-85.

Benbow, C.P. (1992). "Mathematical Talent: Its Nature and Consequences", in N. Colangelo, S.G. Assouline and D.L. Ambroson, Eds. *Talent Development:* Proceedings from the 1991 Henry B. and Jocelyn Wallace National Research Symposium on Talent Development, pp. 95-123.

Bloom (l985). *Developing Talent in Young People.* New York: Ballantine.

Bramley, P. (1991). *Evaluating Training Effectiveness—Translating Theory into Practice*, McGraw-Hill Book Company, London.

Chau, P. (2001). "Influence of Computer Attitudes and Self-efficacy on IT Usage Behavior". *Journal of End User Computing*, 13(1), pp. 26-34.

Chou, H., and Wang, T. (2000). "The Nuance of Learning Style and Training Method on Self-efficacy and Learning Performance in WWW Homepage Design Training". *International Journal of Information Management*, 20, pp. 455-72.

Compeau, D.R. and Higgins, C.A. 1995. "Computer Self-efficacy: Development of a Measure and Initial Test". *MIS Quarterly* 19(2), pp. 189–211.

Corno, L. and Kanfer, R. (1993). "The Role of Volition in Learning and Performance" in L. Darling-Hammond, Ed. *Review of Research in Education*, 19 (pp. 301-42). Washington, DC: American Educational Research Association.

Davis, F.D. (1989). "Perceived Usefulness, Perceived Ease of Use, and User Acceptance of Information Technology". *MIS Quarterly* 13(3), 319-40.

Doll, W.J. and Torkzadeh, G. (1988). "The Measurement of End User Computing Satisfaction". *MIS Quarterly* 12(2), pp. 259-74.

Fishbein, M. and Ajzen, I. (1975). *Belief, Attitude, Intentions and Behavior: An Introduction to Theory and Research*. Addison-Wesley, Reading, A.

Flore. "Challenges of Financial Education in Insurance Sector." *OECD Conference on Financial Education*, 2006.

Hayashi, A., Chen, C., Ryan, T. and Wu, J. (2004). "The Role of Social Presence and Moderating Role of Computer Self Efficacy in Predicting the Continuance Usage of E-Learning Systems". *Journal of Information Systems Education*, 15 (2), pp. 139–54.

Leduchwicz, T. (1982). "Trainer Role and Effectiveness: A Review of the Literature". *International Journal of Manpower*, pp. 2-9.

Leidner, D.E. and Jarvenpaa, S.L. (1995). "The Use of Information Technology to Enhance Management School Education: A Theoretical view". *MIS Quarterly*, 1, pp. 265-91.

Piirto, J. (1995b). "Deeper and Broader: The Pyramid of Talent Development in the Context of the Giftedness Construct". *Educational Forum*, 59, pp. 364-69.

Randall, S. (1982). "Communication and Performance in the real World, simulation and laboratory". American Psychological Convention, Washington, DC: August 27.

Silverman, L.K. (Ed). (1993). "Counseling the Gifted and Talented". Denver, CO: Love.

Torrance, E.P. (1987). "Teaching for Creativity". In S. Isaksen (Ed.), *Frontiers of Creativity Research: Beyond the Basics*, pp. 190-215. Buffalo, NY: Bearly Ltd.

Zimmerman, B.J., Bandura, A. and Martinez-Pons, M. (1992). "Self-motivation for Academic Attainment: The role of Self-efficacy Beliefs and Personal Goal Setting". *American Educational Research Journal*, 29(3): pp. 663-76.

Planning and Managing Human Resources (ISBN: 9780874257182), Human Resource Development Press, 2002.

The Human Capital Edge (ISBN: 9780071378833), McGraw-Hill.

The Strategic Development of Talent, 2d rev.ed. Rothwell, William J. and H. C. Kazanas. HRD Press, Inc., [c]2003.

Attracting and Retaining of Human Talent

21

Nalin Jayasuriya

"Modern companies should be communities, not battlefields. At their heart lie covenants between executives and employees that rest on shared commitment to ideas, to issues, to values, to goals and to management processes."

—Max De Pree, Chairman of Herman Miller, Inc.

A big challenge that several organizations face, both locally and globally, is the capacity building of organizations to attract and retain talented people. Much has been written on these areas and much has been said...but application, well, that's a different ball game.

Consider a 'love marriage'. The man adopts his best—planned strategy to win the favour of the woman he loves, even leading into marriage. In the event that he depends upon that single strategy to continue with the smooth maintenance of his marriage, the union could possibly end in disaster, i.e. separation or divorce. Therefore, he will require to adopt the second strategy to keep (maintain) his marriage. In the organization, too, management must learn to adopt two strategies, one for attracting talented people to the organization and the second, to retain them in a fast-paced, challenging working environment.

Attracting Strategy

It is important for organizations to build up the necessary criteria/factors that make them appear attractive in the market place. Some of these factors would be—

(a) *The establishment itself,* i.e. the stability, number of years in business, numbers of staff employed, character of the organization and the Goodwill behind its name.

(b) *Credibility,* i.e. the delivery of the promise. To be seen as a dependable supplier of goods and/or services. Reliability and the assurance of not being turned back of a customer was to go back with a problem, even after a year or two of receiving a service.

(c) *Type of product/service,* i.e. how long such products and/or services exist in a changing market place; the innovative and dynamic nature of the product or service offered. Do the products/services enjoy market leadership?

(d) *The pay and benefits.* Are the company remuneration packages and benefits in keeping with the industry/market average or higher. Pecuniary and non-pecuniary rewards for superior performance, built into the working system of the organization so that people can earn as much as they deserve.

(e) *Employer of good repute,* i.e. what is the reputation that the company enjoys? Is the organization seen to be one that is concerned for people development and career prospects, ethical and upholding good values? Positive word-of-mouth reports form staff. This is where the employees sing praises about their organization in public and among their contacts and friends. The word will spread!

(f) *Professionalism,* i.e. is the company professionally run, adopting the state-of-the-art technology, processes and world-class management systems? Is the company non-discriminatory, considering just and equitable outcomes from corporate decisions.

(g) *Corporate responsibility,* i.e. is the company seen as one that respects social responsibility and the law of the land. Is the company contributing towards cleanliness in the environment. Have high regard for Environment, safety and health.

People Factor

Fostering enthusiasm and teamwork builds effective teams committed to organizational goals. It further encourages and empowers people to achieve, establishes challenging performance standards, creates enthusiasm, a feeling of investment and a desire to excel, fosters collaboration among team members and among teams.

People love to achieve when there is reward and celebration. Hence, organizations must recognize, reward and celebrate individual and team accomplishments. The way to go is to—

- Acknowledge and celebrate team accomplishments.
- Reward people for good performance.
- Inspire people to excel.
- Let people know when they are performing well.
- Recognize the contributions of people from diverse backgrounds.

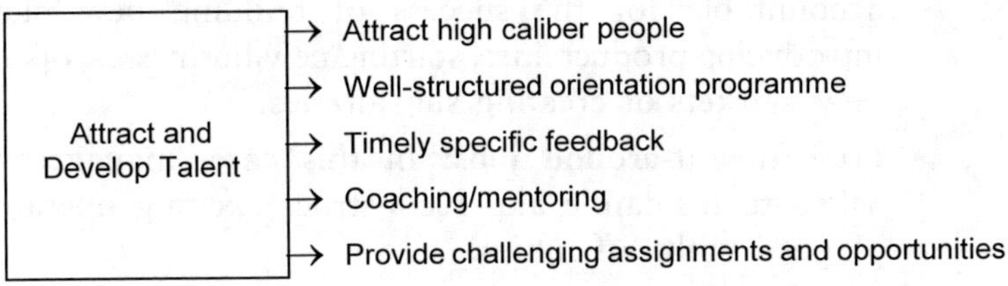

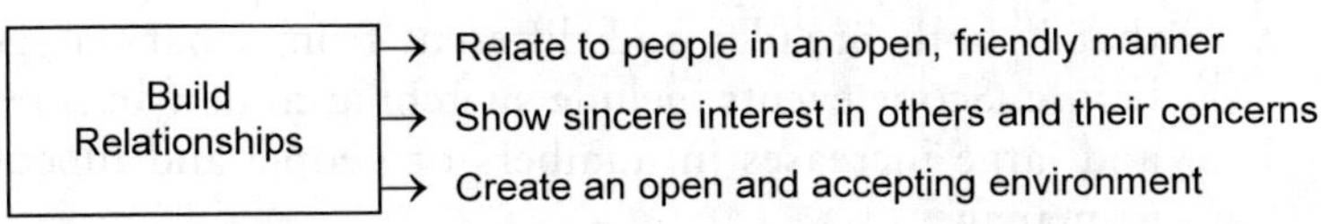

All strategies aimed at maintaining a delighted, enthused and committed workforce must be aimed at kindling employee's mind and heart. This mechanism must be built into the company's performance management and development mechanism.

Development Strategy

The Key three types of experiences that are especially important in development are—

- **Hardships:** Such as missed promotions, divorce or serious business mistakes.
- **Working with other people:** Good and bad, boss and subordinate.

- **Job assignments:** Especially those that stretch the person. Job assignments are the single most important development experience. Turning point jobs involving financial and personal risk, are best. There are five basic types of jobs in this category.
- **Projects and task forces:** These ate discreet, temporary assignments on major problems facing an organization. They are typically taken on as short-term assignments in addition to one's current job.
- **Line-to-staff-switches:** In these assignments, managers leave line jobs for a stint in a staff role.
- **Starting from scratch:** Here, managers create a business venture from nothing or almost nothing. They are accountable for the success of building new plants, introducing product lines, starting new businesses, opening new markets or creating subsidiaries.
- **Fix-it/turn-it-around jobs:** In this case, managers are asked to dismantle and reconstruct exciting operations plagued with difficulties.
- **A leap in Scope:** This involves an increase in responsibility that is both broader and different from what has gone before. Scope events include switching to new businesses and large increases in numbers of people and functions to manage.

Several companies globally, adopt the 'development strategy' in order to energies the enthusiasm and motivation of their talented staff. New opportunities, new challenges and new expectations help the employees rejuvenate. This, in turn, helps in retaining their top performers. For example, certain Multinational companies send their middle managers on short assignments to other operations within the region or, sometimes, outside the region, i.e. the Brand Manager of a MNC in Sri Lanka may be sent on a one-year assignment to Indonesia to help support the similar line or the same "brand" in Indonesia.

Likewise, a manager from the Indonesian operation may be sent to India or Malasia. When such managers return to their own country operations there is a lot of value they could add to the business, as well as a lot of value in their own personal growth.

Retention Strategies

- Establish a climate of openness and trust where employees are encouraged to bring out the differences in the open and resolve them, without backlash or consequence.
- Constantly look for ways to provide skills, resources and experiences that will allow staff to handle more challenging work.
- Recognize achievement, reward and celebrates.
- Foster enthusiasm and team work.
- Devise development activities into small steps that lead to an ultimate goal.
- Progressive pay and benefits in order to further motivate the high performer. Brake away from fixed salary scales and pay for performance. There are several methods of computing pay, e.g.:

  1. Point-factor-job evaluation

     (a) Managers prepare detailed job descriptions for all positions in the company.

     (b) Each job description is then rated according to common factors, such as working conditions, problem solving requirements, knowledge required to perform the job and accountability performance.

     (c) Each job accumulates points based upon how much each factor the job contained.

     (d) The resulting total point score is then used as a basis for establishing a salary level for each job. Jobs with high point scores are paid more than jobs with low point scores.

     (e) The point-factor base pay can be coupled with an annual merit increase that is linked to individual performance appraisals.

2. Pay-for-skill systems

(a) Pay-for-skill compensation system tie base to the skills an employee possesses in particular specialty. In general there are two types, i.e. (i) increased knowledge-bases system (tie pay to the depth of skills a person possesses in a particular speciality); and (ii) multi skilled systems (tie pay to the breadth of skills people have and/or the range of jobs they can perform across the organization.

- Build relationships between top management and all other levels with the view of creating a sense of ownership. Value suggestions and comments and respond to them wherever, it is practical.
- Career path setting supported by need-based training and development offered.
- Properly communicated visions, business directions and goals.
- Conduct a quarterly, bi-annual or annual performance appraisal for all staff. Train managers on giving and receiving open and honest feedback.
- Involvement in a job enriching project or in job rotation, thus killing the monotony of repetitive or routine work.
- Invest in training and development; relate the training budget as a percentage of payroll scales. This way we can relate the impact of training on the development of the business. Most Sri Lankan companies, when facing a down-trend will first cut the T & D budget. This is the most unfortunate!
- Adopt a strategic way to manage performance and retain the employee. Here is how we may do it—
  - (i) Develop high standards for consistent management and performance.
  - (ii) Provide guidance needed to perform at high levels of competence.
  - (iii) Provide opportunities for identifying each person's strengths and development needs.

(iv) Help employees assume greater responsibility for their own career development.

(v) Enhance communications between managers and employees.

- Have a practical and tested "grievance handling" mechanism which is simple and understood by all staff.
- Establish a performance related bonus scheme.
- Consider retention bonuses for identified top performers, to be paid after completing the first-three years in employment.
- Involve employees in decisions that affect them at work.
- Genuine attempt to convert employees into **business persons,** i.e. where there is a shared vision, a shared mindset and where the employees have a sense of direction as to where the organization is heading.
- A transplant goal and objective setting is recommended and where people can size up their achievements or failures against the companies expectations.

This way, people will have a greater buy-in-to a company's performance appraisal processes and could see more clearly 'what's in it for them'. To take this process forward a specimen integrated performance management plan is given below:

INTEGRATED PERFORMANCE MANAGEMENT PLAN

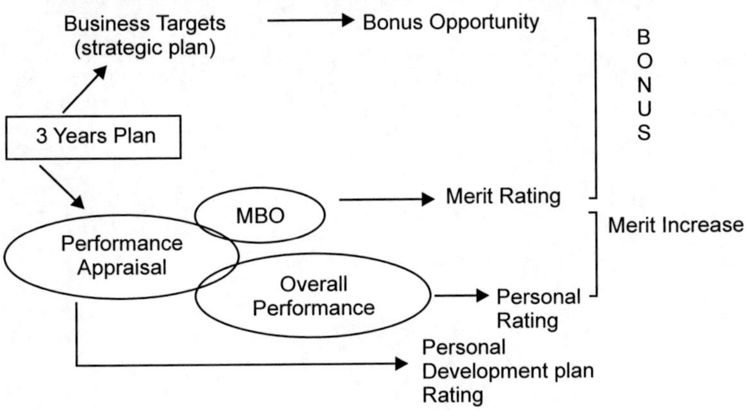

PART – 6
TALENT MANAGEMENT— CHALLENGES AND OPPORTUNITIES

Talent Retention: The Most Critical Issue in Contemporary HR Challenges

22

Rupali Singh and *Anshu Dawar*

Introduction

"People have become the key competitive differentiator in today's knowledge-based economy, but addressing these human performance or 'people issues' is still a vexing management problem for many corporate leaders, regardless of location, industry, or type of company."

Employee Retention: A Winning Mantra and the Need of the Hour Too...!!!

Ritz Carlton, an international hotel chain based its world-wide success on a simple philosophy: 'To take care of customers, you must first take care of those who take care of customers.' The result has been maximised efficiency and effectiveness since satisfied employees deliver high service value. Of course, the natural result is that their satisfied customers create sales and profits for the company.

How do companies in the Cayman Islands create this change? How do they care for their human resources and in so doing, maximise effectiveness? They can do this by paying attention to factors relating to individual employee's performance, employee motivation, and employee retention.

The performance of an individual employee is a major determinant of organizational success. However, when few employees know how to perform their jobs, when there is high turnover, or when employees work ineffectively, they become a liability and put the organization at a competitive disadvantage.

'Employees' are often seen as the front-line staff of the business, and through their work the organization succeeds or fails. However, the efficiency and productivity of front-line staff is often determined by a key manager. If key managers do not develop their staff, the business cannot succeed. The significance of key managers is often overlooked when considering the performance of an organization's human resources.

In management studies, the formula determining performance is: Individual Performance equals Ability times × Effort × times Support (IP = A × E × S). In many work environments the support component seems to have disappeared, and the emphasis has been only on ability and effort.

In the psychological contract between employee and employer, the employer often forgets their role as supporter in this partnership. With greater emphasis being placed only on employees' ability and effort—without employer support—it is more likely to lead to poor performance and even the inappropriate dismissal of an employee. Such a scenario is not a good example of organizational development. Employers should be cognizant of their role in providing support if they hope to create productive work environments.

Productive organizations support the performance of individuals. Organizational support can be provided in many forms: training and development, equipment and technology, setting clear performance standards, support from management and co-workers—to name a few. When an organization's support is added to the employee's ability and effort, the business will be more profitable, and just as importantly, it will be seen as a caring organization. The end result will then be maximised effectiveness.

In management theory, motivation is seen as 'complex and individualised' but organizations will need to develop uniform strategies and tactics to address equity across the organization and set clear expectations for their employees. Leaders and motivators will have to openly display elements of fairness and justice.

As part of the changing workplace, employers will need to find out what employees expect from their jobs and whether the rewards they receive are desirable and 'fair'. How does the organization do this? A first step would be to do an internal assessment of the organization. This would involve investigating the causes of low productivity, inefficiency and high employee turnover.

By talking and listening to employees, looking at the current methods used by the organization to bring about change, and seeing whether the methods used are effective or not, a sense of the reality of the organization can be reached. Most importantly, through this process, the organization will be seen as promoting a culture that supports change and motivates its employees. The impact that job satisfaction has on organizational commitment cannot be minimised. Employees need to know that their interests and concerns are being addressed if they are to be motivated and productive.

The final factor in caring for our human capital and maximising effectiveness is retention. Every employee that stays with an organization means one less person to recruit, select, and train. It is also important to note that organization and individual performance are enhanced by the continuity of employees who know their jobs, co-workers, organizational culture, services and products, and the organization's customers.

There are many reasons why employees leave organizations. Some factors are uncontrollable—employees leaving the islands, an employee going back to school, or individuals being dismissed for work-related violations. However, there are factors that can be influenced by the employer and it is these factors that need to be addressed.

Organizations that intend to maximise their efficiency and reduce turnover must deal with employees' concern. When investigating the potential for productive growth and profits that motivate and develop their human capital, several questions must be addressed. Does the organization have a positive culture that faces challenges, and values change? Is there a culture of trust where diverse opinions in seeking solutions to problems—internal and external—are encouraged and respected? Does compensation and promotion reflect performance? Are there opportunities for professional and personal development? Is there an appropriate balance between work and family?

Businesses with the potential for future growth, and enhanced profitability will take the responses to such questions into account in developing, progressive, productivity-enhancing approaches to developing its human resources.

With the Cayman economy facing a wave of change that will require improved productivity and efficiency, it must develop the country's human resources. By recognizing that Cayman's greatest resource is it people, its will be the development, motivation and retention of its human resources that will ensure its future success.

Staff Retention and Talent Management are Top HR Challenges for 2006

There are ample empirical proofs that establish the fact that staff retention and talent management will be the top HR issues facing businesses for the rest of 2007-08. A survey of 250 HR professionals, by HR consultancy Right-Coutts, reveals that 41 per cent cite the retention of key staff as their organization's most critical issue this year.

Recruiting enough talented individuals is also a hot topic, with 39 per cent of respondents making this issue a high priority. Just 12 per cent believe employee engagement is the top issue, which is a worrying trend, according to Edna Agbarha, head of talent management at Right-Coutts.

Strategies to maintain and develop employee engagement are currently not receiving enough attention and as a result this is having a knock on effect on the attraction and retention of key talent. Businesses need to address this issue sooner rather than later in order to avoid storing up trouble for the future. The research also indicates that despite new government guidelines requiring employers to take a certain amount of responsibility for staff wellbeing, many organizations are still not effectively tackling stress in the workplace.

Talent War Shifts to Battle for Retention

Despite recent corporate staff cutbacks, 80 per cent of global business leaders believe that "people issues" are more important today than they were three years ago, and 68 per cent believe that retaining talent is far more important than acquiring new blood, according to a new study.

The study, by Accenture and titled "The High Performance Workforce: Separating the Digital Economy's Winners from Losers", found that most companies continue to struggle with retention because they are relying on salary increases and bonuses to prevent turnover.

Leading companies have discovered that providing employees with a comprehensive range of career and skills-development opportunities is the key to attracting and retaining the kind of flexible, technology-savvy workforce needed to succeed in the digital economy.

The findings are based on interviews with nearly 500 senior executives from companies in eight countries on three continents and spanning 10 major industry groups. Almost half of the survey participants—47 per cent—identified themselves as senior executives of traditional, or "brick-and-mortar" firms, 39 per cent identified themselves as senior executives of "click-and-mortar" companies, and 14 per cent identified themselves as senior executives of pure-play Internet businesses, or "clicks."

Regardless of the type of company, however, the majority of changes were compensation-related. More than half of the executives in the study said they altered salaries, bonuses or stock options in their quest to attract and retain talent, while only 27 per cent reported that they adjusted their companies' policies to provide employees with advancement opportunities within their organizations.

The ongoing retention problem suggests that money itself is not the answer. In fact, Accenture's research indicates that companies can improve retention rates and improve employee performance by making it easier for workers to find new opportunities within an organization, and by developing the skills and knowledge of all talent, regardless of their position in the company.

For example, leading companies in the area of talent retention are:

- Using an inclusive approach to firm-wide strategy development by involving employees in company decision-making processes. In fact, 60 per cent of executives who described their companies as "leaders" in change said they use such an inclusive strategy-development method.
- Moving to project-oriented approaches, in which all employees can work on diverse, limited-term assignments, rather than being sequestered within a single department or function.
- Developing "talent exchanges", which connect employees and other resources with appropriate projects, roles and positions across the company.
- Instituting "real-time" goal setting, performance measurement, and skills-development programs to ensure that people always know where they stand and to address performance issues and skills gaps before they become a problem.
- Embracing a wide range of emerging information technologies—including personalized employee Web portals, business simulation, and relearning—to increase the efficiency and effectiveness of their training and development efforts.

Building a Strategy to Keep Good People

The search for a highly skilled electrical engineer to head product development had been long and time consuming. The high-tech firm had proceeded carefully, interviewing several candidates. While dozens applied for the job, only two or three met the full criteria.

The company was not about to gamble its future on the wrong choice. Management was resolved to expend, whatever time and resources were necessary to find the right person. The position required a true visionary who could lead the company's development efforts into the next century.

The person they selected was a superb technician, innovative and thoughtful, aware of both opportunities and pitfalls involved in marketing new products. He had a tremendous way with people, as well. The vice-president of engineering was thrilled with the find.

Now, 18 months later, just as the product development team was reaching the expected levels of innovation and effectiveness, the VP received the disappointing news. The director handed in his resignation, effective the end of the month. The company would have to begin the search process anew.

The VP's frustration was palpable. What had gone wrong? Why was the director leaving so suddenly? All the time and care that had gone into the selection, and now this. He wondered what he could do to guard against a similar experience with the next hire.

Turnover Rates are Rising

Stories like this are common in Silicon Valley and other high-tech corridors. In industries such as software and entertainment, some companies experience turnover rates as high as 35 per cent. Recent data suggest that turnover among professional, technical and managerial ranks is increasing in more traditional industries, as well.

Once You have Found Them, Never Let Them Go (or Almost Never)

With all the talk now about the end of cradle-to-grave employment and how often today's workers change jobs, some managers may feel that retention is a lost cause. Employees will go away and you can't stop 'em, right? Wrong. There are, in fact, many ways to keep them. One set of tips came from Diane Arthur, president of Arthur Associates Management Consultants, at a recent American Management Association seminar. She began with a discussion of the overall process: understanding what makes employees want to stay, why they may want to leave, and fostering a "retention environment". She then focused on more specific techniques, such as alternative work arrangements.

Two Sides of the Same Coin

Why do people stay, and why do they leave? The knee-jerk reaction is that these are two different questions—employees stay because it's a great company, but they leave for their own personal reasons. That's a nice, comforting rationale, because it lets the company off the hook. But the truth is, say Arthur and others; employees leave because the company isn't giving them what it would take to make them stay.

They'll stay if they're motivated by management, given opportunities to learn and grow, shown that their contributions are needed, and convinced that they are valued and appreciated. They'll leave if too many of those demonstrations are given short shrift or neglected entirely. Arthur states the foundation: Recognize and reward employees in personal, timely, thoughtful ways tailored to both the individual and his or her performance results.

That's the What; What's the How?

For example, she related, MacDonald's restaurants created a "Speedy Bucks" program in which gift certificates are used as a timely reward system for all employee levels. Managers who perform well are given certificates for Nordstrom, American Airlines, or Ritz Carlton hotels, while "crew" workers receive credits good at Wal-Mart or J.C. Penney. MacDonald's results prove the program works, since turnover is down even in this still-tight labor market.

Programs like those reward not just star performers but also what management consultants William M. Mercer Inc. called "the heart of the workforce" in a recent survey. More than half the responding companies reported that they were focusing as much on rank-and-file employees that Mercer described as "reliable, competent, and consistent performers" as on top producers, who compose only about 15 per cent of any employee body. Since the general population so greatly outnumbers the stars, performance improvements among these workers will bring better bottom-line results to any company. Individual rewards appropriate to all levels include incentive compensation and stock options.

Results of three other national surveys—from Hewitt Associates, the American Compensation Association, and the Conference Board—jive with Mercer's findings, especially on the subject of employees' pay. Even at executive levels, significant compensation increases are coming from bonuses, not base salaries. The most common forms of so-called variable pay, according to Hewitt, are special recognition awards (offered by 54 per cent of respondents), business incentives (53%), individual performance awards (45%), and stock options or ownership programs (36%). Another technique to motivate workers you want to keep is to administer pay increases—be they bonuses or permanent increases—more often than once a year, perhaps as often as every quarter, in functions that HR finds difficult to staff. This approach addresses Arthur's recommendation that rewards be timely.

Help Employees Work When and Where They Want

Like Arthur, however, Mercer consultants stress that the real key to retaining employees is fostering mutual trust, loyalty, and connection to the organization—feelings not always engendered by cash or stock awards.

Arthur asserts that alternative work arrangements—schedules and agreements that allow employees to balance their careers with family life and other interests—are extremely important to today's workforce. Telecommuting is the most common alternative: For employers, it lowers costs, boosts productivity, expands the potential recruiting audience, and facilitates diversity by allowing people who cannot commute to join the staff. For employees, it avoids typical office interruptions, enables people to work during "off hours" while caring for children or elders during the normal workday, and permits them to dress as they please. For both employer and employee, eliminating the daily commute reduces traffic congestion and motor vehicle accidents.

Another alternate arrangement is job sharing, in which (generally) two employees divide the time and responsibilities of one full-time job. Typical job sharers are parents, older workers, and students. Benefits of the scheme include a broader range of skills available for the work, more energy from both workers than either might have alone, reduced absenteeism, and less on-the-job time spent on personal matters by both.

The familiar flextime allows employees to work a full complement of the same hours each week but modify the schedule to vary from the usual 9 to 5. For example, a few employees might work from 7 a.m. to 3 p.m., while others arrive at noon and leave at 8 p.m. One advantage for employers is that an office can feature extended coverage. Compressed work weeks are a variation on this theme: Workers are on the job for four longer days instead of five shorter ones, leaving a day a week when they can attend to personal business and avoid the commute. Sabbaticals, in which long-term employees take off for six months or a year without pay to obtain further education or pursue other interests, are still another option. And so-called V-time, or temporarily reduced work schedules, usually involves allowing one or more full-time employees to switch to part-time for six months or a year.

Arthur also encourages succession planning, a method of grooming top performers for positions of greater responsibility. While that sounds like a program designed to achieve strategic business goals, it turns out that it's also a very effective way of rewarding employees that management has identified as must-keeps; in short, it functions as a good retention program. Arthur describes a typical program this way:

- Identify your top performers, using such metrics as productivity, competencies, and ability to work with a team.
- Maintain their profiles in a database.
- Work with each to map out an ambitious career path.
- Help each one manage his or her career.
- Assess each for individual vulnerabilities to be lured away, and act to strengthen their commitment in appropriate ways.
- Frequently discuss with them how their current job responsibilities relate to their long-term goals.

- Negotiate ways of expanding or refining their jobs to fill in missing skills or appeal to special interests.

How it's done at One Company

At Capital One, a large financial services company headquartered in Falls Church, Virginia, one foundation of an extensive retention program is semi-annual surveys of employees' opinions and experiences at the firm. Spokesperson Diana Don reports that survey questions cover a broad range of issues, from whether or not the staff member understands the company's vision and goals to specific details about his or her work environment. Sample results are that 91 per cent of employees say the company is a fun place to work, and 95 per cent report they have confidence in senior management. (According to consultants at Hewitt, the nationwide benchmark for such confidence among employees is only 75 per cent.)

Capital One has grown very rapidly in recent years, hiring 4,000 new employees in 1998 and 5,000 in 1999. A key business goal after such an extensive and expensive recruitment effort, is to hang onto the talent and energy the company acquired. Along with surveys, other ways of "listening to associates" include "Town Hall meetings", in which top management of Capital One meets with all employees in one of the firm's 10 locations, and "Village meetings," in which all employees in a location meet with local managers to ask questions and discuss the state of the business.

As a result of employees' responses in all these forums, HR identified education, training, and development as a top priority. Some of management's responses include enhancing the tuition reimbursement program to provide 100 per cent payback to staffers, establishing what the company calls IT University to offer the latest computer programming and other high tech training, and creating a division in HR that's devoted to competency-development planning. Based on specific competencies identified as necessary for each function, each employee works out an individual Development Action Plan to further his or her interests and correct deficiencies. Each is provided with a customized package of books, courses, and other material available from a wide variety of vendors and targeted to the employee's particular goals. Such tools can range from an inexpensive workbook to help the individual assess his or her conflict management style to a nine-month course in heading up effective work teams.

Don speculates that however, important training and development are among the 15,000 Capital One employees, other concessions to workers' wishes are also meaningful. For herself, the adoption of a "business casual" dress code that applies not only five days a week but also to headquarters employees was a genuine bonus.

Keep It in Perspective

Now that you have hired them, what do you do to keep them? Stay in tune with the market and your people. As the incumbent employer, you have the best opportunity to assess and fulfill your employees' wants and needs. But you also have the greatest chance to disappoint those employees by failing to meet their expectations. Don't lose sight of why people joined; when that is gone, they will follow. If you get complacent, someone will come along and treat your company like their team's farm system.

We always tell candidates: "do your job well and either your company will reward you or your industry will". That is truer than ever. You must recognize and reward the people who contributed to your success. It's not enough to let them keep their job. Companies are not competitive today simply because they were last year or even last month. Someone, somewhere is willing to pay a premium for your staff; something makes employees receptive to the inevitable call of the headhunter, and amenable to looking, listening, interviewing, considering and ultimately resigning to join another firm.

If you know what drives your players then you know how to keep them happy. If your salary scale is skewed, fix it or don't hire money-motivated people, and don't fret when they leave. They don't fit your system, and as Darwin and Lee Iacocca said (more or less), adapt or perish. However, if too many quality employees are leaving, it's time to challenge your own assumptions. Since most people won't willingly trade a good situation for a bad one, even if a smooth-talking solicitor sidles up and spins a tale of Internet gold, employers must lose the denial mechanism and stay alert for shifts in the mood and climate. If Dilbert cartoons have been popping up around the office, stop laughing at the jokes about "all those other companies" and do some meaningful soul searching.

How to Keep the Competition from Stealing Your Staff

In 1998, a Pittsburgh food-processing company hired a 25 years old man for an entry-level sales position. The company proceeded to train the employee, and provided him with a company car, expense account, and complete benefits package. Two years later, a rival food company from Dayton, Ohio, approached the employee. With hopes of profiting, not only from the employee's training, but also from his customer contacts, the competitor offered the man a substantial raise in salary and a signing bonus. He accepted, and in his new position, managed to convince many of his old customers to divert their business to his Dayton employer. As a result, the Pittsburgh company not only lost a valuable employee, but also suffered a serious decline in sales.

Sound familiar? Unfortunately, it's an all-too-common situation in American business. Many employers even regard this kind of loss as an inevitable consequence of free enterprise. But does it have to be? Is there anything employers can do to protect themselves?

While most companies wouldn't consider doing business without insuring their assets against damage or loss, their true business assets—their customers and customer goodwill—remain vulnerable. There is a solution, and it's remarkably easy to implement. In the example above, the Pittsburgh company could have prevented or at least deterred its Dayton competitor from hiring the employee by utilizing one simple document—an employment non-competition agreement.

Get it in Writing

In an employment non-competition agreement, an employee agrees not to compete with the employer, within a defined geographic territory, for a specified period of time after the employee leaves the employment of the employer. A non-competition agreement is typically obtained at the beginning of the employment relationship, although it may be secured at any time. Employment non-competition agreements are also called "restrictive covenants" and "covenants-not-to-compete".

Be Reasonable

State law determines specific steps that an employer must take in order to obtain a valid employment non-competition agreement. Under the law of most states, including Pennsylvania, an employment non-competition agreement is enforceable if it is (1) ancillary to an employment relationship, (2) supported by adequate consideration, and (3) reasonably limited in time and geographic scope.

The first requirement is easy to satisfy. A non-competition agreement that an employee enters into with his employer is, by its nature, ancillary to an employment relationship.

An employer can meet the second requirement—that the agreement be supported by adequate consideration—by requiring the employee to enter into the agreement at the time of hire. The employer's agreement to hire the employee is adequate consideration to support a non-competition agreement. On the other hand, in many states, including Pennsylvania, an employee's mere continued employment is not adequate consideration to support a non-competition agreement. Accordingly, if a non-competition agreement has not been obtained at the time of hire, the employer must provide the employee with a pay increase, promotion, new employment benefit or some other improvement, in order to obtain a valid non-competition agreement from the employee.

Don't Hang on Too Long

The third prerequisite for a non-competition agreement—that the covenant be reasonably limited in time and geographic scope—poses the greatest challenge for employers. The law provides no definitive guidance concerning what is a reasonable period of time for a non-competition agreement to remain in effect; the law similarly provides no definitive guidance concerning what is a reasonable geographic territory in which a non-competition agreement may apply. Instead, the law suggests that the reasonableness of a non-competition agreement is to be determined on a case-by-case basis, and that a number of factors affect whether the agreement will be found to be reasonable. Of those factors, the principal one is what restrictions in time and territory are reasonably necessary to protect the employer's legitimate business interests. Other factors include the nature of the employer's business, the position the employee holds, the training provided by the employer, the employee's access to customers and confidential business information, the length of employment, the geographic area in which the employee works, and the geographic area in which the employer does business.

Courts generally will find that non-competition agreements lasting one year or less are reasonably limited in time. Agreements lasting between one and five years may be found to be reasonable or unreasonable, depending on the circumstances. Courts generally will find that non-competition agreements lasting for more than five years are not reasonably limited in time.

Non-competition agreements that are limited to the geographic area in which the employee actually performed services for the employer generally will be found to be reasonably limited in geographic scope. Courts typically will not enforce worldwide or nationwide covenants, or covenants that cover a geographic territory broader than the area in which the employee performed services for the employer.

Protect your investment: Almost any employer has a legitimate business interest in preventing recently departed employees from competing. Employees may have access to business information that reasonably can be regarded as confidential. An employee who leaves to go to work for a competitor may intentionally use that confidential business information. Alternatively, the nature of the former employee's new position may be such that he cannot avoid using the information in performing his new duties. Naturally, a company has a legitimate business interest in preventing its former employees from engaging in competitive employment that may result in their revealing or using confidential information.

Most employers make significant investments in their employees. Employers may invest in employee training, and may pay expenses that enable employees to develop customer relationships and industry knowledge. In many cases, a competitor gains an unfair competitive advantage if it is able to divert the dividends of these investments by hiring the employer's personnel. A company has a legitimate business interest in preventing others from gaining this unfair competitive advantage.

Why Not Keep It Confidential?

An employer may utilize confidentiality agreements and confidentiality policies in an effort to protect its proprietary commercial information. In reality, however, these agreements are of limited value in preventing the harm caused by a former employee's competitive activities. It generally is difficult for an employer to detect—and even harder to prove—a violation of a confidentiality agreement or policy. Employees who have gone to work for a competitor will not call their former employer to report that they are using the employer's trade secrets. Moreover, even if the employer were able to prove that a former employee has violated a confidentiality agreement or policy, the only sanction a court would likely impose would be an order requiring the employee to return all confidential information and not to utilize that information further. Confidentiality agreements and policies thus afford little protection to employers.

Discourage Job Jumping

Non-competition agreements, on the other hand, afford employers significant protection. An employee who has entered into a non-competition agreement may be disinclined to seek out employment with a competitor, either out of a desire to abide by his agreement or out of fear of the consequences. A non-competition agreement thus may deter an employee from even applying for employment with a competitor.

A non-competition agreement may also deter a competitor from recruiting or hiring an employee who is bound by that agreement. Whenever possible, businesses usually attempt to avoid the trouble and considerable expense of litigation. During the interview process, a company generally will ask a prospective employee whether he has signed a non-competition agreement. If the employee has, the company typically will think twice before hiring him. The company may very much desire to hire the employee, but may not want to become embroiled in litigation with the individual's employer. So even in cases where a non-competition agreement doesn't deter an employee from seeking out employment with a competitor, the agreement may deter the competitor from hiring the employee.

Nothing to Lose

The benefits of deterrence come at little cost to an employer. An employer can reap these benefits simply by requiring employees to sign non-competition agreements at the time of hire. The benefits of deterrence accrue without the employer's having to endure the cost and inconvenience of litigation.

Non-competition agreements also protect employers from unfair competition in a second significant way. They provide employers with a means to enjoin unfair competition through court proceedings. Contrary to a common misperception, courts will enforce non-competition agreements, provided that the agreements satisfy the three prerequisites set forth above. Moreover, in Pennsylvania, even if a court should find that a non-competition agreement is unreasonably broad in time or geographic scope, the court has the ability to modify the time or geographic restriction and to enforce the non-competition agreement as so modified. A court typically enforces a non-competition agreement by issuing an injunction, restraining the employee from continuing to work for the competitor. Thus, even if the existence of a non-competition agreement does not have the desired effect of deterring an employee from applying for employment with a competitor or of deterring the competitor from hiring the employee, the agreement provides the employer with a mechanism to stop the unfair competition.

An Ounce of Prevention

Confidential business information, customer relationships, and customer goodwill are important assets to any company.

As with other corporate assets, a company should insure against potential damage to these important assets. Employment non-competition agreements constitute insurance that is inexpensive and relatively easy to obtain. Employers should take advantage of this insurance by securing non-competition agreements from their key employees.

Conclusion: Is Your Company Losing Olympians But Keeping Non-Qualifiers?

With today's emphasis on employee retention, organizations often put as much effort into keeping under-performers as they do their superstars, according to career services firm Lee Hecht Harrison. But this mistake can be avoided by classifying employees into four groups and taking different approaches with each.

LHH's Chief Operating Officer Bernadette Kenny said companies should first answer such questions as: Which employees have core and secondary skills? Who are the key players and top performers? Who are most versatile? Who have raw talent? Who are ready to go? Then all employees may be placed in categories:

Gold Medal Contenders: Individuals who fit and are positioned properly.

Olympic Qualifiers: Individuals who fit but need to be repositioned.

Olympic Hopefuls: Individuals who can potentially fit somewhere in the organization.

Non-Qualifiers: Individuals who don't fit or who don't want to fit.

Organizations have a different responsibility towards each group as indicated. Moreover, organizations should be sure employees know what they must do to advance their own careers: "Employees not only have a right to know how they're doing, but the company also benefits from giving clear direction about how individuals can better meet corporate needs".

REFERENCES

American Conference Institute (1998). "High Tech Employee Retention Conference". Presentation by Computer World, Chicago, IL.

U.S. Department of Labor. Bureau of Labor Statistics.

Critchley, R.K. (2006). "The Ageing Workforce—to Rewire or Rust". Paper prepared for the TAFE NSW International Centre for VET Teaching and Learning.

Donaldson, Craig (2006). Companies Need to Flick on Talent Switch Human Resources, 31 October.

Duttagupta, R. (2005). "Identifying and Managing Your Assets: Talent Management". *Intellectual Asset* Magazine.

Frank Fredric and Taylor, Craig (2004). "Talent Management: Trends that will Shape the Future". *Human Resource Planning*, Vol. 27, pp. 33-41.

PART – 7
TALENT RETENTION AND DEVELOPMENT

Employee Retention: By Way of Management Control Systems

23

Shailesh Rastogi and *Vikas Tripathi*

Introduction

Gone are the days when the entrepreneurs were the only important stakeholder in the business organizations. Now there has been a shift from entrepreneur to people as the most important part of any organization that believes or longs for sustainable growth in the organization. People have become a very important stakeholder in any organization. But as the benefits takes precedence over loyalty and professionalism creeps into the organizations and it becomes unyielding task to retain talented people in the organizations.

Evolution is a continuous process. Organizations are also systems and every system evolves with time. Organizations do not operate in vacuum. Organizations are integral part of markets which are also larger systems; ergo they are also subject to evolution. Organizations are evolving and so as the markets are evolving. Earlier we were sellers' market but now we are a buyers' market. Earlier business organizations did not bother much about what is being made, whether its price is correct or not and whether it is value for money to the buyers or not. But situations have evolved and changed drastically by now (It is our meticulous attempt to equate evolution with change). Competition has also taken its root in full swing and it is the customers who are ruling the roost now. This could be a point of debate whether competition does more good or harm but one thing is for sure that it mounts unsurpassable pressure on organization to bring efficiency in everything the organization does. Moreover, who proactively does this corrective exercise, gets the first movers advantage and this brings an addition edge to the organization over its competitors. Otherwise it hardly takes a short span of time for an organization to come to cropper from a commanding position.

This pressing need to bring efficiency in all the things which an organization does, also force organization to introduce many a new things. Human Resources Management is one such thing. Before such time organizations did not have much time to look towards such important factor of production so seriously. Gradually the organizations are coming to terms with this fact that ultimately it is its people who make all the difference in the value creation in or for the organization in long-run. Rising contribution and importance of services sector in the India's GDP has merely facilitated and endorsed this fact. These new economy organizations who are our new bellwether for economic growth and development have taken note of this fact at the earliest that without concentrating upon people they can't remain in business for long. In other words it can also be said that they were left with no other option but to look forward towards the people in the organizations. Because these new economy organizations are operating in such an environment where capital stock has been relegated to second rung over human capital who have acquired the top most priority.

Even the traditional economy organizations are also no longer untouched from such a situations. As our economy has come out of clutches of bureaucracy and red-tapism and cut-throat competition is new order of the day, these traditional organizations are also feeling the heat. Though, it is the new economy organizations that are bearing the maximum burnt in terms of high attrition rate, the traditional economy organization are also gradually coming to terms with the problem of relatively rising attrition rate. The situations gets further exacerbated owing to this fact that the most talented people are the fist who leave the organizations. The less talented and less productive people either prefers to stay in the organizations or they are last to alight the ship. Knowing the problem is the first step in curing the disease. At this point it becomes germane to take into consideration the causes of attrition in the business organizations.

Causes of Employee Attrition

There could be many reasons for one to leave an organization. After all one has to work in every situation whether he works in this organization or in a new organization, therefore it is imperative to have the idea about why at all someone leaves an organization and joins the another one. Had the employee been not interested in the work the story would have been altogher different. But if this is not the case and the person concerned is still working it means something was unusually difficult or terribly wrong in the previous organization.

This world is not heaven nor is the people gods who are living in the world. Both, this world and people are imperfect. It means their problems are also not going to be perfect. Rather everything the people, the organizations and the problems of people who work in the organizations all are imperfect. Therefore, we have to look towards them not as if we are looking towards perfectionists but as if we are looking towards imperfect ones. Now we are in position to concede that their reasons for leaving the organization may or may not be real. But in most of the cases it could easily be understood that whatever had been the reason for leaving, the employee was ultimately dissatisfied with the organization and decided to quit. In fact a dissatisfied employee is worse than not having an employee at all because when one is not satisfied he does more harm than the good for the organization. He disseminates the virus of dissatisfaction to other employees of the organization. Besides this he also does not do his works up to the mark and continuously grumble against the organization which sets a bad example to other members of the organization.

Here we can start thinking for a solution to the problem in hand. Hitting such a problem head-on has two approaches. One way is to look at the various reasons for dissatisfaction and looking for how to cure them individually or collectively. The second approach could be to look for ways and means that how the employees could be kept satisfied so that they do not feel dissatisfied at all. This second approach is a better way of looking at the problem because instead of saying that the glass is half empty we are concentrating on saying that the glass is half filled. There are couple of questions which comes up easily as we start talking about the second approach of making satisfied, because we know this very well that people are not saint that they are going to behave in most decent manner and only good things are expected of them after all as we have said earlier that except God all the other things are imperfect and incomplete in this world.

It means that if we follow the second approach, we are basically talking that everyone could be satisfied. Here my proposition is that yes it is very much possible to keep everyone satisfied but he may or may not be happy. Being satisfied and being happy are two different things. All those who come for work, they do come for work. They may not be happy with their lives, they may not be happy with their spouses and they may not be happy with any damn thing, but when they are ready to work they should definitely deserve to be satisfied with their work. Some people may differ with us on this count on this grounds that there are some people who are bad and they simply don't want to work, not to speak of their satisfaction. It is the proper or improper placing of people which makes all the difference. It is not the subordinate who may be labeled as shirker is bad but the boss who does not know how to use his subordinate may be questionable much more than the subordinate. I am bringing our attention towards inwards from out wrong habit of looking outward for anything and everything. So I am taking this for granted that no one is bad in the whole world if we place employees in a proper manner. Someone may not be suitable for some organization but he would definitely be pretty useful for some other organization. Means, this suitability could be taken care of very seriously at the time of recruitment and even later on also. But, if someone is fit-in in the organization, this issue that some employee is bad does not exist at all. He should simply be placed at the proper work so that he would also be productive. It means everyone who is willing to work in the organizations is a genuine case for getting satisfaction with his work. In spite of this fact people leave the organization because they are dissatisfied from the organization. Therefore, it is high time for introspection.

A threadbare analysis of causes of dissatisfaction leads me to this conclusion that in organizations only two things—Reward and Punishment are relevant as far as the satisfactions or dissatisfaction is concerned. Here again I would reiterate the point that no one is perfect so there would be neither perfect problems nor are their perfect solutions exist. But the biggest source of dissatisfaction in the organizations is due to not having fairness in the execution of both rewards and punishments. We can easily understand this by taking simple example that if somebody commits a mistake and he is punished for the same he would not feel bad (though he may not be happy with this) as long as he is the culprit. But, if has not committed the mistake and he gets punishment which would lead to grave dissatisfaction. Same is applicable to reward and punishment system in the organization.

According to us the best solution to the problem of talent retention is to bring fairness in both the systems of organizations; fairness in the system of reward as well as in the system of punishment.

Having subjectivity in the system of reward and punishment is the major reason for not having fairness. The next obvious question is how to remove the subjectivity from the organization and to bring objectivity in the system. Here comes the Management Control System (MCS) for rescue which is also one of the latest tools for planning and for better control in the business organizations. MCS is fully capable of bringing the objectivity in the system which would automatically remove the subjectivity from the system of reward and punishment of the organization.

Management Control System (MCS)

A management control system is a logical integration of techniques for gathering and using information to make planning and control decisions, for motivating employee behavior, and evaluating performance. The purposes of a management control system are—

- to clearly communicate the organizations' goals to the employees,

- to ensure that managers and employees understand the specific actions required of them to achieve organizational goals,
- to communicate results of actions across the organization,
- to ensure the employee/managers can adjust to the changes in the organization.

A well designed management control supports and coordinates the decision-making process and motivates individuals throughout the organization to act in concert. The first and most basic component in a management control system is the organizations' goals. Because the focus of the management control system is on motivating decisions that help achieve the organizations goals. A basic adage of management control system is that "you get what you measure". It means the measures of performance will influence managers' decisions; therefore measure of performance should be consistent with the organizations goals.

To design the management control system that meets the organizations' goals or organizations needs, the whole job of designing is done in four stages. (Fig. 23.1)

Stage 1: Identifying Responsibility Centers

Under this stage the whole organization is divided into responsibility centers and for every responsibility center their goals are decided and responsibilities are also fixed.

Stage 2: Developing Performance Measures

For every responsibility center the performance measures are fixed. Means if some responsibility has been assigned then the method of their measurements are developed at this stage. Unless we measure the performance, no objectivity could be introduced in the system. To practically implement this performance measures, Key Performance Indicators (KPIs) should be developed for every responsibility center. KPIs are measurement of the performance in a very clear cut and quantifiable terms.

Stage 3: Monitoring and Reporting

After having fixed the responsibility centers and having placed the KPIs in place the job of MCS just begins. Because this system needs continuous reporting and monitoring so that it is ensured that everyone follows the system to the fullest and if there seems to be any need of improvements in the MCS itself that could also be introduced.

Stage 4: Rendering of Rewards and Making People take Corrective Actions

After having gone through the first three stages up to the reporting, the next obvious stage is to render rewards to those

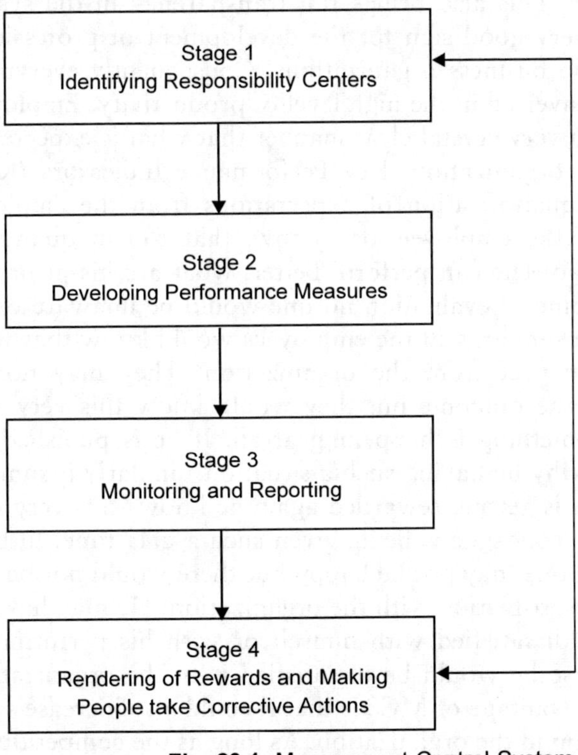

Fig. 23.1: Management Control System

who perform better than expected. Besides this, the next step is taking corrective actions for those performances that are found to be low and taking the decision of even firing to those who are either far below expectations or are not having the scope of improvement at all.

Talent Retention by Management Control System

As the organizations introduces the MCS in the system of rewarding and punishment, a positive feel factor starts taking its root at the workplace. Subjectivity also goes away. Policy of appeasement, sycophancy, and favoritism also gets sidelined and objectivity starts taking its place in the whole system. MCS is one such system in which the top management also ties its hand. Unless the performance is as per the objectivity of MCS, no one could be rewarded despite the willingness of the top management. This also brings full transparency in the system which is a very good sign for the development of professional culture in the business organizations. Consequently everything would be converted in the high level of productivity. Employees also know in very crystal clear manner that what is expected of them in the organization. Key Performance Indicators (KPIs) also brings quantification of expectations from the employee and in turn the employee also know, that too in quantified terms, that how he can perform better, what are his priorities, etc. At the time of evaluation no one would be unaware of his performance similarly all the employees would know that what they could expect from the organization. They may not be happy with the outcome but they would know this very well that why something is happening at all. If he is punished, he knows that why he having such a situation, similarly if some of his colleague is getting rewarded again he knows this very well that why his colleague is being given such a gala time. In both the situation one may not be happy but there would not be any room for dissatisfaction with the organization. He may have all rights to be dissatisfied with himself or with his performance but in no case he would be dissatisfied with the organization. The added advantage of MCS is that it could also increase sense of competition in the organization. As long as the competition is healthy, it would definitely benefit the organization in more than one ways. Here we are hitting the problem of employee attrition from two sides. On the one side we are making the employee more satisfied and on the other side we are creating an environment of competition so that employee would get less time to think of anything else. MCS is not only capable enough to have employee attrition reduced but it would also have the potential to bring high level of productivity in the organization. Both the things omen good for the organization in the long run.

Conclusion

There is no system which is cent per cent fool proof. It can't be expected that just by introducing the management control system (MCS) all the problems related to the employee retention is going to be removed altogether. But with all sincerity it could be expected with MCS that it has the potential to solve many such problems in the business organizations. One caveat which is attached with every system is applied here also that unless the system is properly executed in letter and spirit we can never expect good results in short-run and rich dividends in the long-run. Because developing one MCS is in itself a mammoth task but successful implementation of MCS is even much more arduous than the mere developing of MCS.

REFERENCES

Anthony, Robert N. (2007). *Management Control System*, 12th ed. New York: McGraw Hill.

Besanko, David et al. (2004). *Economics of Strategy*, 3rd ed. New York: John Wiley & Sons.

Bossily, Larry and Ram Charan (2002). *Execution: The Discipline of Getting Things Done*, New York: Crown Books.

Dent, Jeremy F. "Global Competition: Challenges for Management Accounting and Control." *Management Accounting Research* 7, No. 2 (June 1996), pp. 247-69.

Govindrajan, Vijay et al. (2005). *Ten Rules for Strategic Innovations: From Idea to Execution*. Boston: Harvard Business School Press.

Horngren, Charles T. et al. (2005). *Introduction to Management Accounting*, 13th ed. Delhi: Pearson Education.

Marciariello, J.A. and C.J. Kirby (1994). *Management Control System*, Engelwood Cliffs, N.J: Prentice-Hall.

Shank, John K. and Vijay Govindrajan (1993). *Strategic Cost Management*, New York: Free Press.

A Study of Talent Retention Practices in BPOs

24

Aneesya Sharma and *Ekta Sikarwar*

INTRODUCTION

"A love of precision is not a skill, nor it is knowledge. It is a Talent."

A tone deaf will never be able to appreciate the music of maestros. Only a seasoned jeweler would know that all that glitters is not real! And only those who can recognize the worth of a diamond can value it, for others it's just a stone! Talent is easily what others find difficult.

Intelligent employers always realize the importance of retaining the best talent. Retaining talent has never been so important in the Indian scenario; however, things have changed in recent years. Retention of key employees and treating attrition troubles has been now become important to companies, as it is critical to the long-term health and success of any organization. It is a known fact that retaining the best employees ensures customer-satisfaction, increased product sales, satisfied colleagues and reporting staff, effective succession planning and deeply imbedded organizational knowledge and learning.

Employee retention matters as organizational issues such as training time and investment; lost knowledge; insecure employees and a costly candidate search are involved. Hence, failing to retain a key employee is a costly proposition for an organization.

The BPOs in India face an enormous challenge in reducing attrition rate and this being a nascent industry needs to draw parallels. When there are so many benefits associated with BPO industry.... When there are so many privileges for the BPO employees than what makes them to change the company/

industry? Is it only MONEY that matters or anything else as well?

OBJECTIVES OF THE STUDY

The objective of the present study is to determine the current attrition rate in BPOs, reasons and factors impacting retention and challenges that HR professionals or top management face in managing talent. In this study the prevailing retention practices in BPOs are to be assessed and evaluated. The innovative strategies are also proposed that these companies can adopt to get a better solution and also looking at the common myths associated with this HR practice.

Methodology of the Study

To know about retention strategies adopted by various Indian BPO companies (especially the call centers) the internet and print medium like magazine and news paper were used in which the interviews of HR managers were published. The reason behind choosing call center segment of BPO is, Customer care based call center activities constitute for more than one third of the total employment and revenue in the BPO segment (Babu P. Ramesh, 2004).

HIGH ATTRITION—A BIG CHALLENGE FOR BPO INDUSTRY

The IT enabled services (BPO) industry is being looked upon as the next big employment generator (Nasscom predicts 1.1 million job requirement by the year 2008). It is however no easy task for an HR manager in this sector to bridge the ever increasing demand and supply gap of professionals. Unlike his software industry counterpart, the BPO HR manager is not only required to fulfill this responsibility, but also find the right kind of people who can keep pace with the unique work patterns in this industry. Adding to this is the issue of maintaining consistency in performance and keeping the motivation levels high, despite the monotonous work. The toughest concern for an HR manager is however the high attrition rate.

In India, the average attrition rate in the BPO sector is approximately 30-35 per cent and, in two years, it will face a shortage of 30-40 per cent, according to the recent study of

Associated Chambers of Commerce and Industry of India (Assocham).

Why People Leave?

In spite of the salaries and facilities being high (especially for a graduate who starts his/her career with a BPO company) the average attrition rate is very high in this industry. In an industry like BPO, the work can often be monotonous and opportunities for career growth minimal. So when opportunities beckon, the high rate of attrition is not surprising. However, there are some common reasons that especially cause people to leave. In this night shifts, money, inability to handle various types of stress, monotonous work; company policies, lack of career growth, problems with those in senior positions, higher education, misguidance by the company, no personal life, etc., as some of the most common reasons listed by BPO employees for quitting jobs.

Managing Talent—Challenges for HR

First quite often in their bid to attract talent HR oversells the organization to the new recruit. It is easy to recruit good talent but very difficult to retain them specially if the foundation of the relationship has been based on misrepresentation on the truth.

The next challenge for both the HR and the employee is to ensure that there is clarity in the communication of roles and responsibilities. Finally, having ill structured compensation packets.

CONTEMPORARY RETENTION STRATEGIES

Companies have different kinds of strategies adopted to tackle the problem of retaining human capital. It ranges from cash incentives to career concern for the employee.

As only 5 out of 150 employees become team leaders in a year, companies like Daksh Services and Global Vantedge believe that cash incentives are a great way to get employees to stay on (Shelley Singh, 2003). Companies like GE, Wipro Spectramind Offer Management Diplomas and MBA courses to their employees, as most fresh graduates want to study further. (Shelley Singh, 2003).

Exl Service.com and ICICI one source hires outstation candidates (Mainly Non-Metros) and put them in shared company accommodation. Also for leading call centers like 24/7 customer and M source E non-metro talent currently constitutes nearly 25-35 per cent of total hiring, and the main reason for this to happen is to reduce attrition rate (R. Raghavendra, 2003).

Many companies like HCL Tech BPO Services, GTL, Tracmail, and Vertex India use various psychometric tests to get people who can work at night and can handle the monotony. They also believe that giving career counseling and planning career paths to its employee help to control attrition.

Some other BPO majors like Wipro's Spectramind believe that recruiting the undergraduates itself is a strategy to control attrition. Spectramind removed the graduation prerequisite for their employees in order to keep human resource level from waning (Sharvari Joshi, 2003).

Leaving alone the legal and mandatory benefits such as provident-fund and gratuity, other strategies that are designed by the BPOs for providing benefits to the professionals include.

Group Medi-claim Insurance Scheme which is to provide adequate insurance coverage of employees for expenses related to hospitalization due to illness, disease or injury or pregnancy in case of female employees or spouse of male employees.

Subsidized Food and Transportation: BPOs provide transportation facility to all the employees from home till office at subsidized rates or even at zero cost. Lunch is also provided free of cost.

Company Leased Accommodation: Some of the companies provides shared accommodation for all the out station employees. The purpose is to provide to the employees to lead a more comfortable work life balance.

Recreation, Cafeteria, ATM, Gym and Concierge Facilities: The recreation facilities include pool tables, chess tables and coffee bars. BPOs companies also have well equipped gyms, personal trainers and showers at facilities.

Corporate Credit Card: The main purpose of the corporate credit card is enable the timely and efficient payment of official expenses which the employees undertake for purposes such as travel related expenses like Hotel bills, Air tickets, etc. Cellular phone/Laptop are provided to the employees on the basis of business need.

Personal Health Care (Regular medical check-ups): Some of the BPOs provide the facility for extensive health check-up. For employees with above 40 years of age, the medical check-up are given once in a year.

Loans: Many BPO companies provide loan facility on different occasions like, during the times of medical emergency, at the time of their wedding, also new recruits are provided with interest free loans to assist them in their initial settlement at the work location.

Educational Benefits: Many BPO companies have this policy to develop the personality and knowledge level of their employees and hence reimburse the expenses incurred towards tuition fees, examination fees, and purchase of books for pursuing MBA, and/or other management qualification at India's topmost Business Schools.

Performance Based Incentives: In many BPO companies they have plans for, performance based incentive scheme. The parameters for calculation are process performance, i.e. speed, accuracy and productivity of each process. The Pay for Performance is high as 22 per cent of the salary.

Regular Get Together and Other Cultural Programs: BPOs also organizes cultural program as and when possible but most of the times, once in a quarter, in which all the employees are given an opportunity to display their talents in dramatics, singing, acting, dancing, etc. Apart from that the organizations also conduct various sports programs such as cricket, football, etc. and regularly play matches with the teams of other organizations and colleges.

Wedding Day Gift: Employee is given wedding day gift voucher worth Rs. 2000 to Rs. 7000 based on their level in the organization.

Employee Referral Scheme: In several companies employee referral scheme is implemented to encourage employees to refer friends and relatives for employment in the organization.

Employee Stock Option Plan: Some BPOs also give ESOP scheme to their employees to make them more loyal to the company they work.

In spite of these benefits that are given through innovative strategies, people still leave BPOs at a faster rate and retaining them has become a real challenge for the HR managers. Now, the actual question, what types of retention strategies are required to solve this problem and retain the human capita, which is a crucial resource in the high growth IT-ITES industry in India (www.nasscom.org).

TACTICS FOR IMPROVING RETENTION

There are certain myths or misconceptions related to the talent retention which are need to be understand by the organizations to improve retention. The five most valued talent retention interventions are—

(1) 'Retention and Attrition'—Two Different Metrics

Most of the organizations are still reeling under impression that employee retention is the answer to attrition woes but the fact is attrition and retention are different and do not complement each other. Attrition indicates the number of employees left the organization through retirement, resignation or death. It may be voluntary and non-voluntary. But retention looks at ensuring that critical and core employees stay with the organization.

So the companies should try to find out the relevant attrition rate by classifying it into the various categories. The employees who left the organization by getting dissatisfied should be identified. Employees leaving for genuine reasons like marriage, death, higher studies, family and health problems, locational advantages should be excluded. This can be effectively done by conducting Exit interview. This gives organization a sense of the drain they are facing in key manpower and helps them to prepare retention plans.

Retention on the other hand is ongoing and continuous process and related to current employees. Retention is precaution, not cure and should not be the outcome of attrition. So in order to improve retention the companies should monthly conduct a internal survey of employees so that satisfaction level can be determined and preventive measures can be adopted to improve the satisfaction among employees.

(2) 'Talent Retention' is not 'People Retention'

Unlike most of the organizational policies and practices; the retention practices cannot be implemented or applicable for all employees. It is not feasible also for a mid sized organization. So organization need to identify its core and critical employees it would like to retain and role out retention plans for them specifically for them. The employees who are necessary but not core/critical and their attrition has minimum impact on the performance of the organization can be excluded or ignored.

(3) Retention Plans—One Size does not Fit All

As we already know that individuals have different needs and satisfaction level according to the Maslows need hierarchy. So while preparing retention plans companies should try to identify the individual employees needs and expectations. Organizations need to understand which retention practice would suit to its employees' individual specific needs and frame out the specific policies rather than a general plan.

It is very pertinent to say that all employees cannot be satisfied or motivated by giving more monetary benefits or higher salary. Although it will work as a exit barrier up to a certain extent but sometimes more important is the career growth and development opportunities. One should remember the Hertzberg theory of HR. Employees are motivated when they involved in the area of their interest. So company should identify the motivational factors for individual employees and plan accordingly.

(4) People Leave 'Managers' not 'Company'

Gurt Coffman and Marcus Buckingham in their research clarify that 'Managers play critical role in an organization's ability to tetain talented people. Anything the supervisor or manager does to make an employee feel unvalued will contribute to turnover. So employees should be appreciated for their work and managers try to help, guide and support them.

(5) Right Selection is the Key of Retention

The procees of retention starts at the very beginning of the selection procedure. The selection of the right people can play a very important role to retain people within the organization. Companies should try to select only those people whose individual objectives are align with the organizational objectives and their needs and expectations can be satisfied within the organization. Employees who are able to adjust with the unique work patterns of BPO industry. Everything regarding company policies should be disclosed at the time of selection process so that no dissatisfaction arises in the later stages.

CONCLUSION

It is to be concluded that in spite of giving so much benefits BPOs are facing high attrition rate as compared to its counterparts. The suggested strategies are not exhaustive but can produce better results if properly implemented. Although the 100% retention is not possible in any organization yet more steps should be taken by companies to retain people.

REFERENCES

Anoop K. Kamat. "Ten Retention Myths", *HRD News letter*, Vol. 23, Issue 5, Aug 2007.

Babu, P. Ramesh (2004). "Cyber Coolies in BPO: Insecurities and Vulnerabilities of Non-Standard Work". *Economic and Political Weekly*, January 31st, p. 492.

Joshi, Sharvari (2003). "BPOs have Undergrades in their Sights", *Times of India*, 2003, 17th December, p.1.

Raghavendra, R. (2003). "BPO Firms Head Hunt in Smaller Cities". *The Economic Times*, 8th October, p.10.

Singh, Shelley (2003). "Keeping 'em from Straying", *Business World*, August, pp. 25-27.

http://economictimes.indiatimes.com/articleshow/247047.cms

http://www.nasscom.org

http://economictimes.indiatimes.com/articlesshow/286800.cms

http://www.indiastat.com
www.bpoindia.org
www.hr.com
http://www.callcenterservicesindia.blogspot.com
www.bpowatchindia.com

Talent Retention—The New Imperative?

25

Priti Suman Mishra

Introduction

Today, India is the hottest destination for any company that wants to outsource its business processes. But what can be the reason for India being so popular with the companies worldwide? The attractiveness of India can be contributed to three basic factors-cost, people and environment. India ranks first among a host of desirable nations in terms of cost (which includes employee cost, infrastructure cost, management cost and the tax structure). It beats all its competitors on the people front as well. The people factor is evaluated on the lines of size of the job market, workforce education level, language barriers, past outsourcing experience and employee retention. When it comes to environment (which includes country risk, infrastructure, cultural compatibility, proximity, etc.). However, India lags behind countries like Canada, Australia and Ireland. Breakthrough developments in the information technology, cut-throat global competition, rapid organizational re-structuring, emerging market economies and growing realization of the importance of customers were some of the drivers of the new business paradigm. Outsourcing is the byproduct of this paradigm change. In general when a company decides to focus on its core business and outsource its non-core operations such as customer care, finance, payment services, HR, administration, insurance claims and of late content development to vendors or other organizations which deal in them, it is called business process outsourcing (BPO).

The IT Enabled Services (ITES) [1] and Business Process Outsourcing (BPO) [2] constitute the fastest growing industry in

India. BPO industry is considered to be a part of the ITES industry. The Indian ITES sector is expected to generate nearly 2 million jobs in the country in the next few years. The revenues from this industry, which stood at \$1.4 bn in 2002, are expected to rise sharply to \$24 bn by 2008 according to a Nasscom-McKinsey report. India is projected to increase its market share to fifty-one per cent by March 2008 of global outsourcing (Pradhan and Abraham, 2005). Likewise the banking and financial services sectors in the US are observed to have made savings of US \$8 billion in the last four years by Outsourcing to India (Chandaran, 2003).

The scenario, however, is not as rosy as it looks, for this sector with enormous potential. Like any other industry during its growth phase, this industry is also going through its share of turbulence. The fact that the growth has been very sharp has added to its problems. However, all these ups and downs would help the industry in stabilizing and maturing. At least that's what experts and past experiences say.

The Challenges of Growth

The major challenges being faced by the ITES or BPO industry in India can be classified into internal and external challenges. The internal challenges include shortage of competent managers for the middle and senior management and the high attrition rates. The external challenge is in the form of opposition from the US politicians and the UK labor unions against shifting of the BPO operations by local companies to India. The threat of real competition from other players like Philippines also exists, but doesn't seem to need our immediate attention. We should look at these issues.

A speaker at the ITES-BPO Track at Nasscom 2003 commented that it is not ITES, but HRES. That succinctly explains the importance and value attached to the 'people' aspect in this service industry. The fact that this industry is still in its nascent stage in India has led to the dearth of experienced middle management level team leaders and senior managers. Nasscom President Kiran Karnik agrees that shortage of middle and senior level managers is in fact a critical issue. Entry-level recruitment and employment has not been a problem with so many fresh graduates with good language skills, available readily in the job market. The problem is more intense for the third-party outsourcing companies which have just ventured into this business. They cannot even invest in training, given their financial and other constraints. Captive BPOs like GE and American Express, which are established players in the business, have no such problems. They in fact invest substantially in training their managers.

However, they have been facing a problem of a different kind. Their middle and senior level managers are being poached by the new entrants to the industry. Everyone agrees that hiring from competition is a cyclical process and will not help the industry grow, but with very few options available, they resort to the easiest solution-poaching.

That brings us to the next issue—high attrition rates. Attrition means not only loss of talent, but also includes the cost of training the new recruits. The attrition rate in the industry has been hovering around 35 per cent, which is quite high for any industry. An average Indian call center employee works with a company for 11 months, whereas an average UK call center employee stays in a company for 3 years. Call centre jobs are often referred as "electronic sweat shop", "battery hens", etc. by the media and academicians as well. V.V. Giri Labour Institute research on labour practices in call centers recently (2005) have equated this industry as "19th Century Prisons" or "Roman Slave Ships". However, Holman Study (2003) on three British call centers has challenged these connotations. Holman concluded that call center work compared favorably with shop floor manufacturing and clerical work. It is expected that the attrition rates would come down once the growth stabilizes. Steep growth is one of the reasons for the high attrition rates, according to many in the industry.

According to a survey by People—One Consulting, an employee's leaving the organization happens typically in the first couple of weeks of joining. The reasons are many—high stress levels, monotonous nature of the job, demand-supply disparity and lack of career growth potential on the professional front; loss of identity, mismatch with normal cycle, complete change of life style and lack of comfort on the personal front. Add to this, the 'poaching' strategy being adopted by the players in the industry. What else can we expect, but an attrition rate of 35 per cent?

Exploring Attrition Problem in BPOs

Attrition is "the normal reduction of the workforce caused by employees leaving the organization for reasons of retirement, death, or resignation" (*National Performance Review*, 1997).

HR management in BPO is vital as staff satisfaction translates directly into money quiet quickly in BPO industry. So there is a need to reinvent and rework on HR strategies for retaining staff, as real cost of employee attrition is loss of skill and cost of restraining. Bleuel (2001) reports that instead of revitalizing the organization, attrition created a phenomenon identified by Leonard Schlesinger and James Heskett as "the cycle of failure". The cycles involve a chain of consequences beginning with employee dissatisfaction and ending with organizational inefficiency, poor service quality, high customer turnover and decreased profitability. Attrition means not only loss of talent, but also includes the cost of training the new recruits. Many experts are of believe that all these challenges can turn out to be a real dampener in the growth of this industry. This only raises the responsibility of "Finding the right candidate" and building a conducive work environment which will be beneficial for the organization. It is expected that the attrition rates would come down once the growth stabilizes. The industry players are trying out all the tricks in the book to tie down their employees and keep them locked in a safe.

They have been offering excellent infrastructure facilities in the form of ergonomically designed work stations and spacious, airconditioned offices. They have been offering industry specific benefits like 24/7 cafeterias and home pick-up and drop facilities apart from regular benefits like retrials and loans at low interest rates. They have been arranging special weekend parties and offering incentives like tickets to exclusive music shows and dance parties. Some players are also sponsoring the higher education of their employees. This is one of the best ways of retaining a skilled employee for 2-3 years with a company. All this really goes well with a typical employee, who is in his early twenties, fresh out of college and unmarried. The industry has been quite benevolent on the compensation front as well. According to a Hewitt Associates survey conducted last year, the highest salary increase in the Asia Pacific region was in India. Within the country, it was the ITES industry which recorded the highest growth of 14 per cent. The variable pay component varied in the range of 15-70 per cent, which is exorbitant, to say the least.

All these measures are at the organizational level. At the industry level, companies have tried to get into informal agreements with competitors to avoid poaching. Though these agreements have no legal sanctity, they are based on mutual faith of the companies and code of ethics. For example, GE, HSBC, Nipomo, Microsoft, etc. informally agreed that they would not recruit someone who has worked for less than a year with his employer or someone who has switched 3 jobs in 2 years. Similarly, Trammel, Infowavz, Tran Works, Epicenter and Global Telesystems have all entered into an informal understanding to arrest poaching.

In spite of all these measures, the attrition rates have remained high. All these attempts by the employers have resulted in only partial success. Experts feel that appropriate staffing strategies and managing employee morale are the key areas. Recruiting the right kind of people not only at the entry level but also for the middle management level can be a big contributing factor. Any fresh graduate in need of a job would say that working during odd hours and adapting to a new life style is not a problem, but when it actually comes to adapting to a completely different way of life, they find it difficult to reorient themselves. Adequate care should be taken in choosing and employing candidates in the entry level positions. Companies should also be willing to invest in training employees to take up higher responsibilities as team leads and managers. A strong middle and senior management helps in arresting attrition at the lower levels and consolidates the organizational culture and character.

Another important area of concern is the limited growth potential for an employee in this industry. Organizations should concentrate on individual career growth of employees and succession planning in the organization. Planning for growth both vertically and horizontally can bring a little reprieve to the employees. Horizontal growth can be in the form of promoting the employee from simple to more complex processes within the organization. This will enhance the learning of the employee and make him "feel-good".

All companies, regardless of size, are struggling with how to keep employees from leaving for more money or better opportunities. Studies consistently show that even though employees may say they are leaving for more money, when those same employees are asked several months later why they really left, the money factor is about 5th or 6th on the list. The first few reasons include lack of recognition, disagreement with the culture or direction of the company, poor treatment by their boss, lack of excitement about their growth prospects, and poor relationships with co-workers.

Retention strategies have to be viewed holistically against the total systemic framework of talent management that encompasses the 'talent', the 'corporation' and the 'environment'. Attrition and retention should be seen as reciprocal phenomena, which have an inverse relationship with each other. Recruitment and needs for downsizing must also be considered in conjunction. An understanding of the inherent considerations of an individual who wishes to join a company and continue to stay, and potential compulsions, which push him away, would help.

The company's brand image crowns the list of the priorities for the job seeker, other important considerations being; the pay package and other pecuniary benefits, the class and quality of people that work in the company, the challenges of the job and attractiveness of the position and designation, the opportunities for career growth and professional development and the kind of technology, he would be exposed to. Dissatisfaction in any of these aspects causes severe cracks to appear in the bonding. Anxieties and apprehensions arising from restructuring, movements, marginalization, power politics, change of boss, change of tasks and responsibilities, mergers and acquisitions, etc. could be instrumental in taking decisions to leave.

While on the one hand, a compelling brand image, astute leadership within the organization, an enduring culture and an environment that is trusting, caring and nurturing, credibility, transparency, empowerment, responsiveness and creative policies on compensation, recognition, etc. would exert a positive influence on the subject talent, on the other hand, compliance, control, rigid power structure, knee-jerk changes, unexciting and drab jobs, unjust discrimination, unrealistic deadlines and poaching would be debilitating.

The retention strategies should be designed such that the retentive forces are maximized and the debilitating forces minimized. Today's labor force is different. Supervisors must take responsibility for their own employee retention. If they don't, they could be left without enough good employees. A wise employer should learn how to attract and keep good employees, because in the long-run, this workforce will make or break a company's reputation. Keeping all these considerations, this study has been undertaken to give an insight to this challenge of managing people in BPO sector.

Objectives

The present study aimed to explore the following issues—

1. The reality of attrition problem in BPO sector, and
2. To study how people are managed in BPOs, particularly management of recruitment process, training and development process, compensation system, motivation of employees.

Method

Participants

This research contains extensive study on the Indian BPO industry wherein 6 contact center were taken as sample of study and various parameters from the perspective of OB and HRM were taken in Indian BPOs. 100 employees from four BPOs-Info Vision, PCS, Daksh, EXL Service, RT Outsourcing, located in

NCR of Delhi participated in the study. In this 20 were Team leaders/HR managers and 80 were BPO executives. They were in the age bracket of eighteen to thirty-two (mean = 23.04 yrs). Gender proportion was fifty-seven per cent males and forty three per cent females. Surveyed BPOs were of different sizes, doing business in different domains, some were domestic and some were international.

Data Collection

Data were collected using both qualitative and quantitative measures. A questionnaire involving 5-point scale ranging from strongly agree to strongly disagree was used. This questionnaire included a 5-point scale containing five items for each reason related to HR and a total of 50 statements. Items were modified, where necessary, to suit the present study.

Focus group discussions and in-depth interviews were used to collect the qualitative data. Two focus group discussions of an hour each with eight call handlers/CCEs of a small call center (total strength was, 100) in their premises once and then in the nearby coffee shop were conducted. To supplement the information base, in depth interviews were also conducted from 20 agents, mostly individually and on the two occasions in a group of 2-3 persons.

Results and Discussion

Venn Diagrams, Pie Chart, Bar graphs were used to analyze questionnaire data. Subjective data were also used to enrich our information base and get a holistic picture of the BPO sector's reality with an emphasis on rising attrition rate.

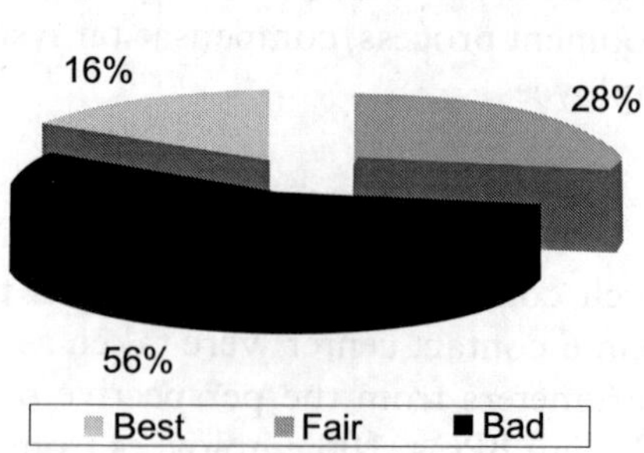

Fig. 25.1: Rate the call center with any other job

(I) Salary issues—16% (II) Work shifts—18.5%
(III) Growth—12% (IV) I + II—28%
(V) II + III—7.5% (VI) I + III—9.5%
(VII) I + II + III—8.5%

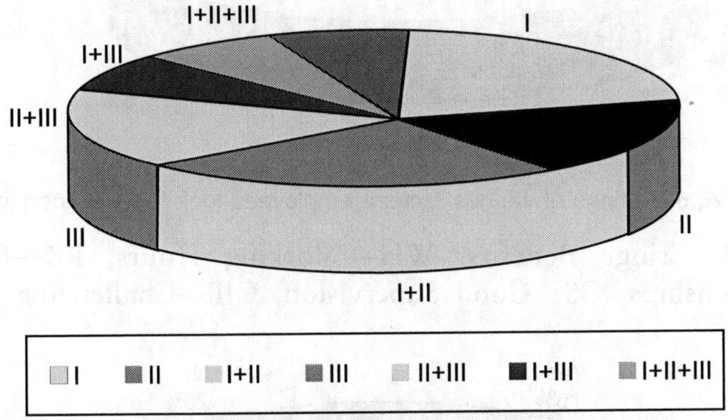

Fig. 25.2: Reasons for leaving the previous job

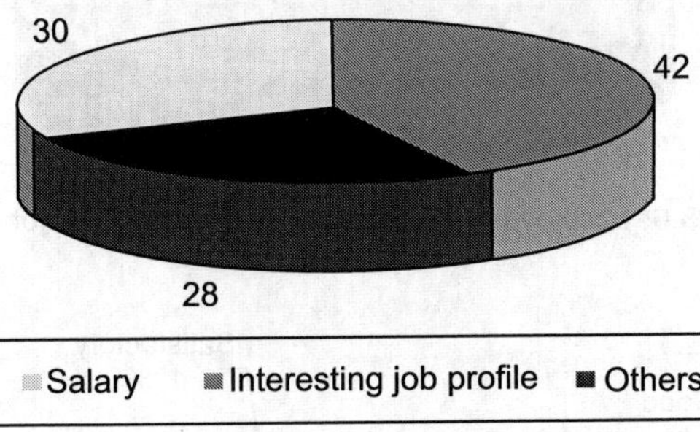

Fig. 25.3: Reasons for joining a new company

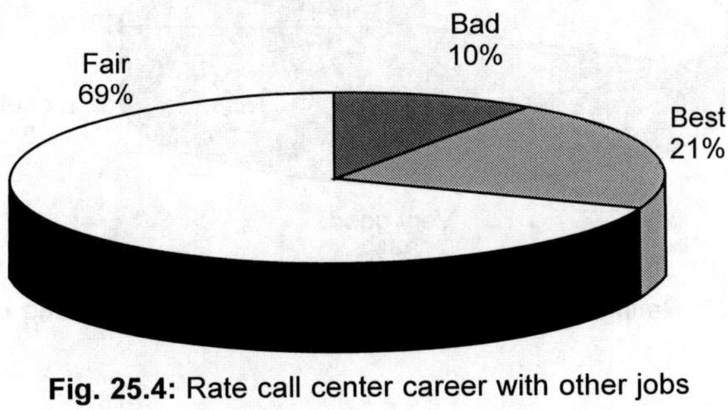

Fig. 25.4: Rate call center career with other jobs

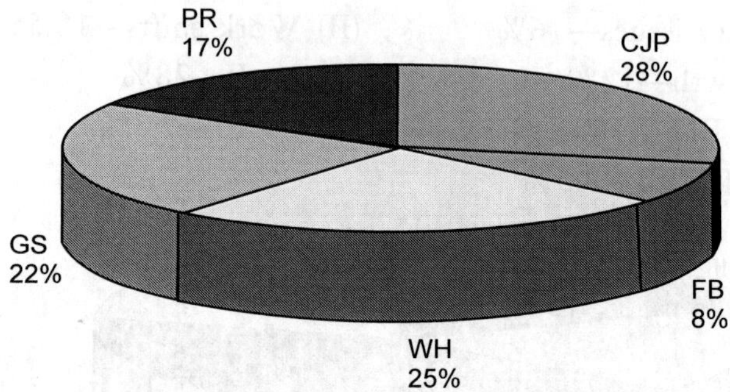

Fig. 25.5: Ratings of various factors, employees look for in a good job

FB—Fringe Benefits, WH—Working Hours, PR—Peer Relationships, GS—Good Supervision, CJP—Challenging Job Profile.

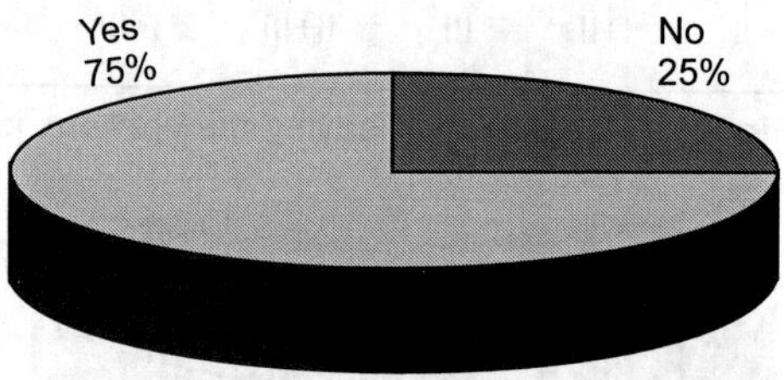

Fig. 25.6: Employees whether satisfied with their job profile

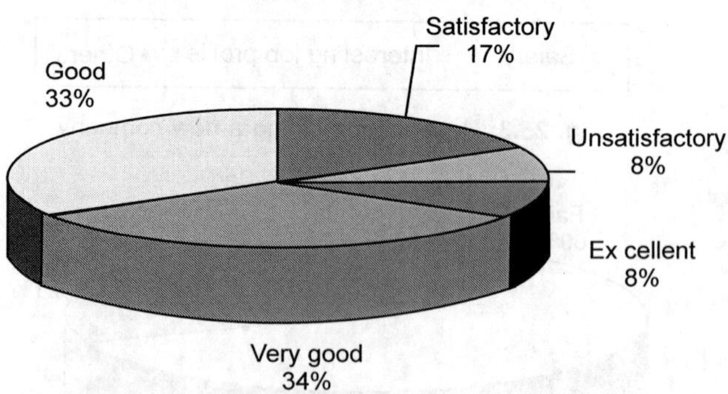

Fig. 25.7: Rating of OB policies and practices in the existing company

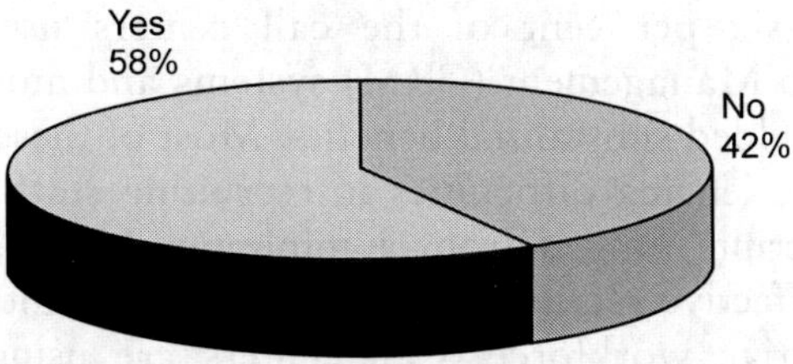

Fig. 25.8: Views on career paths whether worked out or not

According to this study undertaken it was found that most challenging aspects of call center jobs that should be taken care of by HR managers are company infrastructure, technical problems, and working hours. 18 per cent of call centers in the sample are open twenty-four hours a day a week. 'Time to answer' remains the most critical indicator of employment condition. The mean number of calls taken by an Agent each day is seventy-eighty: of course this varies significantly with the type of call center and sector. Flexible working arrangements remain a critical issue in many calls centers affecting the recruitment, retention and productivity of staff. Getting the best performance from employees who might only have a part-time commitment to the business is another key challenge before HR managers. 33.33 per cent of employees only agree that there is proper team spirit and coordination among employees in the organization. Most of the employees rated their work place, perks and canteen to be the best. Few others also agreed that there is work pressure, flexible shifts, and strict supervisor's control. 75 per cent of the employees were very satisfied with their existing incentive schemes. Rest wanted a change in their incentive scheme. In addition to this they wanted changes in workspace, infrastructure, career path and hygiene. Most of the employees were not satisfied with their appraisal system.

Our study continues to be on the subject of managing people particularly recruitment, retention, absenteeism and pay in BPOs. This study deals with employment conditions in call centers and the OB practices and policies in call centers, so some of the results of the study provide some interesting facts to counter some of the wilder allegation.

Twenty-six per cent of the call centers use Customers Relationship Management (CRM) systems and most think that they have yielded substantial benefits. Most of these call centers are not experiencing difficulties in recruiting staff and the age for new recruits ranged from a minimum 19 to a maximum 51 years. Effective recruitment is the starting point for a stable and productive workforce. Call centers are using more and more systematic methods to ensure that they recruit the right staff with the right skills. There has been a noticeable increase in the use of assessment centers or consultancies doing resourcing on behalf of the call centers.

The amount of formal training and development has fallen again, but 21 per cent of the sample said that it takes over four months for the new recruit to reach the average standard. Various training programs such as product training program, skill development program, customer care program are undertaken in different call centres. In other responses on training, 89 per cent of centers said that executives were accompanied by a buddy, when they start taking live calls.

The call centers have a formal communication structure in place. On interrogation HR managers identified the factors that have most affected morale positively or negatively. Managerial style is considered to have most influence along with training—but all the factors are considered important. A number of different methods were used to gather information from employees such as group meetings, 'Suggestion' boxes and Staff attitude survey.

Salary rates for executives have risen modestly in line with inflation. Pay for Executives tends to be lower in smaller call centers and executives receive some form of bonus payment. Rates are still highest in the financial services sector and in the larger call centers. In the sample of five call centres, for all sectors, there has been a slight increase in the average "lowest" and "highest" pay for executives. Providing team and/or individual incentive to enhance performance is the norm in many calls centers. Reviewing the incentive scheme at infrequent intervals is done. There is an almost infinite variety of incentive programs such as free group tours, a free 'pizza and beer' night,

Best Employee scheme, White water rafting, Parties and pub coupons, sports and leisure facilities, lunch vouchers and more.

Seventy-eight per cent of call centers have developed their own job competence and use them mainly to support recruitment and the assessment executives. And finally, 84 per cent of the call centers in the sample use Internet to provide information to customers.

Our study continues to be on the subject of managing people particularly recruitment, retention, absenteeism and pay in BPOs. This study deals with employment conditions in call centers and the OB practices and policies in call centers, so some of the results of the study provide some interesting facts to counter some of the wilder allegation.

Organizational structures aims and objectives vary. Only those with a balanced set of performance measures that include effective indicators of productivity, quality and business effectiveness can properly set meaningful targets for individuals, teams and sections, assess performance objectively to compare results with others and measure progress and take corrective action when objectives are not being met.

Number of ideas we should consider for retaining good people

- **Recognizing the importance of listening to the voice of the Customer—The Employees:** Assuming customers are happy without asking them if they're right, is a surefire way to lose customers—and employees—left and right. Talent Magnet organizations can't assume that what they are doing is working; they have to constantly engage in conversations with their workforce through employee satisfaction surveys, anonymous suggestion boxes, company-wide meetings, focus groups, and informal conversations. Importantly, they should also work at creating a culture where honesty and openness is supported, so employees feel safe enough to voice their concerns. Employees should offer ideas, feel free to criticize and commit to continuous improvement. If not, they bite their tongues or find themselves constantly "in trouble"—until they leave. Successful business performance will be achieved by structuring the business to meet customer expectations. Managing outsourced business processes is the key to providing competitive products or services and, along with managing core activities will determine the success of organizations in achieving competitive excellence. (Andrew Sheridan, 1998)

- **Organization culture**: Culture is somewhat like "the operating system" of the organization. It drives the organization and its actions. It guides how employees think, act and feel. Essentially organizational culture is seen in two broad dimensions. The hard dimensions relate to the functional, technical and control aspects, while the soft aspects deal with inspiration, emotion, energy, enthusiasm, collaboration, openness, sense of belonging, etc. A culture that is open, trusting, nurturing, authentic as well as empowering tends to attract and retain top talent. Managers can alter the culture of their organizations by (1) hiring employees who fit well with the new vision of the organization, (2) training employees in skills that match the new vision, or (3) motivating employees to adopt actions and attitudes that are consistent with the new vision.
- **An effective selection process:** Ensures the entry of the right kind of people into the organization, with the desired loyalty and sense of belonging that goes a long way in restricting attrition in the long-run. The type of people one selects should not only fit into the job in terms of skill set but should match the company culture in terms of attitude, personality and commitment. The first step for individual companies is to develop detailed profiles of the kind of people they are after by analyzing the job profiles, career paths, background and experience of their current high performers.
- **Breakeven point:** One of the objectives at this level should be on retention for a specified period of time (breakeven period) so as to recover the cost incurred on the employee. Small Tenure Bond should be there. Once

this period is calculated, strict actions can be taken to ensure that employees do not leave the organization before completion of this minimum time frame. For example, bonds should be signed between employer and employee. To minimize the training cost industry needs to work with the government to introduce courses at a school and college level, which are in line with the requirements of the industry.

- **Ensure you offer competitive compensation and your staff members must feel rewarded, recognized and appreciated:** Frequently saying thank you goes a long way. Monetary rewards, bonuses and gifts make the thank you even more appreciated. Understandable raises, tied to accomplishments and achievement, help retain staff. Commissions and bonuses that are easily calculated on a daily basis, and easily understood, raise motivation and help retain staff. Organization should prioritize employee recognition and then it can ensure a positive, productive, innovative organizational climate. People with positive self-esteem are potentially your best employees. These beliefs about employee recognition are common among employers even if not commonly carried out.
- **Employee should know clearly what is expected from him everyday at work:** Defining job roles would help in mitigating the effects of attrition. Clear documentation of the process and the jobs performed should be done so that the process is not dependent upon an employee. Changing expectations keep people on edge and create unhealthy stress. They rob the employee of internal security and make the employee feel unsuccessful. It is not enough that the supervisor is well-liked or a nice person, starting with clear expectations of the employee, the supervisor has a critical role to play in retention. Anything the supervisor does to make an employee feel unvalued will contribute to turnover.
- **Using humors to boost morale at work place:** In today's uncertain work environment, humor isn't an option; it's

a necessary way to boost morale. When employees clown around, they're not wasting valuable time, they're making use of one of the few tools available to increase and maintain their esprit de corps. Laughter may not change the external reality, but it can certainly help people survive it.

- **Employee recognition rocks:** Managers who prioritize employee recognition understand the power of recognition. They know that employee recognition is not just a nice thing to do for people. Employee recognition is a communication tool that reinforces and rewards the most important outcomes people create for your business. An effective employee recognition system is simple, immediate, and powerfully reinforcing. Employees feel cared about and appreciated. It may seem simplistic, but people who feel recognized and cared about produce more and better work.
- **Talent and skill utilization is another environmental factor your key employees seek in your workplace:** A motivated employee wants to contribute to work areas outside of his specific job description. Best employees, always want to seek frequent opportunities to learn and grow in their careers, knowledge and skill. Without the opportunity to try new opportunities, they feel they will stagnate. A real and genuine interest in people's career aspirations and personal lives should be taken. A career oriented, valued employee must experience growth opportunities within your organization.
- **The perception of fairness and equitable treatment is important in employee retention:** Employees should be treated equitably. There is a value in highlighting specific models or best practices to prevent or eliminate potential arbitrariness and discrimination in compensation practices. Even though benefits are considered integral to any total compensation philosophy and the principles of fairness are applicable, the project's primary emphasis is directed to pay as represented by wages, bonuses,

incentives, stock option, etc. There should be fairness in every aspect.

Conclusion

BPO is the latest buzzword on the Indian business scene. Its economic rationale is well established but people of late have started questioning its human implications. Keeping people is arguably the most challenging aspect of running a business today. The answer lies in the fact that there is no one set of answers. People are different, so their reasons for doing anything are different. Our study reveals that while salaries, perks, challenges, designations, foreign assignments may drive people for sometime, most of the people also seek stability for themselves. Therefore, an HR manager needs to identify and create systems and processes that will retain employees.

In order to be able to implement effective retention strategies, the first step should be to understand the scope of the retention problem that is unique to one's organization. The target group, which is crucial to the company's operations and success, should be identified and the strategies are directed appropriately. It is a paradox that the companies which invest heavily in recruitment and development and make a good job at that, are prone to more risk of poaching. A sound sensing and tracking system to assess the volume and causes of attrition by performance level could be useful. The ability to identify good performers, who are prone to leave for any job or management, related issues and timely intervention to address these issues, could be effective.

Creating and delivering a great employee value proposition is clearly the best way to retain the people. This would encompass building and sustaining a compelling brand image with an appealing culture and inspiring values, tailored to the talent segment that one seeks to attract and retain, offering great jobs and career opportunities, building an effective learning framework, investing in workplace infrastructure, moving on poor performers, instituting effective reward and recognition programs, putting in place innovative compensation schemes. But most importantly, when the organization is successfully able to convey the message that it cares for employees, retention works best.

REFERENCES

Andrew, Sheridan May. "Business Process Outsourcing: A New Test of Management Competence" in *Career Development International*. Vol. 3, 1998.

Blueul, W. Curbing. "Cycle of Failure". Available: http://www.scantronsurveys.com/surveys imple/cycle of failure.htm, 2001.

Chandran. "IT Outsourcing to India Saves Sixty Per cent Costs", *Business Standard*, March 11, 2003.

Holman, D. Call Centres in "The New Workplace: A Guide to the Human Impact of Modern Working Practices". Chichester: John Wiley, 2003.

Pradhan, J.P. and Abraham, V. "Social and Cultural Impact of Outsourcing: Emerging Issues from Indian Call Centre". *Harvard Asia Quarterly*. http://www.fas.havard.edu/~asiactr/haq/200502a001.htm, 30.12.2005.

Talent Retention—Changing Dimensions

26

Somesh Dhamija and *Aruna Dhamija*

Employers in each corner of the world are discussing about how difficult it is to recruit and retain talented people in their organization and how the war for talent retention seems never ending. Even the best efforts by the companies (either big or small) to retain the talented people, have met with limited success. It is no wonder that the talent management is going to be the hot issue in near future for the survival of the organization.

Paradigm Shift

The old paradigm involved asking people to work hard, be loyal and give the best and in return promise a job for reasonably long time, a regular and moderate salary increase and a good chance for a promotion if one did reasonably well. Now the scenario is entirely changed, Jobs are more offered on contract term, no one talks about life time employment, Salary increase are performance driven, hence organizations are also looking for selective retention, keep at least few good employees at any cost strategy.

Why Talent Leave

Most of the managers often has a mistaken belief that reasons to stay and reasons to leave are same, the truth is that reasons for employees to stay are not the same as why they leave. In a recent study on software professionals, it was observed that top most reasons for staying are:

Career Development —28%
Appropriate Salary —20%
Overseas Opportunity—10%

Another Harvard Business School study cited following principal reasons for exit—

Job Content

Level of Responsibility

Company Culture &

Caliber of Colleagues.

Company market image and customer relations are also key important features, which plays an important role in retaining talented employees in the organization. It gives pleasure to work for a company which has a very excited customer base rather then working for complaints ridden company.

Foundations of Retention

To retain talents in organization following foundation stones should be established—

Clear Sense of Direction and Purpose

It is not enough to have a mission statement of the organization, employees should be ensured that organization is continuing its march towards its mission and no one is keeping them in dark about the future of the company.

Caring Managers

Employees need mentors and coaches these days. They needs shoulders to rely upon when they have strong grievances. Friendly attitude of manager develops strong bond of mutual trust and confidence amongst them.

Open Two-Way Communication

An environment of open two-way communication develops harmony and its impact on employee satisfaction can easily be analyzed. A talented employee when given a chance to express his/her views about any important issue, feels associated with the organization.

A Healthy Work Environment

Everyone loves to work in healthy work environment, which now become a luring factor, encourages long-term stay of employee. Despite of other factors employees now gives preference to a healthy work environment in choosing an organization.

Recognition and Rewards

Rewards not awards can be a major factor of employee retention, as at one side rewards becomes a means of recognizing someone's extraordinary performance on the other side it encourages non-performers to enhance their level of performance, whereas awards always develops winners and losers in the organization.

Liberal Training and Development Budget

By providing continuous learning opportunities, organization may go a long way in creating high employee satisfaction especially among high performers, as really talented person is always hungry for knowledge.

Adequate Salary

Organization need not to be top salary payer, Fair wages along with reasonable increments at regular intervals make people to stay.

Designing a Retention Strategy

To retain talented employees, one must have an effective comprehensive retention strategy that addresses following key components—

- Effective Performance Management,
- Challenging Job,
- Career Development Opportunities,
- Recognition & Compensation,
- Work-Life Balance.

Effective Performance Management

Identifying real good performers in the organization is still a big challenge for H.R. professionals, most of the time due to sympathy or any other reason supervisors develops a tendency of hiding bad performance and therefore performance management becomes non-functional. An organization with sound performance appraisal system can successfully maintain high morale of employees, reduces frustration and encourages performance improvement efforts. Effective performance management makes people to know where they stand in organization, therefore consequently becomes a major factor of talent retention.

Challenging Job

A really talented employee cannot continue a monotonous job for a longer time period, howsoever paying it is, as high performers are looking constantly for high challenges on the job, as to be on top of the world. It is therefore a must-to-add challenges in the job profile of talented employees.

Career Development Opportunities

As a common phenomenon of human psychology everyone wants advancement in career. High performers seek and relish higher responsible positions, so H.R. policies must ensure faster growth opportunities. An organization with poor career development opportunities cannot become successful to retail talent for long enough.

Recognition and Compensation

Who would like to get ignored? No one especially the best performers, if there is neglect or a feeling of neglect, it will be motivate them. Most of high performers will leave the job if they get the signals that their work is not being recognized. Similarly even an average employee would not like to work for a lesser sum then reasonable one.

Therefore a judicious mix of recognition and compensation policy is to be considered by H.R. professionals.

Work-Life Balance

Employees often complain for failing to establish viable fit between their personal and professional fronts. This confrontation puts them in stress and strain, which leads to turnover. Organizations today are adopting some unique strategies like flexi time, job sharing and banking of hour, etc. An effective implementation of these strategies can lead to employee retention.

HR Role—A Proactive Approach

Most of HR managers believe in using exit interviews to find out the reasons why the person left, but it is observed and experienced that people often do not tell truth in the exit interviews, moreover it is of no use to cry on spilt milk as once employee decides to leave it becomes very difficult to make him stay in the organization. HR people should take a proactive action, whenever there are symptoms of frustration, before it become too late. Following action plan may show miracles if duly taken care by HR persons in the organization—

- The timing is all important. Develop retention plans from the day one when employee joins the organization. Don't wait until an employee has decided to leave, "can we do something to change your decision". It should be a regular practice to figure out the reasons of employee discomfort, which requires serious involvement of HR staff.
- Provide internal "escape hatches" that allow employees to reinvent themselves, their roles, Careers and circumstances without leaving the organization. Provide them opportunities to move into new geographical areas different teams, new tasks and responsibilities.
- Offer options. Once the organization has invested in recruiting and training a new entrant, the management has a stake in retaining talent. Instead of loosing him, offer valued employee the chance to work part-time or flexi time.
- Facilitate Communication and Coordination across the organization. Treat your employee as your strategic partner. Performance planning as well as transparent evaluation systems that are consistent with the business goals also work for employee.
- Stay Connected, if retaining a talented employee is impossible, then the best policy is to maintain connectivity with him, even after he leaves, put him in your reserve database and make him your external Public Relation Officer. This is an effective way to convert a threat into

an opportunity, as none of the employer can assure lifetime employment, so it is better to develop lifetime affiliation rather then lifetime loyality. It may be worthwhile for HR people to spend energy in communicating that people who left are welcome back. More the HR department will be in touch with former employees, more will be the probability either to get them back in organization or to get more talented people referred by them.

By paying due attention these components and by making appropriate strategies, organization will be able to retain top employees, reduce costly turnover and remain competitive in the marketplace.

A Study on Talent (Faculty) Retention in Educational Institutions under U.P.T.U., Lucknow

27

Dinesh Kumar Sharma and *Moumita Kusari*

INTRODUCTION

The Faculty (Talent) is the main storehouse of knowledge, driving and influencing all activities towards pursuit of excellence. The calibre and scholarship of faculty members influence the quality of teaching and research programs in any academic institution and hence its image among different stakeholders. Characteristics and performance of faculty members, for example, the number of PhDs and research output by faculty play weighty roles in rankings of technical institutions.

Talent (Faculty) is the critical success factor to any educational institution. The challenge of finding, attracting, developing and retaining the right faculty is taking up a major part of management and once the right talent is found; the next demanding job is to retain that faculty. The main reason for attrition lies in rapid mushrooming of technical institutions on account of surging demand of technically trained manpower by fast growing industrial sector of Indian economy; and abysmally low number of PhDs/Fellows in technical disciplines from good institutions opting for the teaching careers on account of possibility of higher incomes from the non-academic career options. Ability of faculty may be insignificant if not matched with desire of students and institution.

Though the education industry is stretched out in the light of privatization of education in Uttar Pradesh; most of the B.Tech., MBA and MCA institutions are found to be ill-equipped to handle the challenges of the workplace. They are mostly equipped with only the theoretical aspects of the issues and lack the application part. The educational system is faulty and does not take industry needs into consideration, resulting in a mismatch between industry requirements and educational preparation.

An institution should exert some efforts and undertake some analysis to determine the monetary, non-monetary interests and preferences of its faculty members, and then attempt to meet these preferences in action. In this context institutions need to dig novel approaches to retain effective faculty members. Looking carefully into many organizations retention strategies are very competitive. Institutions try to provide their best to retain the faculty of their competitors. Though all constituting elements of an institution are important for its success; but it is its enhanced ability to attract and retain the quality faculty that separates it from the other institutions.

There are various factors that affect an individual's decision to change a job. While an employee leaving the job is considered attrition by one organization, it is looked at as talent acquisition by the new organization and to the individual it means a career move, economic growth and enhanced quality of life/convenience or closeness to family, etc. Hence, what is a problem for one may be an opportunity for another. Gone are the days when a faculty would join a college in his mid-20s and would work till his retirement in the late-50s. Today the young professionals hop jobs, especially during the first 4-5 years of their work life. In fact now-a-days faculty members are a restless species who, unlike the immovable Banyan Tree, cannot stay rooted in one place, they need to move on for one reason or another, and the institutions stand to lose. So the faculty retention is one of the primary measures of the health and success of any institution.

In this conceptual paper authors have attempted to bring out faculty retention approaches for achieving competitive advantage. The data have been collected through primary as well as secondary sources. The Questionnaire has been used for primary data, which are divided into two categories, the first category aimed at collecting data from the faculty and the second category aimed at collecting data from the top management, i.e. Directors or Deans. For this purpose 100 faculty members have been selected from 20 institutions (under U.P.T.U) 5 from each having more than one-year stay in the same institute and 20 top management people one from each institute. This paper also contemplates personal experiences of authors and informal discussions with faculty members of various institutions under U.P. Technical University.

Talent management implies recognizing a person's inherent skills, traits, personality and offering him a matching job. A wrong fit will result in further hiring, re-training and other wasteful activities. Talent Management is beneficial to both the organization and the employees. The organizations besides being devoted to predicting success in the immediate job, is also concerned with predicting the future potential.

NEED TO ADDRESS EMPLOYEE RETENTION

The institutes have to bear huge costs associated with the retention of employees. May be some of the factors for attrition is not visible to management reporting but none of them are less real. The management should give due emphasis on the identification of both expressed and implied factors resulting into attrition or turnover within the institution. The institution should maintain the competitive edge for providing the combination of the most cost-effective and high quality manpower. The following can be the different costs incurred to any institution due to increased attrition:

Recruitment Cost

Advertisement cost, internal recruiter's time cost of pre-employment tests for various candidates, etc.

Training Cost

Sending faculties for attending seminars, workshops, conferences and FDP's.

Lost Quality Performance Cost

Increased load of teaching on existing faculty members when more number of employees leave the institute and cost of mistakes the new employees commit during their probation period.

TALENT DEVELOPMENT SYSTEM

The design, care and nurturing of the talent development pipeline depends on the institution's talent development system. This is really a meta-system, since it consists of seven smaller systems, each of which must be aligned with the others. The driver is the human resource strategic planning system, which indicates the talent required to execute the strategic plan. Recruitment and selection, career management, training and development, succession management, compensation and benefits, and performance management systems enable it. Failure in any of these systems either blocks or breaches the talent pipeline and frustrates the ultimate institutional goal of talent sufficiency.

Avoiding the Pitfalls in Talent Development

There are many ways in which the best-intentioned talent development process can go wrong. We just want to identify a few of the more common ones:

- Seeing it as an isolated issue: In truth any separate function cannot run the talent development function. It requires the commitment and personal engagement of senior line management. It won't work unless there is a highly competent and aggressive faculty strength prepared to enable the process, one with excellent systems that they can use to make it work, and with good monitoring and feedback so that they know whether it is working or not.
- Developing talent for yesterday's needs: In a rapidly changing environment it takes time to develop talent for higher positions, it's essential that the institution specifies the talent it needs on a go-forward basis. This is derived from strategic thinking and planning, and then translating

that into producing the talent the institution needs to execute the strategies. This is a very different perspective from one that is based on a historical analysis of what it took to be successful in the past is what it takes in the present.

- Failure to prune: One of the toughest of all tasks is the necessity to tell an individual that he or she is no longer considered to be in the high-potential pool and will be taken out of the accelerated development track of the institute. Yet failure to do this blocks the pipeline. There are, after all, only a limited number of developmental roles in most institutions and continuing the functioning of the institution with the same players like these creates havoc with institutional effectiveness and efficiency.
- Doing it at the wrong level: One of the most natural instincts of the institutes is to hoard talent—after all, they found it and developed it, why not use it? But if talent development is done at anything other than at the total level, we sacrifice great opportunities for enrichment, and getting people loose the experience they want and need for later years. Top talent must be "owned" by the institution and must be encouraged.

TALENT MEASUREMENT

Measuring talent in any organization is a very difficult task because it cannot be quantifiable. In order to measure the talent from the institution point of view the following factors have been highlighted:

- Human Resource Compliance,
- Employment Law,
- Training and Development,
- Performance Management,
- Worker's Compensation/Claims Management.

DATA ANALYSIS AND INTERPRETATION (FACULTY MEMBERS)

Data Analysis (Faculty) **Response in %**

	Strongly agree	Agree	Satisfactory	Disagree	Strongly disagree
Q1.	The current job in this academic institution is satisfactory.				
	18	30	37	12	3
Q2.	The institute uses modern teaching aids.				
	13	33	29	25	0
Q3.	The institute usually sponsors teachers for training programs.				
	19	27	23	31	0
Q4.	Salary structure is comparable with good institutions.				
	10	29	27	24	10
Q5.	Superiors are co-operative.				
	28	36	25	8	3
Q6.	There is good academic autonomy to teachers.				
	14	36	32	14	4
Q7.	Rules and regulations are clear and transparent.				
	0	26	32	31	11
Q8.	Goodwill of the institute attracts you to remain in the institute for a longer period of time.				
	17	30	25	23	5
Q9.	There are performance-based incentives in this institute.				
	0	30	26	18	26
Q10.	The institute promotes the research work.				
	18	22	34	14	12
	Aggregate percentage				
	13.7	29.9	29	20	7.4

The authors have assumed that respondents subscribing to 'strongly agree and agree' options should stay with current organization for a longer period. Satisfactory, Disagree and Strongly disagree category faculty members may leave the institute at anytime, whenever they get little better opportunity. However, strongly agree and agree rating faculty will take the decision having analyzed various pros and cons of available opportunity.

Approximately 52 per cent faculty may leave anytime when they get slightly better opportunity and 48 per cent of faculty will stay with the same institute until they get remarkably better opportunity. It shows that there is an existence of more amount of satisfaction rather commitment among faculty members which detains to retain a longer stay of talent.

About 46 per cent of institutions are using modern teaching aids, leading to higher level of faculty members and 54 per cent of institutions are not using it causing for dissatisfaction. It also shows that most of the institutes are emphasizing on availability of modern teaching aids, showing their inclination towards quality teaching in near future.

Personal growth of the faculty in terms of academic exposure is attached with the growth of the institution. Only 46 per cent faculty said that institute usually sponsor for training programs and 31 per cent faculty said that their institutes are not sponsoring for any training program. Besides having highly sophisticated infrastructure this shows the rigid attitude of institution to hold the allowance of related equipment to develop the skills.

Here comparable salary means not as IIM's, etc. but according to AICTE and UGC and comparable with middle class institutions. Only 39 per cent of faculty agreed that salary structure is comparable while 34 per cent faculty have disagreed. It shows that there is no uniformity in salary structure of the faculty members, which ignites the fear of insecurity and underestimation.

About 53 per cent of faculties said that superior are co-operative and 36 per cent faculty are not happy with their boss. So this shows that superiors follow a fair degree of mutual respect towards their subordinate faculties.

On the basis of autonomy 50 per cent faculty enjoys academic autonomy is being provided and 50 per cent are not fully satisfied. Here according to author's experience maximum of 30-35 per cent of faculty members may have the academic autonomy. Therefore, it seems that the work site atmosphere is good but the extent of academic discretion is still not that high.

Only 26 per cent of faculty said that rules and regulations in their institutions are transparent. About 32 per cent said O.K. and 42 per cent are not satisfied with the rules and regulations of the institute. So it shows that there is sense of fear in faculties boggling their minds regarding the implementation and violation of rules and regulations.

About 47 per cent faculties are staying with same institute due to the goodwill of the institute while 53 per cent said that goodwill of the institute does not provide for staying with the same organization. Goodwill as a tool for attracting faculties serves an important factor but using the same as the only tool for retaining may prove to be a disaster.

None of the faculty members of the sample institutions strongly agrees with performance based incentive in their institution and 30 per cent agreed and 44 per cent disagreed for this statement. It shows that there is a seldom practice of follow-up by the management to know about the performance.

About 40 per cent of the faculty members agreed that their institution is promoting research work while 60 per cent did not. A well-defined plan for career development and growth through research work does not exist till the extent required.

If the average rating of all the ten factors is taken into account then approximately 50 per cent of the faculty members may stay for a longer period of time and rest may leave at anytime, whenever they get slightly better opportunity.

Existence of effective talent utilization scheme within the institution helps the faculty to stay for a longer time. According to the data institutions are lacking on this part which if improved can be beneficial for the retention scheme of the institutes.

Most of the institutes do not have an enriched talent in their store, which makes the achievement of goals very difficult.

More than 50 per cent of the institutes say that the average stay of talent in the institute is favorable. Therefore, it can be said that the average stay of talent within the institute do satisfy the management to declare it as a fair condition but not favorable.

About 70 per cent of the institutes say that they promote research work within the institute. This shows the institute inclination towards faculty development skills which according to data is on a high end but is not consistent with observation of author.

DATA ANALYSIS AND INTERPRETATION (TOP MANAGEMENT)

Data Analysis (Top Management) **Response in %**

	Strongly agree	Agree	Satisfactory	Disagree	Strongly disagree
Q1.	The institute is utilizing the key talent management process to retain the talent (faculty)				
	10	30	30	20	10
Q2.	Institute has the talent what you require for achieving your objectives.				
	20	20	40	20	0
Q3.	The average length of stay of talent in the institute is favorable.				
	10	50	20	20	0
Q4.	The institute is promoting research work and faculty development.				
	40	30	30	0	0
Q5.	Basic infrastructural facilities such as separate sitting place, internet facility, etc. provided within the institute.				
	15	30	25	25	5
Q6.	The extent of strict adherence to the AICTE and UGC norms.				
	30	25	35	10	0
Q7.	The faculty appraisal system within the institution is done frequently.				
	30	20	35	0	15
Q8.	The institute uses modern teaching aids.				
	25	35	35	0	5
Q9.	Institute organizes workshops, seminars and conferences at least once in a year.				
	25	35	30	10	0
Q10.	Goodwill of the institute serves as a driving force for retaining talent.				
	25	35	30	10	0
	Aggregate percentage				
	23	31	31	11	4

Less than 50 per cent of the institutes agree on the availability of the basic infrastructure facilities to the faculty members. It shows that the working atmosphere of the institute with basic infrastructural facilities within makes them attractive enough to hold the talent. But due to the rigid attitude of the institute towards allowing the usage of these facilities the retention rate is heading southward.

According to the data the institute adheres to the AICTE and UGC norms satisfactorily making it difficult to drive the flow of talent towards them.

Only 50 per cent of the institute agrees that the faculty appraisal system is regular. Therefore, it shows that the frequency of occurrence of faculty appraisal system is not fair enough to retain talent.

According to the given data more than 50 per cent of the institute agree that modern teaching aids have been provided. This shows the institute's emphasis on quality teaching, which improves their acceptance level among faculty members.

More than 50 per cent of the institutes emphasize on conduction of different FDP's through seminars, workshops, etc. This enables them to attract and retain talent for a longer period.

According to the data more than 50 per cent of the institute believe that taking goodwill, as the only factor to retain talent may serve to be a disaster in future.

How to Develop a Retention Strategy

The concept of employee retention is not just retaining a single or few employees but it's the future of retaining competitive sustainability of most effective manpower key asset of any organization. Institutions should have a retention strategy, which helps in reducing employee turnover. The retention strategy should be planned by every institution keeping in mind the following aspects:

1. Inculcating Culture of Retention.
2. Proper Career Planning and Succession Planning for the employees.
3. The Placement of faculties to the respective subjects should be in correct outfit.
4. Emphasizing on motivating factors of individuals.
5. Causes for increased attrition in the institution.
6. Recruitment and selection process.
7. Arranging a familiarity visit.
8. Offering an attractive compensation package.
9. Equity in compensation.
10. Creating best physical infrastructure.
11. Help the new faculty in settling.

12. Best colleagues.
13. Quality of students.
14. Academic planning.
15. Time and resources for research.
16. Workload.
17. Transparent performance appraisal of faculty.
18. Involvement in academic decision-making.
19. Faculty freedom.
20. Pro-active retention endeavours.
21. Exit interviews.

1. Inculcating Culture of Retention

Retention strategies should not be isolated and culture of retention implies the length of holding the employees. The culture of retention should prioritize the following:

- Introduce the employees to the organization that it holds high degree of attachment towards them.
- Inculcate the culture in the employees saying—Retention of employee is not a segregated task anymore, but a task for the whole family.
- Involving employees more in planning retention strategies so that they understand their supervisors better.

The following are some of the ways, which can create the culture of retention:

- No role within the organization should be viewed as "ordinary" as everyone should be given the opportunity and the goal of being extraordinary.
- Creation of task in such a way in which the team can take pride in so that they don't have to memorize the things rather get a reason to think that their job is important.
- Celebrate activities, not just performance, i.e. celebrate progress not only the results.
- Allow the employees to play with full discretion so that they can be encouraged to contribute to the students in extraordinary ways.

2. Proper Career Planning for the Employees

Another foreseeable change is in respect of career growth of employees. Amongst the educated faculties with middle class values and aspirations, the urge for promotion is very great. The urge is as much for more emoluments as for the higher status in the social group. This may necessitate development of a well defined career development system for employees at various levels which enable them to enhance their knowledge, develop better skills, ability, etc.

3. Placement of Faculties

When once the candidate joins the duty, the institutions have to allocate a job initially, for which he is selected. After this initial allocation the employee's performance have to be observed after which the necessary training is to be imparted as per the institute decision. After the training is over the employee can be given added responsibility to fulfill based on which the institution may extend the probation or otherwise his services to be regularized and placed permanently.

4. Emphasizing on Motivating Factors

The employees concern to work in the organization should be realized. The employers should become dominant and committed on organizations motivating factors. The factors according to the priorities of employee concerns are as follows:

- Good working environment,
- Feeling of achievement,
- Recognition,
- Separate sitting allocation,
- Career advancement,
- Improvement in quality of work life,
- Strategies like mentoring and other growth needs should be fulfilled,
- Ego gratification should be pre-dominantly successful for senior positions, and
- While applying the retention strategies on employees, the entire life cycle of the employee within the institution

have to be examined, so that the strategies can be applied selectively and appropriately.

5. Identifying the Causes for Increased Attrition

From Employees point of view:

- Leave structure,
- Salary competitiveness, and
- FDP's.

From Employers point of view:

- Being Unethical, and
- Cost-cut oriented attitude.

6. Recruitment and Selection Process

The institute must advertise its faculty positions through multiple-channels like widely circulated dailies, professional magazines/journals, own websites, e-groups, etc. It is always good to prefer comparably young applicants as they can better adapt to the institute's requirements. The institute's authorities should avoid playing a predominant role at the first-level short-listing. The short-listed candidates should then be invited for a research seminar before the departmental faculty, who can give their recommendations regarding the suitability of the candidate for the department. A final opinion can be taken by conducting interviews of the recommended candidates by the outside area experts. Involvement of outside experts at the final stage helps avoid any inbreeding tendencies and nepotism from within the departmental faculty.

7. Arranging a Familiarity Visit

Identification of the top candidate for a position completes only the first-half of the hiring process: once a desirable candidate has convinced the institute to extend an offer, the institute must convince the candidate to accept the offer. An important element in attracting outstanding faculty to the institutes can be to arrange a familiarity visit to the institute for the candidate, his or her spouse and immediate family. During this visit, the particular benefits of joining the institute's community, not only for the candidate, but also for his/her spouse and immediate family should be highlighted.

8. Offering an Attractive Compensation Package

Of course, some technical institutions have gone ahead of UGC or AICTE scales to attract and retain their teaching talent. But even then, brain drain is evident as many good Indian teachers are jumping to overseas management schools. In terms of faculty attraction and retention, the greatest competition comes from the corporate world, with pay scales there being hard to match, and infotech, finance and strategic planning offering a range of opportunities for academics.

Those packages should be multi-dimensional, involving compensation, but also the other monetary resources available to a faculty members like laboratory space, research support, secretarial and research assistant support, liberal start-up research grants, and, yes, sometimes even a reduced teaching load.

9. Equity in Compensation

Having equity in the compensation offered to faculty members according to their relevant past experience and educational qualifications would surely create a just feeling among the faculty community. The institute's authorities should ensure transparency and equity in deciding the increments for the existing faculty and in offering a compensation package to the new faculty.

10. Creating Best Physical Infrastructure

An impressive and supportive physical infrastructure within the campus setting plays a critical role in hiring and retaining the faculty talent. Faculty housing within the campus is the foremost attraction for a faculty joining from a distant place. Other ingredients constituting best infrastructure include: state-of-the-art IT infrastructure, library and laboratory facilities; in-campus school, hospital, super-market, recreational facilities, a good family cafeteria, etc. for the campus residents.

11. Help the New Faculty in Settling

The job is not done when the candidate arrives. The candidate will need to settle down in institute and this is not a problem-free procedure for an outstation candidate. When they arrive, allowing them some days of free stay at the institute's guesthouse till they ready their house should help them. In a non-residential institution, it is good idea to recommend the newly arrived faculty member some reliable realtors, physicians, etc.

12. Best Colleagues

High quality faculties tend to stay at/drift to places where there is no dearth of high quality colleagues to do deliberations on difficult issues. Therefore, institute should ensure that its eligibility criteria for faculty positions should remain stringent and are strictly adhered to. Compromisingly hiring mediocre faculty members does not serve long-term goals. High-quality faculty, in turn, insists on and attracts high-quality staff and students.

13. Quality of Students

This is an obvious, but crucial, issue faced by all the technical institutions. Quality of students plays a vital role in the research and teaching efforts of the institute's faculty. In some technical disciplines the quality of the students impacts the quality of the research more directly than any other resource. Therefore, attracting and maintaining a pool of high-quality students is an important aspect of both retention and hiring of faculty. It is a general observation that institutes attracting quality students have low faculty turnover.

14. Academic Planning

A haphazard academic system disturbs the talented faculties. Hallmark of any successful technical institutions is the attention it pays to academic planning. Institutions must spend time to work out their year-long academic planning in the beginning of the year. The academic load of faculty members should be communicated to them at least three months in advance to allow them to prepare well for their classes. For new faculty members who take their first teaching assignment, some extra time for settling and preparation should be given.

15. Time and Resources for Research

If a teacher does not do research, there is a danger that she will become stale and obsolete. Barring some exceptional persons who are passionate about teaching and who keep themselves up-to-date, faculty research is important to maintain quality of teaching.

Besides the time for the research, faculty needs to be provided with resources for the research. The quality of research support (research space-laboratory and office space, liberal research grants, library holdings, subscription to the electronic research paper databases, travel grants for research activities, and research assistants) is extremely important in attracting and retaining first-rate faculty talent. Institution must create and financially support the joint research opportunities for the faculty with nationally and internationally renowned researchers from other institutions.

16. Workload

The institute should strike a balance between faculty's teaching and research time at the time of workload allocation. Often workload assigned for a faculty includes teaching, research and consulting and administrative activities. Inadequate apportionment of total workload across these three categories would hamper the long-term goals of both institute and faculty.

17. Transparent Performance Appraisal of Faculty

An irregular and untimely faculty appraisal demeans the ability of any faculty to perform better and can be reason for dissatisfaction for the talented faculty members. Institute should adopt and strictly adhere to practice of timely (mid-year and year-end) faculty appraisals. Students' feedback is an essential component of faculty appraisal and need to be promptly communicated to concerned faculty members. The performance measurement parameters should be measurable, transparent and disclosed to all faculty members. An absolutely essential part in retaining faculty is recognition of efforts and accomplishments.

18. Involvement in Academic Decision-making

In many technical institutions faculties are restricted to teaching and their involvement in crucial academic decision-making is minimal or almost negligible. They are not consulted on matters related to acquisition of books and journals for library, recruitment of new faculty members and enrollment of new students. This increases apathy and alienation among talented faculty on all matters relating to institution.

19. Faculty Freedom

Technical institutions should adopt a system of flexi working hours for its faculty members. The emphasis should not be on time spent mechanically inside the institute's premises but on the efficient result oriented performance of the responsibilities assigned to them.

20. Proactive Retention Endeavors

When a faculty member is dissatisfied and has already taken steps to secure an outside offer, it is difficult (but not impossible) to retain him or her. Institutions should proactively identify individuals that have a potential for leaving or being targeted by other institutions. It is important that the area chairs and deans are engaged with their faculty and recognise situations where pre-emptive actions are needed.

21. Exit Interviews

Exit interview is an important tool to get feedback on various issues that plague an institution. Exit interview enables an institute to understand the outgoing faculty's views about the environment, culture, processes and systems, leadership and managing styles, clarity of roles, commitments or attitudes of associates within the organization.

These views may be the most frank and hence the valuable source of information and feedback on current environment in the institution. In a way institute can use the exit interviews to learn more about what it is doing well, what more is needed to still improve the institutional overall environment as is experienced by its faculty members.

CONCLUSION

Availability of suitable and competent talent inside any organization determines the excellence of the same. Different organizations believe in different theories and practices to ensure the right 'availability' of talent. Talent is the key to success in every business. Reciprocity is the key. The employees are a kind of investors in the company and expect a return on their every investment such as hardwork, creativity, etc.

The institutions should be seen as employer of choice by competing on various aspects such as compensation, benefits and others given as above. High potentials must be carefully managed. Generational differences continue to pose new challenges to today's employers, which must be carefully handled.

In order to be able to implement effective retention strategies, we should be first able to understand the scope of the retention problem that is unique to one's institution. A sound sensing and tracking system to assess the volume and causes of attrition by performance level could be useful. Finally the institutions need to be protective about the employees—the stronger institution's possessiveness—the longer are the faculty member's retention.

REFERENCES

"A Study on the Status of Women Faculty in Science at MIT". *The MIT Faculty Newsletter*, Vol. 11, No. 4. 1999. (http://web.mit.edu/fnl/women/women.html)

"Employee Retention—Talent Management" by Isukapally, Mythri Alliance Business Academy (http://ssrn.com/abstract=948142)

"Frustration of Talent: A Study in Scarlet" by Malcom Goodman, Durham University Business School.

"Leveraging Talent: Spin off Strategy at Industrial Research" by Sally Davenport, Adrian Carr, and Dave Bibby.

"Nine More Ways to Find and Retain Best Tutors" by Prof. Mohan, IIM, Lucknow, Nov. 26, 2006.

"Patterns and Priorities in Indian Research and Development" by R. Chidambaram (*Current Science*, 10 October 1999).

Paul, Rhea. *Faculty Development: Nurturing Our Future*. Faculty Focus, Spring 1997 (www.oaa.pdx.edu/CAE/FacultyFocus/spring97/nurturing.html)

"Ten Ways to Find and Retain Best Tutors" by Prof. Mohan, IIM, Lucknow, Nov.15, 2006.

"University Education in Science" Indian Academy of Sciences, December 1994.

University of California—Irvine Faculty Recruitment Manual. Accessed, July 2003. (http://advance.uci.edu/media/FacRecManualWeb3.pdf)

University of Colorado Boulder. Faculty Recruitment and Retention Task Force Report. May 2001. (http://www.colorado.edu/AcademicAffairs/fac_recruit/index.html)

University of Washington Academic Human Resources: Resources for New and Prospective Employees. Accessed, July 2003. (http://www.washington.edu/admin/acadpers/procedures/careers.html)

University of Washington Advance Center for Institutional Change. Recommendations to Chairs for Facilitating Dual Career Hires. Accessed, July 2003. (http://www.engr.washington.edu/advance/resources/dual_career_hires.html)

University of Washington College of Arts and Sciences Climate and Community Project. Accessed, July 2003. (http://depts.washington.edu/asccp)

University of Washington College of Arts and Sciences Faculty Development Program. Accessed, July 2003. (http://www.artsci.washington.edu/services/Personnel/Juniorfaculty)

University of Washington College of Arts and Sciences Promotion and Tenure Workshop Handout. Accessed, July 2003. (http://www.artsci.washington.edu/Services/Personnel/promtenguide.htm)

University of Washington College of Engineering Faculty Professional Development Opportunities. Accessed, July 2003. (http://www.engr.washington.edu/advance/workshops/20030227-development opportunities.pdf)

University of Washington Faculty Recruitment Toolkit. Accessed, July 2003. (http://www.washington.edu/admin/eoo/forms/ftk_01.html)

Bibliography

"A Study on the Status of Women Faculty in Science at MIT". *The MIT Faculty Newsletter*, Vol. 11, No. 4, 1999.

A. Green, and H. Lauder, *High Skills: Globalization, Competitiveness and Skill.*

Acemoglu, D., Johnson, S., Robinson, J.A. (2001). "The Colonial Origins of Comparative Development: An Empirical Investigation". *American Economic Review, 91,* 1369-1401.

Acemogul, D., Johnson, S., Robinson, J.A. (2002). "Reversal of Fortunes: Geography and Institutions in the Making of the Modern World Income Distribution". *Quarterly Journal of Economics,* 117, forthcoming.

Ahmed, Feroz (2007). "Hair to Grow: Ponytails and Pets are Lemon Tree Hotel's Tools for Keeping Employee Morale High", (Retrieved from http://www.businessworld.in/content/view/1732/1793/)

Al Ehrbar (1998). *EVA: The Real Key to Creating Wealth*, New York; John Wiley & Sons, 1998.

Alien, Natalie J. and Gresaffe, Douglas B. "Employee Commitment to the Organization and Customer Reactions: Mapping The Linkages", *Human Resource Management Review*, 11 (2001), 209-36.

Ambler, T. and Barrow, S. (1996). "The Employer Brand". *Journal of Brand Management*, 4(3), 185-206.

American Conference Institute (1998). High Tech Employee Retention Conference. Presentation by ComputerWorld. Chicago, IL.

Andrew, Sheridan May. "Business Process Outsourcing: A New Test of Management Competence" in *Career Development International*. Vol. 3, 1998.

Anthony, Robert N. (2007). *Management Control System*, 12th ed. New York: McGraw Hill.

Armour, Stephanie. "Higher Pay May be Layoff Target," *USA Today*, June 22, 2003.

Armour, Stephanie. "More Men Train to be Nurses, Midwives, Secretaries," *USA Today*, July 10, 2003.

Article of Mr. A. Aravamudhan. Executive Vice-President—HR, TVS Lucas.

Article of Salma Aliakbar: faqs@cnkonline.com

"Attracting and Retaining Talents—HR Challenge", Balasaheb Sonawane, *NIPM* 25th WRC Souvenir.

"Attrition Rate Increases 14 per cent in Asia", http://www.ciol.com/content/developer/2006/106101204.asp

Awasthi, Raja and Talreja, Vishakha (2007). "Hospitality Hit by Staff Checkout", *The Economic Times*, 26th August, 2007.

Babu, P. Ramesh (2004). "Cyber Coolies in BPO Insecurities and Vulnerabilities of Non-Standard Work". *Economic and Political Weekly*, January 31, p. 492.

Baird, L. (1985). "Do Grades and Tests Predict Adult Accomplishment?" *Research in Higher Education*, 23(I)-85.

Balu, Rekha, "The New Face of Leadership," *Fast Company*, May 2001.

Beck, T., Demirguc-Kunt, A., Levine, R. (2002). "Small and Medium Enterprises, Economic Growth and Development". World Bank Mimeo.

Beck, T., Demirguc-Kunt, A., and Levine, R. (2002). *Law, Endowments and Finance*. Working Paper.

Beck, T., Levine, R., Loayza, N. (2000). "Financial Intermediation and Growth: Casuality and Causes". *Journal of Monetary Economics,* 46, pp. 31-77.

Becker, Brian E. et al. (2001). *The HR Scorecard: Linking People, Strategy and Performance*. Harvard Business School Press.

Benbow, C.P. (1992). "Mathematical Talent: Its Nature and Consequences". In N. Colangelo, S.G. Assouline, and D.L. Ambroson, Eds. *Talent Development:* Proceedings from the 1991 Henry B. and Jocelyn Wallace National Research Symposium on Talent Development, pp. 95-123.

Bennis and Biderman (1997). *Organizing Genius: The Secrets of Creative Collaboration*.

Bernes, K. (1999). *A Synergistic Model of Organizational and Career Development*. Edmonton, AB: Life-Role Development Group.

Berry, L.L. and Parasuraman, A. (1991). *Marketing Services Competing Through Quality*. New York: The Free Press.

Besanko, David et al. (2004). *Economics of Strategy*, 3rd ed. New York: John Wiley & Sons.

Bhagwati, J.N. (2003). "Borders Beyond Control." *Foreign Affairs*, Jan/Feb.

Bloom (l985). *Developing Talent in Young People*. New York: Ballantine.

Blueul, W. Curbing the "Cycle of Failure" Available: http:// www.scantronsurveys.com/surveys imple/cycle of failure.htm, 2001.

Bonabeau, Eric and Valdis Krebs. "Model Behavior," *Optimize*, October 2002.

Bossily, Larry and Ram Charan (2002). *Execution: The Discipline of Getting Things Done*, New York: Crown Books.

Boyd, J., Levine, R., Smith, B. (2000). *The Impact of Inflation on Financial Sector Performance*. University of Minnesota, Mimeo.

Bramley, P. (1991). *Evaluating Training Effectiveness: Translating Theory into Practice*, McGraw-Hill Book Company, London.

"Britain: Skills Filled," *The Economist*, February 7, 2004.

Brown, Jeff and Lindy Williams 2003. "People: HR's Bottom-Line Asset," in *Human Resources in the 21st Century*, eds. Marc Effron, Robert Gandossy, and Marshall Goldsmith, John Wiley & Sons, Inc.

BSE Training Institute (2001). *Fundamental Analysis*, BSE Stock Exchange Publication.

Budman, Matthew. "Will We All be Unemployed?" *Across the Board*, January 1, 2004.

Bulkeley, William M. "IBM Now Plans Fewer Layoffs from Outsourcing," *The Wall Street Journal*, July 29, 2004.

Caira Rosanna (2000). "Hold'Em High: An Investment In Your Employees", *Resort Magazine*, September, 2000.

Cairncross, Frances (2002). *The Company of the Future*. Harvard Business School Press.

Campbell, Kenneth G. (1999). "Retaining Employees: Six Steps to Success." *Global Perspectives*.

Cappelli, Peter. "What Labor Shortage?" Knowledge@Wharton, August 27, 2003.

Cappelli, Peter. "A Market Driven Approach to Retaining Talent." *Harvard Business Review*, January 2000.

Cappelli, P. (2000). "A Market Driven Approach to Retaining Talent", *HBR*, January-February, 2000.

Carman, J.M. (1990). "Consumer Perceptions of Service Quality: An Assessment of the Servqual Dimensions", *Journal of Retailing*, 66(1): 33-55.

Case Study—*Harvard Business Review*, South Asia, 2007.

Castells, M. (1998). *The Information Age: Economy, Society and Culture*, Vol. 3.

Caudron, Shari. "How HR Drives Profits." *Workforce*, December 2001.

Census Releases Immigrant Numbers for Year 2000, Center for Immigration Studies, June 4, 2002.

Chakraborty, Sujata (2002). "The Taj's Stars Shine Bright". (Retrieved from http://www.tata.com/0_our_commitment/

employee_relations/articles/20021115_taj_starshine_bright.htm).

Chalamwong, Y. (2004). *The Migration of Highly Skilled Asian Workers in OECD.*

Chambers, Elizabeth G. et al. "The War for Talent." *McKinsey Quarterly*, 1998.

Chandran. "IT Outsourcing to India Saves Sixty Per Cent Costs", *Business Standard*, March 11, 2003.

Chartered Institute of Personnel and Development (2004). "Recruitment, Retention and Turnover 2004", Survey Report, London: CIPD. Available at: http://www.cipd.co.uk/surveys

Chatman, Jennifer A., Jeffrey T. Polzer, Sigal G. Barsade and Margaret A. Neale, "Being Different Yet Feeling Similar", *Administrative Science Quarterly*, December 1998. Hewitt Associates 25.

Chau, P. (2001). "Influence of Computer Attitudes and Self-Efficacy on IT Usage Behavior". *Journal of End User Computing*, 13(1), 26-34.

Chou, H. and Wang, T. (2000). "The Nuance of Learning Style and Training Method on Self-efficacy and Learning Performance in WWW Homepage Design Training". *International Journal of Information Management*, 20, 455–72.

Compeau, D.R., Higgins, C.A. (1995). "Computer Self-efficacy: Development of a Measure and Initial Test". *MIS Quarterly,* 19 (2), 189-211.

Coonradt, C. (1984). *The Game of Work*. Orem, UT: Liberty Press.

Dabholkar, P.A., Thorpe, D.I. and Rentz, J.O. (1996). "A Measure of Service Quality for Retail Stores: Scale Development and Validation", *Journal of the Academy of Marketing Science*, 24(1): 3-16.

Das, J.P. (1998). *The Working Mind: An Introduction to Psychology*. Sage Publications, New Delhi.

Davidson, Paul, "Tacit Finds Matches in Company Email," *USA Today*, June 14, 2004.

Davis, F.D. (1989). "Perceived Usefulness, Perceived Ease of Use and User Acceptance of Information Technology". *MIS Quarterly*. 13 (3), pp. 319–340.

Dent, Jeremy F. (1996). "Global Competition: Challenges for Management Accounting and Control." *Management Accounting Research* 7, No. 2 (June 1996), pp. 247-69.

Djankov, S., La Porta, R., Lopez-de-Silanes, Shleifer, A. (2002). "The Regulation of Entry", *Quarterly Journal of Economics*, 117, pp. 1-37.

Djankov, S., La Porta, R., Lopez-de-Silanes, Shleifer, A. (2003). "Courts", *Quarterly Journal of Economics*, 118, 453-517.

Doll, W.J., Torkzadeh, G., (1988). "The Measurement of End User Computing Satisfaction". *MIS Quarterly*, 12 (2), 259–274.

Dolliver, Mark, (2003). "Just Think How Cheery They'd Be If They Weren't Discriminated Against," *Adweek*, December 1, 2003.

Dubey, M.P., Sunil K. Agrawal, Arun Mohan Sheery (2005). "MSME Impact in Global Economy: Technology Incubator," WAMSME International Conference, Romania, 17th May-19th May.

Dubey, M.P. (2006). "Benchmarking of Technology Park/ Incubator: The New Paradigm for MSME," IASP Asia Conference, Isfahan 2006, Iran. 1-8.

Dubey, M.P. (2007). "Software Technology Parks/Incubators and Their Impact on Growth of MSME using the Neural Back-intelligent Propagation Network," Korea, 24-27 October, 2007.

Dubey, M.P., Sunil K. Agrawal, Manu Pratap (2006). "Benchmarking of Incubator", ISPA Global Meet, Korea.

Dubey, M.P., (2005). "Technology Incubator", ISBE 2005, Black Poll, UK.

Dubey, M.P., (2006). "Benchmarking of Incubator", *Inmantec*, 99-107, ISBN 81-903615-0-3.

Dutta, Suvrokamal (2007). "India Marches Ahead to Emerge as the Largest Economic Power of the World". (Retrieved from http://www.merinews.com/catFull.jsp?articleID =125876)

Duttagupta, R. (2005). "Identifying and Managing Your Assets: Talent Management". *Intellectual Asset Magazine.*

Dwivedi, R.S (1983). "A Comparative Study of Managerial Styles, Leadership and Trust among Indian Managers", *Lok Udyog* 27(1), 7-17.

Dychtwald, Ken, Tamara Erickson and Bob Morison. "It's Time to Retire Retirement," *Harvard Business Review*, March 1, 2004.

Dychtwald, Maddy. *Cycles*, The Free Press, 2003.

Easterly, W., Loayza, N., Montiel, P. (1997). "Has Latin America's Post-Reform Growth Been Disappointing", *Journal of International Economics,* 43, pp. 287-311.

The Economist, (2003). "Economic and Financial Indicators", 17 May, 367(8324), p. 112.

"Employee Retention—Talent Management" by Isukapally, Mythri Alliance Business Academy http://ssrn.com/ abstract=948142)

Employer Perspectives on Global Sourcing, Hewitt Associates, 2004. and also see Gandossy, Robert and Tina Kao, "Overseas Connections," *Across the Board*, November/ December 2004.

"Engagement & Retention", *HRD Newsletter*, Vol. 23, Issue 3, June, 2007.

Engerman, S., Sokoloff, K. (1998). "Factor Endowments, Institutions, and Differential Paths of Growth among New World Economies". In Haber, S.H. (Ed.). *How Latin America Fell Behind*, Stanford University Press, Stanford, CA, pp. 260-304.

Enlightening Books on Talent Management: A List by Elijah Chingosho. Chingosho, Elijah.

Ewing, M.T. et. al. (2002). "Employment Branding in the Knowledge Economy". *International Journal of Advertising*, 21(1), pp. 3-22.

Facts on Women at Work, International Labour Organization, 2003.

Financial Express. "Rural India will be Growth Engine: Purwar" 22nd March, 2005, Net Edition.

Fishman, Charles, "The Anarchist's Cookbook," *Fast Company*, July 2004.

Flore. "Challenges of Financial Education in Insurance Sector", OECD Conference on Financial Education, 2006.

Foot, M. and Hook, C. (2002). *Introducing Human Resource Management* (3rd edition) Prentice Hall.

Frank, Fredric and Taylor Craig (2004). "Talent Management: Trends that will Shape the Future". *Human Resource Planning*, Vol. 27, pp. 33-41.

Friedman, E. (2000). "Dodging the Grabbing Hand: The Determinants of Unofficial Activity in 69 Countries". *Journal of Public Economics,* 76, 459-93.

Frincke, Jessica (2006). "2006 US Job Retention Poll Findings", *SHRM Research*, September 2006.

Fullerton, Howard N. and Mitra Toossi. "Labor Force Projections to 2010," *Monthly Labor Review*, November 2001.

Gandossy, Robert, and Tina Kao, *Channels to Anywhere*, Hewitt Associates, 2004.

Gary Dressler. *Human Resource Management*, Prentice Hall India Ltd.

George, W.R. and Gronroos, C. (1989). "Developing Customer Conscious Employees at Every Level—Internal Marketing", in Congram, C.A. and Friedman, M.L. (eds), *Handbook of Marketing for the Services Industries*. New York: AMACOM, pp. 85-100.

George, W.R. (1990). "Internal Marketing and Organizational Behavior: A Partnership in Developing Customer-conscious

Employees at Every Level". *Journal of Business Research*, 20, pp. 63-70.

Giese, K. (2003). "New Chinese Migration to Germany: Historical Consistencies and Global Survey Predicts Upsurge in Telework," ITAC (International Telework Association & Council) *Telework News*, Issue 3.3, Summer 2003.

Globalization: Analyzing the Economics. Chicago: University of Chicago Press.

Govindrajan, Vijay et. al. (2005). *Ten Rules for Strategic Innovations: From Idea to Execution*. Boston: Harvard Business School Press.

Gratton, Lynda, (2003). "Free to Choose," in *Human Resources in the 21st Century*, eds. Marc Effron, Robert Gandossy, and Marshall Goldsmith, John Wiley & Sons, Inc.

Greer, C. (2000). *Strategic Human Resource Management—A General Managerial Approach* (2nd edition), Prentice Hall.

Gregerson, Hal B., Morrison, A.J. and Black, J.S. "Developing Leaders for the Global Frontier", *Sloan Management Review*.

Grow, Brian, "Hispanic Nation," *Business Week* Online, March 15, 2004.

Gupta, Saurabh (2006). "Hotels without Hoteliers!" (Retrieved from http://www.hvs.com/ Jump/?aid=2741)

Hallberg, Kristin (2001). "A Market-Oriented Strategy For Small and Medium-Scale Enterprises". IFC Discussion Paper # 48.

Harari, O. (1998). "Attracting the Best Minds". *Management Review*, 87(4), pp. 23-26.

Hart (1999). "Different Approaches to Bankruptcy". Harvard Institute of Economic Research Working Paper No. 1903.

Harvard Business Review on Finding and Keeping the Best People. Harvard Business School Press, 2001.

Hayashi, A., Chen, C., Ryan, T., Wu, J., (2004). "The Role of Social Presence and Moderating Role of Computer Self Efficacy in Predicting the Continuance Usage of E-Learning Systems". *Journal of Information Systems Education* 15 (2), 139-54.

Heet, Justin A. *Beyond Workforce 2020: The Coming (and Present) International Market for Labor*, Hudson Institute, 2004.

Hewitt Associates has conducted extensive research on the movement of work around the world. e.g. Hewitt's *Channels to Anywhere: The Supply Chain for Global Talent White Paper and Global Sourcing: Managing the Flow of Work and Talent Research Highlights* (2003).

Hewitt has conducted extensive research on the characteristics of DDG companies. e.g. Hewitt's White Paper "Building the Management and Organizational Disciplines to Grow" (2004).

Hewitt's Human Capital Foresight TM service uses predictive analytics to turn a company's massive amount of HR data into actionable insights on how key characteristics of human capital impact the bottom line.

W.A. Cornelius. *Highly Skilled: High-Tech Braceros' in the Global Market.*

Hofstade G. *Motivation, Leadership & Organization*, McGraw Hill, New York, 1984.

Hollifield, *Controlling Immigration: A Global Perspective*. Stanford: Stanford.

Holman, D. Call centres in " The New Workplace: A Guide to the Human Impact of Modern Working Practices". Chichester: John Wiley, 2003.

Horngren, Charles T. et al. (2005). *Introduction to Management Accounting*, 13th ed., Delhi: Pearson Education.

http://advance.uci.edu/media/facrecmanualweb3.pdf

http://depts.washington.edu/asccp)

http://economictimes.indiatimes.com/articleshow/247047.cms

http://economictimes.indiatimes.com/articlesshow/286800.cms

http://searchwinit.bitpipe.com/rlist/term/IT-Workforce.html search.techrepublic.com.com/searchtalent+management.html

http://web.mit.edu/fnl/women/women.html

http://www.artsci.washington.edu/services/Personnel/Juniorfaculty

http://www.artsci.washington.edu/services/personnel/promtenguide.htm

http://www.callcenterservicesindia.blogspot.com

http://www.colorado.edu/academicaffairs/fac_recruit/index.html)

http://www.coolavenues.com/know/hr/s_4.php

http://www.coolavenues.com/know/hr/sandeep_1.php3

http://www.deloitte.com

http://www.engr.washington.edu/advance/resources/dual_career_hires.html)

http://www.engr.washington.edu/advance/workshops/20030227-development_opportunities.pdf)

http://www.indiastat.com

http://www.interbiznet.com

http://www.leadershipadvantage.com/increasedcompetition.html

http://www.marceffron.com

http://www.nasscom.org

http://www.newtmn.com

http://www.psc-cfp.gc.ca/ppc/assessment_cp10_e.htm

http://www.sei.cmu.edu/cmm-p/version2/faq.html

http://www.skylinevillege.com

http://www.washington.edu/admin/acadpers/procedures/careers.html)

http://www.washington.edu/admin/eoo/forms/ftk_01.html)

J.P. Meyer and N.J. Allen, (1991). "A three-component Comceptualization of Organizational Commitment" *Human Resource Management Review* (1991). 1, 61-89

John P. Meyer and Lynne Herscovitch, "Commitment in the Workplace: Toward a General Model", *Human Resource Management Review*, 11 (2001), 299-326.

Hymowitz, Carol, "In the Lead: Baby Boomers Seek New Ways to Escape Career Claustrophobia," *The Wall Street Journal*, June 24, 2004.

"Innovation: Remote Working in the Net-Centric Company," The Economist Intelligence Unit Executive Briefing, July 15, 2003.

"Innovations in the Software Industry", in A.P. D'Costa and E. Sridharan (eds). *India in the Global Software Industry: Innovation, Firm Strategies and Development.*

Jackson, R. and Osmond, N. (2003). "How To Recruit and Retain Older Staff", *People Management.* Vol. 9, No. 10, 15 May, pp. 46-47.

John, Hagel III. "From Push to Pull: The Next Frontier of Innovation," *The McKinsey Quarterly*, 2005. Number 3, pp. 82-91.

Johnson, Lauren Keller. "Four Practices for Great Performance," *Harvard Working Knowledge*, August 23, 2004.

Kaihla, Paul. "The Coming Job Boom," *Business* 20, September 2003.

Kaliprasad, M. *Cost Engineering*, Vol. 48, No. 6, June 2006.

Kanungo, R.N. and M. Mendonce (1996). *Ethical Dimensions of Leadership*, Sage, Thousand Oaks.

Karoly, Lynn A. and Constantijn W.A. Panis. *The 21st Century at Work*, Rand Corporation, 2004, and Thomas J. Donohue, "Falling Behind," *Training*, October 2003.

Kaufman, D., Kraay, A., Lobaton, P.Z. (1999). "Governance Matters". World Bank Policy Research Department Working Paper No. 2196.

Kaye Thorne & Andy Pellant, (2007). "The Essential Guide to Managing Talent", Kogan Page India.

Khandelwal, R. (2002). "Winning The Retention Game", *Human Capital*, Vol. 5, No. 9, February, p. 40.

Kinlaw, D. (1999). *Coaching for Commitment* (2nd ed). San Francisco: Jossey-Bass Pfeiffer.

Klapper, L. and V. Sulla (2002). "MSME Around the World: Where Do they Matter Most?" World Bank Mimeo.

Kotlu, P. (2003). *Marketing Management*, New Delhi: Prentice-Hall of India.

Kumar, S. (2001). "A Magnetic Attraction", *Human Capital*, Vol. 5, No. 7, December, p. 44.

La Porta, R., Lopez-de-Silanes, F., Shleifer, A., Vishny, R. (1998). "Law and Finance". *Journal of Political Economy,* 106, pp. 1113-55.

La Porta, R., Lopez-de-Silanes, F., Shleifer, A., Vishny (1999). "The Quality of Government". *Journal of Law, Economics and Organization,* 15, pp. 222-79.

Lance A. Berger, Dorothy R., *The Talent Management Handbook: Creating Organizational Excellence by Identifying, Developing, and Promoting Your Best People.*

Leduchwicz, T. (1982). "Trainer Role and Effectiveness: A Review of the Literature". *International Journal of Manpower*, 3, pp. 2-9.

Leibfritz, Willi, "Retiring Later Makes Sense," *OECD Observer*, January 13, 2003.

Leidner, D.E., & Jarvenpaa, S.L. (1995). "The Use of Information Technology to Enhance Management School Education: A Theoretical View". *MIS Quarterly*, 1, pp. 265-91.

Lloyd, S. (2002). "Branding from the Inside Out". *BRW*, 24(10), pp. 64–66.

Lockwood, Nancy R. "The Aging Workforce," *HR Magazine*, December 2003.

Loughlin, Catherine, and Julian Barling. "Young Workers' Work Values, Attitudes, and Behaviours," *Journal of Occupational and Organizational Psychology*, November 2001.

Lowell L. Bryan, Claudia I. Joyce and Leigh M. Weiss. "Making a Market in Talent," *Indian Management*, June 2006, p. 82.

Luft, J. and H. Ingham. *The JOHARI Window: A Graphic Model of Interpersonal Relations*, University of California, Los Angeles, 1955.

Luge, Arthur, and Jakuknwski, Patricia. *Responsible Assertive Behaviour*, Campaign III: Research Press, 1976.

Magnusson, K. (1997). *Radical Change in the World of Work: Counsellor's Guide*. Edmonton, AB: Alberta Human Resources and Employment.

Mainiero, Lisa A. and Tromley, Cheryl L. (2003). *Developing Managerial Skills*, Prentice-Hall of India Private Limited, New Delhi.

Malcom Goodman. *Frustration of Talent: A Study in Scarlet*, Durham University Business School.

Malone, Thomas W. *The Future of Work*, Harvard Business School Press, 2004.

Marciariello, J.A. and C. J. Kirby (1994). *Management Control System*, Engelwood Cliffs, N.J: Prentice-Hall.

Martin, Susan F. "Heavy Traffic," *The Brookings Review*, Fall 2001.

Media Release (2002). "Human Energy from Hospitality Sector", *The Economic Times*, 18 November, 2002.

Media Release (2002). "Taj employee loyalty at 80 per cent: Survey" *Financial Express*—November 24, 2002.

"Meeting the Challenges of Tomorrow's Workforce", Supplement to *Chief Executive Magazine*, August/September 2002.

Mehta, Ambika (2005). "From Poaching Salmon to Poaching Hotel Employees!". (Retrieved from http://www.hvs.com/staticcontent/library/102405/)

Meyer, John P. and Herscovitch, Lynne (1991). "Commitment in the Workplace: Toward a General Model", *Human Resource Management Review*, Vol. 11, pp. 299-326.

Michael, Argyle. *The Psychology of Interpersonal Behaviour*, Penguin Books, 1967.

Mishra, A.K. and Wagh, Ajay. "Retention Strategy: Vital for Building Present and Future Capabilities", *Management Insight*, Vol. 1, No. 1, December, 2004, p. 46.

Mullich, Joe. "Hiring Without Limits," *Workforce Management*, August 2002.

Mullich, Joe. "They Don't Retire Them, They Hire Them," *Workforce Management*, December 2003, p. 115.

Naidu, Venugopal (2007). "Reducing Employee Turnover in Hospitality". (Retrieved from http://www.articleclick.com/Article/Reducing-Employee-Turnover-In-Hospitality/600)

Natalie, J. Alien and Douglas B. Gresaffe. "Employee Commitment to the Organization and Customer Reactions: Mapping the Linkages", *Human Resource Management Review*, 11 (2001), pp. 209-36.

Nayyar, D. (1994). *Migration, Remittances and Capital Flows*. Delhi, Oxford.

Nilkantha, V. and S. Ramanarayan (1990). "Managers in the Middle: A Case of Underdevelopment and Underutilization", *Vikalpa* 15(2), pp. 3-12.

——.*Organizational Behaviour,* Stephen, P. Robbins. Prentice Hall of India Pvt. Ltd.

Steven L. Mcshane, Mary Ann Von Glinow, Radha R. Sharma, *Organizational Behaviour*, Tata McGraw Hill.

Pandit Satyakam Vidyalonkar. *The Holy Vedas*, Clarian Books, New Delhi, 1998.

"Patterns and Priorities in Indian Research and Development" *Current Science*, 10 October 1999.

Paul, Rhea. "Faculty Development: Nurturing Our Future". *Faculty Focus*, Spring 1997 (www.oaa.pdx.edu/cae/facultyfocus/spring97/nurturing.html)

Phillips, G.M. and Wood, J. T. *Communication and Human Relationships—The Study of Interpersonal Communication*, Macmillan Publishing Company, New York, 1983.

Piirto, J. (1995b). "Deeper and Broader: The Pyramid of Talent Development in the Context of the Giftedness Construct". *Educational Forum*, 59, pp. 364-69.

Planning and Managing Human Resources, ISBN: 9780874257182, Human Resource Development Pr. 2002.

Pradhan, J.P. and Abraham, V. "Social and Cultural Impact of Outsourcing: Emerging Issues from Indian Call Centre". *Harvard Asia Quarterly*. http://www.fas.havard.edu/~asiactr/haq/200502a001.htm,30.12.2005.

Prasanna Chandra (2001). *Financial Management*, Tata McGraw-Hill Publishing Company Limited, New Delhi.

Raju, PVL KBS Kumar. *HRM Recruitment & Retention*. ICCAI University Press.

Raghavendra R. (2003). "BPO Firms Head Hunt in Smaller Cities", *The Economic Times*, 8th October, p. 10.

Ramalingaswami, Vulimiri and Jonsson, Urban and Rohde, Jon (1996). "The Asian Enigma". *The Progress of Nations*. New York: UNICEF.

Ram Marlapalle, "ABCDnRoadmap to Attract and Retain the Talent", *NIPM* 25th WRC Souvenir

Randall, S. (1982). "Communication and Performance in the Real World, Simulation and Laboratory". American Psychological Convention, Washington, DC: 27 August.

Rao, T.V. "Old Pillars of People Management", *Indian Management*, June 2006, p. 80.

Rao, V.S.P. *Human Resource Management*, Excel Books, 2003.

Raphael, Todd. "At Google, the Proof is in the People," *Workforce Management*, March 2003.

Reddi, Venkat Laxma (2000). "Homing in on Their Staff", *The Hindu*, 2nd February, 2000.

Ritson, M. (2002). "Marketing and HE Collaborate to Harness Employer Brand Power". *Marketing*, 24 October, p. 24.

S. Radhakrishan, *Bhagvadgita*, Blackie & Son (India) Ltd., Bombay, 1977.

Sahay, Arvind (2007). "How to Reap Higher Profits with Dynamic Pricing", *MIT Sloan Management Review*, Summer, 2007.

Salter, Chuck. "Calling JetBlue," *Fast Company*, May 2004.

"Solving the Real Productivity Crisis," *Fast Company*, January 2004.

Schneider, F. (2000). The Size and Development of the Shadow Economies and Shadow Economy Labor Force of 18 Asian and 21 OECD Countries: First Results for the 90s.

Schneider, F., Enste, D. (1998). "Increasing Shadow Economies All Over the World—fiction or Reality". A Survey of the Global Evidence of Its Size and of Its Impact from 1970 to 1995", IMF and University of Linz, August 21.

Schwartz, Karen. "Some Finding Retirement is only Temporary," *Chicago Tribune*, March 17, 2004.

Schwartz, Peter. *Inevitable Surprises*, Gotham Books, 2003.

Semler, Ricardo. *The Seven-Day Weekend*, Penguin Group, 2004.

Shank, John K., and Vijay Govindrajan (1993). *Strategic Cost Management*, New York: Free Press.

Shari, Caudron. "How HR Drives Profits", *Workforce Management*, December 2001, pp. 26-31.

Joshi, Sharvari (2003). "BPOs have Undergrades in Their Sights". *Times of India*, 2003, 17th December, p. 1.

Singh, Shelley (2003). "Keeping 'em from Straying," *Business World*, August, pp. 25-27.

Sherry, A. (2000). "Put Branding Iron into Your Image". *Business Review Weekly*, 22(28), p. 66.

Silverman, L.K., (Ed). (1993). *Counseling the Gifted and Talented*. Denver, Co: Love.

Skimmer, B.F. *Analysis of Behaviour*, McGraw Hill, New York, 1967.

Society for Human Resource Management and the *Wall Street Journal* Job Recovery Survey, 2003.

Solomon, Charlene M. "Putting HR on the Score Card" *Workforce*, March 2000.

Speizer, Irwin, "By Adding More Women to its Workforce, HP sees Customer Needs More Clearly," *Workforce Management* Online, September 2004.

Speizer, Irwin, "Hilton Tries to Clone the Model Employee," *Workforce Management* Online, August 2004.

Sriram, Yogi (2006). "Service with a Smile", (Retrieved from http://www.tata.com/ 0_our_commitmentemployee_relations /articles/20060824_vision_HR.htm)

Srivastava, V.N. & Gupta, Shuchi. "Managing Organizational Talents. *Synthesis*, January-June, 2004, Vol. 1, No. 2, pp. 56-66.

Stadler Christian (2007). "The Principles of Enduring Success" *Harvard Business Review,* July-August, pp. 62-72.

Nasreen, Taher. *Talent Magnets*, ICFAI University Press.

Talent Management Systems: Best Practices in Technology Solutions for Recruitment, Retention and Workforce Planning by Allan Schweyer.

"Talent Management—The New Mantra for Corporates", *The Hindu*, April, 2007.

"Talent Management", *HRM Review*, ICFAI University Press.

Talreja, Vishakha (2007). "Hotels Address Talent Crunch in Lively Ways", *The Economic Times,* 20th July, 2007.

Taylor, Craig R., "Retention Leadership," *Training & Development*, March 2004.

Temple, Paul, "No Retirement for Boomers," *Workforce*, July 2000.

"Ten Retention Myths", Anoop K. Kamat, *HRD News Letter*, Vol. 23, Issue 5, Aug. 2007.

"Ten ways to find and retain best tutors" by Prof. Mohan, IIM, Lucknow, Nov. 15, 2006.

The Analyst, Chartered Financial Analyst, ICFAI, University Press Dec, 2006.

"The Challenge of Age: The Change Agenda", Chartered Institute for Personnel and Development, November 2003.

The Human Capital Edge, ISBN: 9780071378833, McGraw-Hill.

Torrance, E.P. (1987). "Teaching for Creativity". In S. Isaksen (Ed.), *Frontiers of Creativity Research: Beyond the Basics*, pp. 190-215. Buffalo, NY: Bearly Ltd.

Tuglan, Bruce and Brealey, Nichloas. "Wining the Talent Wars" U.S. Department of Labor. *Bureau of Labor Statistics*.

Pareek, Udai. *Training Instruments in HRD & OD*, Tata McGraw-Hill Publishing Company Limited, Second edition, 2002.

Udai, Pareek. *Understanding Organizational Behaviour*, Oxford University Press.

University of Colorado Boulder. Faculty Recruitment and Retention Task Force Report. May 2001.

"University of Washington Academic Human Resources: Resources for New and Prospective Employees". Accessed, July 2003.

"University of Washington Advance Center for Institutional Change: Recommendations to Chairs for Facilitating Dual Career Hires". Accessed, July 2003.

"University of Washington College of Arts and Sciences Climate and Community Project". *Accessed*, July 2003.

"University of Washington College of Arts and Sciences Promotion and Tenure Workshop Handout". Accessed, July 2003.

"University of Washington College of Engineering Faculty Professional Development Opportunities". Accessed, July 2003.

"University of Washington Faculty Recruitment Toolkit". Accessed, July 2003.

Urkude, Ashish Manohar. "Faster Development of India: Using Rapid Time Compression Technologies, Techniques, Tools and Talents", Annual Technical Paper Meeting, 2005, The Institute of Engineers (India), Nagpur, pp. 47-52.

Urkude, Ashish, Manohar Ph.D. Thesis, submitted to Nagpur University in 2002, "Management of Indigenously Built Small Car Market in India with Special Reference to Customer Behaviour", Chapter 1, Introduction, "Table: Jobs Associated with Automobile Industry", pp. 14-21.

V.V. Ramani, and K. Guruswam, *Talent Management—Concepts and Cases*, August 2003.

V. Rama Devi. "Job Satisfaction among University Teachers", *SCMS Journal of Indian Management*, Vol. III, No. IV, Oct.-Dec. 2006, pp. 87-94.

Veiga, John F. (1988). "Face Your Problem Subordinates Now", *The Academy of Management Executives*, 1988, Vol. 2, pp. 145-52.

Wallace, Patricia. *The Internet in the Workplace*, Cambridge University Press, 2004.

Ware, James and Charles Grantham. "The Future of Work," *Journal of Facilities Management*, September 2003.

Weber, Gretchen, "Adelphia's 'Rent to Own' Recruiting Solution," *Workforce Management*, August 2004.

Weiss, Michael J., "To Be About to Be," *American Demographics*, September 1, 2003.

"What's Behind the 4-Minute Mile, Starbucks and the Moon Landing?" Knowledge@Wharton, July 14, 2004.

whitepaper.optimizemag.com/cmpoptimizemag/search/tabsortbrowse/research/1767/26/2/index.jsp

whitepaper.techweb.com/.../Performance%20Management%20Tutorial%20 On%20 Talent%20 Management

Wood, R. (1999). "How To Cope with the Applications Avalanche", *Competency*, Vol. 6, No. 3, Spring, pp. 21-23.

www.bersinassociates.com

www.bestemployeraustralia.com

www.bpoindia.org

www.bpowatchindia.com

www.bsbmumbai.org

www.chartcourse.com

www.cnbc.com

www.dqindia.com

www.eei.org/meetings/nonav_2005-10-02-cs/garzich_employeeengagement

www.garnet.acns.fsu.edu

www.google.com, Neil Barber, Director, Maritz Research (ISPI Europe, Sept 2003).

www.greatplacetowork.com

www.growth-insights.com

www.haygroup.cz

www.hays.com.au/news/ausworkplace/issue5.aspx

www.hewittasia.com/hewitt/ap/australia/index.htm

www.highretention.com

www.hospitality.org

www.hr.com

www.hrmguide.com

www.iimb.ernet.in

www.investopedia.com

www.learn2007.com

www.lrc.ie/viewdoc.asp?m=&fn=/documents/symposium04/mariemoynihan.

www.management-issues.com

www.moserbaer.com

www.perterkeen.com/emgbp007.htm

www.plateau.com/prod/talent-management.htm blogs.zdnet.com/BTL/?p=4332

www.reliabilitycareers.com

www.saipantribune.com

www.shrm.org/hrmagazine

www.talentmgt.com/columnists/full-potential/2007/september

www.tcs.com

www.theglobeandmail.com

www.vital-learning.com/documents/April26

www.wikipedia.com/talent

"You Can Do Anything, But Not Everything", *Fast Company*, May 2000.

"Youthful Demographics of Developing Countries may be Their Economic Salvation," *Institute of Public Affairs Review*, March 2003.

Zimmerman, B. J., Bandura, A., and Martinez-Pons, M. (1992). "Self-motivation for Academic Attainment: The Role of Self-efficacy Beliefs and Personal Goal Setting". *American Educational Research Journal*, 29(3): 663-76.

Contributors

Masood Hasan, Director, GLA Institute of Business Management, Mathura, U.P., India.

Jai Prakash, Director General, GLA Group of Institutions, Mathura, U.P., India.

Solai Baskaran, Alliance Business School, Bangalore, Karnataka, India.

Ashish Manohar Urkude, Alliance Business School, Bangalore, Karnataka, India.

Neha Agrawal, Alliance Business School, Bangalore, Karnataka, India.

Deepak Dixit, Department of Management Studies, GLA Institute of Technology and Management, Mathura, U.P., India.

Rachna Srivastava, Department of Management Studies, GLA Institute of Business Management, Mathura, U.P., India.

C. Karthikeyan, Deputy Director, Sree Narayana Guru Institute of Science and Technology, Mannam P.O., North Paravur, Ernakulum District, Kochi, Kerala-683520, India.

P.N. Ramchandran, Principal, Nehru College of Engineering and Research Centre, Pampady (P.O.), Thiruvilwamala, Thrissur District, Kerala, India.

Ashish V. Gadekar, Department of Management, Anand College of Engineering, Keetham, Agra, U.P., India.

Rimalini Ramesh Band, Department of Mechanical Engineering, Hindustan College of Science and Technology, Farah, Mathura, U.P., India.

Manika Sumani, Department of Management, Anand College of Engineering, Keetham, Agra, U.P., India.

Seemant Kumar Yadav, Department of Management Studies, GLA Institute of Technology and Management, Mathura, U.P., India.

Vijay Goyal, Department of Management Studies, GLA Institute of Technology and Management, Mathura, U.P., India.

M.P. Dubey, Joint Director, Software Technology Parks of India (STPI), Deptt. of IT, Ministry of Communications and Information Technology, Govt. of India, Ganga Software Technology Complex, Sector-29, Noida, U.P., India.

Atul Narang and Yogita Narang, BMAS Engineering College, Keetham, Agra, U.P., India.

Yogita Narang, BMAS Engineering College, Keetham, Agra, U.P., India.

Uma Sreedhar, Alliance Business Academy, Bangalore, Karnataka, India.

Vibhuti N. Bajpai, Department of Management Studies, Galgotias College of Engineering and Technology, Greater Noida, U.P., India.

Dhirendra Kr. Tripathi, Department of Management Studies, Advance Institute of Management, Ghaziabad, U.P., India.

Anil Kumar Goyal, Department of Management Studies, Galgotias College of Engineering and Technology, Greater Noida, U.P., India.

Satendra Kumar Yadav, Department of Management Studies, GLA Institute of Technology and Management, Mathura, U.P., India

Bhavesh P. Joshi, Department of Management Studies, Army Institute of Management and Technology, Greater Noida, U.P, India.

G.S. Rawat, N.M.S.N. Dass College, Budaun, U.P., India.

Vikas Kumar, University of Petroleum & Energy Studies (UPES), Dehradun, Uttarakhand, India.

Gitanjali Singh, Department of Management Studies, GLA Institute of Technology and Management, Mathura, U.P., India.

S.S. Narula, Director, Bharat Institute of Technology, Meerut, U.P., India.

Bhawna Jaiswal, Department of Management, Bharat Institute of Technology, Meerut, U.P., India.

Rakesh Kr. Agrawal, Institute of Management Technology, Ghaziabad, U.P., India.

Pragati Swaroop, ICFAI National College, Ghaziabad, U.P., India.

Shubhada Mohan Kulkarni, In-Charge Director, Institute of Management and Research, Jalgaon, Maharashtra, India.

Sanchita Ghatak, Jaipuria Institute of Management, Lucknow, U.P., India.

Satyendra Kr. Singh, International Institute for Special Education, Lucknow, UP., India.

Nalin Jayasuriya, Managing Director and CEO, McQuire Rens and Jones (Pvt) Ltd., Sri Lanka

Rupali Singh, Department of Management Studies, Mangalmay Institute of Management & Technology, Greater Noida, U.P., India.

Anshu Dawar, BMAS Engineering College, Keetham, Agra, U.P., India.

Shailesh Rastogi, Department of Management Studies, GLA Institute of Technology and Management, Mathura, U.P., India.

Vikas Tripathi, Department of Management Studies, GLA Institute of Business Management, Mathura, U.P., India

Aneesya Sharma, Department of Management Studies, GLA Institute of Technology and Management, Mathura, U.P., India.

Ekta Sikarwar, Department of Management Studies, GLA Institute of Business Management, Mathura, U.P., India.

Priti Suman Mishra, NIILM, Badarpur, Faridabad, Haryana, India.

Somesh Dhamija, Department of Management Studies, GLA Institute of Professional Studies, Mathura, U.P., India.

Aruna Dhamija, Department of Management Studies, GLA Institute of Professional Studies, Mathura, U.P., India.

Dinesh Kumar Sharma, Department of Management Studies, Galgotias College of Engineering and Technology, Greater Noida, U.P., India.

Moumita Kusari, Department of Management Studies, Galgotias College of Engineering and Technology, Greater Noida, U.P., India.